Conservation of Building and Decorative Stone

Volume 2

Butterworth–Heinemann Series in Conservation and Museology

Series Editors: *Arts and Archaeology*

Andrew Oddy
British Museum, London

Architecture

Derek Linstrum
Institute of Advanced Architectural Studies, University of York

US Executive Editor: **Norbert S Baer**
New York University, Conservation Center of the Institute of Fine Arts

Consultants: **Sir Bernard Feilden**

David Bomford
National Gallery, London

C V Horie
Manchester Museum, University of Manchester

Colin Pearson
Canberra College of Advanced Education

Sarah Staniforth
National Trust, London

Published titles: Artists' Pigments c. 1600–1835, 2nd Edition (Harley)
Conservation and Exhibitions (Stolow)
Conservation and Restoration of Works of Art and Antiquities (Kühn)
Conservation of Building and Decorative Stone (Ashurst, Dimes)
Conservation of Glass (Newton, Davison)
Conservation of Historic Buildings (Feilden)
Conservation of Library and Archive Materials and the Graphic Arts
(Petherbridge)
Conservation of Manuscripts and Paintings of South-east Asia (Agrawal)
Conservation of Marine Archaeological Objects (Pearson)
Conservation of Wall Paintings (Mora, Mora, Philippot)
The Museum Environment, 2nd Edition (Thomson)
The Organic Chemistry of Museum Objects (Mills, White)
The Textile Conservator's Manual (Landi)

Related titles: Manual of Curatorship
Materials for Conservation
Museum Documentation Systems

Conservation of Building and Decorative Stone

Volume 2

Editors

John Ashurst DArch FSA(Scot)
Principal Architect, Research and Technical Advisory Service,
Historic Buildings and Monuments Commission for England;
Chairman Standing Joint Committee on Natural Stones (UK)

Francis G. Dimes MSc BSc MIGeol FGS
Private Consultant
Formerly Institute of Geological Sciences, Geological Museum, London

Butterworth–Heinemann
London Boston Singapore Sydney Toronto Wellington

 PART OF REED INTERNATIONAL P.L.C.

First published 1990

© Butterworth-Heinemann Ltd, 1990

British Library Cataloguing in Publication Data

Conservation of building and decorative stone
Vol. 2
1. Stone buildings. Conservation
I. Ashurst, John, *1937—*
721'.0441

ISBN 0–7506–1269–X

Library of Congress Cataloging-in-Publication Data

Conservation of building and decorative stone.

(Butterworths series in conservation and museology)
Bibliography: v. 1, p.
Includes indexes.
1. Stone buildings—Conservation and restoration.
2. Building stones.   I. Ashurst, John.   II. Dimes,
Francis G. III. Title.   IV. Series,
TH1201.c66 1989   691'2   88–34056
ISBN 0–7506–1277–0

Laserset by Scribe Design, Gillingham, Kent
Printed and bound by Hartnolls Ltd, Bodmin, Cornwall

Contents

Corrigenda

Page 34	Column 1, line 15 up: read 'should never be cleaned ...'.
Page 36	Figure 1.7, last line of caption: read 'slurried in lime mortar'.
Page 47	Figures 1.53 and 1.54: transpose the captions.
Page 83	Column 1, line 21 up: read 'about 5% C_3A compared with ...'.
Page 86	Column 1, lines 5–7 down: read 'Wedge chisels should never be used because they may tend to stress the joints ...'.
Page 136	Column 2, line 18: note that TBTO is already banned in some countries; the application techniques described are equally relevant to other biocides.
Page 137	Column 2, lines 12–13: read 'aluminium oxide powder'.
Page 149	Figure 8.23, line 6 of caption: read 'Cleanstone Ltd'.
Page 154	Figure 8.37, line 5 of caption: read 'based on EDTA'.

1

Methods of repairing and consolidating stone buildings

John Ashurst

Introduction

A stone building of any age and condition requires an experienced practitioner to assess its real state and its repair and maintenance requirements. The objective of this and subsequent chapters is to assist the general building practitioner to become more familiar with the problem of stone construction and the various repair and maintenance options, rather than to discuss matters of general survey and inspection.

There are as many dangers associated with unnecessary or incorrect interference with masonry structures and surfaces as there are associated with neglect. Whilst the interference problem is not new it is tending to take over from neglect as the prime enemy of historic stone buildings in the more affluent areas of the world. Typical examples of harmful intervention include:

1. Introduction of massive concrete stitching or beams into cracked but stable masonry
2. Introduction of large quantities of cement grouting
3. Introduction of large quantities of polyester or epoxy resin grout
4. Unnecessary replacement of worn and heavily weathered stones
5. Widening of original joint widths and spalling of arrises by the use of cutting disks and wedge-shaped chisels
6. Superficial pointing of joints with cement-rich or resin-based mortars
7. Alteration of original joint profiles
8. Damage by air-abrasive and disk cleaning
9. Residual damage associated with acid and alkali cleaners
10. Use of inappropriate surface treatments, such as water repellents, consolidants and anti-graffiti coating of the wrong type

In some cases the work carried out will not be physically harmful, but when stones are replaced unnecessarily or the original joint profiles are altered this will have a de-valuing effect on the building.

The keys to good masonry conservation are undoubtedly experience in problem recognition and diagnosis, competent specification, minimal physical intervention and maximum technical site skills. Clearly these desirable elements need the involvement of more than one discipline, but it is likely that the central co-ordinating discipline will be the architect's.

On pages 2–3 the architect's plan of approach to a masonry building is suggested in the form of various action options. Unless the problem is very simple, however, the architect should involve the archaeologist, art historian, specialist engineer, analytical chemist, masonry technician and stone or sculpture conservator at an early stage.

The need to examine minutely and to record before anything is altered or repaired is paramount. In some situations there may be no money available for any work for many years. In these cases recording should be given a high priority. Photography, photogrammetry and monitoring are all important, sometimes critically so, but so, still, is the making of drawings, the taking of moulds and casts and the making of accurate templates of original profiles. Although there are some highly sophisticated recording techniques, and in some parts of the conservation world there is so much specialized technical back-up that simple site observation becomes relegated, there will never be a substitute for close site observation based on long experience. All techniques must be subordinate to and supportive of personal site survey.

Sites with ruined masonry and roofed and occupied masonry buildings have various repair and maintenance requirements in common, but ruined

1

REMEDIAL WORK TO MASONRY : SCOPE AND OPTIONS

Inspection and diagnosis of condition can usefully be considered in the following categories :-

A : THE WALLS [structural condition] **B :** THE STONES [individually]

C : THE JOINTS

A : THE WALLS

Are they leaning, bulging, twisting, fracturing ? If so, the reasons must be known. Are the structural problems real and "live", or have they already been resolved ?

CAUSES OF PROBLEMS may be :

- UNEQUAL SETTLEMENT [inconsistency in the bearing capacity of the ground, mining sub-sidence, unequal loads from different building elements]
- COLLAPSE OF ARCHES VAULTS or BUTTRESSES [knock-on effects from destruction of essential supports or counter-thrust elements]
- GENERAL INSTABILITY [due to structural alterations, explosion, earthquake, robbing of stones, washing out of wall core and joints]
- INAPPROPRIATE STRUCTURAL INTERVENTION [stresses imposed by rigid restraints and ties, unecessary buttressing, strong resin-based or cementitious grouts]

REMEDIAL WORK TO WALLS

Must be preceded by detailed site investigation and survey, including accurate monitoring. Work should not be visually obtrusive and must not impose new problems on the fabric. Remedial work may include :-

- SECTIONAL UNDERPINNING
- PILING
- STITCHING ACROSS FRACTURES

- INSERTION OF HIDDEN WALL HEAD BEAMS , RING BEAMS , ANGLE BEAMS

- INSERTION OF HIDDEN LINTOLS AND HANGING SYSTEMS FOR ARCHES

- GROUTING BY GRAVITY OR LOW PRESSURE WITH LIME, FLY ASH, WHITE CEMENT

Full records of all structural interventions must be kept ; some on-site monitoring may need to continue indefinitely

B: THE STONES

Are they spalling, scaling, splitting, powdering, disfigured by staining and pitting? If so, the reasons must be understood, using laboratory analysis if necessary.

CAUSES OF PROBLEMS may be :

- ACID ATTACK ON BINDING MATRIX OF STONE [especially calcareous, dolomitic, argillaceous and ferruginous sandstones and marble]
- SULPHATE SKIN FORMATION ON LIMESTONES [especially in sheltered zones]
- CONTOUR SCALE FORMATION ON SANDSTONES [especially in saturation zones]
- OTHER SALT CRYSTALLISATION [associated with rising damp, cement grout, incompatible stones]
- FREEZING   • FIRE DAMAGE   • WEATHERING OUT OF SOFT BEDS
- WEATHERING OUT OF VENTS AND SHAKES • INCORRECT BEDDING
- RUSTING OF IRON CRAMPS • COMPRESSION FRACTURES
- STAINING AND EFFLORESCENCE AFTER CLEANING

  DISCOLOURATION, PITTING AND SPALLING ASSOCIATED WITH SURFACE TREATMENTS [especially traditional pore-blocking treatments]

REMEDIAL WORK TO STONES

Must be preceded by a comprehensive survey with adequate diagnosis completed on all damage and decay. Study of thin sections and salt analyses may be needed; identification of stone type and any treatment or unusual soiling must also be made. An elevational record with large-scale profile details is necessary on which each stone is identifiable and referenced. This record may be a measured survey, corrected photography or a photogrammetric survey. All work and treatment must be recorded.
Remedial work may include :-

- Modification of external environment [providing weather protection, re-routing water channels, introduction of damp-proof membranes, dirt removal]

- Modification of internal environment [humidity, temperature controls, restriction on visitor numbers]

- CUT OUT AND REPLACE OR RE-FACE WITH MATCHING STONE [to original profiles]

- CUT OUT AND PIECE-IN WITHIN EXISTING STONES, IN MATCHED STONE

- CUT OUT AND FILL WITH MORTAR [lime based fills for limestone, epoxy or acrylic based fills for sandstone etc., ensuring fills are permeable and impose no new stresses]

- DRILL, GROUT AND PIN FRACTURED STONES

- CUT OUT AND BUILD UP REPAIR IN TILE COURSING

- PROVIDE WEAK, PROTECTIVE PLASTER }
- PROVIDE SACRIFICIAL PLASTER } the constituents and porosity of these plasters are designed to take up moisture and salts in solution without rapid failure

- CLEAN AND PARTIALLY DESALINATE [leaching packs of paper pulp, attapulgite or sepiolite clay, CMC and solvents]

- USE A WATER REPELLENT [silicone or stearate based repellents are only very rarely useful. Competent diagnosis of the cause of damp is essential]

- USE A CONSOLIDANT
e.g. limewater for limestone. Alkoxysilanes are promising consolidants : TETRAETHOXYSILANE [TEOS - ethyl silicate] gives good penetration and consolidation without water repellence. ETHYLTRIMETHOXYSILANE [ETEOS] consolidates and imparts water repellence. Acrylic resin may be added to both to impart surface hardness. METHYLTRIMETHOXYSILANE (MTMos) is usually used in conjunction with a catalyst such as acrylic resin or lead soap Although primarily suitable for sandstones, alkoxysilane consolidants have been used successfully on siliceous and argillaceous limestones and even on magnesian limestones.
NOTE : CONSOLIDANTS MUST NOT BE USED UNLESS THE CAUSE OF DECAY AND THE CONSTITUENTS OF THE STONE ARE FULLY UNDERSTOOD ALL OTHER OPTIONS SHOULD BE CONSIDERED FIRST

C: THE JOINTS

Are they partially or wholly open, deeply weathered, loose and powdery? Have they been re-pointed in unsuitable, impermeable mortar?
CAUSES OF PROBLEMS may be :-

- POOR CARBONATION OF MORTAR • SATURATION AND FREEZING

- SOLUBLE SALT CRYSTALLISATION • SHRINKAGE AND CRACKING
[from contaminated aggregates, marine environments, rising damp, flue gases]   [from wet mixes or use of strong hydraulic limes/cements or oil mastics]

- MASONRY BEE BURROWING AND BIRD ATTACK • ESTABLISHED IVY GROWTH

REMEDIAL WORK TO JOINTS

Must only be carried out when the absence or failure of mortar is adversely affecting stones or walls, or where strong, sound mortar is causing decay or is visually destructive. Original mortar should be sieve-analysed and new mortar should incorporate matching aggregates and be designed to suit the condition of the stones first and the exposure of the wall second. Work may include :-

- RAKE OUT, TAMP AND POINT • CUT OUT, TAMP AND POINT • SAW OUT, PLUG AND POINT
[open joints or inadequate mortar] [dense, unsuitable mortar]   [fine joints - under 3mm]
- RAKE OUT, PLUG AND POINT   O CLEAN OUT AND PLUG AND POINT
[special joints with weathering problems]   [local damage by birds or bees]

masonry in particular requires a special approach and treatment which demands a close co-operation between archaeologists, architects, engineers and stone masons.

Treatment of monument sites

Ruined masonry buildings, especially those classified as ancient monuments, have special problems. They may be of considerable archaeological and historical importance, which would be lost in whole or part if neglect continued or demolition took place or, on the other hand, if clumsy, inappropriate repairs or ignorant restorations were carried out. Archaeologically important sites may consist of standing, partly ruined walls, or an open or wooded site with all surviving masonry below the modern ground level, or, most commonly, a combination of both.

Development of inner city areas frequently exposes even more problematical remains in the course of rescue archaeology. Usually, because of building programmes, nothing but recording and removal of finds can take place; exceptionally the value of an uncovered site is such that modifications to the proposed building are possible. These situations call for particular care in temporary reburial.

Walls below modern ground level

These walls may be exposed as the result of a planned archaeological investigation and the sole intention may be to record what is there and to backfill. Alternatively, the site may be discovered or opened fortuitously by road or drainage works or by building development, and 'rescue archaeology' will then be needed to record ahead of destruction. In neither situation will much maintenance of the masonry exposed be required.

Other circumstances, however, may require the excavated walls to remain exposed to view. In this case a programme of consolidation and repair, followed by some plan for maintenance, should be instituted as soon as possible. Stones and mortar which have lain for centuries in saturated ground or dry sand may have survived in excellent condition due to these stable environments. Once exposed, however, they may begin to show signs of deterioration fairly quickly as exposure to wind, sun and rain sets up wetting and drying cycles and the destructive crystallization of soluble salts begins to take its toll. Winter conditions bring the additional hazard of frost to walls saturated with water, and substantial losses may occur in one night.

Availability of finance, skilled labour and professional supervision will determine how quickly consolidation can begin. Delays will almost certainly be involved, and temporary protection must then be provided appropriate to the risks of exposure. Such protection may range from geotextile sheets and sand or 'duvets' of straw or polystyrene weighted down, to temporary boxing filled with polystyrene beads, to temporary scaffold frame structures that can double up as protection for the excavation or maintenance team and may even be heated.

Walls standing above ground level

Unroofed and often ruinous buildings which stand above ground level require the attention of an experienced team of specialists, not only to investigate, excavate and record, but also to strengthen and consolidate what survives. When funds and expertise are limited, it is essential that the necessary first-aid is carried out to ensure that further collapse, disintegration or vandalism are kept to a minimum. Emergency work may include the provision of secure fencing, formwork to support vaults and arches in danger of collapse, and strutting and shoring to support leaning and bulging walls. Wall head protection may also be necessary; see below. Features of particular value may need to be protected by temporary roofs.

Much of the final consolidation will consist of stabilizing double skin walls of ashlar, or the consolidation of exposed mortar and rubble fills. The latter are much more difficult to consolidate to a visually acceptable standard than walls with facework and head intact. Core filling may have become exposed by many years of neglect, by deliberate destruction, or by the robbing of dressed facework for use elsewhere. Common problems resulting from this neglect or destruction are:

1. The thickness of the original wall has been reduced and the wall may have become unstable.
2. The core filling is frequently of inferior stones and mortar, with a high percentage of mortar exposed. Such surfaces often have poor resistance to weathering and encourage the development of organic growth.

Considerable experience is needed to 'read' corework when a substantial quantity of the face is missing. The survey and recording of untouched core before any work commences is of great importance; even superficial treatment can obscure or destroy the last traces of, for instance, the size of an opening, the bearing of a beam or indications of alteration or rebuilding. The impressions made in the corework by the tails of missing stones will often yield much information, such as the pattern of previous coursing, or the existence of a former vault or line of corbels.

The initial survey should include the archaeological examination of the adjacent ground. Often this

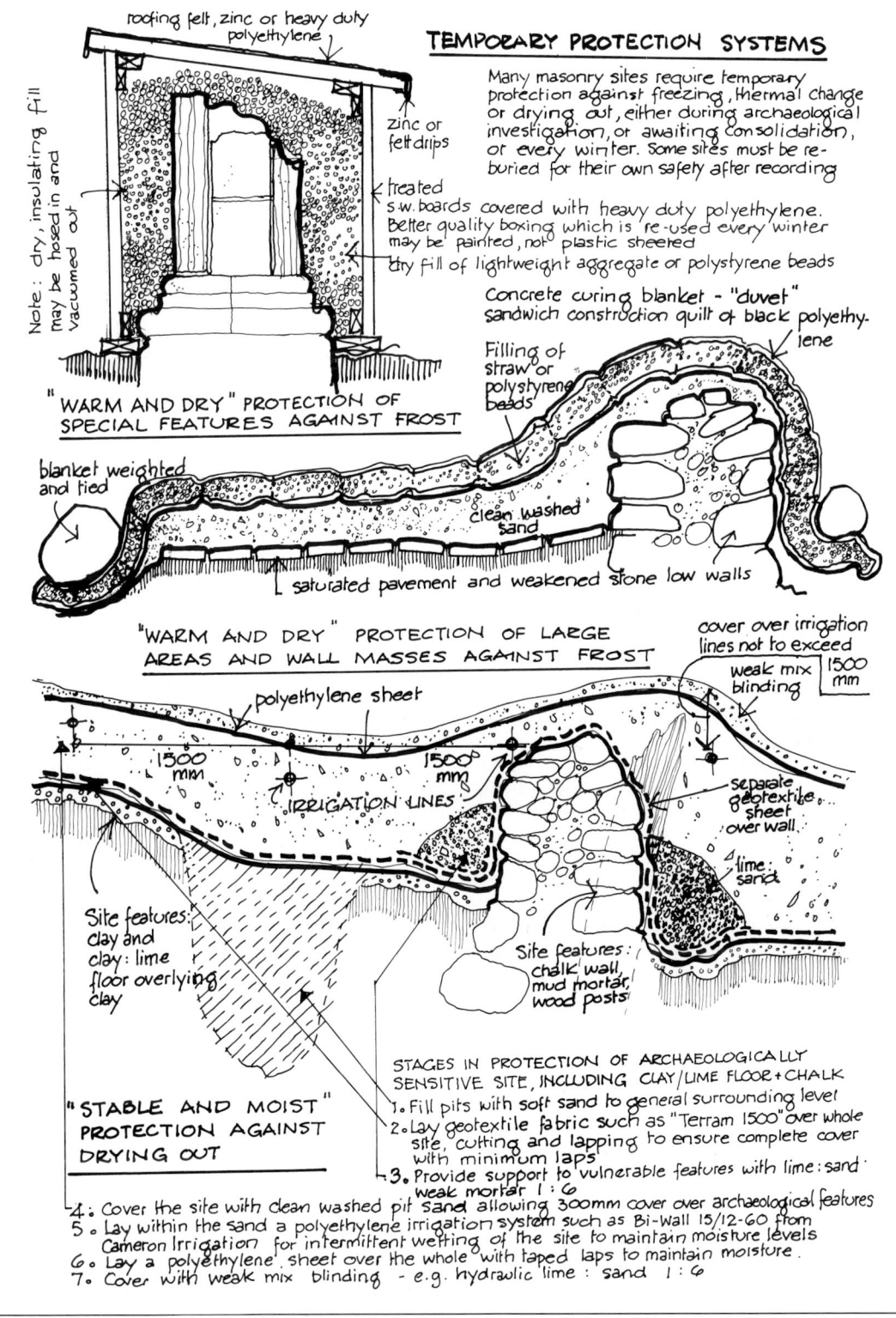

TEMPORARY PROTECTION SYSTEMS

Many masonry sites require temporary protection against freezing, thermal change or drying out, either during archaeological investigation, or awaiting consolidation, or every winter. Some sites must be re-buried for their own safety after recording

roofing felt, zinc or heavy duty polyethylene

Note: dry, insulating fill may be hosed in and vacuumed out

zinc or felt drips

treated s.w. boards covered with heavy duty polyethylene. Better quality boxing which is re-used every winter may be painted, not plastic sheeted

dry fill of lightweight aggregate or polystyrene beads

"WARM AND DRY" PROTECTION OF SPECIAL FEATURES AGAINST FROST

Concrete curing blanket - "duvet" sandwich construction quilt of black polyethylene

Filling of straw or polystyrene beads

blanket weighted and tied

clean washed sand

saturated pavement and weakened stone low walls

"WARM AND DRY" PROTECTION OF LARGE AREAS AND WALL MASSES AGAINST FROST

cover over irrigation lines not to exceed 1500 mm

weak mix blinding

polyethylene sheet

1500 mm

1500 mm

IRRIGATION LINES

separate geotextile sheet over wall

lime sand

Site features: clay and clay: lime floor overlying clay

Site features: chalk wall, mud mortar, wood posts

"STABLE AND MOIST" PROTECTION AGAINST DRYING OUT

STAGES IN PROTECTION OF ARCHAEOLOGICALLY SENSITIVE SITE, INCLUDING CLAY/LIME FLOOR + CHALK
1. Fill pits with soft sand to general surrounding level
2. Lay geotextile fabric such as "Terram 1500" over whole site, cutting and lapping to ensure complete cover with minimum laps
3. Provide support to vulnerable features with lime:sand weak mortar 1:6
4. Cover the site with clean washed pit sand allowing 300mm cover over archaeological features
5. Lay within the sand a polyethylene irrigation system such as Bi-Wall 15/12.60 from Cameron Irrigation for intermittent wetting of the site to maintain moisture levels
6. Lay a polyethylene sheet over the whole with taped laps to maintain moisture.
7. Cover with weak mix blinding - e.g. hydraulic lime:sand 1:6

will reveal stones that have fallen from the wall and may be replaced. Sometimes quantities of stone tracery, vault ribs and tilestones will also be found. These can provide valuable information about the building. It is important to record them in the exact positions in which they have fallen.

Plants, shrubs, later buildings and insertions and heavy soiling may all obscure evidence surviving in the core. However, their incautious removal can destroy the evidence altogether.

Consolidation by taking down and rebuilding

Some core consists of loose stones and other aggregate in a largely disintegrated matrix of mortar, soil and the roots of weeds. After a photographic record has been made and dimensions and levels taken, the stones should be lifted off and cleaned. This operation should be carried out over a few metres at a time. The top of each stone should be numbered in its take-down sequence. In some cases, the arrangement of the stones may be traced through onto a sheet of untearable plastic film. The stones and film can then be given reference numbers to assist in the reassembly. The condition and type of core will determine whether this technique is practicable or not.

The cleaned stones must be rebedded in a mortar which is a good visual match with the original surviving core. The mortar must be resistant to weathering and not too dense or impermeable for the stones forming the filling. Where stones that have no weather resistance were used as fill in the past, a compromise must be made: replacement stones of at least similar appearance and size, but with a better resistance to wetting and drying cycles and to frost, should be used. The aim in rebuilding is to reproduce the same outlines as found, modifying only as necessary to avoid water traps and pockets. Results resembling a garden rockery or rubble facework can be avoided by technical expertise based on study and familiarity with the true appearance of untouched core.

Sometimes it is necessary to insert new core to support sections of the original wall or features that are in danger of collapse. Other methods of support have been used from time to time, including delta metal brackets and straps, which can be pre-formed to profiles of, for instance, traceried heads or lintels. Page 7 illustrates the insertion of a concrete stitch behind the facework to tie the masonry together across an open fracture. Page 8 shows methods of providing support to the damaged heads of arches.

Treatment of wall tops

The treatment of the wall tops of ruined buildings is of particular importance. These areas, which have become exposed to the weather through the loss of roofs, now have to take on the role of parapets. What is more, they must be parapets without copings, unless the visually disastrous and archaeologically confusing expedient of setting coping slabs on levelled wall-tops is followed. In the wall top consolidation, therefore, modifications must be made in lifting and re-setting to ensure that water is shed as rapidly as possible and that there is no risk of ponding. On very thick wall tops a lead-lined sump is sometimes formed with a lead downpipe carried through the core to some convenient outlet. This should only be considered in exceptional circumstances, and the sump must be fitted with a strong, secure wire balloon or grid of fine stainless steel or non-ferrous metal mesh, to avoid blocking with leaves or bird excrement.

Temporary wall coverings (accepting that 'temporary' may mean many years) may be provided by mortar 'blankets', isolated from the historic masonry by a thin sheet of polyethylene and include a reinforcing mesh of alkali-resistant fabric. Non-ferrous wire anchors may be used to secure this rendering into the wall top. Carefully designed and colour-matched mortar blankets provide good and usually acceptable protection for wall tops; if necessary they can be broken up and removed from the historic level at a later date. In less severe climates the mortar blanket may be of a weaker mix than the wall core and be used without an isolating membrane, as was done in the so-called Temple of Saturn in the Forum at Rome.

Where the climate permits, another form of wall capping suitable for low walls in rural situations is turf set, or allowed to grow, on a reinforcing net of synthetic land mesh pegged into the heart of the wall with glass-fibre or non-ferrous wire pegs. The use of mesh makes it easier to remove the turf if further examination of the wall is required at a future date. Mesh has sometimes been used on rough dry stone or on stones which were originally clay-mortared, to form a kind of gabion by stretching it from wall base to wall base and pegging it into the core. However, this is a first-aid procedure only and should not be seen as a permanent method of consolidation. Page 9 illustrates different types of wall topping.

Removal of woody weeds

Where sites are covered with woody species of weeds, the Building Research Establishment recommends control by spot spraying with glyphosate. This is a non-selective herbicide, so care must be taken to protect non-target species from drift. The spray equipment should also be kept for glyphosate

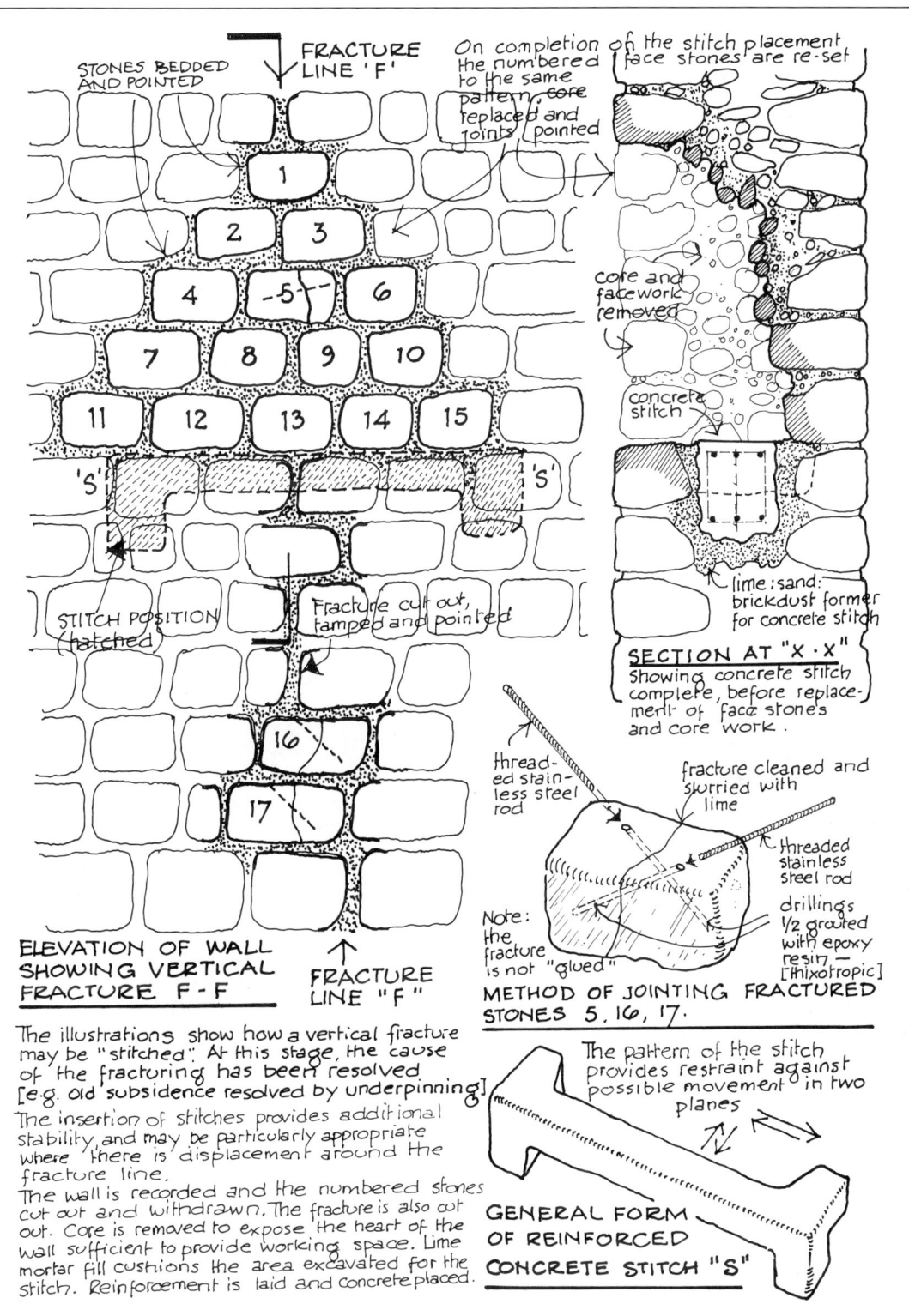

STONES BEDDED AND POINTED

FRACTURE LINE 'F'

On completion of the stitch placement the numbered face stones are re-set to the same pattern, core replaced and joints pointed

core and facework removed

concrete stitch

lime : sand : brickdust former for concrete stitch

SECTION AT "X·X"
Showing concrete stitch complete, before replacement of face stones and core work.

1 2 3 4 -5- 6 7 8 9 10 11 12 13 14 15

'S' 'S'

STITCH POSITION (hatched)

Fracture cut out, tamped and pointed

16 17

ELEVATION OF WALL SHOWING VERTICAL FRACTURE F-F

FRACTURE LINE "F"

threaded stainless steel rod

fracture cleaned and slurried with lime

threaded stainless steel rod

drillings ½ grouted with epoxy resin — [thixotropic]

Note: the fracture is not "glued"

METHOD OF JOINTING FRACTURED STONES 5, 16, 17.

The illustrations show how a vertical fracture may be "stitched". At this stage, the cause of the fracturing has been resolved [e.g. old subsidence resolved by underpinning].

The insertion of stitches provides additional stability, and may be particularly appropriate where there is displacement around the fracture line.

The wall is recorded and the numbered stones cut out and withdrawn. The fracture is also cut out. Core is removed to expose the heart of the wall sufficient to provide working space. Lime mortar fill cushions the area excavated for the stitch. Reinforcement is laid and concrete placed.

The pattern of the stitch provides restraint against possible movement in two planes

GENERAL FORM OF REINFORCED CONCRETE STITCH "S"

8

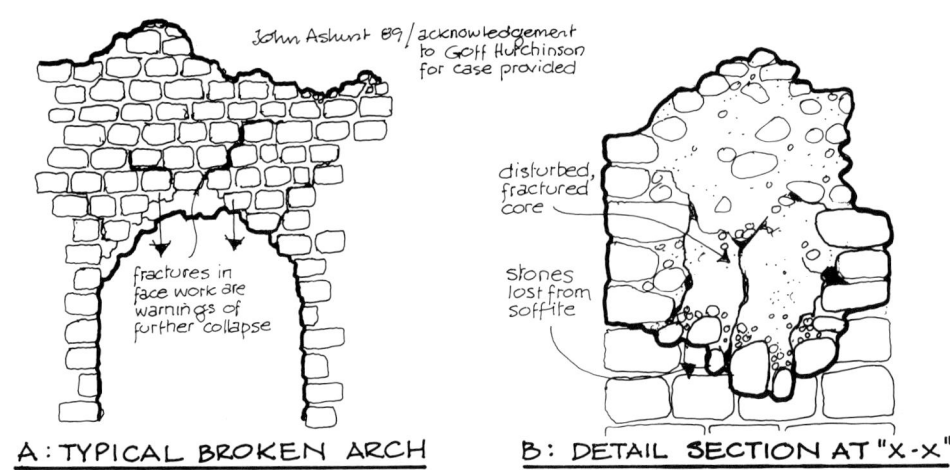

John Ashurst 89 / acknowledgement to Goff Hutchinson for case provided

fractures in face work are warnings of further collapse

A : TYPICAL BROKEN ARCH

disturbed, fractured core

stones lost from soffite

B : DETAIL SECTION AT "X-X"

Broken heads of openings are a common feature of ruined masonry buildings. Further failure represents a major hazard and can constitute substantial losses of historic fabric

These situations are sometimes resolved by unsatisfactory permanent propping. A more acceptable solution is to form surface supports in phosphor bronze or stainless steel straps. These are profiled to the ruined soffite of the opening using a template. The straps act as permanent "false-work" when bedded under the arch. Unfortunately, they are usually obvious [Example 'E']

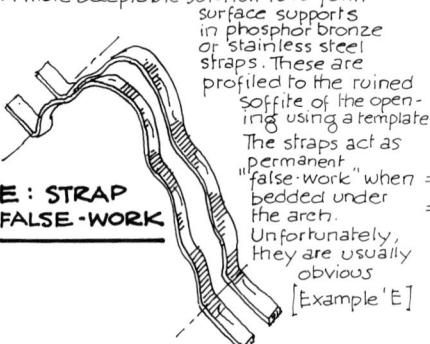

E : STRAP FALSE-WORK

coarse sand fill

core profile recorded before core is excavated

bitumen coating

stainless steel-hanger

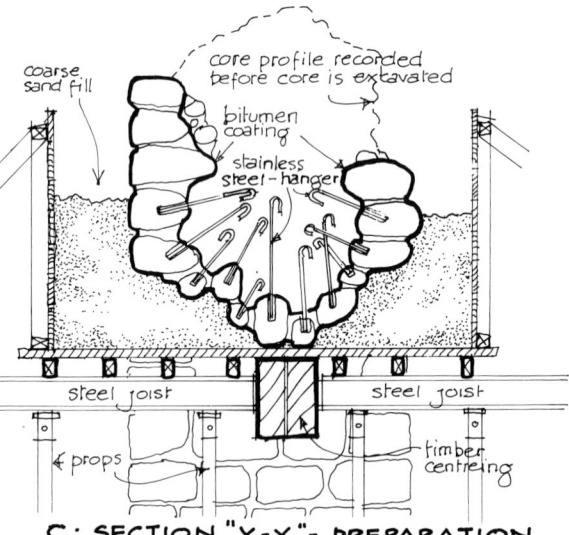

steel joist   steel joist

props   timber centreing

C : SECTION "X-X" - PREPARATION

Details B-C-D illustrate a system of inserting a secret lintol

B : shows the condition as found Careful recording and numbering of all the stones takes place at this stage

C : full support for the broken arch head is provided in the form of temporary centreing. Steel joists, props and timber bearers support a platform and boarded, strutted timber sides form a sand-box. Coarse sand is packed in to provide full support for all the stones.

The core is carefully lifted out in sections to expose the back of the stones. Each stone is drilled to receive a threaded stainless steel hook bar set in epoxy resin. The stones are bitumen coated at the back. Reinforcement is placed and concrete is poured to form a lintol from which the stones are now hanging.

core replaced to original profile

top and bottom reinforcement

concrete pour 1

concrete pour 2

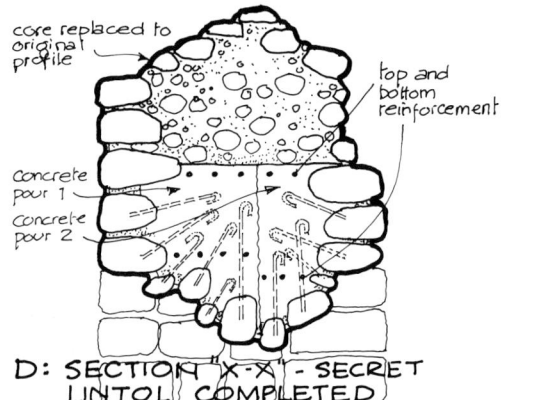

D : SECTION "X-X" - SECRET LINTOL COMPLETED

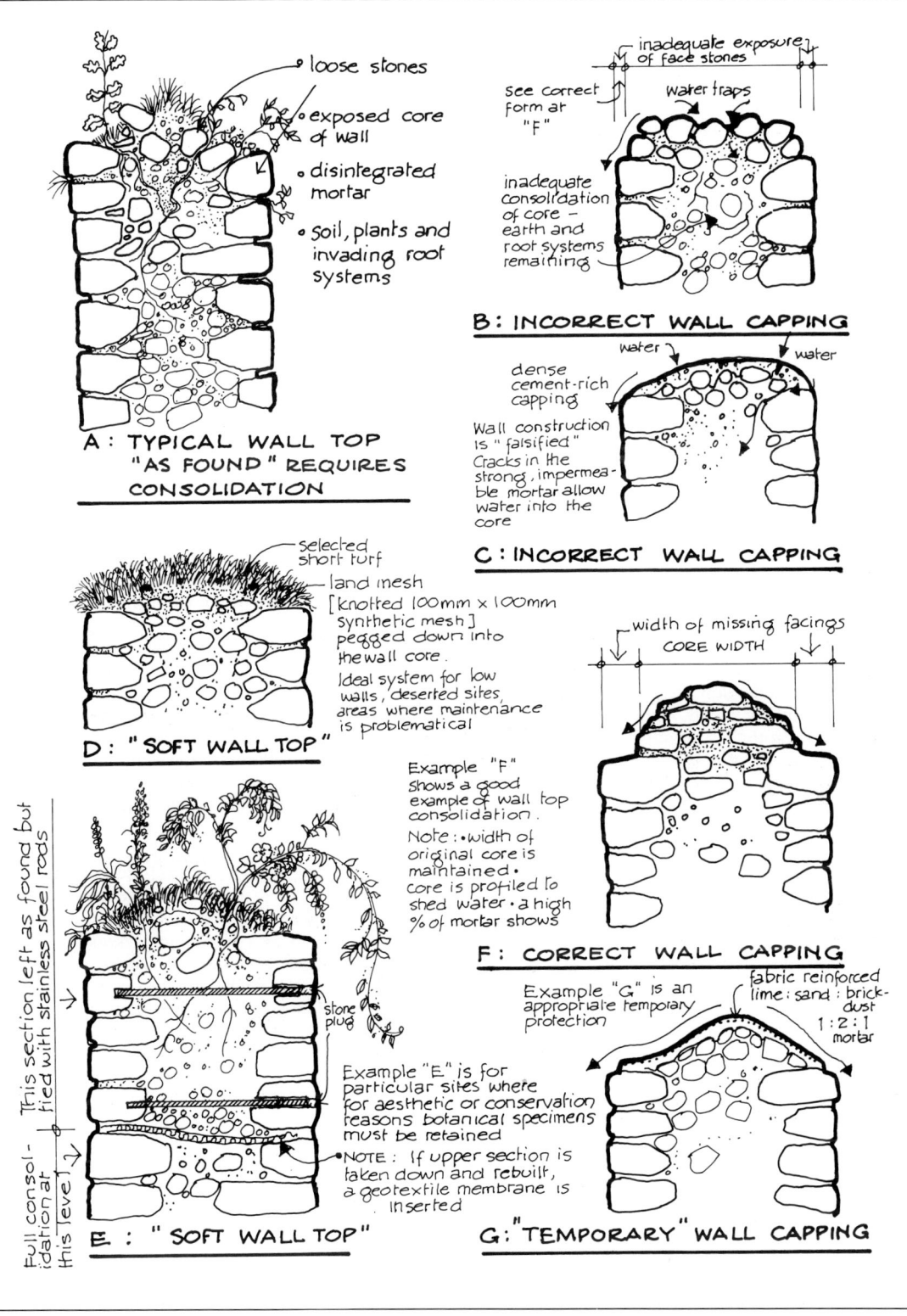

- loose stones
- exposed core of wall
- disintegrated mortar
- soil, plants and invading root systems

A : TYPICAL WALL TOP "AS FOUND" REQUIRES CONSOLIDATION

inadequate exposure of face stones

see correct form at "F"

water traps

inadequate consolidation of core — earth and root systems remaining

B: INCORRECT WALL CAPPING

water   water

dense cement-rich capping

Wall construction is "falsified" Cracks in the strong, impermeable mortar allow water into the core

C : INCORRECT WALL CAPPING

selected short turf

land mesh [knotted 100mm x 100mm synthetic mesh] pegged down into the wall core.

Ideal system for low walls, deserted sites, areas where maintenance is problematical

D : "SOFT WALL TOP"

width of missing facings

CORE WIDTH

Example "F" shows a good example of wall top consolidation.

Note: • width of original core is maintained • core is profiled to shed water • a high % of mortar shows

F : CORRECT WALL CAPPING

Full consolidation at this level

This section left as found but tied with stainless steel rods

stone plug

Example "E" is for particular sites where for aesthetic or conservation reasons botanical specimens must be retained

• NOTE : If upper section is taken down and rebuilt, a geotextile membrane is inserted

E : "SOFT WALL TOP"

Example "G" is an appropriate temporary protection

fabric reinforced lime: sand : brick-dust 1 : 2 : 1 mortar

G: "TEMPORARY" WALL CAPPING

application only, in order to avoid accidental contamination. Site clearance for archaeological investigation may be facilitated and field sites may be kept accessible to visitors by these means. It is worth remembering, however, that the presence of undergrowth, especially brambles, sometimes forms the best and most economic protection of unexplored or only partly explored sites from inquisitive amateurs.

Where walls stand above ground, control of woody weeds may be more essential. Whilst there are many circumstances in which small flowering plants may enhance the appearance of masonry walls without adverse effect, some creepers (especially in maturity) and trees are obviously undesirable. This is because their root systems feed on the wall core and disrupt stones. In particular, ivy (*Hedera helix*) should not be left on walls, because of its rapid growth and the searching effect of its aerial roots. These intrude into joints and rubble fill, converting originally substantial walls into an unstable mass of loose stones and decomposed mortar. In occupied buildings, mature creepers may cut out light, inhibit drying out and obscure the condition of the walls.

Whatever means are employed to kill the disruptive growth, digging out the roots is laborious but inescapable. The survival of even small pockets of woody root may allow the plant to re-establish itself or may create a void in the wall as the organic matter decomposes. Stones will normally have to be lifted out and reset, following the general advice already given. If the plant has its main root system established in the ground (a large ivy, for instance), the following procedure should be adopted.

1. Cut out a 1 metre (3 ft) section of the main stem between 300 mm (1 ft) and 1 metre (3 ft) above ground level, taking care not to let the saw slip against the masonry.
2. Spray the plant with a herbicide such as an ester formulation 2, 4, 5-T, and leave it to die. After the cutting the plant would die of its own accord without the spray treatment, but a well-established specimen might survive between one and two years on the wall.
3. Cut a frill girdle around the parent stem and coat all the exposed surfaces with a paste made from ammonium sulphamate crystals. The root system may then be left to die. This method is preferable to the more traditional process of drilling the stump and pouring in a corrosive acid. If the acid process is used, the drillings must be securely plugged afterwards. Ammonium sulphamate should not be used on masonry surfaces, especially limestone, where, in association with lime, it would become a nitrogenous fertilizer.
4. The dead plant on the wall must be removed carefully. Attempts to pull off well-established

plants with a rope are always hazardous and can result in the collapse of walls with weakened cores. Roots in the wall must be cut out and pursued, if necessary, deep into the core. If they are left to decay, voids will be created in the wall, threatening its later stability. Local grouting, wedging of blocks, tamping and resetting of stones must be anticipated in this kind of remedial work.

Coexistence of masonry and plant growth

In some situations botanical specimens, natural habitats and valuable, mature climbing plants of historical/horticultural importance have substantial claims on conservation and may well be valued more highly than the masonry against or on which they are growing. Cooperation between the conflicting interests is a necessary part of the solution. Whilst it is true that vegetation is not generally the friend of historic masonry, it is possible to contrive an acceptable co-existence by planning and control.

In no circumstances should plants be allowed to enter masonry joints, to interrupt the collection and discharge of rain-water or to take hold of a roof. Within this restriction, however, arrangements can be made by judicious cutting back of plants at the right season to introduce a climbing frame against a masonry wall. This should be a light grid of aluminium (painted with epoxide paint) or stainless steel, carefully fixed into joints or plugs in the stones with long expanding stainless steel bolts passing through sleeve spacers. The object of such a construction is to allow the climbing or spreading plant to grow against a screen. A useful gap of 50–100 mm (2–4 in) between the screen and the masonry face can usually be achieved, and the frame facilitates the 'disciplining' of the plant. Although such an installation can be seen as a considerable security risk on occupied historic buildings, it can be argued that mature plants on walls are also a security risk. Climbing grids can be linked to alarm systems.

On ruined sites the need to keep high-level wall tops clear of vegetation has already been made clear. An interesting experiment is currently in hand at Jervaulx Abbey in Yorkshire on lower ruined walls. The Jervaulx site is important botanically, and preservation of the masonry has consisted of consolidating the walls from ground level only up to within three or four courses of the broken wall tops. Consolidation consists of grouting, tamping and pointing to achieve a solid construction. There is a 'soft' wall top containing soil, grass and established flowering plants and small, wild shrubs. Although such wall tops are obviously moisture-holding and there is a frost-risk to the mortar, the experiment is promising. 'Soft' wall tops should not be left on walls over four metres (13 ft) high which are not readily accessible for maintenance.

Treatment of historic masonry

Good masonry practice is not always in harmony with the aims of stone conservation. The trained mason and the owner of an old stone building may be in agreement on the replacement of all heavily weathered, disfigured or damaged stones; the mason's approach may be in the best traditions of repair and maintenance, and the owner may want to see a complete and pristine building. Conservation, however, is about minimum replacement and minimum, or no, restoration.

Cutting out existing stones

In the context of conservation a moderate, sensible balance must be reached between the extensive, speculative restorations of the nineteenth century and the reaction-opinion that to insert any new stone at all in an ancient wall is debasement and dishonesty. The criteria for deciding which stones in an old masonry structure should be replaced include:

1. *The value of the stones.* The intrinsic value of any worked stone in a building varies considerable with the age of the building and the quality and condition of the detail. The approach to a decayed eighteenth century rusticated ashlar is usually, for not very well defined reasons, rather different to the approach to a twelfth century door moulding. The ashlar will certainly involve less speculation if it is replaced than will the medieval detail. The ashlar can usually be replaced with accuracy from well known matching examples.

It is difficult to determine 'value' and to make rules about it. Perhaps it is sufficient to say that copies should not usually be attempted of carving and sculpture too distant from us in time and culture, especially where the original work is characterized by subtle freedom of line and form. Sometimes the value of individual stones, especially in Renaissance and later work, is subordinate to the value of the architectural design of the building. The line of a string with its important, unbroken shadow may be considerable of far more importance than the preservation of a few decayed stones in its length.

2. *The function of the stones.* The function of any stone which is under consideration for replacement must be clearly understood. Decaying stones which have a structural role and on which the stability and survival of other stones or other elements of the structure depend have a clear priority for replacement, almost regardless of their intrinsic value. Typical stones in this category are quoin stones, arch and vault springers and decayed ribs.

Stones which have a protective role provide another essential function. Examples in this category include copings, buttress and plinth weatherings and label mouldings. The replacement of these stones if they are decayed is essential for the survival of the stones below them.

3. *The timing of the replacement.* The expense of a scaffolding is, in itself, an encouragement to replace 'border-line' stones which might or might not survive until the next scaffold access in twenty, fifty or one hundred years. No one in this situation likes to leave a doubtful situation which may require emergency scaffolding a few years after consolidation and repairs had, supposedly, been completed. A.D.R. and M.B. Caroe[1] suggest, in the context of the English parish church, that the life of the stones should be considered in relation to likely scaffold access intervals as follows:

- Low aisles: stones with 25–30 years estimated life should remain.
- Towers: stones with 50–70 years estimated life should remain.
- Spires: stones with at least one hundred years of estimated life should remain.

Estimated life depends entirely on the experience of the architect and his masons, who should use their knowledge to balance their concern for the building with the need to preserve for posterity as much original fabric as possible.

4. *Alternative remedial work.* Alternatives to removing stone must always be considered first. Such measures may simply involve attention to open joints or the provision of a lead flashing or discreet gutter over a label mould and stop. They may also include the removal of an impermeable cement pointing, or a surface treatment designed to protect with a sacrificial layer or deeply penetrating consolidant. In this category, too, may be the design and provision of a protection screen or roof over, for example, a rood or tympanum.

In the face of over-enthusiastic restorationists demanding a new building it should be remembered that it is replacement, not retention of original fabric, that has to be justified.

Once decisions have been made, based on the above criteria, on which stones are to be replaced, these will need to be indicated on a record drawing or photograph, or ideally on a photogrammetric survey drawing. They must also be clearly marked on site with an indelible marker. There is no satisfactory short-cut to on-site marking of individual stones, which is best carried out in the company of a stone mason who will understand the practical implications of cutting back the selected stones. Once a decision has been taken on replacement, the most economical and sensible way of carrying out the work must be determined. In general, new stones will need to be 100 mm (4 in) on bed, unless the stones are very small or only local piecing-in of a larger stone is taking place, but it is often cheaper to remove an old stone completely than to face it with a new 100 mm (4 in) skin. During the marking up procedure notes should also be prepared for the specification of necessary temporary supports which may simply be wooden plates and blocks or, when lintels, arches and vaults are involved, full centering.

The physical process of cutting out the old stone will vary according to the situation. The old stone may still retain some vestige of moulding or carving and it may be retained for a museum. Alternatively, it may be a faceless, scaling lump which is simply to be broken up and disposed of. In either case care is required to ensure that the adjacent surviving stones are not damaged. Cutting of perimeter joints may be carried out with a masonry saw or a diamond cutting disc mounted on a power tool. If the old stone is to be retained the cut will first be made by a diamond disc in the case of a fine joint and hard mortar, or with a plugging chisel in the case of a wide joint and lime mortar. In both cases the cut should be finished with the help of the saw. If the stone is to be wasted it may be drilled out after the initial cutting or broken up with a hammer and chisel.

Smaller-scale piecing in will involve cutting into an existing stone to remove a pocket of decay. Piecings may be very small in good quality work, for example 20 mm (0.8 in) square on face. The cut out must be made with small, sharp chisels and small saw blades to a neat, square profile.

Large stones may be 150 mm (6 in) on bed. Bonders whose tails are to be bedded into core work may be larger. If a large area is to be faced up with new stones it is essential that the new 'skin' should be cramped back with a staggered grid of stainless steel fishtail cramps.

Replacement stones

New stone should match the original as closely as possible. In Chapter 3 criteria relating to selection are discussed. In many cases a substitute stone will have to be found. In these cases some knowledge of the characteristics of original and new stones is necessary. In the UK, the Building Research Establishment has published books on the durability of French and British limestones and British sandstones and Magnesian Limestones.[2].

Stones must be carefully matched to original sizes

Piecing-in

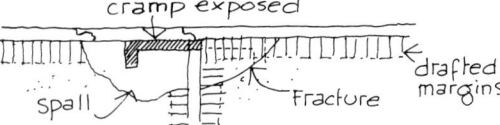

Typical problem   Rusting iron cramps cause the splitting and spalling of ashlar faces

Typical solution   The spalls, and incipient spalls, are cut out, the cramps removed and substituted and new, matching stone is pieced-in.

Note In a situation of this kind the whole wall should be examined for potential failures. The cramp failure may be isolated due to a positioning too near the wall face or due to a faulty joint which has allowed water to enter locally; alternatively, it may be the first sign of wholescale failures over the wall. The stages described represent the execution of the best quality work. Short cuts may be thought appropriate in any given similar situation, but it is important to remember that short cuts often involve an element of gambling and frequently lead to inaccuracies.

Specification and procedure

1.   Determine the overall size of the stone pieces required to make good the damage. Each stone must be repaired independently with no bridging of joints.

2.   Select a matching stone for the piecing-in. The stone must be as close as possible to the original in colour, grain size, shell content and other particular characteristics. The pieces must be geologically compatible with the host stones and placed in the same bed. Colour differences which will be corrected by natural weathering should be accepted.

3.   Reduce the two pieces for the repair down to the required size with the joint and bed faces finished fine and true (see note 16).

4.   Offer the prepared pieces up to the damaged wall and scribe the areas to be cut out using a tungsten tipped or hardened steel scribe and using the new pieces as a template.

5.   Cut out the damaged stone with tungsten or fire-sharp tools to expose the cramp, providing a slight undercut to the joint faces. The scribe line should be removed by the cutting tools leaving a sharp, true, clean edge to the socket being formed. Cut round the old cramp with a sharp quirk, lift out the cramp, brush out all rust and scale and form new shoulders for a new cramp.

6.   Fix locating pins into the back of the new pieces. The size and number of these pins is determined by the size of the piece to be fixed, but normally there should be a minimum of two. Drill the back of each piece to receive the pins (e.g. 25 mm in a 50 mm piece). Wash out the drill holes to ensure

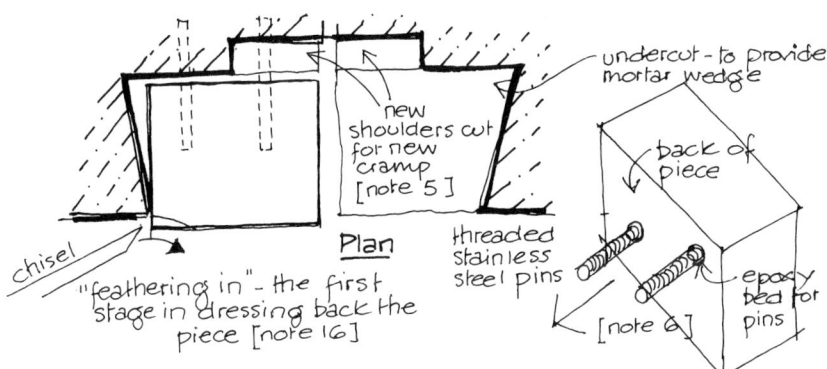

that they are free of dust and that no slurry remains in the holes. Form a template in zinc or hardboard to fit the back of the pieces and mark the position of the holes on the template.

Select and cut to size suitable pins (e.g. threaded stainless steel or ragged phosphor bronze 4–3 mm diameter). On no account should ordinary ferrous pins be used. When the stone pieces are dry, fill the drill holes no more than two-thirds full with a thixotropic epoxy grout such as SBD Epoxy Plus Anchor Grout. Place the template on the back of the piece so that the template holes overlie the holes in the piece, and drop in the pins. The purpose of the template is to hold the pins true and square while the resin cures (e.g. 2–4 hours). Ensure that no displaced resin is in contact with the template.

7. When the resin has cured, offer the pieces up to the socket again. Mark the ends of the newly fixed pins with wax chalk to enable corresponding marks to be transferred to the back of the socket.

8. Drill out the hole positions now marked to a suitable depth to receive the pins (e.g. for a 30 mm pin projection on the back of the piece, drill out 35 mm). Thoroughly remove all dust and slurry from the drill holes and the socket. A hand-held water spray with a fine pencil jet and an off-cut of threaded rod is a good combination to scrape out all the slurry from the holes. It is essential not to rely on washing out alone, as any remaining film of slurry will adversely affect the bond.

9. Offer up the pieces of the socket again to ensure that the fit is good and that the pins are properly aligned. At this stage, final trimming and sharpening of the arrises with a fire-sharp chisel may take place if required.

10. Thoroughly soak the new pieces in clean water.

11. Wet up the joint faces and surrounding faces of stone in the socket using a hand spray and clean water. Ensure, by temporary plugging or other means, that the holes formed for the pins remain dry.

12. Slurry the surfaces of the socket and the pieces which come into close contant with each other. The slurry should be a finely sieved paste of lime putty and white refractory brick dust (suitable for limestone) or hydraulic lime and stone dust (suitable for sandstone) and should, by the choice of fine, staining sands or dusts, endeavour to provide as close a match as possible to the host stone.

13. Fully fill the drill holes with thixotropic epoxy anchor grout.

14. Offer up the slurried piece and ease it into the socket with a sawing motion to ensure full contact of all surfaces until the piece is fully home.

15. Sponge off any slurry on the face of the work at once.

16. After an adequate curing time, which should be at least 24 hours, surface dressing or finishing of the piece may be undertaken. In general, most new pieces will require some dressing at this stage, which may range from simple carborundum rubbing to the full replication of the tooled surface of the host stone. The amount of stone left proud of the surface will be dicated by the finish required. To avoid damage to the edge of the new pieces during tooling back, the edges should first be feathered down flush.

Note Stones should not be bedded in resins. Resins such as the familiar epoxies, polyesters and acrylics set up impervious or relatively impervious barriers against which water in the wall will be checked. Staining and salt crystallization will almost inevitably follow. Quality piecing-in should, in time, be almost indistinguishable from the host stone. Note also that if the wall is to be cleaned, this cleaning should take place before the piecing-in is carried out, to avoid the risk of staining the new pieces.

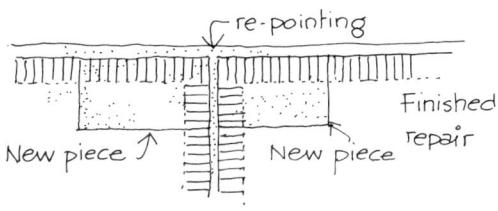

Note: dowells (shown ╫) are recommended as there is little keying between sawn stones

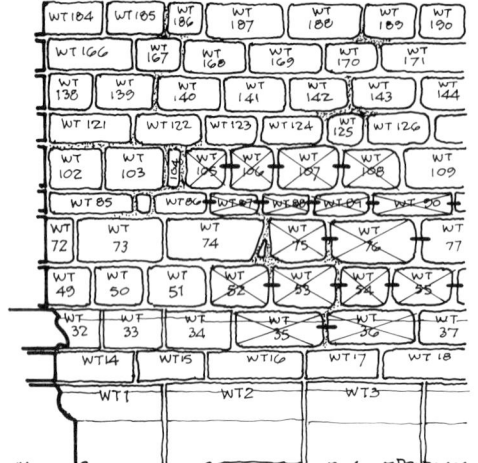

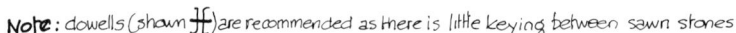

NEW STONES ARE DIMENSIONED "L × B × H"

true dimension

weathered profiles of old stone

BED

"A"

CORRECT FACE LINE OF WALL

NEW STONE

OLD STONE

"B"

PART ELEVATION Showing <u>all</u> stones identified by a code number on a drawing or survey photograph. The condition of each stone is considered individually and as part of the wall. The crossed stones have decayed extensively and are to be replaced. Areas for pointing are hatched

STONES are marked insitu for removal with an indelible marker or incision. They are similarly recorded on a survey document. New stone for replacement must be geologically compatible and of similar grain size and colour. Dimensions are taken as "A" and "C". These must be the <u>true</u> dimensions and not weathered or restoration dimensions. Careful note should be made of any surviving tooling, which should be matched on the new stones. If no such evidence survives a fine, textured, rubbed finish is recommended. This is achieved with a hand-held block of the same stone and a uniform size coarse sand abrasive. This will "mellow" the face without artificiality or speculation about tooling patterns. At the very least, all saw marks must be removed. Sharp arrises off the saw can be translated into "pencil-rounds" in the same way to good effect. New stones will stand proud of the old if the correct face line is maintained. Where necessary, water traps in the form of ledges should be subtly weathered 'off', as at "B", not covered with thick mortar fillets.

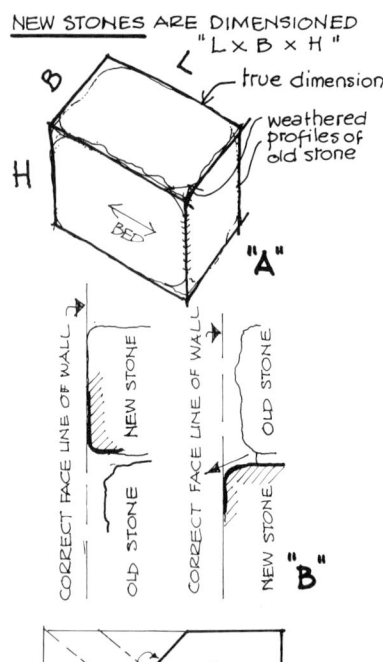

ships cut with snips and snapped

profile scribed onto zinc sheet

"C"

JOINT MOULD FOR WT 35 AND WT 36

CUTTING OUT is generally from the bottom up, a course or part of a course at a time. This will avoid major collapse if a separation between face and corework occurs. The sequence of cutting out, and indenting, is as follows:—

[WT] 35·36·53·55·54·52·76·75·89·87·86·88·70·107·105·106·108·

The method of cutting out is to work from the centre of the stones breaking them with points and chisels and working towards the edge. The cavities should be well-washed out and, if salt migration has been a problem it is recommended that the cavity is lime:sand slurried and bitumen coated.

JOGGLES AND DOWELS AND CRAMPS tie the

stones into each other and to the wall core. Plain ashlars are cut in the joint beds with straight joggles and the moulded stones with Y-joggles. These correspond to horizontal dowel holes as shown at "D" and "E". The top beds of the stones are morticed to receive stainless steel fishtail cramps which are bedded into the core. It is vital not to form skins of consolidated masonry which are not properly bonded or tied back.

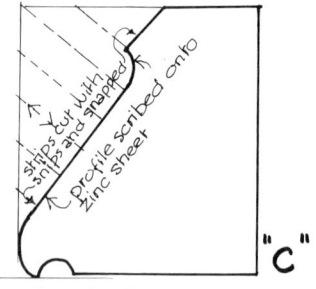

grout   grout

dowel hole

"D"

JOGGLES Moulding Ashlar

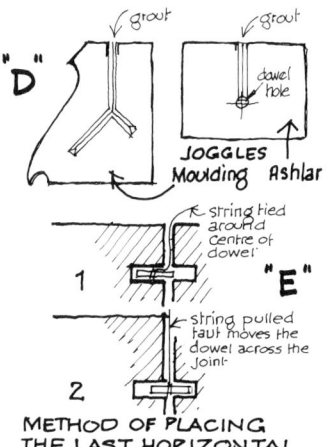

string tied around centre of dowel

"E"

1

string pulled taut moves the dowel across the joint.

2

METHOD OF PLACING THE LAST HORIZONTAL DOWEL

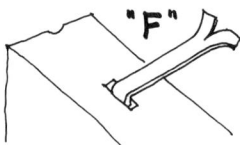

"F"

POINTING AND GROUT-ING are the last stage. The top joint is dry packed while grouting takes place of the final course.

and profiles. Where possible the original finish should be matched, except when, for reasons of historical accuracy, the repair stone is deliberately left to a simpler profile or with a distinctive finish. Sometimes the original profile may not be readily determined, especially when there has been extensive weathering or where there has been a succession of repairs and replacements perhaps over several hundred years. To make a copy of a copy is almost always a mistake, because details can become less and less accurate. In such cases the advice of a competent archaeologist must be sought, so that profiles can be taken from the original stones where possible. Such information may only survive in one small, sheltered area; if so, its value is extremely high and the making of an accurate copy is essential. A profile may be drawn *in situ* directly onto a zinc or tough plastic insert where this can be slipped into a joint carefully sawn out with a small masonry saw. If a joint does not occur in the run of desired moulding a fine saw cut may be made through the moulding itself. In exceptional circumstances it may be necessary to take a squeeze mould in clay and to produce a good cast from which the profile may be taken. From these and from face measurements the bed moulds (plans of the stones) and joint moulds (profiles) can be prepared as drawings and as zinc or acrylic sheet templates. These drawings and templates must be carefully and indelibly marked so that their identity and location are in no doubt. They should be kept safely after the work is complete as part of the building records, and hung or pinned up, not left lying.

Today the replacement stones are sawn to size and may be partly machined to reduce the time which must be spent on hand working. The moulds and templates are then used to mark out the stone in pencil. Further reduction takes place with hammer and punch, mallet and claw tool, mallet and chisel and perhaps drag. As much use as possible may be made of compressed air tools to reduce the time involved. When the stone has progressed with its job card through the production line it should be clearly marked with its job reference and location and packed in polystyrene and straw to protect it from damage during transit and handling. Limestone and marble may receive a temporary protective slurry of lime and stone dust which can easily be cleaned down on completion of fixing. Although straw is a cheap and traditional packing, when wet it can stain light coloured stones. Synthetic packaging is increasingly used, and in many ways is preferable but it must be effective. To spoil expensively produced stones through carelessness is an unforgivable waste of money and shows scant regard for the work which has gone into their production. On arrival at the site the new stones must be stored off the ground (with air spaces between them) to prevent absorption of water and salts from the ground, and with heavy-duty polyethylene sheets over them to avoid saturation from rain.

Placing the new stones

The stones can be raised into position by hand, hoist, or hand winch depending on their weight and location in the building. The cavity or open bed to receive them should be carefully cleaned out and a mortar bed spread onto the wetted old stone. The new stone must also be dampened to avoid the risk of dewatering the mortar. The mortar may be a 12 mm (0.5 in) thick bed with coarse sand and grit to match the original mortar, or no more than a fine buttering with masons' putty. The stone should be handled into position and eased into the correct alignment with the aid of the lubrication provided by the wet mortar. Very heavy stones may have temporary additional support in the form of lead or slate packs. The top bed joint and the perpendicular joints may then be stopped up on the surface with clay ready for grouting. Grout pouring holes and proving holes (exit points to indicate the grout flow) are left in the joints. The grout should be lime with a low sulphate fly ash or lime and a pozzolanic additive such as HTI powder; it must *not* be a cement grout, which is brittle when set, extremely hard and notorious for staining from alkali salts. Mortar staining of new light coloured limestones is a constant problem; the recommended grouts and the protective slurry left on until completion of the work should avoid the worst risks.

Where a background of core or brick cannot, for some reason, be treated with an isolating paint such as sanded bitumen the new stone may itself be painted on all but its face to avoid contamination from salt laden moisture in the old wall. Such a treatment must stop 25 mm (1 in) short of the face to avoid any risk of discoloration from the paint. The condition of the wall, the reason for the decay and likely moisture movements will influence the decision on painting, but it is generally considered to be a sensible procedure.

New stones, when not to be grouted up as described above, must be bedded but not pointed until the work has settled in. If the stone is a sill or lintel the bedding mortar may initially be placed under bearing points only and subsequently tamped and pointed, but this procedure relates principally to new work rather than replacement. Even so, pointing of the outer 25 mm (1 in) should be left until all the bedding work has settled.

Sometimes new stones, or new stone faces, may be spot-secured with an epoxy adhesive. A typical example of this is the halving of decayed mullions in traceried windows, where the decayed stone is cut back to the glass line and half mullions are glued to the face of the surviving internal half. Excellent as modern resin adhesives may be, it is always unwise to rely on the interface bond alone. The halving technique relies, therefore, on dowell pins of stainless steel, phosphor bronze or even glass fibre.

In some situations the use of pins and epoxy mortars has enabled valuable masonry features to be saved which otherwise would have been lost. An illustration of this is the securing of the traceried windows of the Temple Church in Bristol. They were shattered during the blitz of World War II when the roof burnt off as incendiary bombs dropped into the nave and the use of fire hoses produced a thermal shock. Thirty years later the tracery was a fragile jigsaw of pieces retained in position only by rusting ferramenta and softwood corsets bolted together. The alternatives were total replacement or *in situ* stitching together of the pieces. Careful drilling down the length of the mullions and through the tracery bars enabled grouping with an epoxy mortar and stitching with pins of glass fibre to take place. The spalls and lacunae were then built up in phosphor bronze wire and matching mortar. A similar technique was used to hold back the fire-shattered external face of the Norman masonry in Westminster Hall.

The drilling and injection of holes to receive resin and reinforcement requires great care and thoughtful preparation of the site. The viscosity of the resin should permit the drill hole to be filled adequately under the pressure from a gun or a hypodermic syringe. Fine fissures may be grouted with a very thin, low viscosity resin, but the useful mobility of such materials is also a risk; it is not possible to control or to 'pull back' the grout once injected, so adequate precautions must be available in the form of latex paint 'facing', modelling clay for plugging runs, and swabs and solvents. Latex paint can be brushed onto the surface in one or preferably two applications, and can be peeled off on completion of the work.

After holes have been drilled, they must be flushed out with a solvent, or, if drying time is available, with water. Flushing out is best achieved with the same apparatus used to inject the resin. Small holes may sometimes be cleared of dust by blowing out with a small tube. One of the problems especially associated with smaller holes is the entrapment of air when the resin is injected. If a hypodermic syringe is used, a length of tube or plastic drinking straw, cut to the depth of the drilling, can be attached to the end of the hypodermic and filled with resin before insertion into the hole. In this way, the hole will be filled from the deepest point back to the surface. The amount of resin injected into the hole must take account of the displacement that will occur when the reinforcement is inserted. Unless the hole is very small in diameter, the resin should not come too close to the surface. For a hole 6 mm (0.25 in) in diameter, prepared to take a 3 mm (0.125 in) rod, the hole should be injected for approximately two-thirds of its depth. Pins should be sized before injecting resin. The heads of the pins should not be closer to the surface than 6 mm (0.25 in) for small diameters, or 12 mm (0.5 in) for large diameters, allowing the outer 6–12 mm (0.25–0.5 in) to be filled with a fine matching mortar.

Redressing stone

The removal of the original face from the surface of an old stone wall is a drastic process and one that is quite alien to the normal principles of conservation. Although the practice should be resisted while there is any hope of conserving the original face, there are some circumstances when it may be justified—for instance, where the face of the stones has become badly disfigured by blistering, splitting or spalling, or by poor quality, superficial repairs. There are many examples where redressing has taken place on a large scale, especially in the English cities of London and Oxford, where there was no satisfactory alternative. However, there are many other examples where redressing has been used as a cosmetic treatment, with the object of re-introducing uniformity and creating a 'new' appearance. Destruction of an original face for such reasons is always to be discouraged.

Successful redressing demands a high level of expertise, especially where mouldings and columns with entasis are involved. Recent examples of successful redressing can be seen at All Souls College, Oxford, and at Woburn Abbey, England, where the decayed, original clunch face has been taken back with compressed air chisels and hand rubbing. Other redressing tools include combs and drags.

A more sophisticated system for putting a new surface on badly decayed and disfigured limestone was employed recently on a Palladian-style building in Cirenester, England. Ian Constantides (St Blaise Ltd) developed a system with Diamant Boart Ltd based on the latter's standard drilling rig. The system was modified to lock into the scaffold. A two-speed 2.1 kW motor powered the machine which 'dressed' the surface with an electro-plated, diamond-faced grinding disc. Approximately 6 mm of stone was removed from the surface and approximately 12 square metres could be redressed from one position of the rig. Clearly, the use of such a system is limited to simple, flat surfaces and does not eliminate the need to work by hand, but it can produce a very accurate, close finish compatible with the original fine rubbed surface.

There is no technical reason why redressing should not take place, although many masons are opposed to it and E.G. Warland, in his *Modern Practical Masonry*,[3] claims that the quarry sap drying from the freshly quarried block leaves 'a deposit of crystals which fills, or partly fills, the pores of the stone, thus forming a film on the surface. The removal of this film greatly reduces the weathering properties of the stone'. The long history of reworked and redressed stone does not bear out this claim, and Schaffer[4] discounts it altogether. What is certainly true is that weathered stone is usually very tough to work and very demanding on the tools.

The hardening of a freshly quarried stone from the face is a well known phenomenon. The moisture present in the stone contains some of its natural cementing matrix in solution. (This is discussed more fully in Volume 1, page 33.) Traditionally, the more the stone could be worked in its 'green' state, the more receptive it was to cutting and carving. The finished stone would then be seen to harden in a very satisfactory way. If the finished faces of sculpture received a thin plaster of lime gesso while the stone was still drying out, the plaster hardened onto the face and became a superb and very durable ground for polychrome. Traditional practices of this kind, coupled with the failure of thin sulphate skins after exposure to a polluted environment and the observation of powdery stone and small crystals immediately below the skin, are likely to have reinforced the 'essential surface' idea. It would be an easy step to link the relatively tough sulphated surface on a weak limestone with a protective skin provided centuries before.

Redressing of the arrises of sandstone blocks is a common solution to the problems of contour scaling exacerbated by lime leaching from core work through the masonry joints. This situation is typically identifiable by a margin of decay around each stone, sometimes accompanied by efflorescences and splitting parallel with the arrises. Redressing is commonly carried out to improve the appearance and to reduce the occurrence of water traps. However, a curious rusticated appearance may result, or a rough surface patterned with claw or drag marks may be left if the work is carried out by an inexperienced operative. Limited redressing coupled with piecing in with new stone is often a satisfactory compromise.

Wholescale redressing should not be attempted where the stone is weak or of poor quality. There are nearly always alternatives to redressing even in the most problematical situations.

Repairing with tiles

The use of clay tiles as an alternative to piecing in with new stone is of some antiquity but was adopted and developed for philosophical reasons under the influence of the Society for the Protection of Ancient Buildings. The insertion of tiles, bedded in lime mortar and limewashed or left exposed or sometimes rendered, was seen as a way of carrying out an 'honest' and readily identifiable repair which could not be confused with original work. The technique has some specific technical advantages, too.

Powys[5] says: 'The material [tile] is very durable, the surface is plastic and can be modelled to fit adjoining stones, it is so keyed to the stone backing as to become part of it, and the finished texture and colour are not objectionable, and "weather" pleasantly.' In the absence of appropriate stone for repair or the appropriate masonry skills, a further advantage may be claimed in that cutting away and building up in tiles may be carried out with a readily available material using relatively unskilled labour.

Repairs of this kind can be structural or only cosmetic. Complete mullions may be built up in tile, or jambs or quoins may be rebuilt by blockbounding courses of tiles into the stone behind. Alternatively, minor damages or lost faces may simply be covered in tile pieces and rendered. The informal line which Powys describes as the 'plastic surface' and which can be drawn between the heavily weathered faces of adjacent surviving and remaining stones overcomes one of the problems of attempting to marry in a new piece of stone.

Understandably, this repair method does not often appeal to stonemasons nor to many architects and building owners. It may be seen as the thin end of an unattractive wedge, leading to a ridiculous hotch potch of materials which will finally rob a building of its dignity and interest. There is no doubt, however, that tile repairs have saved stones in the past and will continue to do so. The technique has an established place in masonry conservation.

Rendering external masonry surfaces

If there is sound evidence for the existence of external rendering at the period of building then re-rendering in a suitable material may be justified on historical, visual and maintenance grounds. The wall construction of much church building in Britain, for instance, consists of dressed stone quoins, jambs and arches, and areas of random coursed or uncoursed stones which were rendered to keep walls weatherproof. The rendering may have failed and not been replaced, or it may have been deliberately stripped off and all the joints laboriously pointed in ignorance of the original design and intent or merely for visual preference. There is often a temptation to remove rendering from old walls, especially when extensive, ugly patching up has been carried out in a dense mortar; indeed if an old wall has been re-rendered with an impermeable cement-rich mortar it is often good sense to remove it and replace it with a more permeable lime render. Dense renders always crack and admit water into the body of the wall. The water cannot escape except, perhaps, through the inside face. Successful rendering must inhibit the direct penetration of water through the joints but be capable of absorbing and then yielding moisture through evaporation without detaching from the wall surface.

Matching the rendering

Careful study should be made of what original, or likely original, plaster survives. If the evidence is slight it may be difficult to tell if a thin or a thick rendering existed or if, as is so often the case with undressed or roughly dressed stones, the thick mortar joints were simply extended as a slurry over most of the stone face. In these cases the line of any dressed quoin or jamb stones in relation to the infill masonry may be some guide, as may be other buildings of similar age and construction in the area. In some cases the rendering may have extended over dressed stones as well as infill, although not usually over mouldings. Some help may be found from old paintings or prints.

Surviving areas of render may be analysed to determine binder:aggregate ratios and to assist in the identification of aggregates for matching purposes. The design of new rendering, however, although seeking to be a good visual match for the old, should be based more on known good practice than on results of analysis. Samples of the new rendering should be laid on the wall and approved when dry for colour and texture.

Preparing the wall

Preparation procedures for most situations tend to follow the same principles. They may be summarized as follows:

1. Brush down all wall surfaces with a stiff bristle or non-ferrous wire brush to remove scales, loose mortar and algae and lichen. Wash off with mains-pressure water through a hose, or high-pressure water through a lance. When dry, treat with a biocide.
   Or de-scale walls with a high-pressure, low-volume water lance at 500 psi to remove all loose scale and loose mortar. When dry, treat with a biocide.
   Or clean all wall surfaces with a wet-head system compressed air and abrasive to remove all loose scale and loose mortar. Finish the work by flushing with water alone. When dry, treat with a biocide.

2. Deep tamp all open joints with lime mortar. Dub out cavities in lime mortar and small stones or pieces of clay tile, leaving a rough surface for keying to the render.
3. Form a bridging over wood, metal, concrete (or other material which is significantly dissimilar in porosity to the general background) with stainless steel expanded metal secured with stainless steel screws and washers, *or* with a spatterdash coat of hydraulic lime aggregate; 50% of the material should be of approximately 5 mm (0.2 in) size, the remainder graded down.
4. Thoroughly dampen the substrate immediately before applying the undercoat and all subsequent coats with water from a hose or lance to cut down the risks of suction and de-watering the rendering mix.

Mixes for rendering

Although the variations on substrate and exposure combinations are endless, some typical situations which involve rendering stone surfaces include:

1. Thick, rough textured rendering on sound stone rubble.
2. Thin, smooth textured rendering on sound stone rubble.
3. Rendering on weak, friable backgrounds.
4. Rendering on strong, impermeable backgrounds.

Thick, rough textured renderings have the best chance of survival when correctly specified. They have good drying-out characteristics and are least susceptible to shrink crazing and cracking. Two or three coats are usual for masonry.

Thin, smooth textured rendering on sound stone rubble may be carried out in the same mixes but in one or two coats only and omitting the stones and some of the hair. The principal differences are in some of the application techniques, described below. The render coat thickness and finishing coat should be in the order of 6–9 mm and 4–6 mm respectively.

Rendering on weak, friable backgrounds presents particular problems of adhesion which can only satisfactorily be overcome with the aid of fabric reinforcement and anchors. Mixes should be of the lime type only, as above, but if the exposure is moderate to severe the HTI proportion may be doubled and the lime:aggregate ratio kept at 1:2.5 for render and finishing coats. Reinforcement in the form of stainless steel or other expanded metal is possible but will necessitate a greater thickness of rendering than may be desirable. An alkali-resistant glass fibre woven fabric, with anchors into masonry joints, is therefore recommended.

Table 1.1 Mixes for thick, rough textured renderings

Type one: Cement compo. These may be used on sound backings in quite severe exposures.

		Cement	Lime	Aggregates (sharp sand, pebbles and small stones) Sand:stones
Render coat (up to 9 mm (⅜ in) thick)		1	1	6:0
Floating coat (up to 9 mm (⅜ in) thick)		1	1	6:0
Butter coat	*either*	1	1	6:0
	or	1	2	9:0
Finishing coat	*either*	1	1	3:3
	or	1	2	5:4

The butter and finishing coats combined can be up to 12 mm (½ in) thick.

Type two: Hydraulic lime. These mixes may be used on slightly weaker backgrounds in moderate to severe exposures.

	Cement	Hydraulic lime	Aggregates Sand:stones
Render coat (up to 9 mm (⅜ in) thick)	0.5	2	5:0
Floating coat (up to 9 mm (⅜ in) thick)	–	2	5:0
Butter coat	–	2	5:0
Finishing coat	–	2	3:3

The butter and finishing coats combined can be up to 12 mm (½ in) thick.

Type three. Lime. These mixes may be used on weak to moderately strong backgrounds in sheltered to moderate exposures.

	Lime	Pozzolanic additive (HTI)	Aggregate Sand:stones
Render coat (up to 9 mm (⅜ in) thick)	1	0.1	2.5:0

A hair or synthetic alkali resistant fibre reinforcement is often to be recommended, beaten in to the render coat at 5 kg/m³ of coarse stuff (lime:sand). The hair must be clean, well combed (natural hair) and chopped to 50 mm to 150 mm lengths.

	Lime	Pozzolanic additive (HTI)	Aggregate Sand:stones
Floating coat (up to 9 mm (⅜ in) thick)	1	0.1	3:0
Finishing coat	1	–	2:1

The lime rendering would traditionally be limewashed (see Appendix 1).

Table 1.2 Mixes for thin, smoother renderings

Type one: Two coat

	Pozzolanic additive (HTI)	Lime	Aggregates (fine sharp sand and stone dust)
Render coat	½	1	2
Finish coat	¼	1	2

Type two : One coat

	Pozzolanic additive (buff coloured brick dust	Lime	Aggregates (fine sharp sand and stone dust)
	½	1	1½

Rendering on strong, rather impermeable backgrounds such as granite, basalt or flint is often, mistakenly, carried out in dense, cement-rich mixes. In these cases, although the strong mortar will not damage the background, an inefficient rendering results which lets water in through shrinkage and movement cracks and traps it in the wall. Adhesion is often poor initially and these dense renderings tend to detach in large areas. Unless an overall backing of stainless steel expanded metal is used, a haired or fibre reinforced undercoat is recommended on a spatterdash render coat. PVA (polyvinyl acetate) bonding agents are often used to overcome the natural bonding problem, but bonding agents based on SBR (styrene butadiene rubber) are preferred in conditions which are likely to remain permanently damp. Type one, two or three mixes may be used as appropriate to the exposure, but types two or three are preferable. Suitable mixes are given in Tables 1.1 and 1.2.

Techniques of mixing and application

Storage of lime putty and aggregates in wet, air-tight conditions is strongly recommended, unless hydraulic lime is used. Hydraulic lime and sand must be mixed together dry before water is added. Cement or HTI powder must only be added to wet lime putty and sand mixtures just before use. Hair or fibre should be beaten into the wet mix when appropriate, chopped to lengths and added to quantities as specified above. Water ratios must be kept as low as possible.

Typical procedures are described below for the thick, rough textured rendering and the thin, comparatively smooth textured rendering which are likely to be found covering rubble masonry.

Rough textured rendering

This is also known as rough-cast, wet-dash or harling.

1. Prepare the wall.
2. *For patch repairs.* Cut out detached and bulging areas to regular, square-edged shapes, preferably between architectural elements before preparing the wall.
3. Apply a rendering coat with a laying-on trowel on to a damp substrate to the general levels required but not exceeding a 9 mm (⅜ in) thickness. Iron the coat hard on to the wall and finish with a comb scratcher to provide a key.
4. Protect the rendering coat from rain and hot sunshine or direct draughts. Allow to dry as slowly as possible and ensure that the coat has completely dried out before the next stage.

5. Wet up the rendering coat with a hose and spray attachment sufficient to ensure a damp substrate.
6. Apply a floating coat with a laying-on trowel to the damp substrate and finish with a comb scratcher to provide a key.
7. Repeat stage 4.
8. Repeat stage 5 on the floating coat.
9. Apply a butter coat to aid the adhesion of dashed material to the damp substrate with a laying-on trowel. While the butter coat is still soft and sticky, throw on the finishing material from a board or shallow box using a dashing trowel with a wrist flicking action. As large an area as possible should be covered in one operation. If a wall must be divided up by day working limitations, every attempt must be made to work between plinth and eaves, or between windows. Accidental bunching up of aggregates should not be corrected by attempting to spread the stones out with a trowel but by taking off, re-buttering and re-dashing.
10. Repeat stage 4.
11. Limewash if required.

A different finishing coat, which is simply a coarse textured version of the render and float coats, can be substituted for the butter coat. The finishing coat should be about 6 mm (¼ in) thick, finished either with a cross-grained wood float or about 10 mm (⅜– ½ in) and scraped down with a fine-toothed saw blade after a slight stiffening of the rendering has begun to take place. The latter technique is a common continental practice which has the advantage of removing any slight surface shrink crazing and any patchiness in the form of laitence, leaving a uniform, slightly rough textured face.

Smooth textured, thin rendering

Whereas the thick rendering may cover all but the most prominent irregularities, thin renderings spread over rubble between dressed stones will show much of the form of the stones underneath.

1. Prepare the wall.
2. For patch repairs follow stage 2.
3. Ensure that the substrate is damp enough not to de-water the thin render. Iron on one thin coat of lime and sand gauged with HTI powder (see Table 1.1) with a small trowel, pressing hard into all contours of the wall. Compaction is absolutely essential to the success of the render. Work is necessarily slow, and re-wetting of the substrate may be necessary. Protect the work area from strong sunlight.
4. Press on with pads of damp sacking or other coarse, absorbent cloth. This technique leaves a slightly rough texture.

THREE COAT THICK RENDERING TO WEAK BACKGROUND

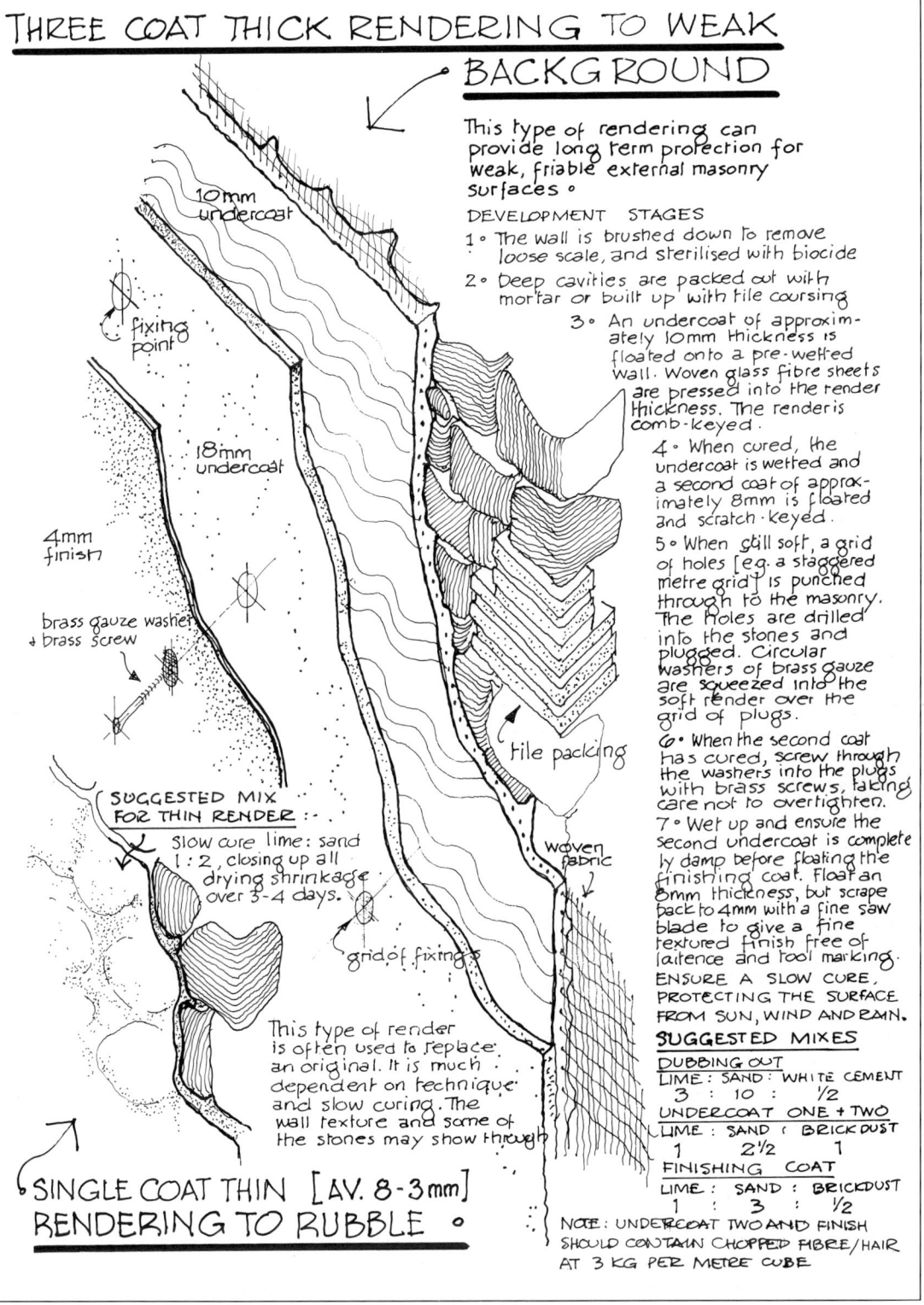

10mm undercoat

fixing point

18mm undercoat

4mm finish

brass gauze washer + brass screw

SUGGESTED MIX FOR THIN RENDER :-
Slow cure lime: sand 1 : 2, closing up all drying shrinkage over 3-4 days.

grid of fixings

This type of render is often used to replace an original. It is much dependent on technique and slow curing. The wall texture and some of the stones may show through

tile packing

woven fabric

SINGLE COAT THIN [AV. 8-3mm] RENDERING TO RUBBLE

This type of rendering can provide long term protection for weak, friable external masonry surfaces.

DEVELOPMENT STAGES

1. The wall is brushed down to remove loose scale, and sterilised with biocide
2. Deep cavities are packed out with mortar or built up with tile coursing
3. An undercoat of approximately 10mm thickness is floated onto a pre-wetted wall. Woven glass fibre sheets are pressed into the render thickness. The render is comb-keyed.
4. When cured, the undercoat is wetted and a second coat of approximately 8mm is floated and scratch-keyed.
5. When still soft, a grid of holes [eg. a staggered metre grid] is punched through to the masonry. The holes are drilled into the stones and plugged. Circular washers of brass gauze are squeezed into the soft render over the grid of plugs.
6. When the second coat has cured, screw through the washers into the plugs with brass screws, taking care not to overtighten.
7. Wet up and ensure the second undercoat is completely damp before floating the finishing coat. Float an 8mm thickness, but scrape back to 4mm with a fine saw blade to give a fine textured finish free of laitence and tool marking. ENSURE A SLOW CURE, PROTECTING THE SURFACE FROM SUN, WIND AND RAIN.

SUGGESTED MIXES

DUBBING OUT

LIME	: SAND	: WHITE CEMENT
3	10	½

UNDERCOAT ONE + TWO

LIME	: SAND	: BRICK DUST
1	2½	1

FINISHING COAT

LIME	: SAND	: BRICKDUST
1	3	½

NOTE: UNDERCOAT TWO AND FINISH SHOULD CONTAIN CHOPPED FIBRE/HAIR AT 3 KG PER METRE CUBE

5. Ensure that the work is protected from rapid drying, if necessary by laying on thin, damp cloths or cotton wool. See also description of the lime method in Chapter 9.

Painting rendering

If the colour of a rendering can be satisfactorily achieved as the result of selection of aggregates, this is obviously preferable to introducing any form of paint. Where applied colour is necessary to follow existing conditions, the new rendering must be dried out completely before application. In average drying conditions, protecting the work from rain and direct sunlight, a 25 mm (1 in) thickness of rendering will take about four weeks to dry. Paint systems which can be applied to new rendering soon after this period are:

Limewashes
Lime casein paints
Distemper (size-bound)
Distemper (oil-bound)
Cement paints
Emulsions
Silicate paints

These paints are also likely to be the most suitable for matching early surviving examples. Paints which provide a tough, impervious envelope, especially those which are sprayed on, should always be avoided for historic buildings both on grounds of appearance and because no envelope can ever be complete. Water and salt trapped behind a tough paint film will result in loss of adhesion and can increase dampness in a building and the risk of persistent deterioration behind the paint.

Painting stone direct

If the stone is to be painted or limewashed directly, the substrate should be prepared in the same way as for rendering. Similarly the paint system used should be from the list given above. Limewash is likely to be the most usual finish (see Appendix 1). Paint systems on masonry must, as an absolute minimum requirement, be vapour permeable. In the past, soiled or disfigured masonry has sometimes been painted to improve the appearance, and the same temptation will sometimes persuade building owners to cover up a problem, especially where cleaning has failed. Whilst this is not a course of action to be recommended, if there is no acceptable alternative a system must be selected which can be removed without abrasion or caustic strippers.

Repair with mortars

Repair of stone with mortars, or plastic repair as it is traditionally known, is useful to conservators of stone as an alternative to cutting out and piecing in with new stone. Unfortunately the reputation of such repairs has suffered from inadequate specification, misuse and inexpert handling. Plastic repair is thought of as a cheap option to repairing with stone, but the cheapness relates very often to poor quality workmanship. Properly prepared and placed plastic repair is not cheap, except that its use may sometimes mean the avoidance of such expensive items as temporary supports for vault and arch stone replacements or reduce the amount of cutting out required.

Plastic repairs are of particular interest and importance to conservators because the technique frequently permits the retention of more original material with much less disturbance than would be possible for the execution of conventional masonry repairs. In this respect the familiar description of the method as 'dentistry repair' is very apt. The careful removal of decayed material, the cleaning and sterilization of the cavity and the placing, compaction and finishing of the amalgam are common to the repair of both teeth and stone. The analogy may be extended further; if careless filling of imperfectly prepared cavities is carried out much energy and expenditure will have been wasted and failure will occur in a predictably short time.

Failure of plastic repairs may be both cosmetic and mechanical. In particular, mortar repair material coloured with pigments, or feather-edged to ragged areas of decay or finished with steel trowels, is often visually disastrous. Over-strong mortars, mortars relying on bonding agents instead of mechanical keying, or large surface areas in exposed positions, will be mechanical failures.

Although there are exceptions, plastic repair should always be carried out by a stone mason or a stone conservator, because their familiarity with the material should give them a feeling for the repair which other trades and disciplines will not necessarily have.

The following criteria will affect the decision to use a plastic repair.

1. Will the use of mortar enable more original material to be retained than if stone is used?
2. Will the use of mortar avoid disturbing critically fragile areas?
3. Will the use of mortar avoid the removal of structural elements such as vault or other arch voussoirs?
4. Will mortar perform satisfactorily in the intended context, i.e. is it capable of weathering adequately? Would cast stone be more appropriate?

Lime mortar for limestone repair : 1 lime putty : 2½ sand and stone dust (1 : 3 finish)

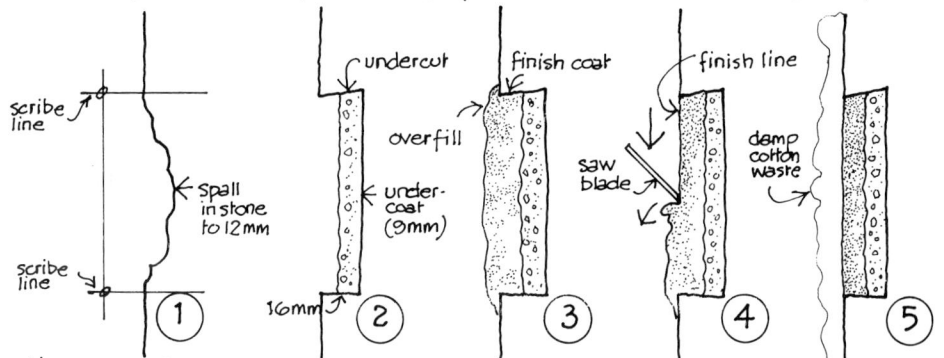

1 Line out a rectangular shape enclosing the whole of the damage. Scribe the area using a steel rule.
2 Using fire-sharp small chisels, cut back to a uniform sinking of 16mm, undercutting at the top and sides.
  Wet up the cavity and fill to 9mm with backing mortar. Iron in hard, cover and allow to cure slowly.
3 Wet up the remaining cavity and overfill with finishing mortar, ironing in hard until no shrinkage appears.
  Ironing may be repeated over 2-3 days with non-setting (non-hydraulic) lime
4 Scrape back with a fine hacksaw blade to finished line, leaving a laitence-free, uniform texture
5 Cover with damp cotton waste and allow to cure slowly.

PATCH REPAIR OF STONE USING MORTAR

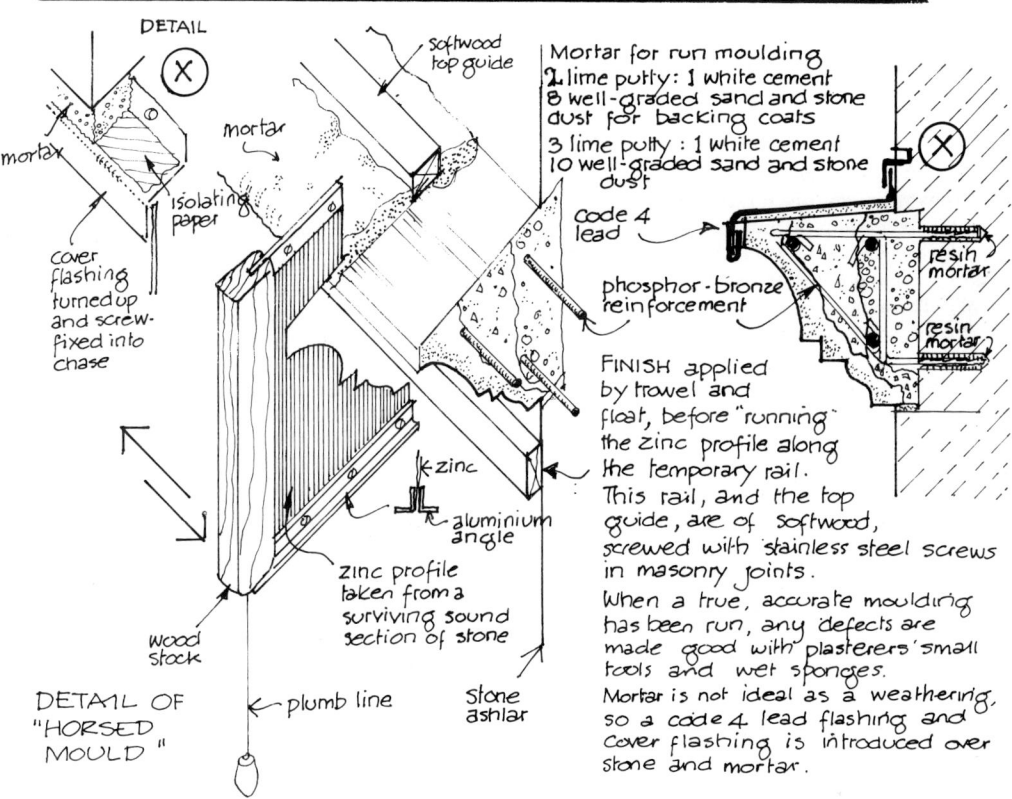

Mortar for run moulding
2 lime putty: 1 white cement
8 well-graded sand and stone dust for backing coats

3 lime putty : 1 white cement
10 well-graded sand and stone dust

FINISH applied by trowel and float, before "running" the zinc profile along the temporary rail.
This rail, and the top guide, are of softwood, screwed with stainless steel screws in masonry joints.
When a true, accurate moulding has been run, any defects are made good with plasterers' small tools and wet sponges.
Mortar is not ideal as a weathering, so a code 4 lead flashing and cover flashing is introduced over stone and mortar.

DETAIL OF "HORSED MOULD"

REPAIR OF MOULDING USING MORTAR

5. Are the areas to be repaired small enough to be repaired with mortar? Would rendering be more appropriate or should a large replacement of stone with matching stone be accepted?
6. Will mortar provide a visually better repair than new stone in the context of heavily weathered, softened outlines?
7. Are the appropriate skills available to produce high quality mortar repairs?

If, after consideration of these factors, it is decided to proceed with mortar repairs, wholly or partially, the following procedures should be put into operation.

1. Prepare a schedule of stones to be repaired with mortar or with stone.
2. Prepare samples of mortar to match the various conditions of weathering on the building. Weathered stones exhibit a subtle variety of colour which must be matched in the repairs. Much plastic repair suffers from an unnatural uniformity. The repairs must be prepared as samples on a piece of stone or tile, not in a wooden mould.
3. Cut out the decayed areas.
4. Wash and sterilize the cavity with water and formalin.
5. Saturate the cavity with water using handsprays to prevent dewatering of the repair mortar.
6. Place the selected repair mortar, compacting in layers not exceeding 9 mm (⅜ in) in thickness in any one application. Allow each layer to dry out before rewetting and placing the next layer.
7. In cavities exceeding 50 mm (2 in) in depth and extending over 50 mm (2 in) square surface area, drill and fix non-ferrous or stainless steel reinforcements. These may vary between simple pins and armatures. The most common materials are copper, phosphor bronze and stainless steel wire. After drilling to receive the reinforcement the holes are filled with an epoxy mortar before embedding the wire; 18 mm (0.7 in) of cover should be allowed for any reinforcement.
8. The repair may be finished directly to the required profile using a wood or felt-covered float, or with a damp sponge or coarse cloth. Ingenuity will provide other finishing tools appropriate to the texture of the finish required. Unsuitable tools to be avoided are steel trowels or dry, absorbent pads. Steel trowels will leave an undesirable and unnatural laitence on the surface, and absorbent pads will risk the removal of water from the repair too soon. An alternative repair finishing method is to build the repair up proud of the required profile and then to work it back after an initial set has commenced on the surface with a fine saw blade or purpose-made scrapers.

Mortar repairs must be protected from direct sun or other rapid drying conditions. This may be achieved with damp cotton wool pads on small-scale repairs or with damp sacks on larger areas. Care taken during preparation and after placing of the repair will avoid one of the most common problems associated with this kind of work, the appearance of fine shrinkage cracks during drying.

Different mixes may not always provide quite the variation in colour required. In this situation, stone dusts may be added to the face of the repair before a set commences. This is very skilled work and is best avoided unless the repairer is particularly skilled. This and other aspects of high quality mortar repair, especially of limestone, are described in detail in Chapter 4.

A number of proprietary mortar repairs are available. Some of these have proved to behave well on weathering and they may be useful where on-site matching expertise is questionable. Unfortunately, to be successful, the repair mix has to be matched in a laboratory to samples of stone provided by the client, and it is difficult to vary the potential strength of the repair. A match which involved a number of site visits from a laboratory would become very costly. There is no doubt that the most desirable way of forming mortar repairs is to use on-site expertise throughout.

It should be noted that while most of the plastic repair mortars are based on a lime binder, repairs to sandstones may be better carried out using a cement binder and a plasticizer, or a masonry cement. This is because sandstone which is already decaying may further deteriorate in the presence of lime washing into the edges of the prepared cavities. This problem is described in Volume 1, Chapter 7, in the context of incompatibility of sandstones and limestones. A comparison of mortars of equivalent strengths is given below, using a variety of binders.

Plasticizer	Portland cement	Lime	Masonry cement	Aggregates
–	1	3	–	10
yes	1	–	–	8
–	–	–	1	7

The high proportion of aggregate to binder in the cement:aggregate mixes is a further advantage when matching a strong coloured sandstone. The mortar mixes need not be as strong as shown above for many small-scale repairs, but preparation must always ensure that the grains of sand and stone dust are adequately coated with the binder paste.

Although plastic repairs should not be used for areas of extreme exposure it may be possible to use them in strings and cornices if a lead flashing is provided as well. A limited amount of experience indicates that plastic repairs of exposed elements such as balustraded parapets may perform well if they are subsequently treated with a catalysed silane consolidant.

Plastic repair using resin binders

Whilst it is true that some of the worst mortar repairs in the last decade have been those based on epoxy mortars, there is an important potential in the use of resin binders, especially for the dentistry repair of sandstones. In particular, Mr Jack Heiman of the former Commonwealth Experimental Building Station in Sydney, Australia, has carried out preliminary studies on epoxy/quartz sand blends using very small proportions of epoxy (for example 1:12, 1:16 resin:sand by weight). The performance of these mortars in Australia and in Britain is currently being compared with the performance of sandstone originals, especially in conditions of wetting and drying, heating and cooling and during salt crystallization cycling. In general, behaviour of the resin-bound sandstone mimics is much closer to original sandstone than mimics with cementitious paste binders. The appearance, too, is much better than traditional lime/cement based repairs, as the full colour potential of the aggregate can be exploited. The permeable resin mortar, carefully matched and properly cut in, avoiding feathering, has an undoubted role to play in dentistry repair.

Replacement with cast stone

The British Standard (BS 1217:1975) specification for cast stone defines it as 'any product manufactured from aggregate and cement and intended to resemble in appearance and be used in a similar way to natural stone.' Although there are no savings on on-site labour or on disruption for fixing when cast stone is used in place of natural stone, economies are achieved when repetitive elements need to be produced. In some situations, cast stone may be preferable to natural stone for the replacement of copings, ridges and chimney caps where the environment is particularly demanding and aggressive. Cast stone has also been used extensively in England as a substitute for some forms of stone slate. Casts of varying quality have also been used extensively as *in situ* replacements for sculpture which has been removed to some place of safety.

Cast stone used as a building element may either be homogeneous or may consist of a facing material and a backing concrete. Where reinforcement is included for structural or handling purposes it is recommended that this is stainless steel or bronze alloy with a minimum 10 mm (0.4 in) of cover. If untreated mild steel or even galvanised steel is used, a cover of 30 mm (1.2 in) is recommended.

Good cast stone can be immensely durable but it is subject to the same weathering processes and, eventually, to similar forms of decay as natural stone. Unfortunately its appearance is liable to become less and less stone-like with passing years and its very durability will count against it visually unless the surface is masked by organic growth. The repetitive precision of replacement mullions or balusters in cast stone can be very detrimental aesthetically in a weathered stone facade. Cast replacements of sculptural elements are sometimes desirable for architectural completeness or as landscape features; in such cases the most important point is that the original is not stained or damaged by the moulding process, and a careful inspection must determine how safe the operation will be. It may be necessary to consolidate the original to enable it to be used in this way (see Chapter 9). A silicone rubber is recommended as the moulding medium. Individual moulds should be kept to as small as sensibly possible, especially where there is undercut detail, and the surface should be treated with a barrier which will not stain. Liquid detergent has been found safer in this respect than many proprietary barrier treatments. A good quality cast should always be made and retained for further moulding processes, because the moulds themselves will deteriorate with age and use, even when kept in rigid 'mother mould' casing. The original should not need to be subjected to the hazards, however small, of moulding more than once. Some cast replacements are, of themselves, of considerable interest beause of their age or originality.

Providing protection

Providing protection on the building should always be considered as an alternative to repair or replacement. Protection may be in the form of a new architectural element such as a small roof over a piece of sculpture or a complete porch over a door. Care must be taken that the new element does not create additional problems, such as run-off from new roofs creating drip and splash patterns, or undesirable changes in relative humidity at different times of the year, especially under glass, polycarbonate or other plastic sheet. Occasionally the cover may be a complete new structure in itself, such as that proposed for Sueno's stone in Aberdeenshire, or in a ruined building a new roof may be put back on the line of the old, as at Howden Minster Chapter House with long term beneficial results for the carved and sculpted stones inside. These are, of course, important architectural decisions as well as protective measures and must be fully and professionally assessed.

Protection in the form of lead dressings is a much simpler expedient which may be introduced discreetly to assist stone elements with a particularly difficult weathering job to do. Thus a Code 4 flashing may be dressed over a small string, label mould or transom neatly fixed into a carefully prepared chase,

Gravity system

The grouting apparatus required for filling large voids consists of one or two open galvanized iron pans with outlets in the bottoms. A union with 38 mm (1.5 in) diameter galvanized pipe is fitted to the outlet, which in turn is connected by means of couplings to several lengths of 38 mm (1.5 in) diameter rubber hose, terminating in a galvanized iron nozzle 19 mm (0.75 in) in diameter and fitted with a stopcock. Each grout pan is provided with a wooden plug about 460 mm (18 in) long to fit into the hole in the pan bottom and with a plunger in the form of a rubber cup on a wooden handle. This plunger is used when the grout is flowing, to give an added impetus to the flow in the event of an airlock or other stoppage in the tube.

Preparation

Small holes are drilled into the wall where voids have been located, or are anticipated. They should be about one metre (3ft 3in) apart horizontally and 500 mm (1ft 8in) vertically on a staggered pattern. As the holes are drilled, they should be washed out thoroughly with clean water, by pouring in at the top holes and continuing to pour until the water runs out clean at the bottom. During this process, note should be taken of the joints through which the water runs out. Before grouting begins these joints must be tightly filled with tow or clay, pressed well into the joint to a depth of 38–50 mm (1.5–2 in). The nozzle of the delivery hose is then inserted into the lowest hole and plugged round with tow.

Operation

The assembly of this simple equipment is shown on page 27. To operate it, two men are stationed at the upper level with the grout pans. They regulate the flow of grout into the delivery hose from one pan and mix the grout in the second pan ready for use, so that a continuous operation can be carried out. A third man is stationed at the lower level, to open and close the stopcock on the nozzle as required. Ample supplies of water and grout components must be kept on the scaffold.

When the grout has been mixed to the right flow consistency in the pan, the wooden plug is withdrawn and the grout flows down the delivery hose. The stopcock on the nozzle is then opened, allowing the grout to flow into the wall, until the grout level in the wall has risen sufficiently to begin to flow out of the series of holes immediately above. These holes may then be stopped up, the grout cut off and another section of wall prepared, or grouted, while the first begins to set. After the initial set, the tow or clay can be stripped out of the joints in readiness for pointing at a later stage. The next lift can then be grouted in the same way. One metre should be taken as the maximum lift at a time, to avoid the build-up

of pressure from liquid grout behind loose face stones. A pressure of about 0.98–1.28 kgf/cm² (14–18 lbf/in²) (10–12 ft) is obtained in the hose when the pan is placed about 3.5–4.5 m (11.5–15 ft) above the point of inlet.

Pumped systems

Hand and power operated pumps usually consist of a mixer, diaphragm pump, suction and delivery hoses and metal nozzles fitted with stopcocks. Hand-operated pumps are recommended for ancient masonry in unstable conditions. The compact nature of these assemblies usually permits the equipment to be located adjacent to the work in progress and cuts down on the hose lengths required.

Preparation

Preparation is similar to that needed for the gravity system. The nozzles are fitted into the holes and plugged around with tow. The lowest nozzle is usually then coupled up to the delivery hose.

Operation

One man will be required to operate the mixer, one to operate the pump and one to open and close the stopcock as required. When all is ready, the stopcock is opened on the nozzle and the pump started. The level of the grout rising up the wall is indicated by the seepage of grout from weep holes, which can then be plugged with clay. Hidden grout flows may sometimes be identified by sweating of the wall surface as water is forced through under pressure.

When the grout reaches the next line of nozzles, the lower stopcock can be closed and the delivery hose can be removed and coupled to the nozzle above. The lower nozzle can be left in position until the grout has set.

The maximum pressure obtained depends upon the model being used, but a range of 10–15 kg/cm² (140–210 lbf/in²) is usual. Much lower pressures are obtained with hand-operated pumps. Hand-operated pumps have a capacity of 18–45 litres/minute (4–10 gal/min). Power-operated pumps have a capacity of 1400–1800 litres/hour (300–400 gal/h).

The aerated pressure system (Aerocem) is useful in large scale grouting, especially where tunnels and vaults are involved. The apparatus consists of a compressor, mixer, pressure vessel, air lines and delivery hose, with a wide variety of nozzle designs suitable both for pointing and grouting. The pointing finish is unsatisfactory and messy if left from the nozzle, but can be acceptable if followed up with pointing tools.

The preparation of the walls for grouting is the same as that used in the gravity system. Metal nozzles are fitted into drilled holes and plugged round with tow. The spacing of the holes will vary with the condition of the masonry, but could be set, for example, 0.5 m (18 in) apart vertically and 1.25 m

(4ft 6in) apart horizontally. The point positions should be staggered as before.

During operation, one man is stationed at the nozzles to open and close the stopcocks, one man at the pressure vessel to ensure that the correct pressure is maintained, and one man at the mixer to prepare the next grout batch.

Vacuum grouting

Vacuum grouting is a relatively recent development which has considerable potential for structural consolidation and for the conservation of architectural detail and sculpture.

During the electrification of the Dacca-Chittagong railway in 1972, the late Mr Jimmy Milne evolved a system of applying resins to brick and stone bridges under vacuum. As so often, an emergency situation, in this case the transport of vital supplies by rail and the need to adept bridges to carry high speed trains, provided the stimulus for the idea. Patent applications were registered world-wide and the system is now known as the Balvac process (Balfour-Beatty).

In the United Kingdom the system was used on another railway bridge, the eighteenth century Causey Arch at Tanfield, County Durham. In this case, the traffic across the bridge was originally horse-drawn on rails, and carried coal to the River Tyne. Water percolation, open joints, salt crystallization damage and freezing of saturated masonry was causing considerable damage, especially to the inner ring of the single-span, three-ring arch. Vacuum sealing of a complete structure of this kind would have involved enormous practical problems. The sandstone arch was therefore prepared for local vacuum application and injection by tamping the open joints with conventional mortar, sealing the mortar face with resin and by drilling holes into the inner ring, which were then capped with nipples. A vacuum pump was applied to the nipples in turn, to remove air and water. This was followed by resin injection under low pressure. Structural grouting under vacuum is fraught with problems, but there is no doubt that it can sometimes provide an answer where straightforward injection under pressure will not work, or is too hazardous.

The application of vacuum techniques to smaller, freestanding objects is a subject which has now been quite extensively explored, especially by Kenneth Hempel. In the early 1970s, Mr Hempel, then of the Victoria and Albert Museum, London, began to use the Balvac system. He subsequently introduced various modifications which enabled it to be applied to valuable and, in some cases, fragile pieces of sculpture.

For eight years before the Balvac process was patented, the Victoria and Albert Museum had been brush applying silane monomers to decaying sculpture, on some occasions with considerable success.

Before the silane monomers were applied the sculpture was dried out as much as possible, sometimes under ventilated black polyethylene shrouds, during the summer. Before treatment, the dry stone was painted with cellosolve and left overnight in preparation for the silane monomer, which was applied by brush, mixed with equal parts of cellosolve and two to eight parts of water. Brush application was continued until no more silane was absorbed. Up to 80 mm (3.25 in) penetration was achieved in this way. Application under vacuum presented a way of improving the consolidation by increasing the depth of impregnation and extending the absorption time by omitting the solvent and water and thus delaying polymerization.

In the procedure developed by Hempel, which is still sometimes used, the sculpture is placed on a non-porous base which extends well outside the surface area of the base of the stone to be treated. A fine polypropylene mesh is cut and fitted over the sculpture, followed by a clear polyethylene shroud, which is cut and sealed to form an envelope. The shroud is sealed at the top around a vacuum head and at the bottom to the non-porous base with a mastic cement. The polyethylene shroud is turned up all round the base to form a trough. When the vacuum is applied, the shroud clings tightly to the surface of the sculpture as the air is removed. At this stage, the consolidant is poured into the trough at the base and the shroud is pierced below the surface of the liquid. The consolidant can then be seen to move up the sculpture within the vacuated shroud, until it reaches the vacuum head. The vacuum is then switched off, allowing any consolidant which is not absorbed to flow back to the base. The vacuum is applied a second time to cover any area which has been missed. Impressive depths of impregnation of up to 300 mm (1 ft) have been achieved in this manner.

One of the hazards to fragile sculpture is the pull exerted by the shroud under vacuum, which can cause damage. Hempel modified his system to overcome this problem by carefully wrapping the sculpture in cotton flannelette, secured to sound surface with very small spots of latex. At the base, the flannelette is secured to the non-porous base with polyester cement. Instead of being enveloped in a polyethylene shroud, the flannelette is painted with a rubber latex, which cures to form a continuous skin. A vacuum head is sealed into the latex skin at the highest point, but the consolidant is introduced through a perforated polyethylene tube at the base. This is linked by a supply line to a polyethylene reservoir, which is fitted with a tap. When the vacuum is applied, its meter will register at once if the seal is successful. Any holes must be sealed with a puncture repair kit, consisting of small squares of polyethylene painted with latex. When pressed over a hole, the polyethylene can be peeled off the patch. After the vacuum has been held successfully for about an hour, the reservoir tap is turned on and the advance of the consolidant up the surface of the sculpture can be seen through the latex skin. The vacuum is maintained for ten minutes after the consolidant has reached the head, after which it is switched off and reapplied as before. On the following day, the latex and flannelette 'suit' can be cut away with a sharp scalpel. Impregnations of between 25–150 mm (1–6 in) have been achieved in this manner.

Some of the successful consolidations carried out by this process can be seen on the fifteenth century Porta della Carta in Venice, which was restored (1976–1979) by K. and G. Hempel, as part of a complex and delicate overall cleaning and consolidation programme. The Carrara marble sculptures of Prudence, Fortitude and Temperance were consolidated under vacuum in the laboratory. The figures of Justice, Charity, the Doge Foscari and two angels were treated *in situ*.

Repair of stone roofs

Stone slates, properly called 'tilestones', are perhaps the most distinctive of the many forms of roof covering found on traditional buildings. In *The Pattern of English Building*, Alec Clifton-Taylor defines their special quality by describing the effect of stone slates on a roof as 'complete visual harmony, both with the architecture of the buildings of which they form a part and with the landscape in which they are placed'. This harmony is due largely to the fact that both the tilestones and the stones from which the buildings are constructed were obtained from the same geological formations, so that, in composition and colour, there is often a close similarity.

Since the early nineteenth century, when mechanical means of producing roof coverings were developed, both thatch and stone roofs have been replaced by lighter, more regular roofing materials. Welsh slates, pantiles, plain tiles and, more recently, concrete and asbestos roof coverings have replaced traditional stone roofs. This often has a damaging effect on the character and appearance of the building. The decline of stone roofing undoubtedly also relates to the practical difficulties of maintenance and repair, the decreasing number of craftsmen capable of laying a stone roof and the steadily declining availability of both new and good quality secondhand stone slates. Surviving stone roofs are often important visual components in many urban and rural settings and their loss would seriously affect the appearance of numerous towns and villages throughout the country.

The laying of stone slates is a craft tradition of considerable importance, which demands not only a high standard of workmanship, but also an understanding of the variable characteristics of the material with which the roofer is working. Stone slates are obtained from stone deposits which allow the splitting of the stone along the bedding planes into thin sheets, capable of being used for roof coverings. These stones, generally sandstones, split or laminate quite easily along straight lines, giving a fairly smooth-faced finish which allows one slate to be bedded upon another quite evenly. The slates are laid in diminishing courses. The large eaves slates are several feet wide. The slates decrease in size up to the courses near the ridge, where the slates are considerably smaller. Traditionally, the slates are hung with oak pegs, which are driven into holes in the heads of the slates made with a pointed pick-end. The slates are fixed to riven oak laths, except where a peg hole coincides with a rafter position. In that case the slate is nailed with a large round-headed, non-ferrous nail. At the eaves, under-eaves slates are bedded directly onto the wall and the first course of slates laid over these, with the tails meeting. At the ridge, the roof is finished with ridge stones cut from the solid, either laid dry or bedded on mortar. Ridge stones vary in size and angle, according to the pitch of the roof.

In the past, before waterproof felting was available, various devices were adopted to make the stone slates, which were laid on open battened roofs, more weatherproof. One of the earliest methods was to drive moss into the joints, known as 'mossing'. Another method was called 'torching' or 'tiering'. Torching was a mixture of sand and slaked lime, to which beaten cow hair was added. This mixture was applied to the underside of the slated roof, either at the top of the laths (single torched), at the top and the bottom (double torched), or entirely filling the space between the laths (fully torched). The torching not only acted as a means of preventing rain and snow from penetrating the roof, but also cemented the wooden pegs firmly in position, preventing them from twisting and moving. Torching has been replaced, in recent years, by the use of bituminous roofing felt.

Many of the defects which develop in old stone roofs are attributable to the method in which the roof is laid, rather than to the deterioration of the roofing material. The most common failures occur in the wooden pegs, which shrink and dry out with age, allowing the slates to slip. Another common failure is in the laths, which tend to deflect under the weight of the stone slates. Often, the roof timbers themselves may have bent under the weight of the covering early in the life of the roof, but unless the timbers are cracked, or are badly infested with death-watch beetle or dry rot, this is not necessarily a cause for concern. In many older buildings there is a considerable margin of safety provided by timbers whose scantlings are far in excess of the structural requirements. If, however, the laths and pegs have generally failed throughout the roof, then there is no alternative to re-roofing.

Signs of a defective roof covering include areas of bitumen painted over the stone slates, the presence of bitumen impregnated fabric covering the entire roof, or the external pointing of the stone slates with cement mortar. These signs indicate water penetration and imply that the original mossing or torching has failed. The bituminous covering is the most unfortunate, as it blurs the outline of the stone slates and renders their re-use impossible in all but hidden locations. Also, like external rendering, a damaged bituminous covering can help to trap water inside the roof covering, increasing the effect of even a small fault, which cannot be seen. The result will only be apparent when serious damage occurs.

If a stone roof needs attention, it is essential to consult a specialist roofing contractor who is familiar with stone roofing techniques. The principles which apply to Welsh slating and plain tiling do not necessarily apply to stone roofing. A suggested specification for stone roofing is outlined below.[7]

1. The existing roof covering should be carefully removed and the slates carefully stacked in preparation for sorting for re-use. All badly laminated and spalled slates should be rejected, but those which are damaged by fractures should be stacked separately, for possible re-use after re-dressing. Ridges should be carefully lowered and stacked. They should never be dropped to the ground.

2. All leadwork should be removed from the roof and only re-used if it is in good condition. The leadwork should be renewed in lead of adequate weights, for example, in BS 1178 Code 4 (1.80 mm) for flashings and minimum Code 5 (2.28 mm) for gutter linings.

3. Roof timbers should be cleaned down and all loose debris and accumulated material removed from the roof space. The timbers should then be repaired and treated as required. The replacement of original roof timbers should be kept to a minimum.

4. Sound salvaged slates should be carefully cleaned down, sorted to length and thickness and arranged in stacks corresponding to the various lengths. The slates should be stacked vertically, standing on their heads (with the peg holes to the ground). The length of each slate should be measured from the peg hole to the tail and sorting to length should precede sorting to thickness. Each stack of sorted slates will then constitute one course of stone slates. The number of slates required for the eaves course should be established by measuring the length of the building and then by checking this dimension against the combined widths of the longest slates. If there are insufficient large slates of one size, then the slates can be dressed to the length of the next largest size, which will then become the eaves course.

5. When sorting has been completed, the roof should be covered with reinforced untearable roofing felt to BS 747 (type IF), with a minimum vertical lap of 150 mm (6 in) and, where lengths are joined, a minimum horizontal lap of two spars width, fixed with 25 mm (1 in) galvanized clout nails.

6. New battens treated with preservative should be fixed as required to replace missing or defective material. Typical sizes are 38 × 19 mm (1.5 × 0.75 in) secured with 50 × 25 mm (2 × 1 in) eaves course battens and fixed with 63 mm (2.5 in) nails. For pegged slates counter battens will be required under the slating battens. Double battens are recommended for pegging to prevent the peg moving due to shrinkage or twisting. Pegs should be of seasoned oak, treated with a suitable preservative. Sometimes a tough plastic peg is used, especially in conjunction with a combined plastic sleeve and double washer where the nail/peg hole has become enlarged.

7. Re-slating should proceed using the sound slates previously removed, with deficiencies made up with sound, second-hand slates of matching type, thickness and, where possible, colour. The slates should be fixed in regularly diminishing courses. A double course should be laid to the eaves, fixed and positioned to give a minimum of 75 mm (3 in) overhang beyond the outer face of the wall. Each course of slates should overlap the second course below by 75 mm (3 in) and each horizontal joint below should be similarly lapped by a minimum 75 mm (3 in). The slates should be pegged, or nailed with 63–75 mm (2.5–3 in) heavy gauge copper nails, driven into the centre of the batten. The largest slates should be double nailed. No nails should penetrate the thickness of the batten.

8. The stone ridges should be re-bedded on a cement:lime:sand mortar (in the proportions 1:1:6) and supported at the joints with small wedges of stone. This traditional mix may be improved by using a styrene butadiene rubber additive with the gauging water. This additive should also be used to point up the ridge. The junction of roof and abutments should be finished with lead soakers and flashings and pointed in SBR modified mortar. Traditionally this lead was pointed into stone with an oil

mastic based on linseed oil and sand with litharge.

9. The gutters should be re-fixed with the roofing felt carried over into them.

10. The contractor should, wherever possible, leave on the site an assortment of sound slates to enable localized repairs to be carried out when necessary.

Repair of slate roofs

True slates provide a much lighter roof covering than tilestones. They form a good waterproof roof when properly laid, close butted and accurately lapped vertically and horizontally. The failure of slate roofs is generally as a result of the deterioration of fixings, although the slates themselves are brittle and vulnerable to impact. They may be lifted and detached in gale-force winds.

As with any other stone there is a range of durability. Slates containing significant amounts of calcium carbonate, which is attacked by acids present in the atmosphere, are likely to be of poor durability. However, calcium sulphate can be formed from calcite and pyrite present in the slate by regular wetting and drying, and atmospheric sulphate is not necessarily the sole cause of decay.

Deterioration often occurs under the laps where moisture is held by capillarity. Replacement or refixing of even single damaged or slipped slates is important. If left unattended, damage may result to the roof structure. Unfortunately the expense of access in order to refix a few roof slates is frequently well in excess of the cost of the repair, and neglect is all too common.

Slates are often pegged with wood or nailed direct to close boarding, or to battens, with copper or iron nails. Commonly a slate roof which was intended to be wholly copper nailed was fixed with iron as the work progressed. Replacement nails should be of copper, or tin alloy. Where oak pegs were used to hang the slates on battens these nails can be used as substitutes. Enlarged holes can be reduced by making an epoxy-slate powder amalgam filler and drilling to form the desired size of hole. New holes in old slates should always be drilled and not punched through, to avoid the risk of shattering.

Original, hardwood pegs were frequently trimmed from green, unseasoned wood. They did not endanger the slate when driven through, but lost their wedging effect as they dried out. For this reason the re-use of unseasoned hardwood pegs is undesirable. On the other hand, seasoned hardwood may damage the slates during driving in. For these reasons, seasoned, good quality softwood pegs, treated by immersion in timber preservative so that they will be rot-resistant and retain their tight hold on the slate, are often substituted.

Individual slates which have slipped may be secured with slating hooks. New slates may be fixed in the same manner without cutting nails. Although hooks may be visible they allow minimum interference with the roof and avoid some of the risks to good slates when cutting nails with a ripper.

Large-scale failure of fixing almost inevitably means the stripping and relaying of the roof using as many new slates as necessary. It is important that the coursing pattern is maintained and that any polychromatic designs or special shaped slates are retained.

Another method of securing stone slate on slate roofs which has been used in a limited way over the past two decades is to fix a resin-impregnated glass-fibre membrane to the back of the slates or, alternatively, to attach a resin block to the back of the slate to act as a hanging nib. The first system involves the slating battens, and it is claimed that they remain sufficiently flexible to accommodate normal roof movements. The second is less of a commitment in that each slate remains free to move or to be replaced. Both systems rely on adhesion to the underside of a laminated slab, which may be seen as an inherent weakness, but both allow relatively inexpensive repairs to be carried out without access to the external slopes.

A number of Local Authorities in the UK have accepted a patented process, the 'Roof-Bond' system, for inclusion under House Improvement Grant schemes.

A third system secures slipped slates and provides insulation by covering the underside of the slates with an adhesive polyurethane foam. Like the glass-fibre sheet method this is a major commitment which, however successful initially, is likely to make future replacement of damaged slates very difficult. The foam and glass-fibre systems are visually undesirable, increase the fire loading, and can encourage the retention of moisture in encapsulated wood and in stone slates, which may subsequently become more frost vulnerable. Although some foams are reversible in theory, the likelihood of their removal is very small until a problem has been well established.

Stone paving

Stone has been used extensively as an external and internal paving material since prehistoric times. As paving it is subjected to some of the most severe deterioration processes. In addition, it may have to withstand the effects of pedestrian and/or vehicular traffic concentrated in specific zones. Street paving, including kerbs, roads and pavements (sidewalks) is very vulnerable to damage and liable to loss through replacement with substitute materials. Internal paving is primarily at risk on stairs and thresholds. All paving can be damaged by poorly prepared or carelessly disturbed substrates.

One of the most troublesome modern aspects of maintaining external stone paving is the constant need for access to services below the paved surface and the problems associated with heavy vehicles. For example, small basalt or granite setts are often lifted with a pick and shovel to expose a defective drain. The surface is then back-filled with poorly compacted material and the setts are relaid by road-gangs or service maintenance engineers with no appropriate skills and, in some cases, no interest beyond the service repair they have completed. These repaired areas are frequently disfigured by slurrying the joints with cement mortar. They soon show signs of subsidence, creating hazards for vehicles and pedestrians. Paved footways which are similarly disturbed are especially vulnerable to cracking after poor rebedding and rocking under the wheels of vehicles mounting the pavement, especially when large slabs are involved. Slabs are commonly broken or have their edges damaged during careless lifting. The attractions of tarmacadam, asphalt and cheap concrete paving slabs in terms of economy and fast servicing are obvious enough, but these materials are visually disastrous and their use causes an enormous loss of the historic characteristics of a street or area of old buildings.

An ideal arrangement to avoid disturbance during repairs would be to contain all services below roads and pavings in adequately sized ducts spanned by slabs or tray-profiled covers in which units of setts or cobbles or some lighter and sympathetic material can be bedded. Large slabs covering services should be fitted with slots for lewis pins so that they can be lifted mechanically without recourse to leverage. Unfortunately this ideal can only rarely be achieved. Sewers, gas lines, water mains and later electrical and telephone services have arrived at different periods and their maintenance is the responsibility of different authorities. The best solution is for long-term plans to be made to phase the grouping of services when possible. In the meantime, careful excavation and reinstatement remains the responsibility of road crews. In areas where there are still considerable areas of original or early and interesting paving, a plea must be made for at least one competent supervisor to oversee all disturbance and reinstatement work with the support of a small gang who carry out all the re-setting work. Protests about the increased time of operation with added inconvenience to traffic and increased costs to the ratepayer must be balanced, against the value of the conservation approach and the preservation of the original environment.

Paving specifications

Backfilling normally provides an unstable base for paving and is frequently followed by subsidence, displacement or cracking of units. A well-compacted sub-base of broken stone or brick of 100 mm (4 in) gauge topped with similar material of 25–50 mm gauge should be laid first and blinded with fine, well-graded stone aggregate to correct contours and profiles. The compacted thickness of the sub-base should be at least 150 mm (6 in). The sub-base should be covered with a 75 mm (3 in) thickness of 50 mm hoggin topped off with 13 mm (0.5 in) of fine hoggin well rolled or otherwise compacted.

Typical specifications for surface finishes

Granite or basalt setts. These vary in size, but 100 mm cubes or wedge-shaped square or rectangular sizes such as 100 mm × 125 mm × 180–250 mm (4 × 5 × 7–10 in) are common. Setts may be laid in regular lines or in concentric rings (fans) for decorative effect. The setts are trimmed to shape and laid tight-butted or sometimes with 6 mm wide joints. They are rammed home with wooden rammers or laid out on the compacted sub-base into sand or onto a 25 mm bed of cement:sand mortar in the proportion 1:3. The setts which are jointed should then be vigorously brushed over with a dry 1:6 cement:sand mortar, or 1:3 hydraulic lime:sand mortar. All the surplus should be swept away and the paving watered with a fine mist spray.

Limestone and sandstone setts. These are usually laid in the same way as granite but should be edge bedded and jointed in hydraulic lime:sand 1:3. Only very tough stones are suitable for paving.

Cobble stones. Cobbles are traditionally made of a very durable sandstone and have been water-worn into approximately spherical or flat shapes with well-rounded edges. Approximately even sizes graded between 40–50 mm (1.6–2 in) and up to 100–120 mm (4–5 in) are common. Split cobbles are also used. Cobbles are typically laid on a 100 mm (4 in) bed of 1:2:4 semi-dry concrete using 19 mm (0.7 in) nominal aggregate. The cobbles are set, as tightly butted as possible, into the base to no more than 14 mm of their depth and compacted with a heavy wooden mallet. A dry grout of cement:sand in the proportions 1:2 is then brushed in around the cobbles to achieve the desired level, which is often determined by adjacent paving. The surface is then watered with a fine mist spray. Rapid-hardening cement is sometimes used. Although the mortar bed is important to grip the cobbles, a more visually pleasing mortar will be obtained using hydraulic lime:sand 1:2.

Stone flags. Limestone, sandstone or slate flag stones of specified size, thickness and finish, with edges sawn at right angles unless otherwise described, are usually laid on a 25 mm (1 in) thick bed of semi-dry lime-sand mortar which is well compacted to a true and level surface. Old slabs are usually only worked level on one face (and four edges), so the base must be thick enough and accommodating enough to take the irregularities and provide support at all points. Modern replacements are six sides sawn. Lime:sand mortar 1:2.5 should be brushed dry into all the joints, sprinkled with water and protected from rain and hot sun under ventilated covers, such as sheet material laid on bricks. For tough, durable stones hydraulic lime:sand 1:3 is recommended. Cement is not necessary and should be avoided.

When pavements are repaired, flags of a similar size and pattern to the old flag should be used. For new infills a general recommendation is that no less than 25 slabs should be used to cover 10 m² (100 ft²) of surface area. If precedent demands very large slabs some form of perimeter sleeper wall will be advisable. Slabs of large size, say 2 m (6.5 ft) square, will be 100–150 mm (4–6 in) thick and extremely heavy, so that lewis holes must be left for mechanical lifting.

Paving in light traffic areas

Much paving was traditionally bedded direct on the soil or a levelling base of sand. If there is only to be light pedestrian traffic there is no need to change this. Even joints may be simply filled with sand, although from a mainenance point of view a weak binder of lime is advisable (say lime:sand 1:4 or 1:5).

Marble and decorative limestone paving

Marble and decorative limestone paving, whether used internally or externally, should not be bedded on cement mortar. A white cement:white lime:silver sand base and jointing of 1:1:8 is typical good practice and will avoid the staining and possible damage arising from alkali salt migration. A reliable damp-proof membrane is also required. Internal marble should be cleaned with powdered detergents or abrasive scouring methods.

A peculiarity of marble paving (or any thin marble slabs) is the phenomenon of stress-release where there has been inadequate seasoning of the stone. A number of examples are known where thin (20 mm (0.8 in) thick) marble slabs have distorted and cracked, producing either humped or dished profiles. The removal of confining stresses during the quarrying operation may lead, gradually, to expansion towards the marble's original condition. Extremes of cold and heat can accelerate the process of de-stressing. Micro-cracking from stress relief can largely be avoided by the storage of the block for a few months.

Deformation may also be linked to weathering in damp, polluted environments. Recrystallization phenomena associated with acidic solutions washing the crystals of calcite in the marble may bring about upward buckling as well as dishing effects. Unfortunately, the distortion of thin slabs cannot be remedied and they must be replaced with seasoned stone. This problem is a relatively modern one, linked to fast delivery and laying times and the sophisticated sawing which produces very thin slabs economically.

Wear problems

Problems of wear associated with the modern tourist industry must inevitably lead to restricted circulation and covering of valuable areas, however unpopular this may be. The seriousness of the problem may be seen externally at such important sites as Pompeii and the Acropolis at Athens, which have to contend with a phenomenal amount of foot traffic. At such sites as S. Maria Maggiore in Rome the resistance to constant wear of the constituent stones in a polychromatic scheme varies, so that the red and green porphyries stand proud of marble and travertine. In these situations decks, raised walkways externally and carpets with thick, absorbent underlay which are turned and vacuum-cleaned regularly internally must be tolerated. Our increasingly conservation-conscious society will not, in the end, thank us for allowing our monuments to be 'visited to destruction'.

References

1. Caroe, A.D.R. and Caroe, M.B., *Stonework: Maintenance and Surface Repair*, Council for the Care of Churches, London, 1984
2. BRE Digest 269, *The Selection of Natural Building Stone*, Building Research Establishment, 1983; D.B. Honeyborne, *The Building Limestones of France*, Building Research Establishment Report, HMSO, London, 1982
3. Warland, E.G., *Modern Practical Masonry*, reprinted by the Stone Federation, London, 1984
4. Schaffer, R.J., *The Weathering of Natural Building Stones*, Department of Scientific and Industrial Research Special Report 18, HMSO, London, 1932 (available from Building Research Establishment, Watford WD2 7JR, England)
5. Powys, A.R., *Repair of Ancient Buildings*, reissued by the Society for the Protection of Ancient Buildings, London, 1981
6. Clifton-Taylor, A., *The Pattern of English Building*, 2nd edition, Faber, London, 1977
7. Derbyshire County Council, *Traditional Stone Roofing*, Design and Conservation Section, County Planning Department, Derbyshire County Council

Figure 1.1 Corfe Castle, Dorset, is constructed of some of the finest quality masonry found in medieval castle building in England. Although deliberately slighted by the Parliamentary army in the civil war of the seventeenth century it remains a testimony to the technique of double skin core-filled construction carried out by master builders

Figure 1.4 Vertical fractures, split and exposed wall core and broken wall heads require possible stitching, grouting and wall-top weathering. The first essential is to record the condition and the position of all the stones, including those which have fallen (Jervaulx Abbey)

Figure 1.2 Castle Acre Priory is a good example of a ruined building consolidated 'as found' with very little added or taken away but with corework and wall tops consolidated and internally reinforced. Decorated stones and stones with tooling survive in a good state of preservation. Each stone has an intrinsic value in its original position

Figure 1.3 Jervaulx Abbey in Yorkshire is typical of roofless and otherwise depleted construction where survival is dependent on structural intervention and weatherproofing. The failure of one structural element at this stage in the building's deterioration can have a knock-on effect of considerable magnitude

Figure 1.5 Developing fractures may take decades to become serious, but may also fail with surprising rapidity, especially when temperature extremes, such as a long dry summer or severe freeze-thaw cycling at the end of the winter, interfere with the normal equilibrium. Recording and monitoring of fractures, and temporary support, are desirable if not essential

36

Figure 1.6 Successful consolidation of ruined masonry requires an understanding of the roles of facework and corework. At Goodrich Castle, on the Welsh border of England, core has been accurately consolidated with a high ratio of mortar visible and with water traps eliminated. The facing stones have been tamped and pointed where necessary

Figure 1.8 Occasionally it is necessary to introduce new stone into ruined buildings. In this illustration of Cleeve Abbey in Somerset, three new stones have been corbelled out to provide a discreet support for the arch. They have been carefully selected and professionally bonded in

Figure 1.7 An exposed wall head at Corfe Castle in Dorset illustrates the proper treatment of corework. The main points to note are: (1) the core does not extend over the area which was once occupied by face stones, (2) the impression of the tails of missing stones has been made in the core profile, (3) the core shows stepped 'course lines' reflecting the coursing of missing facings and (4) the mortar to stone ratio is high and the stones themselves have been slurried in lime water (work of St Blaise, Evershot)

Figure 1.9 Falsework provides temporary support for this archway at Jervaulx Abbey, Yorkshire. To the left of the arch, masonry is missing, with the result that the arch has become distorted by an unequal thrust from the right. To counteract this, corework will be rebuilt on the left-hand side to provide an opposing thrust. No attempt to rebuild or alter the arch is made

Figure 1.10 Masonry elements, once properly consolidated, can be re-aligned if necessary. This shored-up section of wall at Fountains Abbey, Yorkshire, was leaning due to settlement. It was supported as shown (left), grouted, tamped and pointed until fully consolidated. After archaeologically supervised excavation under the footings the leaning wall was jacked up into a vertical position and underpinned with masonry and concrete

Figure 1.11 The nave arcade of Fountains Abbey in Yorkshire illustrates the effects of water washing through the mortar core of the drum piers. Unprotected wall heads allow the ingress of water which carries calcium carbonate and sulphate into the sandstone ashlars and mouldings. Apart from the encouragement of decay in the sandstone, the major risk is that progressive washing out of the core will threaten the stability of the piers and walls

Figure 1.12 Replacement of mortar in wall cores to achieve structural integrity of double skin, core-filled walls is achieved by grouting. In this illustration a wall which has lost core and bedding mortar is being prepared for grouting. The blocks are being levelled and secured by oak wedges driven into the joints. The bottom four courses have been plugged with tarred hemp, pushed in with a pointing key as a temporary seal

Figure 1.13 The grout (liquid mortar) is being introduced by a gravity system. The grout pan, hung in a timber cradle, is located on a scaffold about four metres above the grout points. A hose conducts the grout from the bottom of the pan to the grout point. A wooden plug closes and opens the grouting line. The solids in the grout are kept in suspension by continuous stirring. The force cup standing on the cradle is used to clear any blocking in the line

Figure 1.14 Below the grout pan at the base of the wall the hose delivers the grout into the wall through a galvanised feed pipe fitted with a stop cock. When the pan plug is lifted and the stop cock opens the grout flows into the wall and rises up to proving holes left at one half metre height. The dark patch is left by escape of water during the preliminary flushing out process which must always precede the introduction of grout

Figure 1.15 The grout has filled the voids of the first lift of masonry and is escaping from the proving holes, which are immediately stopped up with tarred hemp

Figure 1.16 Grouting proceeds in lifts of between one half metre and one metre height. When grouting is complete, the tarred hemp is pulled out and the joints pointed up back to the grout line. This illustration (left) shows the bottom section grouted and pointed

Figure 1.17 When structural intervention is necessary, the aim should be to provide the assistance to the wall in as unobtrusive a manner as possible and without imposing new stresses on the wall being repaired or on associated masonry elements. The wall in the illustration above shows distinct bowing at its head, as indicated by the vertical line of the scaffolding. To prevent further movement, a wall head beam is inserted into the wall, spanning between two cross walls

Figure 1.18 A view of the top of the wall shows several stages in the process of installation of the beam. First, all vegetation must be cleared from the wall top. Second, the wall is photographed and the stones numbered as found. Third, the stones are lifted off the top of the wall and the core work between the two lines of facing stones is excavated under archaeological supervision. Fourth, a lime mortar 'cushion' is placed to isolate the tails of the stones from the new concrete. Fifth, the reinforcement cage is placed, section by section. Sixth, concrete is tamped around the reinforcement. Finally, the wall head stones are replaced, from the records, exactly as found. The wall head beam reinforcement is turned into the heart of the cross walls to provide anchorage and restraint

Figure 1.19 Although organic growth on ruined masonry is rightly acknowledged as a problem, there are sometimes situations where plants are also important. Some species thrive on lime-rich substrates and may be considered proper subjects for conservation in their own right. The ruins of Jervaulx are of considerable interest to botanists and the total clearance of the wall tops would be unacceptable

Figure 1.21 Similar problems to those at Jervaulx can exist in the context of occupied buildings, where the garden encroaches on the masonry in the form of ornamental climbing plants. Some decorative climbers can be of considerable age and beauty. A satisfactory compromise can be reached if work is planned to allow pruning at the correct season by the correct personnel. Sometimes a stainless steel grid on 100 mm spacer bolts can provide a discreet climbing frame which allows some maintenance. Climbing plants should not be allowed to invade gutters and roof coverings

Figure 1.20 This illustration shows an experimental section of wall at Jervaulx where the masonry has been consolidated (deep-tamped and pointed up from the ground to within two or three courses of the broken wall head). The wall head zone is left untouched, unless individual stones are loose, to allow the flowering plants to remain in their natural habitat. Whilst this would be a dangerous practice on high walls where access was difficult, it is an acceptable compromise on walls up to about five metres in height

Figure 1.22 Unsupported projections can be supported by corbelling out. Other openings with missing heads may need to be secretly hung from new lintols set behind the face stones. All features, however indistinct or apparently insignificant, must be recorded by archaeological survey (Jervaulx Abbey)

Figure 1.23 The 'Achilles Heel' of the ruined masonry structure is the exposed and weathered-out core, whose disintegration is brought about by water, frost and plant growth. The wall head protection is critical

Figure 1.25 The wall enclosing the Roman city of Silchester has fallen prey to stone robbing, especially at the base of the wall, to exposure to weather and to colonisation by plants. Construction of this kind, small stones with lacing and bonding courses, contains a high ratio of mortar to stone. As such, it is relatively easy for major growths to establish themselves and for root systems to penetrate deep into the wall. This tree has been cut back but must now be carefully excavated from the fragile masonry. The voids left by its removal are packed with lime mortar, tile and stones. The wall section in the second illustration shows the consolidated work, including underpinning with stones which had fallen out at the wall base

Figure 1.24 Tintern Abbey, in Monmouthshire, after wall head consolidation. The core is recorded, lifted and reset as found after consolidation, with one modification: the stones are so placed to shed water off the wall and to eliminate any pockets where water could be trapped or organic debris could accumulate

Figure 1.26 Thousands of metres of exposed wall top at Bolsover Castle, Derbyshire, present a major and ongoing maintenance problem which only re-roofing would solve permanently. Even so, false detail such as coping stones is not introduced and the work is achieved by core consolidation

Figure 1.27 Wall head maintenance is just as critical in an occupied building but the situation is less of a philosophical problem. This building complex in the university city of Oxford has had a long history of repair and maintenance which includes essential replacement of copings and weatherings when they fail but also preserves the architectural integrity by replacement of decayed pinnacles

Figure 1.28 Not all decorative elements are non-functional. These buttress caps on the nave buttresses at Westminster Abbey are both weathering and structural elements, providing the necessary load on the buttress to withstand the thrust of the flying arches

Figure 1.29 The Treasurer's House in York shows how new stone should be introduced into an old facade. The most important weathering element, the cornice, has been substantially replaced and has had a lead flashing installed. Elsewhere, minimum replacement has been carried out, leaving every original stone where possible. New detail is an exact replica of the old and stones are replaced on the same line. The stone is geologically compatible with the original Magnesian Limestone

Figure 1.30 Depending on the type of construction and the bed depth of the original stones it is sometimes expedient and economic to replace only the front face of a stone block, usually between 75 mm and 100 mm on bed. The rusticated sandstone ashlar in the illustration has been faced in this way where the lighter tone can be seen. Facings such as this are sometimes bedded in epoxy or polyester resin, but this is not good practice, since moisture movement is checked against the resin barrier. Fixing should be in the form of threaded stainless steel dowels set in resin, the rest of the interface between new and old stone being coated in lime and white cement

Figure 1.31 Replacement stone of the right kind may be much lighter in colour than the weathered original. The weathered colour can be anticipated by an iron oxide wash if considered essential

Figure 1.32 Minimum piecing-in or minimum replacement can result in an initially startling patchwork. This replacement stone at Durham Cathedral is, however, technically and philosophically absolutely correct. New stone weathers over a period of decades. Owners of historic buildings, and sometimes their architects, must be dissuaded from replacing too much for the sake of uniformity

Figure 1.33 A detail of the original stone at Durham shows a heavily weathered, textured surface which is, nevertheless, perfectly sound and not in need of replacement. Any water traps can be rubbed back using a hand-held carborundum stone. Discreet mortar fillets and fills may be used in deep pockets or ledges provided they are well matched to the stone in colour and are not gauged with water-repellent adhesives

Figure 1.34 The medieval market cross at Chichester in Sussex, largely constructed in Caen stone, has suffered extensively from pollution and crude repairs in dense, hydraulic mortars. The two pairs of trefoils in the illustration were largely reconstructed in Portland cement mortar. The mortar was cut out to a square line on the springing point of the trefoil heads and a limestone insertion secured in its place with stainless steel dowels and a restraint fixing back into the core. White cement and lime were used to grout behind the new piece. Slightly weathered Caen stone below the springing line was repaired in lime mortar (Cathedral Works Organization, Chichester)

Figure 1.35 The replacement of a damaged course of stone above a plinth weathering has been completed, except for the last stone. Because the damage was partly due to water leaching through the contaminated corework, the back of the cavity has been mortar slurried and coated with sanded bitumen. Note that the bitumen is stopped 25 mm back from the face (right of illustration) to prevent staining. The object of the bitumen is to prevent any salt contamination of the new stone

Figure 1.36 The stone is here in place, on bedding mortar with vertical joints filled. Grouting takes place through holes left in the vertical joints until it appears at the hole shown in the top bed (the proving hole)

Figure 1.39 Good quality quoin indents contrast with the work of the non-mason. These stones at Fort George, Scotland, are correctly and accurately sized and neatly tooled to match surviving original stones. The edges of the blocks have a subtle 'pencil-round' to take off the sharpness of sawn arrises

Figure 1.37 Poor quality finishing of indented stones defaces and devalues the building into which they are placed. These quoin stones have been set in, six sides sawn but over-sized. A grinding disc has been applied to the face to achieve the correct line. Because of incorrect tools being used by an operative with no masonry skills the exercise is a waste of money. The stones are misshapen and scoured with disc marks

Figure 1.38 Hand-dressing on site is a skilled operation. In this illustration a mason is putting the final tooled finish on the stone. Note that the new stone is not being dressed back to 'fit' the weathered profile, but is maintaining the correct original line

Figure 1.40 Rebuild of a limestone parapet wall, Richmond Terrace, London. The illustration shows the use of joggles in the joint beds of cornice, blocking course, die stone and coping. With sawn stones the importance of these joggles, into which liquid grout will be run, is paramount. Note the damp proof membrane inserted under the coping, and the chase cut into the face of the blocking course to receive the edge of the lead flashing to the cornice

Figure 1.43 Mortar filling in a redressed surface is one of the most difficult cosmetic activities to achieve successfully and requires considerable skill and investment of time in mortar matching. In this illustration a mortar consisting of one part buff hydraulic lime to five parts stonedust and sand graded down from 600 μm has been designed to match the stone in wet and dry conditions. It is ironed in with small wooden floats and is here being finished with a small float faced with felt. Protection from the weather during curing is essential

Figure 1.41 There is no technical or practical reason for not redressing stone and it has often been used as an economic way of producing a 'new' facade. In construction terms it represent a major loss of original worked surface (if any survived) and can create curious details, such as projecting window dressings at Oxford, which are replacement stones on the original line

Figure 1.44 Contrasting textures of weathered and redressed clunch [limestone] at Woburn Abbey illustrate why, architecturally, the technique of redressing can be attractive. Nevertheless, the first consideration should always be the retention of as much as possible of the original worked face

Figure 1.42 Sometimes uniform-depth redressing will still leave cavities which cannot be left. In fact, redressing tends to accentuate remaining damage, so that mortar filling or limited piecing-in with new stone becomes almost essential

Figure 1.45 Experimental treatment to save the weathered faces at Woburn included cleaning with hot lime poultices, treating the friable areas over two to three days with limewater, grouting behind scales with lime, brickdust and acrylic emulsion and closing up water traps with weak lime, stonedust and brickdust mortar. The brickdust was from white, refractory bricks and graded down from 150 μm

Figure 1.46 Redressing is seen here at Lichfield not for architectural reasons but to remove contour scaling around joints. This is very much an intermediate treatment to exclude water and prevent large scales falling from the walls. It may also 'buy time', before indenting with new stone takes place

Figure 1.49 A major weathering element such as a cornice cannot be repaired in reinforced mortar unless it is to be covered with a lead flashing. Frost has removed this mortar repair within one year

Figure 1.47 Mortar repair or 'plastic' repair has a poor reputation largely because it is too often used as a cheap option to be carried out by operatives with limited expertise and because it is used on too large a scale. Three periods of plastic repair are shown here in different stages of disintegration. All are feather-edged and two are relying on bonding agents to keep them in position

Figure 1.48 Plastic repair is never satisfactory, except on a very minor scale, as a weathering. The mouldings on this buttress have been repaired with a coloured mortar with little preparation or mechanical key. Failure is commencing within two years of completion

Figure 1.50 Good quality mortar repair is not cheap, because the amount of preparation can be as great as for stone replacement. This pierced work at Bristol is being very professionally carried out using a well matched mortar, phosphor bronze wire armatures and considerable practical expertise. In this case, the use of mortar enables more of the original stone to be retained than if a stone replacement was selected

Figure 1.51 Mortar is most often applicable as a 'dental' repair i.e. the filling of small lacunae in such a way that the maximum amount of the stone under repair is retained. The work involves dental tools and plasterers' small tools and requires experience to be successful

Figure 1.54 Colour-matched mortar was built up round the wire armatures and glass fibre rods until the full profile was re-created. The final stage was to dress and rub the cured mortar with masonry chisels and carborundum blocks until an acceptable finish was produced

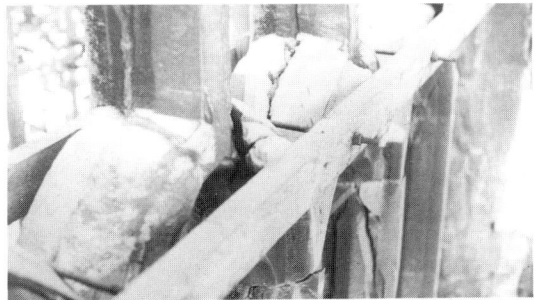

Figure 1.52 Mortar repair in association with surgical techniques sometimes makes it possible to save masonry which otherwise could only be recorded and replaced. During World War II the Bristol Temple Church was burnt out by incendiary bombs. Rapid cooling promoted a shattering of much of the stone, especially the tracery. Subsequent weathering of the roofless building brought the windows to a dangerous condition. Many of them were kept in place only by timber corsets, bolted together

Figure 1.53 The tracery was drilled horizontally and vertically whilst clamping the stone with timber splices. These drillings, after flushing out dust, were grouted with epoxy mortar and glass fibre rods were inserted as a complex stitching system. The ends of all rods were kept within the general line of the tracery. When the resin had cured, a cage of phosphor bronze wire was built up around the rods as an armature for mortar repair

Figure 1.55 This illustration is of a completely reinforced, stitched and repaired window after the removal of the corsets. The repairs are all concealed and the tracery has regained full structural integrity

Figure 1.56 Fire damage and the rapid cooling of masonry by fire hoses created typical fracturing of the Norman period masonry of Westminster Hall in London. The fractures run parallel with the face of the stone at (typically) 5, 10 and 15 mm depths. To secure the stones, all of which bore marks of axe-work and some of which had mason's marks, it was decided to pin the 'plates' of stone back into position. The stones were covered with a temporary, protective latex coating and supported with padded shuttering. A small, diamond disc was used to open the weakened joints, because any impact tools would have destroyed the fragile bond between the 'plates'

Figure 1.57 Drillings were made into the joint thicknesses to a depth of 75 mm, beyond the deepest of the fractures. An average of five drillings were made, each 12 mm in diameter, round the perimeter of each stone. The holes were blown free of dust

Figure 1.58 The drillings were grouted with a thixotropic epoxy placed with a mastic gun fitted with an extension tube, so that the holes could be filled from the back. Each hole was grouted two-thirds full

Figure 1.59 Glass fibre rods, 8 mm in diameter and constructed of continuous glass roving set in polyester resin, were sandpapered to clean and roughen the surface before being pushed fully home. As the rods are squeezed forward, the resin mortar is displaced into the fracture lines wherever they have been intersected by the drilling. When cured, each 'plate' of stone has four to five squeezed resin keys anchoring it to the rest of the block. The drill holes and joints are finally pointed up in lime mortar

Figure 1.60 Horizontal projections such as cornices can act as water catchments, especially when there is inadequate fall and when joints begin to fail. Breakdown of such a major weathering element as this can lead to accelerated deterioration of the stones below. The introduction of a lead flashing to this detail, even if slightly obtrusive visually, would play a major role in extending the life of the building

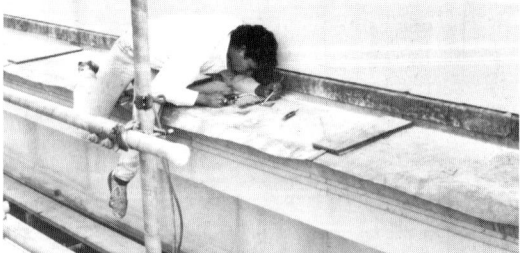

Figure 1.61 The installation of a lead flashing to a wide cornice in progress. Code 6 lead is used for a major projection and sheets are limited to 1.5 m in length. The sheets are welted together, the welts incorporating copper clips. The front edge is also secured with copper clips and intermediate fixings are made into the cornice with lead-capped brass screws

Figure 1.62 The versatility of lead as a protection is illustrated by its use on the chapter house of Howden Minster in Yorkshire. Vulnerable wall heads and decorative detail are covered in Code 6 and Code 4 lead, welt jointed and secured with copper clips and brass screws and washers

Figure 1.63 At Drumlanrig Castle in Scotland it was necessary to take the lead flashing up over the blocking courses of the parapet. Because the detailing of the parapet required each stone baluster to be fixed through the lead, separate cover flashings were provided to each baluster, welt jointed together. This ensured that the lead would not be 'over-fixed' and unable to accommodate thermal movements

Figure 1.64 At Tintern Abbey in Monmouthshire the malleability of lead has been put to good use by bossing over the mouldings of a damaged roundel in the traceried window. This lead dressing, turned down into masonry joints, lead wedged and pointed in, sheds water off a natural collection point and protects the tracery below

Figure 1.65 The splendid tympanum at Kilpeck is in such good condition that it needs little attention other than deflection of water. A Code 4 lead flashing has been dressed carefully over the hood moulding and fixed back into the joint with lead wedges to prevent water running off the wall into the sculpture

Figure 1.66 The church of St Mary the Virgin (1154–1189) at Iffley, Oxford, has an external rubble construction which was once plastered. Evidences of the plaster remained on the face of the stones in sheltered areas. Stripping of external plaster is quite unacceptable in conservation terms but also creates weathering problems because of the difficulty in pointing round rubble which was not intended to be exposed. The rubble can be seen on the south wall

50

Figure 1.67 The west front at Iffley contains a superb portal of six orders with chevron and beakhead enrichment, as well as circular and circular headed window dressings, all moulded. It was decided to replaster for aesthetic and sound maintenance reasons, to provide a weathercoat which would act as blotting paper, absorbing water and releasing it by evaporation but denying it access to the heart of the wall. The plaster had the considerable additional benefit of providing a simple background against which the enrichment could be enjoyed. The decorative stones were cleaned by lime/poultice, consolidated with limewater and given a lime shelter coat

Figure 1.68 The plaster was a single coat of lime putty, sand and stonedust with a light refractory brickdust gauging. It was applied using small purpose made wood floats and standard small tools, pressing and ironing hard into the profile of the rubble. The result is a pleasing and functional weathering coat with a warm limestone colour which follows the texture of the wall underneath

Figure 1.69 The parapet, buttress caps and finials, distinguished by the lighter (cleaner) colour, are a combination of synthetic mortar and cast stones. Cast stone tends to weather differently from natural stone and its quality varies with the expertise of the manufacturers. Although replacement of 'like with like' should always be the objective in the repair of historic buildings, there are sometimes justifications for using limited casting on selected areas. For instance, if there is genuinely no compatible stone available, parapets and other essential weatherings are better replaced in good quality casts than left at risk

Figure 1.70 The danger of accepting casts in place of natural stone is that it may be seen as a quick and easy option. Larger scale production of these cornice sections in concrete with one 'artificial stone' face is likely to encourage unnecessary replacement. Note that even casts should not be stored on the ground in this haphazard manner. They are liable to damage and staining

Figure 1.71 Some cast stone is of some antiquity and should be conserved. This wall contains about 30% of cast stones made up of hydraulic lime and coloured sands. These casts, placed in late medieval construction, are believed to be of very early nineteenth century date and have performed well without damage to the surviving stones

Figure 1.72 Stone paving is often remarkably durable, having been selected for its resistance to impact and abrasion. The largely undisturbed eighteenth century roadway in Italy is formed of basalt setts. The long dimension embedded in sand or lime sand and pozzolana is 200–250 mm to a surface dimension of 100 × 100 mm. The shape is like a wedge or 'nail', enabling it to be driven into the substrate. This is an efficient unit which takes considerable punishment

Figure 1.73 Limestone setts at Eton, England, in a geometric pattern. Pavings of this kind, or in the more familiar granite, are effective as long as they are thoroughly compacted into the substrate. Eighteenth and nineteenth century pavings of this kind, typically 70 × 160 × 160 mm deep will take heavy traffic if the tails are securely in a well packed base of hydraulic lime and sand or cement:lime:sand (1:3 or 1:2:8)

Figure 1.74 Cobble (water washed sandstone) paving in the process of laying at Richmond, Yorkshire. Note the intermediate bay construction to assist laying to falls. Bedding and tamping are the secret of successful laying. Shallow units of this kind need to be bedded in a strong cement:lime:sand base such as 1:1:6, but they should not be pointed in hard, dense mortar. Hydraulic lime:sand 1:4 would be suitable for pointing, leaving the top and shoulder of the cobble exposed

Figure 1.75 The architect Street's paving at Kingston Church, Dorset. This is a good example of stone texture being used in a functional way to assist pedestrian traffic in the ascent of a steep hill. The kerbs and setts are in Purbeck limestone. Note the importance of not flush-pointing. These random size setts are on average 100 mm deep

Figure 1.76 The process of removing soluble salts from masonry is difficult and can never be totally effective. The concentration of salts can sometimes be reduced by irrigation and poulticing to the extent that lime plastering, limewashing or the local use of a consolidant is successful; or the surface may become more stable without further treatment. This picture shows the effects of storing de-icing salt in a single-skin masonry building. The light coloured zones are evidence of active decay on the external wall surface

Figure 1.77 The first stage in the poulticing process involves the preparation of the wall. Not every wall can be treated by this process and it should never be used where valuable plaster or any timber is associated with the wall surfaces. This picture shows the light coloured area of decay, a temporary gutter secured at the bottom of the wall to receive run-off, and an assembly of water sprays playing on the wall surface

Figure 1.78 Moisture measurements are taken from the centre of the wall. When the joints show that the wall is well penetrated by water (up to seven days on a 450 mm [18 in] wall) the poultice medium is prepared. This picture shows the correct consistency of an attapulgite clay which has been added as a dry powder to clean, fresh water. At this stage the clay can be applied to the wet wall surfaces and will cling to the wall when pressed on with a plastering float

Figure 1.79 This shows the attapulgite clay covering the area of decay. To assist in the support of the clay and to ensure good adhesion is maintained for as long as possible, a galvanized wire mesh is pushed into the wet clay and secured with galvanized staples into the masonry joints. A final working over of the surface with a float assists the embedding of the wire, giving a finished thickness of approximately 20 mm

Figure 1.80 An external clay application must be protected from rain, direct sunlight and strong draughts of air. Here, a simple tarpaulin sheet, securely anchored at the eaves and at the base of the wall, provides adequate protection for the poulticed wall. At this stage, the irrigated wall begins the drying out process. The clay is the drying face and will receive salts in solution from the wall

Figure 1.81 As the wall dries the clay poultice also dries and begins to shrink and crack, pulling away from the wall. Salt growths can be seen on the clay face and the reinforcement. With care, by gently pulling out the staples, the clay and wire 'curtain' can be lifted off the wall as shown here. The dry poultice must be removed from site and not allowed to recontaminate any other surface. The wetting and poulticing cycle is normally repeated three or four times to achieve any useful reduction in salt concentration

Figure 1.82 Desalination attempts are little use if the source of soluble salts remains. At Muchelney Abbey, Somerset, the internal cloister wall had suffered from rising groundwater during marine flooding. Since irrigation and poulticing of these walls would only serve to draw up further salts in solution a barrier needed to be introduced. This picture shows the external face of a wall which is approximately 1.5 m thick at base and is of double skin construction with a core filling

Figure 1.84 The internal face of the same wall, after fresh water irrigation and clay poulticing. At floor level is a bituminous felt-lined temporary gutter to collect the water during the spraying process. Between the floor and the horizontal string course is the attapulgite clay during the drying-out stage. The light coloured areas show the deposition of soluble salt in the clay. Four wetting and poulticing cycles were needed to stabilize the surface for plastering

Figure 1.83 A stage in the introduction of a water barrier. Drillings are made through the wall from both sides using the 25 mm diameter, 1.25 m long drill bits seen in the foreground. The wall core is then grouted with a lime:pulverized fuel ash grout to provide continuity through the wall at this level, eliminating any large voids. When the grout has cured, the drill holes are opened again to sufficient depth to insert the feed lines for a pumped silicone resin in solvent. The resin is pumped in from both sides of the wall to establish a damp proof zone against further salt migration

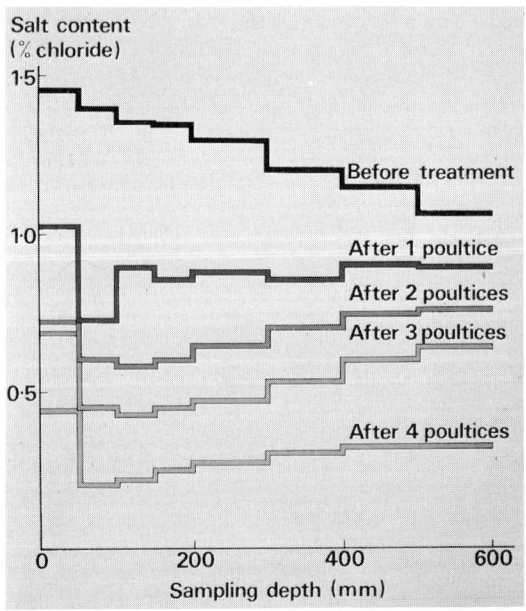

Figure 1.85 This figure, reproduced by kind permission of the Building Research Establishment (UK), shows the reduction of chloride content after four poulticing cycles at the Salt Tower, Tower of London

2

Structural failure and repair

Ralph Mills

Introduction

Before attempting to carry out remedial works to masonry structures, the cause of failure must be determined, bearing in mind that some of the faults may have their origin in the basic form of the construction. Such built-in weaknesses can develop during the life of the structure and may lead to structural failure at a much later date. It is essential, therefore, to diagnose the reasons for failure accurately, in order to avoid unnecessary remedial work.

Foundation failure

Many historic masonry structures have foundations which would be considered inadequate by present-day design standards. However, if such a structure shows no signs of distress and there are no proposals for change of use or for an alteration in the loading pattern, it is unnecessary to improve the bearing capacity. The foundations have proved their ability to transfer safely the loads placed upon them throughout the lifetime of the building. Generally foundations which are satisfactory in an existing situation will only need to be improved if the loading is increased by more than 10%.

Signs of foundation failure can be found by examining the plinth line for differential settlement, or by checking the alignment of masonry joints at wall junctions. The development of cracking in the superstructure should also be assessed, as this may provide further evidence of foundation failure.

The problems caused by shrinkable clays have been widely publicized, particularly the cracking of foundations which can occur in periods of drought. Foundation cracking can also be caused by the removal of nearby trees and shrubs because this will increase the moisture content of the clay and result in local ground heave.

When considering the repair of a masonry structure, the design team is faced with the dilemma of balancing the need to ensure that sufficient remedial work is carried out to secure the safety of the structure against the temptation of trying to achieve too high a safety margin at unnecessary expense.

Structures settle as they are being built and continue to settle thereafter. The rate depends upon the nature of the ground, the speed of the construction and the dead and live loads imposed. This settlement consolidates the ground beneath the foundations, which may eventually provide an adequate load-bearing medium. It would be imprudent to disturb this consolidated ground unnecessarily. If it can be established that differential movement is due to seasonal or moisture variations or shallow foundations, or that only a small increase in bearing capacity is required, then underpinning of the type shown in *Figure 2.1* is likely to be the most appropriate. The base of the masonry must be consolidated to ensure adequate stress distribution, and the excavation and the underpinning should be carried out in the order shown in *Figure 2.2*. This system has the advantage of retaining a large proportion of the existing compacted ground, whilst providing additional depth and bearing capacity to the foundations, thereby minimizing differential settlements. Any further settlement will be resisted by the joint reaction of the consolidated ground and the concrete underpinning.

Chemical grouts can be injected to increase the loadbearing capacity of granular soils, but this method is ineffective for clay or silty soils, because the impermeability of these materials prevents the flow of the grout.

Proprietary piling systems, composed of 'pre-bored' or 'jacked' piles, have been developed for

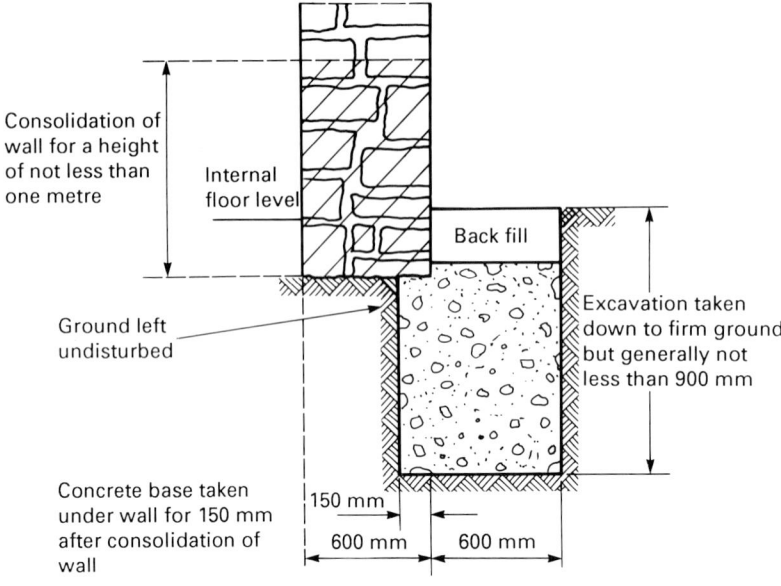

Consolidation of wall for a height of not less than one metre

Internal floor level

Back fill

Excavation taken down to firm ground but generally not less than 900 mm

Ground left undisturbed

Concrete base taken under wall for 150 mm after consolidation of wall

150 mm

600 mm   600 mm

Figure 2.1 Underpinning to walls on shallow foundations

3	1	6	4	2	5	7

Figure 2.2 Order in which foundation underpinning should be carried out

underpinning structures with a minimum of vibration or shock to the surrounding strata. These systems have the added advantage of enabling underpinning to be carried out without the need for dewatering.

Lowering the water table near an existing structure can cause settlement. Therefore piling systems are particularly useful when the water level is above the existing foundation line. Examples of some of the more commonly used types of traditional piling are shown in *Figures 2.3* and *2.4*. A relatively recent development is the introduction of micropiles. These can be either of *in situ* concrete, with external reinforcement in the form of a permanent steel tube, or the well known, friction pile type, with reinforcement embedded in the *in situ* concrete. Pile diameters can be as small as 100 mm and the length can be in excess of ten metres. These piles are usually installed by drilling holes into the ground through the bottom section of the walls as shown in *Figure 2.5*. Installation can be carried out with a minimum of vibration or disturbance to the existing structure. The piles provide good load distribution, whilst ensuring a physical link between the structure and the ground.

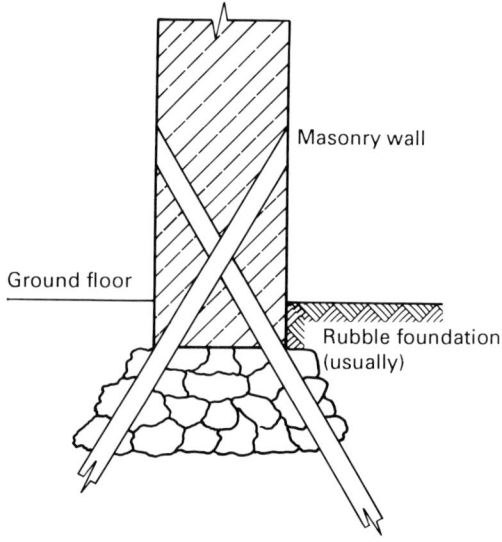

Masonry wall

Ground floor

Rubble foundation (usually)

Figure 2.3 Piles through walls of building

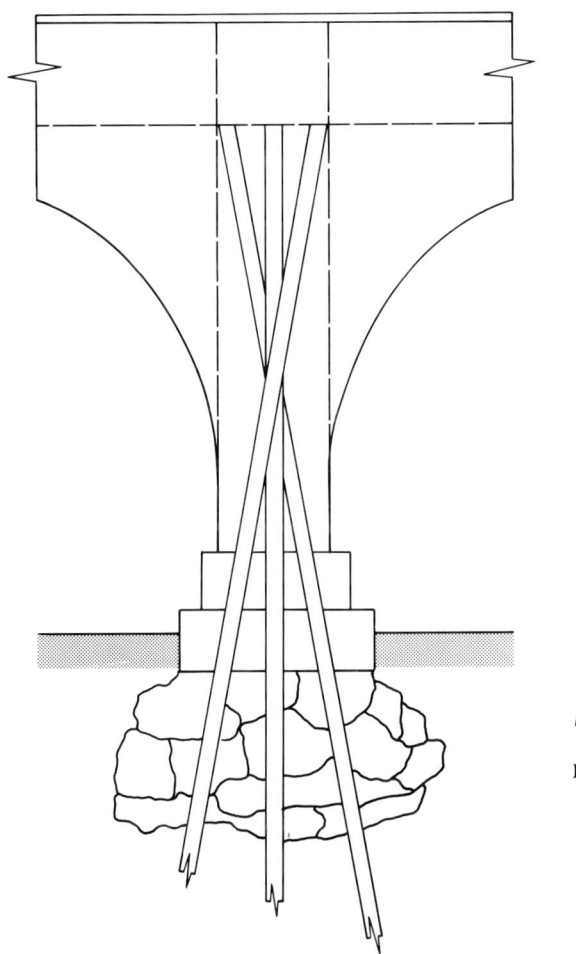

Figure 2.4 Piles through bridge pier

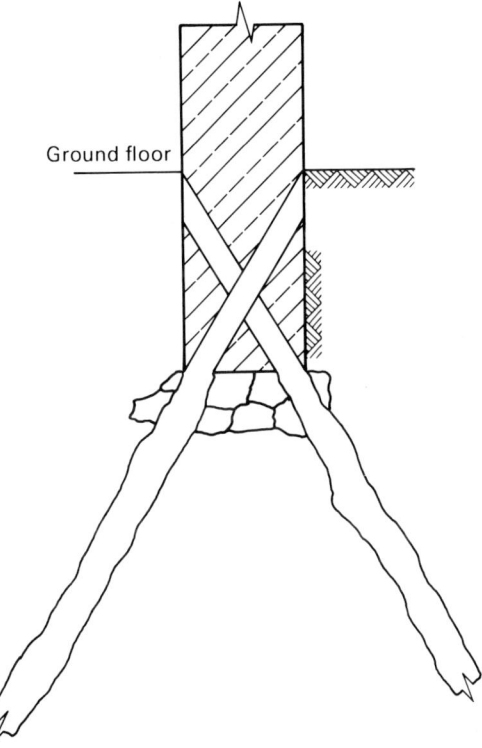

Figure 2.5 In-situ piles through bottom of wall

Structural failure in the superstructure

Factors affecting the strength of masonry struts or compressional members are:

1. *The compressive and shear strength of the masonry units.* In masonry structures, loads are often supported by stone lintels. Whilst these may be relieved to some extent by the arching effect of the masonry above, depending upon the size of unit and the bonding, overloading can occur due to disturbance of the fabric or to differential settlement. Axial compressive forces do not usually present a problem.

2. *The strength of the mortar.* This is usually less than the strength of the stone. However, a mortar of excessive strength can have an adverse effect on the masonry.

3. *The slenderness ratio of the component.* This ratio is determined by the length, form of restraint and cross-sectional shape. A long unit will support a smaller compressive load than a short unit of the same cross-sectional dimensions. A unit which is square or circular in cross-section will support a larger compressive force than a rectangular unit of the same length. The provision of additional end or intermediate restraints will increase the load-bearing capacity of a compressive member. The combination of these properties is expressed as the slenderness ratio, which must be taken into account when designing compression units. Although analytical work is sometimes essential,

it is usually sufficient to have a general under-standing of the importance of the slenderness ratio when proposing measures to strengthen or repair masonry structures. Methods used to reduce the slenderness ratio of masonry elements are described later.

4. *Eccentricity of loading*. A force which is not applied uniformly across the section of a com-pression member, or along its axis, will cause a redistribution of the stresses within the member and will lead to failure either by crushing or by buckling. Horizontal forces due to wind or earth pressures can also produce the same effect. The stresses in masonry structures can, therefore, sometimes be reduced by removing eccentric or horizontal forces. Two simple examples are the provision of a padstone in a wall under a heavily loaded beam, to obtain a more uniform distribu-tion of stresses along the wall, and the support of a beam on a padstone rather than on a corbel.

Tensile members, or ties, are dependent only on the tensile strength of the material and on their cross-sectional area. The slenderness of the compo-nent will not affect the strength, although unsightly deflection may need to be prevented. Masonry structures which incorporate large openings or colonnades can sometimes lack lateral stability. Structural integrity can be provided by introducing diagonal bracing, a structural frame, or cross walls.

Failure of arches

The other important structural form which is often used in masonry construction is the arch. Arches can be used in a simple form to support masonry above an opening in a wall, or in a complex arrangement, such as in a vaulted floor or roof.

The two important properties of an arch are the span and the rise. Although the shape of an arch affects the horizontal forces to some extent, these forces reduce as the rise increases in relation to a given span. Therefore, care must be taken to provide adequate lateral restraint to an arch, particularly one which has a small rise. Where distress indicates horizontal movement of the supports, either the load on the arch must be reduced, or remedial measures (in the form of ties, buttressing or corsetting) must be provided in order to resist further horizontal movement. A corset is usually formed of *in situ* reinforced concrete, placed over the extrados of the arch and keyed into the voussoirs. It is designed to resist the horizontal forces by developing a beam action over the span of the arch. In arches con-structed of voussoir rings of shallow depth, espe-cially where the mortar joints have deteriorated, there is a risk that buckling will develop.

Compression failure

This type of failure is relatively rare and can be recognized by the spalling face of the masonry. However, care must be taken to ensure a proper interpretation of the symptoms. For instance, where a thin joint was required on the face for architectural reasons or for weatherproofing, it was common practice amongst masons to form rough dressed 'hollow beds' in the stones. This meant that only the outer 15–25 mm (0.6–1 in) needed to be finely and accurately dressed. Similarly, stones with a small bed dimension (front to back) were often dressed off behind the face, to enlarge the mortar joint where it would not be seen. In both cases, as minor settle-ment, mortar shrinkage or mortar deterioration takes place, an increasing pressure is placed on the vulnerable front edge of each unit, resulting in spalling. This can appear very similar to spalling caused by a compression failure in the structure. Sometimes, damaged stones which were repaired at the time of construction, especially on the arrises, by glueing pieces together with casein, animal glue, or shellac and stonedust, appear to be suffering from compression damage when spalls are lost as a result of the breaking down of the adhesive bond by weathering. Examination of the surface of the break usually indicates the true reason for the failure.

Masonry defects and weaknesses

It has been common knowledge from the earliest times that sedimentary stone should be set on its natural bed, that is, in the way in which it was originally deposited. However, such stones are still sometimes bedded incorrectly, which eventually results in a tendency to delaminate. In these circum-stances, the damaged stone may have to be replaced, although consolidation and injection with a resin system, sometimes coupled with stainless steel pins, may significantly slow down the deterioration and avoid disturbance of the original structure.

Built-in ferrous metal cramps and ties were often bedded in lead. However, they were sometimes not given such protection, and as a result corrosion has caused the metal to laminate and to split the surrounding stones. If this has happened, the corro-ded metal must be cut or drilled out and the damaged stonework repaired. This can be done with a conventional 'plastic stone' or a resin-based filler, although there will be circumstances where the scale of the deterioration, or architectural requirements, will demand replacement in matching natural stone.

Pointing with a cement-rich mortar can produce the same effect as that caused by forming a hollow bed in the stone. The rich mortar provides a very strong wedge, which causes the face of the stone to spall off under compression.

The role of atmospheric pollution and other agencies of decay and weathering (see Volume 1, Chapter 7) can be responsible for symptoms which may be misinterpreted by the uninformed. For instance, the small cracks naturally present in stone, and referred to as 'vents', can open up after weathering has removed superficial natural bonding. They can look remarkably like fine cracks caused by differential movement of the structure.

The failure patterns caused by some methods of cleaning, the proximity of sandstone to limestone, efflorescence, vegetation and fire must be diagnosed correctly in order to avoid unnecessary remedial work.

Investigation of cracking

Examination of cracking in the internal plaster or external rendering, without cutting chases to expose the basic structure, is a common mistake. Plaster or rendering can conceal built-up doorways or window openings where the infill has not been bonded or toothed into the original work, with the result that cracking can occur along the straight joints. It is a relatively simple operation either to stitch across these straight joints, or to fix one of the proprietary light, expanded metal strips over the joint before replastering or rendering. There will be occasions, both when the masonry is exposed and when it is covered by rendering or plaster, when it may be necessary not to disturb the form of an opening and when stitching will not be appropriate for historical reasons. If the masonry is exposed, the plane of weakness formed by the straight joint can be strengthened by distributing the loads over the

opening by inserting spreaders or ring beams, or, in some cases, by resin injection and pins.

Cracks can also be caused by the differential settlement of adjacent parts of the structure which have been built at different periods. In these circumstances, quite large cracks may be apparent, but, if the structure has reached a state of equilibrium, it will not be necessary to install underpinning. If continuing movement is suspected, accurate monitoring over a period of up to two years will indicate whether or not remedial work is necessary (see below). There can also be variations in ground conditions across the building which may have caused differential movement in the past, but which have reached a state of stability during the lifetime of the building.

Bomb damage, or nearby explosions, can develop planes of weakness in the structure or aggravate an already weakened situation. Most masonry structures have been subject to alterations during their life and the structural implications of their movements have not always been recognized or understood by those carrying out remedial work. For example, bowing and bulging of face walls may have been caused by the removal of cross walls, or the insertion of large openings in cross walls, rendering them ineffective as lateral supports. The reason for the failure must be established. In such cases, suspended floors might, for instance, be used to provide the necessary support, as shown in *Figures 2.6* and *2.7*.

Thick masonry walls are often constructed of two skins with an unbonded rubble core between. If there are sufficient voids within the core, the effective thickness and, therefore, the strength of the wall can be increased by a cementitious grout injection, provided care is taken to avoid a high hydrostatic pressure developing within the wall due to an excessive head of grout. Grouting will be of very little value if the core has been filled, or almost

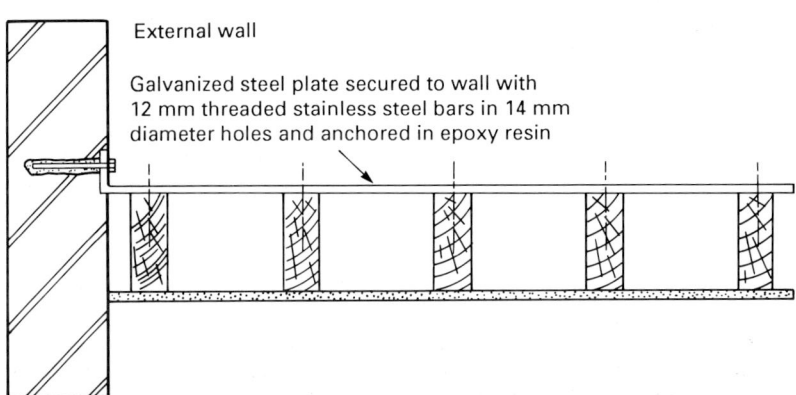

Figure 2.6 Suspended floor providing lateral support to external wall (1)

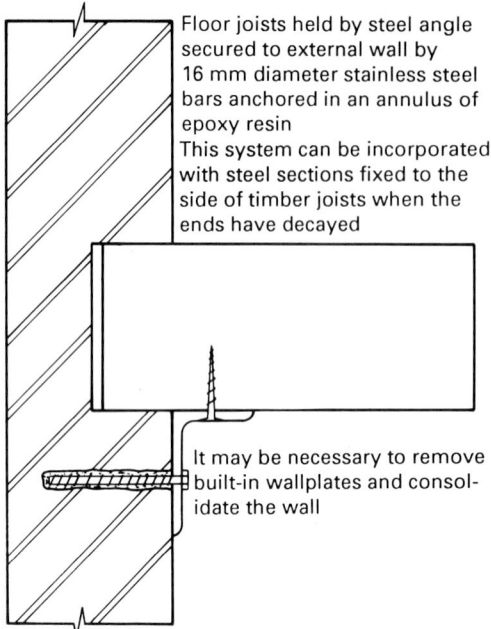

Floor joists held by steel angle secured to external wall by 16 mm diameter stainless steel bars anchored in an annulus of epoxy resin

This system can be incorporated with steel sections fixed to the side of timber joists when the ends have decayed

It may be necessary to remove built-in wallplates and consolidate the wall

Figure 2.7 Suspended floor providing lateral support to external wall (2)

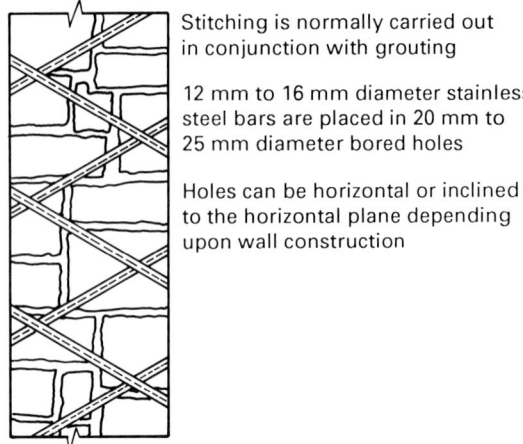

Stitching is normally carried out in conjunction with grouting

12 mm to 16 mm diameter stainless steel bars are placed in 20 mm to 25 mm diameter bored holes

Holes can be horizontal or inclined to the horizontal plane depending upon wall construction

Figure 2.8 Stitching masonry wall

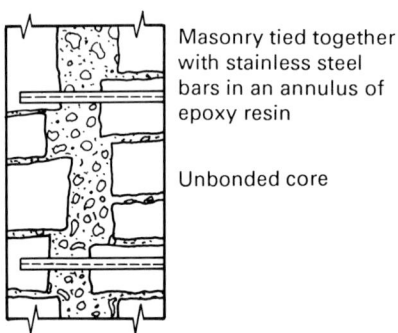

Masonry tied together with stainless steel bars in an annulus of epoxy resin

Unbonded core

Figure 2.9 Masonry tied together with stainless steel bars in an annulus of epoxy resin; unbonded core

filled, with a very soft lime mortar. It is wise, therefore, to drill a number of exploratory holes through the wall in order to properly examine the composition of the core.

Alternative methods of increasing the effective thickness of masonry walls are to stitch, as shown in *Figure 2.8*, or to tie the two skins together. *Figures 2.9* and *2.10* show a number of techniques which are now used to form a tie between two skins of masonry. There are several proprietary systems now being offered by specialist firms, but the technique was originally developed in the UK by the Building Research Establishment in conjunction with the Directorate of Ancient Monuments and Historic Buildings.

There are many masonry structures where the cross walls are not bonded into the external walls and, as a result, the external walls can become unstable. *Figures 2.11* and *2.12* show a number of ways in which to restore stability to such walls.

Where conservation work has been carried out, ties have sometimes been installed because of a misinterpretation of the visible symptoms. For example, walls with a batter have not necessarily moved, and a measurement of both faces for out-of-plumbness, with careful examination at the junctions with any cross walls, will often show that the walls are

structurally adequate. The chancel and nave walls of churches are good examples of walls which are often out of plumb and where unsightly ties have been installed unnecessarily in the past. These ties must not, of course, be removed without very careful study of the structure. If removal is being considered, it is prudent to dismantle the ties gradually, after first installing an accurate system of monitoring and establishing a record of any movement before the ties are disturbed.

Bonding timbers are often found in masonry walls, particularly in walls of random rubble, and it is a great temptation to remove them on discovery. Removal of these timbers, however, can cause a great deal of disturbance to the masonry and, if the timbers are free from decay, it will often be more economic and less disruptive to inject them with a fungicide and leave them in place.

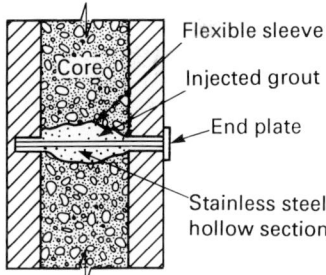

Flexible sleeve

Injected grout

End plate

Stainless steel
hollow section

Resin cartridge pushed to
the end of the drilled hole.
Cartridge broken and resin
mixed when bolt is inserted

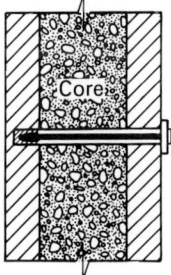

Figure 2.10 Proprietary systems of wall ties

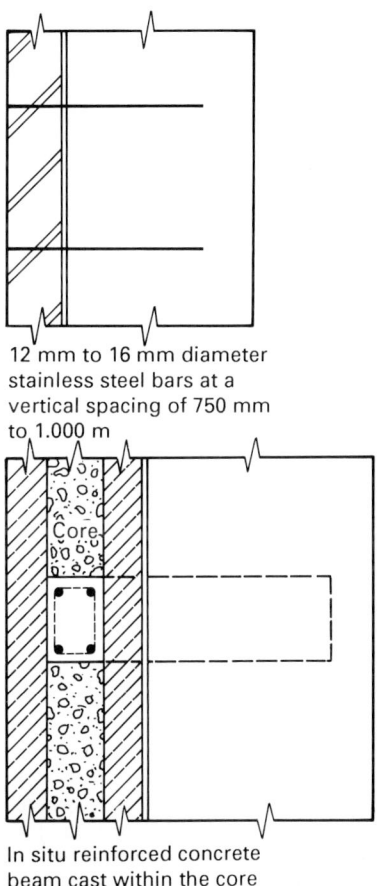

12 mm to 16 mm diameter
stainless steel bars at a
vertical spacing of 750 mm
to 1.000 m

In situ reinforced concrete
beam cast within the core
of the wall by removing
masonry in the inner leaf

Figure 2.11 Reinstating the bond between external and
cross walls (1)

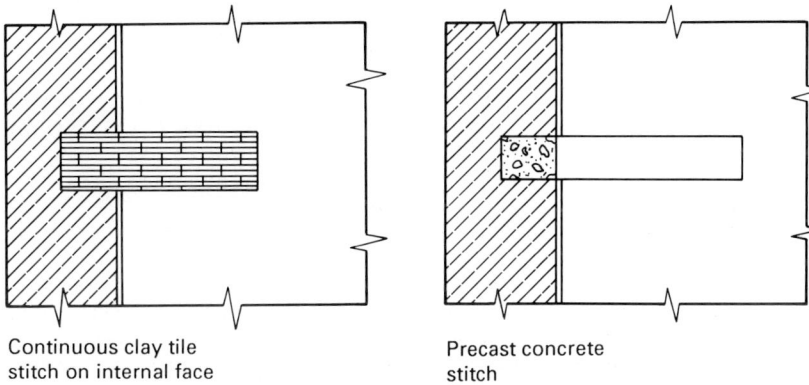

Continuous clay tile
stitch on internal face

Precast concrete
stitch

Figure 2.12 Reinstating the bond between external and cross walls (2)

Monitoring

The implications of cracks in historic masonry structures should not be judged on appearances. Such structures can have cracks of 25 mm or more in width and still be considered structurally adequate. However, assessment of the importance of large established cracks, or the possibility of continuing differential movement, should not be based on visual memory, but on a proper system of monitoring.

Significant results from an accurate monitoring system may take up to two years to obtain, but there can be occasions when such a system is of almost immediate value. For instance, a monitoring system may be able to demonstrate quite quickly that an anticipated structural repair is not required, thus saving money and avoiding unnecessary disturbance of the building. Unfortunately, there have been many examples of the collapse of masonry structures during repair works of questionable necessity where insufficient attention was paid to existing places of weakness. Sensible examination, supported by evidence obtained from monitoring, could have prevented these problems.

The choice of monitoring system will depend upon the location, the defect to be monitored and the nature of the material to which the system is to be fixed. Accuracy is essential and expenditure on labour and materials may vary only marginally between relatively crude and sophisticated systems. However, the possibility of vandalism or accidental damage can be a serious problem in locations where the general public has access. For this reason and in order to avoid disfigurement of a building, monitoring systems should be unobtrusive. Glass and cement tell-tales, which are still sometimes seen on masonry structures despite their ugly appearance and their unreliability, should not be used.

Proposals to carry out work on masonry structures which are scheduled or statutorily listed will need to be approved either by the Secretary of State or by the local authority. Approval can be refused if it is considered that the historic structure would be damaged or significantly altered. An accurate system of monitoring can be invaluable in such circumstances, because it can provide information on the exact extent of the repairs required.

Measuring differential movement

One of the most effective, inexpensive and inconspicuous systems of monitoring differential movement over cracks and planes of weakness is the Demec mechanical demountable strain gauge, which was developed in the UK by the Cement and Concrete Association and is shown in *Figure 2.13*. However, for friable surfaces and for areas where the public has free access, it will generally be necessary to use pins fixed into pre-drilled holes, as shown in *Figure 2.14*. The pins are normally driven flush with the surface and a small hole is then drilled in the head of each pin, as a locating point for the demountable gauge.

Whatever system is used, locating points should not be fixed across cracks in plaster or rendering. These cracks often follow straight joints, or places of weakness in the load-bearing structure, which can be easily revealed by cutting small, neat chases across the line of the crack as shown in *Figure 2.15*. Remedial work can then often be proposed in the form of stitching or grouting, based on the evidence uncovered. Moreover, plaster can move independently from the basic structure, owing to variations

Figure 2.13 Demec demountable strain gauge

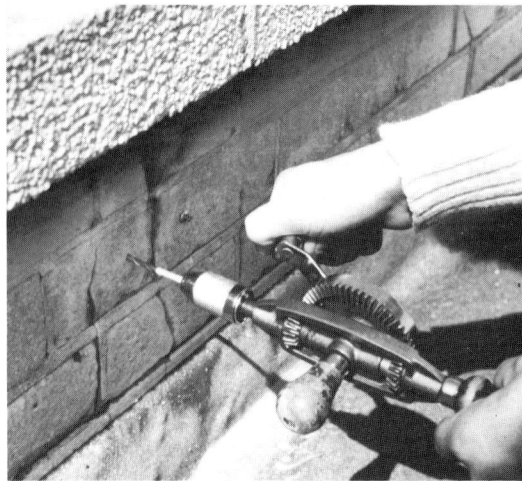

Figure 2.14 Preparing locating point for demountable strain gauge

in temperature. More reliable information, therefore, will be obtained by fixing the locating points or pins to the main load-bearing elements.

Movements of 0.025 mm (0.001 in) are easily detected by the mechanical strain gauge, but it should be remembered that the readings obtained are strain and not absolute movements. In order to obtain the actual movement, the following calculation is necessary;

$$\text{Strain} = \frac{\text{displacement}}{\text{original length}}$$

For the imperial gauge, one division represents a strain of 1×10^{-5} and a movement of 1×10^{-4} in. The corresponding values for the metric gauge are 0.53×10^{-5} strain and 2×10^{-3} mm movement. The

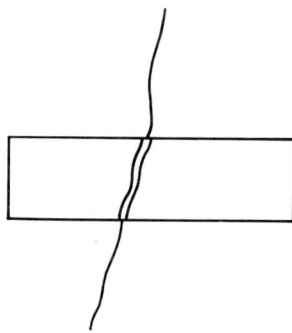

Figure 2.15 Chase cut through plaster across line of crack exposed in basic structure

Figure 2.16 Alternative method of measuring differential movement

pivot on the moving arm is off-centre and the lengths on each side of the pivot have a ratio of 10:8. Therefore, using the metric gauge one division is equal to a displacement of $2 \times 10^{-3} \times 0.8 = 1.6 \times 10^{-3}$ mm. Checking the values,

$$\text{Strain} = \frac{2 \times 10^{-3} \times 0.8}{300}$$

$$= 0.53 \times 10^{-5}$$

An Invar bar is provided, so that a correction can also be made for changes in temperature.

An alternative and less expensive system is to allow the locating pins to project from the surface and to measure the distance between the external faces, using vernier callipers as shown in *Figure 2.16.*

Measuring vertical movement

Vertical movement will only damage a structure if differential displacement takes place. However, in order to provide a reliable record and to avoid misinterpretation, it is necessary, especially for the more important projects, to record absolute movements.

The greatest structural problems in masonry buildings usually occur in areas where coal or salt mining operations have caused subsidence. In these areas a great deal of useful information can be obtained by examining the recorded heights of the Ordnance Survey bench marks. These marks are found on substantial structures, as illustrated in *Figure 2.17*, and the locations are shown on large-scale maps of the area. Bench mark lists, containing fuller and possibly later levelling information, are obtainable from the Director General of the Ordnance Survey in Southampton, England.

Because of the likely distance between the Ordnance Survey bench mark and the structure to be monitored, and also to obtain initial support for the levelling staff, it will usually be necessary to establish an independent datum. Where independent datums are set up, a minimum of three reference points should be provided in order to confirm the stability of the datum being used.

When a satisfactory datum is established, levelling stations can be provided most efficiently by the use of Building Research Establishment levelling sockets. Care must be taken to ensure that the sockets are securely fixed into masonry which is firmly bonded into the wall. This will provide reliable stations, which will indicate accurately any vertical movement which has occurred in the structure. The vertical movements recorded will generally be of such small magnitude that the use of a precise level of the type shown in *Figure 2.18* will be required, combined with a levelling staff equipped with a device to ensure its verticality.

Figure 2.17 Ordnance Survey bench mark

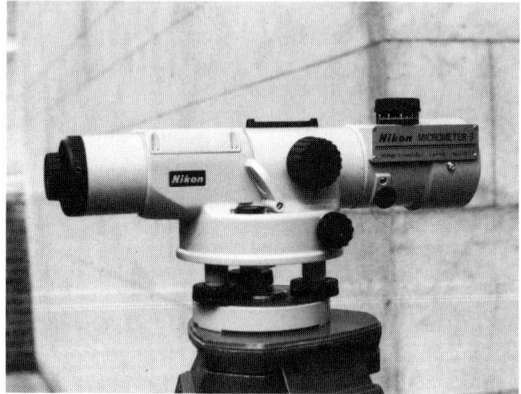

Figure 2.18 Precision level

Measuring movement out of the vertical plane

Plumb bobs are still used to measure movement out of the vertical plane. They can be quite accurate if a plumb bob of sufficient weight is used and it is suspended from a high tensile wire.

There are two main problems in the use of plumb bobs;

1. The readings will generally need to be taken over a relatively long period and there are very few locations where fixed gauging wires can be tolerated. The use of demountable plumb bobs requires an accurate means of location, which will ensure that repeated measurements within the permissible range of variation can be made.
2. The plumb bob will oscillate in the wind, although this can sometimes be prevented by suspending it in a container of oil or water.

Alternatively, a theodolite can be used by sighting on to installed targets or architectural features; this overcomes the various disadvantages of the plumb bob. A five-second variation in the subtended angle will result in an error of approximately 20 mm over a distance of 10.000 mm, which is within the acceptable tolerance limits for this type of work.

The autoplumb is a sophisticated form of plumb bob and is shown in *Figure 2.19*. A target is required at a high level and a station at ground level. The height of the target above ground level should be recorded accurately at the time of installation. The procedure for recording movements is described below.

The autoplumb is levelled in all directions and sited over the ground station, as shown in *Figure 2.20*. Compass readings in all directions are then taken on the high level target. A reading of 10.00 represents a truly vertical line and the rotation of the micrometer drum tilts the line of site away or towards the observer, depending upon the direction of rotation. One revolution of the drum displaces the line of site by an angle having a natural tangent of 0.001. As shown in *Figure 2.21*, b_1 is recorded and deducted from H to give b_2.

In *Figure 2.21*:

H = height of target from ground station
b_1 = height from ground station to centre of focusing control (top telescope)
b_2 = height from the centre of the focusing control (top telescope) to target
d = displacement recorded on micrometer drum

Therefore, $\tan \theta = 0.001 = d/b_2$ for one revolution. Assuming a value of 10.50 m for H and 1.50 m for b_1, b_2 = 9.00 m.

A reading of 9.560 with the instrument pointed in a southerly direction represents a displacement of $10.00 - 9.560 = 0.440$ in a northerly direction. Reversing the line of sights and taking another reading of, say, 10.436 represents a displacement of 0.436 in the northerly direction. For absolute accuracy and with the instrument in perfect adjustment, the two readings should total 20.000. In the example in *Figure 2.21*, the readings total 19.996.

Figure 2.19 Autoplumb

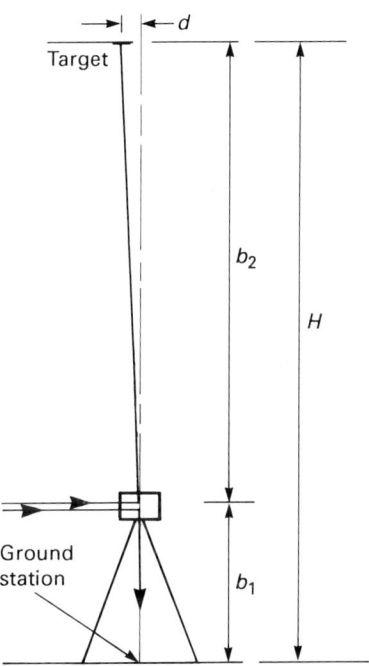

Figure 2.21 Measuring movement out of vertical

Figure 2.20 Autoplumb positioned over ground station

The actual value of $d = \dfrac{0.440 + 0.436}{2} = 0.438$

From $0.438 \times 0.001 = \dfrac{\text{displacement}}{9.000}$

displacement $= 0.438 \times 0.001 \times 9000 = 3.94$mm

By repeating this procedure in an easterly and a westerly direction, the centre of the target can be located in relation to the ground station. The actual positions can then be recorded and the movement plotted on a graph.

Recording the results of monitoring

The recording of monitoring on site is best carried out in tabular form. A proper interpretation can only be made, however, if the results are presented in a graphical form. Typical examples are shown in *Figures 2.22* and *2.23*.

Lasers

The very narrow monochromatic beam from a laser, used in conjunction with one or more targets, is a very reliable way in which to measure deflection or differential movement over a structure, where access can be provided to the laser and to the targets. In most situations, the laser will have to be demountable, but fixed in such a way that it can be re-positioned accurately. The possibility of the targets being accidentally damaged or vandalized should also be considered.

Repair techniques using polyester and epoxy resins

Resins and polymers have been used increasingly over the past twenty to thirty years, but there is no doubt that their full potential has yet to be exploited. Unfortunately, the reputation of these materials has probably suffered because of their use by inexperienced operatives, with disappointing results. Nevertheless, resins and polymers have a valuable role to

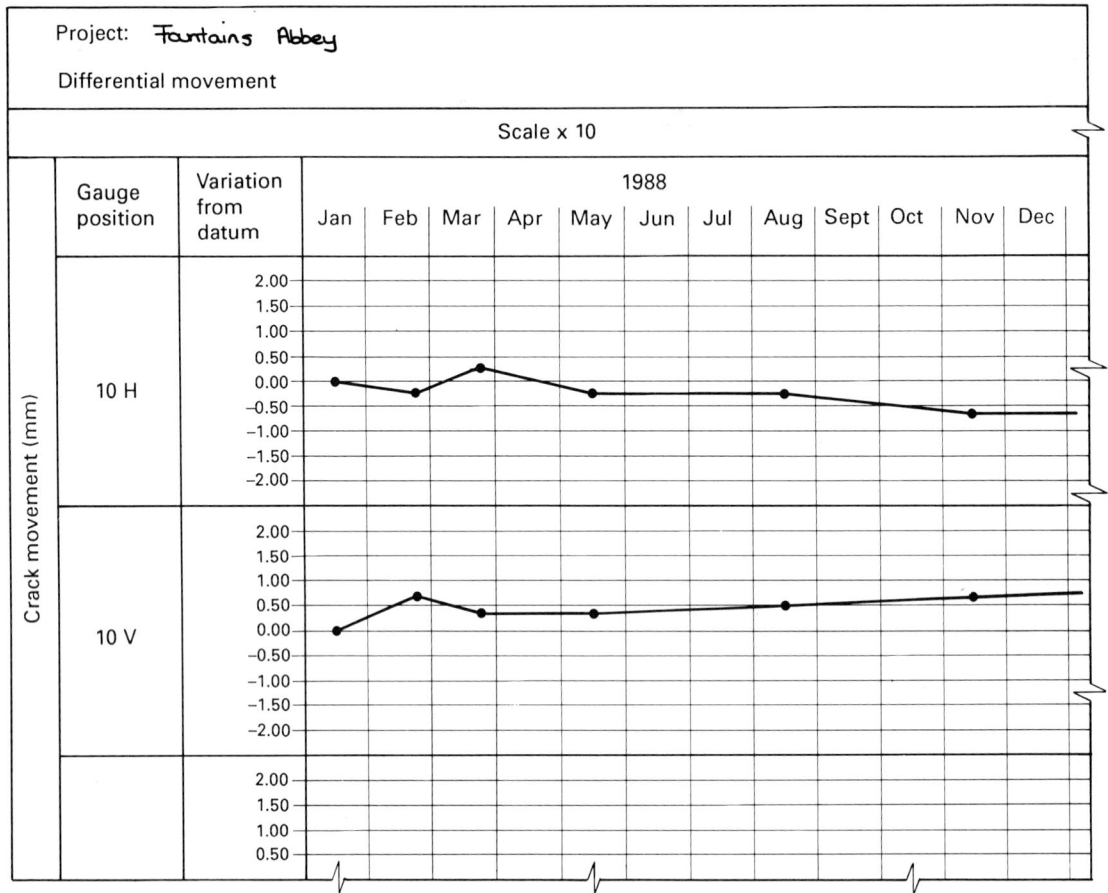

Figure 2.22 Record of differential movement

play in the repair of historic structures, provided that the manufacturer's instructions are followed carefully.

The chemistry of epoxy and polyester resins

Polymerization is the linking together of small, simple molecules to form large units called polymers. It was first developed in Britain during the 1930s. Polymers can be either thermosetting or thermoplastic. A thermosetting polymer is one that can be moulded into the required shape whilst hot, but becomes hard and brittle when cool. It cannot be melted again once solidified. A thermoplastic polymer may be softened and hardened alternatively.

Epoxy and polyester resins are both classed as thermosetting unsaturated polymers because, when cured, the molecular chains are locked permanently together. Unlike thermoplastics, unsaturated polymers do not melt or flow when heated, although they do become more rubbery and gradually lose strength with the increase in temperature. For cured epoxy systems, the heat distortion temperature is in the region of 50 °C (122 °F). If the temperature is allowed to exceed this level, thermosetting polymers will decompose. Unsaturated polymers are composed of organic compounds containing double or triple bonds. Polymers generally have good electrical insulating properties, excellent adhesion and high strength. They are resistant to a large range of chemicals and are impermeable. However, there are chemical differences between epoxy and polyester resins, which give them different properties.

Epoxy resin

Epoxy resin consists of a reactive resin, which cures by the addition of a hardener. It is essential to comply strictly with the manufacturer's recommendation for the proportions of hardener and resin, in order to achieve the required chemical bond and optimum strength. Part packs of the materials should

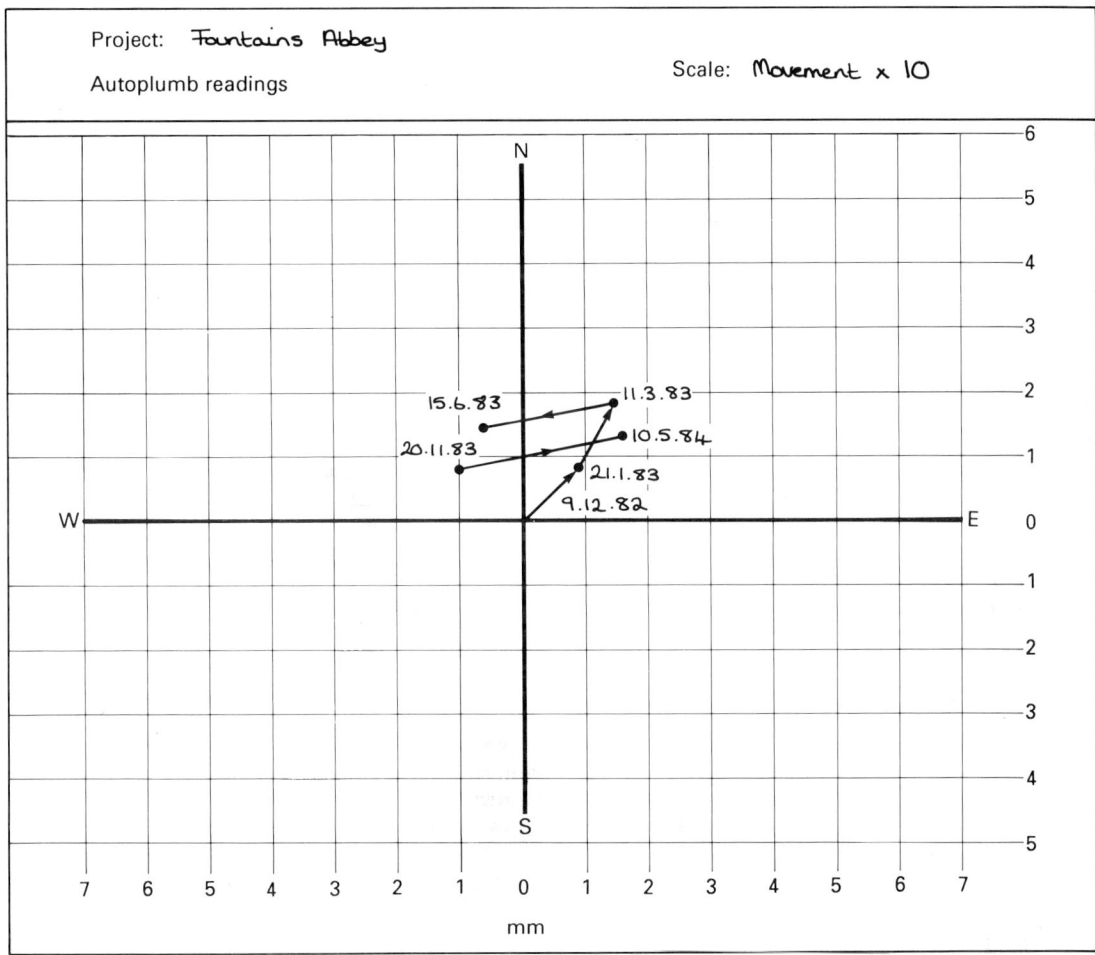

Project: Fountains Abbey
Autoplumb readings

Scale: Movement × 10

Figure 2.23 Record of autoplumb readings

never be used. If the recommended proportion of hardener is increased, in an attempt to produce a high strength resin, the opposite result will be achieved. Because the curing of epoxy resins is an exothermic reaction, during which heat is given off, the rate of cure is temperature dependent and can be assumed to double with an increase of temperature of about 10 °C. Because epoxy resins are poor heat conductors, the rate of cure also depends upon the volume of material used. Although special formulations will cure down to 0 °C, curing will generally stop at temperatures below 5 °C.

Maximum heat evolution usually occurs when the epoxy resin is in a fluid state, although there can be a considerable temperature differential between the set resin and the surrounding structure. Although the volume change between the freshly mixed and the cured resin is small, the subsequent thermal contraction can result in a build-up of stresses between the

resin and the adjacent materials. Therefore, the volume of resin to be placed or injected, the size of the fissure to be filled and the ambient temperature all need to be taken into consideration.

Polyester resins

Polyester resins are generally much cheaper than epoxy resin systems and chemically more simple. The hardener acts only as a catalyst and does not combine chemically, as in epoxy resin systems. The proportioning is therefore not so critical, but this slight flexibility should not be abused.

The curing of polyester is also exothermic, but it differs from the curing of epoxy resin in two significant aspects:

1. The maximum heat evolution occurs resin has set.

2. The change in volume between the freshly mixed and the cured polyester is greater than for epoxy resins.

The effect of these two characteristics is dependent upon the volume of resin injected. They increase the possibility of differential stresses between the resin and the surrounding material and can also be responsible for the development of shrinkage cracking. Specialist contractors, therefore, usually have an understandable preference for using epoxy resins, rather than the cheaper polyester resin. Additionally, polyester resin is not as reliable in damp conditions as epoxy resin.

Application

The proportion of filler for both epoxy and polyester resins can be varied by experienced operatives, but as a general rule the two or three balanced pack systems, which are normally supplied by the manufacturers to suit the requirements of a particular set of conditions, should not be altered. As well as correct proportioning of the constituents, particularly for epoxy resins, adequate preparation of surfaces and proper application of the material is also important in order to obtain optimum bonding. Care should be taken to prevent the material from marking or damaging surrounding surfaces, although new manufacturing techniques have recently produced epoxy resins which can be removed from plain surfaces with a moistened sponge or rag, provided that the resin has not yet cured and there has been no absorption into the surface.

Safety precautions

The need for adequate precautions to be taken to prevent personal injury cannot be overstressed. Some materials present a fire hazard and it may be necessary to enforce regulations governing the storage of highly flammable and liquefied petroleum gases and to prohibit smoking during the handling of these materials. The raw materials should be kept dry and protected from extremes of temperature.

Some materials can cause skin irritation which may, in some cases, accelerate the onset of dermatitis. Therefore, handling precautions should be observed to prevent uncured epoxy resin, or polyester resins and their solvents, from coming into contact with the skin or eyes and from being inhaled. An adequate supply of warm water, mild soaps, disposable hand towels, protective clothing, breathing apparatus and special barrier and removing creams should be provided for the use of the operatives, as appropriate. The provision of proper ventilation is also essential. Solvents must not be used to remove any material which may have come in contact with the skin, as this may increase penetration into the pores and remove essential oils from the skin.

Masonry repairs

Small cracks of less than 0.1 mm can be filled with epoxy or polyester resin using gravity, pressure or vacuum techniques. The method chosen will depend upon the size, nature and location of the repair to be carried out and, also, on whether a specialist or general contractor is to be responsible for the work. Vacuum injection is usually carried out by developing a negative pressure between an enclosing polythene membrane and the masonry to be treated. The negative pressure enables the resin to be conducted from tanks around the masonry into the fissures or cracks which may be present. A vacuum process should only be adopted when the section of masonry under repair can be isolated, because any inflow of air from an adjoining unprotected section can prevent the maintenance of an adequate negative pressure, which is necessary to ensure proper impregnation. The choice between gravity or pressure techniques will usually be dictated by the nature of the work and the size of the fissure or crack to be filled. Specialist contractors will usually recommend some form of pressure impregnation, by using the type of gun shown in *Figure 2.24*, or the simple pump shown in *Figure 2.25*. Grease guns were used in the early days, but they have been superseded by more sophisticated equipment. This has largely overcome the difficulty of controlling the pressures applied and the problems arising from intermittent injection. Pressure guns should be fitted with gauges to ensure accurate use.

Figure 2.24 Pressure impregnation using gun

Figure 2.25 Pressure impregnation using pump

Pressure pots can be used, but these need to be quite large and it can be difficult to determine when the pots are empty and whether the resin is flowing freely, especially at low flow rates.

Whatever equipment is being used, it needs to be mobile in order to avoid long delivery lines. There are obvious advantages in having equipment which allows the continual supply of freshly mixed resin on demand.

Cracking, due to differential movement of the structure caused by foundation settlement or failure of the superstructure, by expansion of embedded and corroding ferrous metal, or by mortar under sulphate attack, can result in the disintegration of joints, the core filling and the masonry units themselves. The repair of mortar joints should be made by raking out, followed by packing and pointing in lime mortar. The integrity of the masonry units can often be restored *in situ* by the injection of epoxy resin. In some cases, the original profile of the unit also can be restored, if required, by using special epoxy mortars. However, this may be inappropriate because of the variation in weathering between surviving stones and the relatively impermeable resin-faced repairs. Embedded and corroding metal should be removed before any masonry repairs are attempted. Once disruptive metal has been removed, epoxy resin repairs can prevent further deterioration of the masonry caused by the ingress of water and subsequent frost action. Cramps can be replaced by using epoxy resins and, where additional strength is required, stainless steel dowels set within an annulus of epoxy resin can prove an effective tie. Repairs of this kind may enable more original material to be retained than would be possible by conventional cutting out and piecing in with replacement stone. They may also be more economic.

The cause of the masonry failure should always be established before repairs are attempted. The rectification of foundation settlements is beyond the scope of this book, but the strength of the superstructure can often be restored by re-establishing the bond between external and cross walls, or between floors and walls, by using stainless steel ties set in epoxy resin. Some typical examples are given in *Figures 2.9* and *2.10.*

Should there be any suggestion that differential movement in the structure has not stopped, it may be better to seal the cracks with a low modulus sealant in order to prevent the ingress of water, rather than to form a rigid area of repair, which may encourage cracking to develop in another part of the structure. If this course of action is followed, it is essential that an accurate system of monitoring is installed.

Separating skins of masonry can be tied together by stainless steel rods set in epoxy resin. This system was first developed in the UK at the Building Research Station, working in conjunction with the Directorate of Ancient Monuments and Historic Buildings. Several proprietary systems have been evolved subsequently. Anchor bolts can also be set in epoxy resin. These have an advantage over expansive mechanical systems because there is no danger of cracking the stone by overtightening.

Repairing cracks in masonry

The cracks should first be examined to determine whether any cleaning is necessary and any loose material present should be removed by flushing out with water or compressed air. Care should be taken to see that small pieces of stone are not displaced, which could cause an unsightly appearance after the injection has been completed. If there are many small fragments of stone in the area of the repair, it will be more difficult to seal the joints effectively in preparation for injection. Sealing can be carried out by one of the following methods:

1. Packing and pointing the vertical and bed joints with lime mortar.
2. Packing and pointing with a polymer modified cementitious stonedust and sand mortar.
3. Adhesive taping of cracks. Taping is unreliable on friable, dusty surfaces and there is a high risk of resin bleeding. This method leaves the cured resin flush with the exposed masonry face.
4. The cracks can be plugged with a material which can be stripped or melted out after completion of the injection. This method enables conventional mortar pointing, matching the face of the stone, to conceal the repair. This is usually the most satisfactory method, allowing a visual check to be made on the effectiveness of the grouting and for the work then to be concealed.

Injection points can then be formed through the seal at a spacing which depends upon the width, depth and length of the cracks (see *Figure 2.26*).

Injection should be carried out systematically in order to dispel air and water in the voids, starting

Figure 2.26 Injecting resin to repair masonry cracks

from the lowest point and maintaining pressure until the resin exudes from one of the injection points at a higher level. Any resin which runs on the face of the masonry must be removed immediately. The danger of runs staining the masonry or curing on the face can be minimized by the application of a synthetic latex skin around the area of repair before injection is carried out. Once the resin has reached the level of a higher injection point, the lower entry point is plugged and injection continued upwards. Injection pressures can be varied over a wide range and can be as high as $2\,N/mm^2$. The viscosity of the resin can be adjusted, in order to prevent loss through internal voids.

Surface repairs in epoxy resin

The success of surface repairs depends to a great extent on the surface preparation and on the choice of formulation related to the performance required. Resin mortars can, if necessary, be made relatively weak and porous. Proprietary materials are available for cleaning the surface of the substrate before the application of epoxy resin. This is necessary if a high bond is to be achieved. Alternatively, an acid cleaning solution for limestone can be prepared by adding commercial grade concentrated hydrochloric acid to clean water, in the proportion of 1 to 4. This acid solution is brushed on to the surface of the substrate with a stiff brush and then washed off with water. Care must be taken not to spill cleaning solutions on surrounding work, or to leave residues in the stone. Pre-wetting the area before the use of acid, in order to reduce absorption, is important.

Metals can usually be cleaned of traces of oil and grease by washing with a detergent, followed by

rinsing with clean water. Mill scale or rust should be removed by grit blasting, if possible, but vigorous wire brushing can be a satisfactory alternative.

The future

Development work is being carried out in the UK, the USA and Japan which is principally concerned with the addition of external reinforcement to structures, such as the strengthening of bridges by bonding steel plates on to existing concrete beams with epoxy resin. Experimental work is also being carried out concerning the effects of curing temperatures, thickness of adhesive layers, fatigue loading and contact with water on the shear and bonding stresses of epoxy resin. The results are awaited eagerly by conservationists and the building profession generally, who perhaps still need to be convinced of the long term effectiveness of these new repair techniques.

The physical properties of epoxy and polyester resin systems

The precise physical properties of epoxy and polyester resin systems are indefinable. However, the following values given in Table 2.1 can be used as a guide when considering the use of these materials.

Table 2.1 Physical properties of epoxy and polyester resin systems

Physical property	Epoxy resin	Polyester resin
Compressive strength (N/mm^2)	40–100	60–100
Tensile strength (N/mm^2)	10–50	10–40
Flexural strength (N/mm^2)	25–60	25–30
Young's modulus E, in compression (N/mm^2)	1000–20000	2000–10000
Percentage elongation to break	0–15	0–5
Linear coefficient of thermal expansion per degree Celsius	$25–30 \times 10^{-6}$	$25–30 \times 10^{-6}$
Linear shrinkage (per cent)	~0.15	–
Rate of strength development	6–8 hours	2–6 hours
Heat distortion per degree Celsius	50–70	60–100

3

The selection of stone for repairs

David B. Honeyborne

Introduction

No doubt any architect responsible for selecting stone for repairing a building of historic or artistic merit would prefer to employ stone from the same quarry and even from the same bed that provided the stone originally, and to ensure that the new stone has reasonably high resistance to weathering.

In many circumstances the origin of the stone is not sufficiently well established for the bed or quarry to be identified. Even if the quarry is known, the working face may have retreated so far that the exposed stone differs significantly from the stone in the building. A change in land-ownership or some other factor may also prevent any further extraction of the stone. The architect is then faced with the task of finding a stone which is a reasonable match with the original, and possesses workability, durability and other properties appropriate for the circumstances.

Selecting new stone to match the original in appearance

To provide a good match, a cut surface of the new stone must be similar in texture and colour to the cut surfaces of its prospective neighbours, both wet and dry. Its appearance must also merge well with the weathered surfaces of its neighbours after long exposure. Unless the architect knows of suitable types of stone from past experience, the best way to make a choice is to look for a good match in other buildings of similar age which are constructed of stone from known quarries that are still in business or could easily be re-opened.

In the rather rare circumstances where the need for repair is foreseen, but the repair is not to be effected for a number of years, it can sometimes be helpful to expose blocks of possible substitutes near the building and observe the appearance they develop. Stone required for very exposed features such as copings, string-courses and sills, should be exposed free from shelter and facing the same direction as those features. Stone that is intended for more sheltered features should be exposed facing the same direction as those features, but comparably sheltered. In all circumstances, the proposed substitute stone should be of the same lithology as the stone it is required to match; that is, limestone should be used to match limestone, sandstone to match sandstone and so on. The use of Magnesian Limestone to match limestone should be avoided as far as possible. The options rationally open to the architect are summarized in the logic flow chart given in *Figure 3.1*.

Organizations such as the British Geological Survey[1] and the Building Research Establishment[2] might be able to help locate appropriate quarries and buildings in the United Kingdom. The Building Research Establishment, the Sedgwick Museum[3] and the British Museum (Natural History) also hold collections of a wide range of building stones, including some foreign stones. However, many of these stones are no longer commercially available. Some commercial organizations, such as the Cathedral Works Organization,[4] have specimens of some currently available foreign stones, particularly from France and Germany. The *Natural Stone Directory*[5] gives addresses of currently operating quarries in the United Kingdom.

Selection for durability

After tentatively choosing a type of stone that will match the existing stonework, consideration should

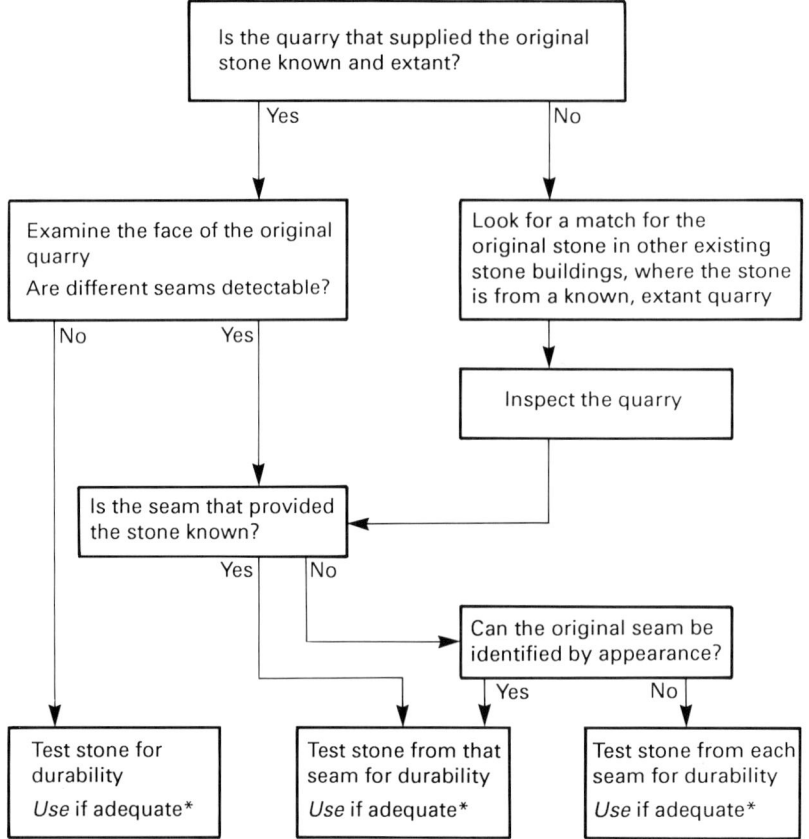

Figure 3.1 Guide for selection of stone for repair of an existing building

be given to the life that might be expected of it once it forms part of the building in question. If the substitute is too short-lived, clearly it should not be used.

The life of a stone depends equally on the aggressiveness of its environment and the intrinsic durability of the stone. This is normally dependent on a combination of chemical, mineralogical and physical factors which cannot be judged from the initial appearance of the stone. Unless wide experience of a particular type of stone leaves no room for doubt about its suitability for use in a particular environment, the architect would be wise to consult a reputable testing organization. However, it should be noted that durability assessment is currently less reliable with magnesian limestones than with other types of building stone.

Determination of the weathering characteristics of a stone is not straightforward. In fact, attempts to

devise satisfactory artificial weathering machines for inorganic materials have so far failed. Instead, testing laboratories in many parts of the world now apply a test system that is appropriate for assessing the particular vulnerability of a stone to the weathering agencies present in the environment in which it is to be exposed. The system has been developed in Britain at the Building Research Establishment and is briefly described in a BRE Digest.[6] Other systems have been developed in the USA, France, Belgium and elsewhere. These systems may be adequate in the countries where they were developed, but are probably not suitable for conditions in Britain, because they do not give enough weight to the hazards of coastal exposure.[7] The British system applies particularly to porous limestones and sandstones, the classes of stone most commonly used in the British Isles. There are special difficulties in applying it to Magnesian Limestones.

Limestones are tested to determine their resistance to the destructive forces associated with the crystallization of soluble salts. Limestones that resist salt crystallization well also exhibit considerable resistance to frost attack and to the secondary destructive processes caused by exposure to acid gases in the air. Descriptions of the test method are given in references 6 and 7. Susceptibility is measured by the mean weight loss of the test pieces after fifteen cycles, or the number of cycles required to reduce the stone to incoherent pieces, if this occurs before completion of the fifteenth cycle. The test conditions must be extremely carefully controlled to ensure that the test results are reproducible. For this reason, at least one set of test pieces of well established durability are included in each test as calibrators. A test specifically carried out to determine whether a limestone is suitable for use in a particular environment should ideally include a calibrator that would fail on exposure to that environment and a calibrator that would survive.

It is important to have some means of defining the different levels of aggressiveness likely to be encountered. In this system, the general environment is divided into four levels of aggressiveness:

1. Low acidic air pollution (rural)—inland.
2. High acidic air pollution (urban)—inland.
3. Low acidic air pollution (rural)—exposed coastal.
4. High acidic air pollution (urban)—exposed coastal.

The *microclimate* is the environment that acts on a block of stone in a building. This depends not only on the general environment, but also on local sheltering and other effects caused by the building itself. The concept of building zones as defined in the French standard for limestones[8] takes this into account. In the French standard, four distinct zones are recognized:

Zone 1 Exterior pavings, where salts from the soil often add a further aggressive element to the environment.

Zone 2 Plinths. Even when there is a damp-proof course, splashes tend to raise the salt content of the stone. However, wetting is less frequent than in Zone 1.

Zone 3 Projecting features such as cornices, sills, string courses and splash courses. These features are substantially wetted more often than in Zone 4.

Zone 4 Elevations under projections.

The micro-climate decreases in severity from Zone 1 to Zone 4.

The ideas of general environment and building zones have been incorporated in *Table 3.1*, which has been taken from reference 7. Limestones are divided into six categories, A to F; the crystallization test is used to determine the appropriate category for each limestone tested. This allows a prospective user to decide where the stone in question may be used. A special case arises when sporadic replacement of blocks in an old building is contemplated and the surrounding stone is already contaminated with salts. The table may still be used in these circumstances, but instead of using the building zone that would normally be applicable, the next lower zone should be used. An exception must be made if the appropriate building zone is 1, because limestone that will survive in Zone 1 must be the best available anywhere. At the other end of the scale, a limestone that is in durability class C or D and is suitable for no better than Zone 4 can be upgraded to Zone 3, if it is covered by an effective flashing. The use of a

Table 3.1 Effects of change of environment on suitability of limestone for various building zones* (from reference 7, reproduced by permission of the Controller, HMSO; Crown copyright)

Limestone type	*Suitability zones for various limestones in a range of climatic conditions*							
	Inland				*Exposed*			
	Low pollution		*High pollution*		*Low pollution*		*High pollution*	
	No frost	*Frost*	*No frost*	*Frost*	*No frost*	*Frost*	*No frost*	*Frost*
A	Z 1–4	Z 1–4	Z 1–4	Z 1–4	Z 1–4	Z 1–4	Z 1 –4	Z 1 –4
B	Z 2–4	Z 2–4	Z 2–4	Z 2–4	Z 2–4	Z 2–4	Z 2[†]–4	Z 2[†]–4
C	Z 2–4	Z 2–4	Z 3–4	Z 3–4	Z 3[†]–4	Z 4	—	—
D	Z 3–4	Z 4	Z 3–4	Z 4	—	—	—	—
E	Z 4	Zone 4	Z 4[†]	—	—	—	—	—
F	Z 4	Zone 4	—	—	—	—	—	—

* Zones referred to are those in French Standard for Limestone
[†] Probably limited to 50 years' life

flashing will similarly upgrade limestones in durability classes E and F where they are to be used in inland, rural areas, but there must be doubt about the wisdom of permitting their use in Zone 3 positions under other conditions, if long trouble-free life is required of them.

There are two serious problems with the crystallization test: it is often difficult to obtain reference stones of the desired proven durability, and the test takes an irreducibly long time to carry out.

Use of interpolative methods when the available reference samples represent only a few of the six limestone classes has been suggested in the literature.[6,7] This would be fairly satisfactory if the classes represented were, say, three steps apart and the crystallization loss rose by approximately equal increments from class A through to class F. Unfortunately, the crystallization loss increases more than linearly as the durability classes are traversed. Even with these disadvantages, this test is still of vital importance, though not so useful as it might be.

Assessment of the durability of *sandstones* is simplified by first eliminating those types where the quartz particles are cemented together by crystals of calcite. These calcareous sandstones are unsatisfactory for long service in urban areas, because even slight attack by acidic gases on the calcite releases many grains of quartz. Immersion of a specimen of sandstone in a solution of sulphuric acid of specific gravity 1.145 for 10 days at a temperature of 16–21°C is sufficient to eliminate susceptible sandstones which are reduced to residual sand grains. Sandstones that survive this test are then normally assessed using the same crystallization test that is used for limestones. If, however, the sandstone is required for long use in an urban coastal district that is exceptionally exposed, or for piecemeal insertions into stone that is already heavily contaminated with soluble salts, the saturated crystallization test—which employs a saturated solution of sodium sulphate instead of the normal 14 per cent solution (specific gravity 1.055)—is more useful. The test is a comparative one and samples of sandstone of well-established durability must be available. The procedure is summarized in *Figure 3.2*.

A suitability-zone table analogous with that shown for limestones can be drawn up for sandstones (*Table 3.2*), but the principles involved are rather different. This is because sandstones are less affected by frost and acidic atmospheric gases, except where the masonry has unusually wide mortar joints or underlies limestone, and are relatively more affected by soluble salts. It should be noted that *Table 3.2* is based on the author's views alone and is backed by less experience than *Table 3.1*. The sandstones are assumed to fit into five durability classes, and the four building zones are defined as in *Table 3.1*. A flashing over a projecting feature will increase the

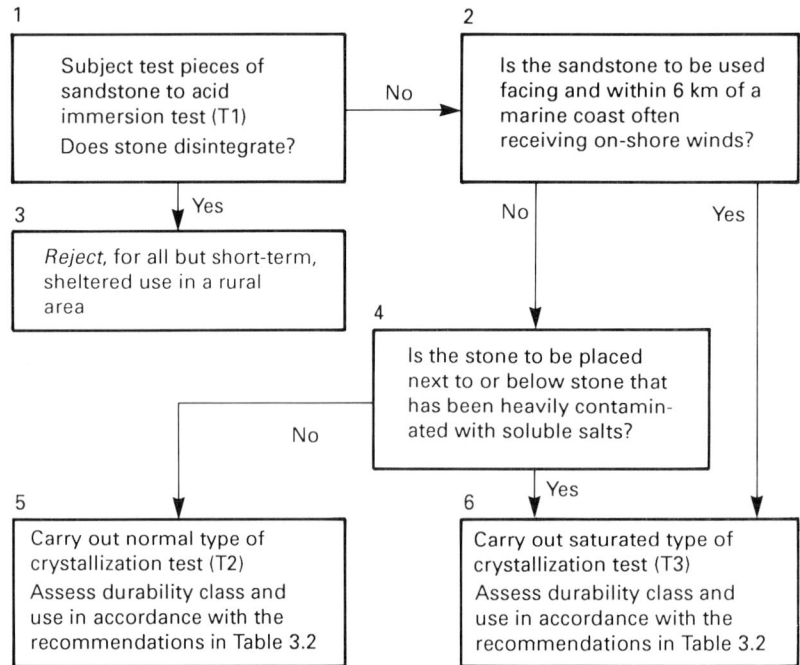

Figure 3.2 Guide for selection of sandstone for repair of an existing building

Table 3.2 Effect of change of environment on suitability of sandstones for various building zones

Sandstone class	Suitability zones for various sandstones in a range of climatic conditions							
	Inland				Exposed coastal			
	Normal joints		Very wide joints or below limestone		Normal joints		Very wide joints or below limestone	
	Rural	*Urban*	*Rural*	*Urban*	*Rural*	*Urban*	*Rural*	*Urban*
A	Z 1–4	Z 1–4	Z 1–4	Z 1–4	Z 1–4	Z 1–4	Z 1–4	Z 1–4
B	Z 1–4	Z 1–4	Z 2–4	Z 3–4	Z 3–4	Z 3–4	Z 3–4	Z 3–4
C	Z 2–4	Z 2–4	Z 3–4	Z 4	Z 4	Z 4	—	—
D	Z 3–4	Z 3–4	Z 4	—	—	—	—	—
E	Z 3–4	Z 4	—	—	—	—	—	—

1. Z indicates building zone as defined in French Standard.[8]
2. When the sandstone is below 'very wide joints' or 'limestone' it is assumed to be in such a position that it will receive rain drips or runs from the joint or limestone.
3. — indicates that the sandstone is not suitable for use in any zone under the climatic conditions indicated.
4. None of the five sandstone classes (A to E) includes calcareous sandstones.
5. For effect of flashings, see text.

effective life of a sandstone when it underlies limestone in an urban region, or is subject to onshore storms but sheltered from direct, driving rain.

Assessing the durability of *Magnesian Limestones* is much more difficult. This class of stone varies significantly in mineralogical composition as well as in pore structure. Therefore there is no one adverse composition that can be simply tested for and eliminated, as with sandstones and calcareous sandstones. Where the main aggressive element is soluble salt attack, a crystallization test may be enough to assess the service life of a magnesian limestone correctly, but where other factors are involved this test is not sufficient. Assessing the durability of a magnesian limestone is an art rather than a science. In the past it was thought that Magnesian Limestones with a composition approaching that of dolomite (45.7% magnesium carbonate; 54.3% calcium carbonate) had the highest durability. Study of the correlation between observed durability, magnesium/calcium ratio and pore structure in magnesian limestones may be useful.

The very low porosity of *slate* ensures that it will not suffer significant attack by frost or soluble salt crystallization. Some slates, however, contain constituents that will be attacked by acidic gases, such as those in urban air. If slate of this kind is used as a roof or mansard roof covering, acidic gas attack can be very serious: the acidic gases dissolve in the rainwater held by capillarity between the overlaps and this acid solution remains in contact with the slate for a long time. A British Standard test system, BS 680,[9] may be used to identify slates that are immune to acid attack. An acid immersion test, a wetting and drying test and a water absorption test are involved. It should be noted that it is widely considered that the acid immersion test deals unduly harshly with the rather thick, slightly calcareous slates from the English counties of Lancashire and Cumbria, and a dispensation clause is given in a footnote to this Standard. Where slate is to be used in block form, as drums for columns or shafts or in thick slabs, no water will be held between overlaps and only the wetting and drying test need be applied. This will eliminate those slates that contain both calcium carbonate and pyrite (iron disulphide). The oxidation of pyrite produces sulphuric acid which attacks the calcium carbonate and causes general loss of strength of the material.

The very low porosity of *marble* ensures that it will also be unaffected by salt or frost attack as long as it retains its original cohesion. However, if marble is subjected to large variations in temperature minute cracks can occur at the boundaries of the calcite crystals. These cracks make the marble more susceptible to acidic gas attack. In severe cases the marble loses cohesion and is said to 'sugar'. In the absence of these minute cracks, acidic gases attack only the external surfaces of the marble. This causes loss of polish but the rate of attack is normally very slow even in urban areas. There is no standard or generally accepted test of a marble's propensity to 'sugar'. It is very difficult to forecast the service life of a marble unless its environment precludes any undue heating and cooling. *Dense limestones* will generally be as durable as marble without any risk of 'sugaring'.

Granites and closely related igneous rocks of good quality are unaffected by any of the three main weathering agencies. However, if they are exposed to frequent large changes in temperature they may well develop micro-cracks. Unlike marbles, they will not become susceptible to acidic gases, but they may become susceptible to salt crystallization attack. There is no standard test, but the experiments done by Hochman and Kessler[11] discussed in Volume 1, Chapter 7, could be used by a competent testing laboratory as a basis for making some assessment of the risk with any particular igneous stone.

Occasionally granites that have undergone some kaolinization have been used for buildings of importance and have weathered rather poorly. Competent mineralogists can recognize such defects if they inspect a potential consignment. These granites usually have greater than normal porosity.

Alternatives to the crystallization test

Because of the difficulties that arise with the crystallization test there have been many attempts to assess the durability of stone based on the values of properties that are more easily measured. Since pore structure plays such an important part in determining durability, properties that are closely related to

pore structure seem to offer the best hope of solving the problem. In fact, some successes have been achieved using such parameters. *Table 3.3* gives a list of some of these properties and some notes about their usefulness. Although very good results can be obtained with a limited number of types of stone, for example Portland stone using microporosity and saturation coefficient, there is not yet any generally applicable system. More research is needed to refine the crystallization test with the aim of developing a test which is not dependent on testing a range of reference samples.

Selection for workability

To ensure that a type of stone is of adequate workability for its intended use it is probably best to ask the opinion of an experienced mason. The French Standard for limestone[8] classifies limestone into hardness groups on the basis of laboratory measurements. The groups are numbered from 1 to 14 on a scale of increasing hardness. These numbers

Table 3.3 Some structural parameters and the durability of stone

Parameter	Description	Comment
1. Porosity	Accessible pore volume expressed as a fraction of apparent volume of stone.	Generally a poor guide to durability but, used in conjunction with (2) it is helpful for indicating the durability of Bath stone. This combination also forms part of the French Standard for Limestones.
2. Saturation coefficient	Volume of water absorbed under some specific conditions (usually 24 hours complete immersion in water at room temperature) expressed as a decimal fraction of the accessible pore volume.	This is a complex function of the pore structure. With (1) it occurs in the French Standard for Limestones and is useful for assessing the durability of Bath stones. With (3) it is very effective in assessing the durability of Portland stones.
3. Microporosity	(a) The fraction of the pore volume that is accessible only via pores less than 0.5 μm in diameter. (b) Alternatively, the fraction of water retained by an initially water-saturated stone after application of a negative pressure of 62.6 kPa.	Very useful in conjunction with (2) for assessing the durability of Portland stones.
4. Capillarity	Defined in the French Standard by $$\frac{100\,M}{S\sqrt{t}}$$ where M is the mass of water absorbed from the beginning of a test in which a cube of cross section area S stands in water. The elapsed time is t.	The constant obtained is a measure of the pore structure. For example, the lower the value, the less water will rise in the stone when standing on wet soil. While the Belgians propose to use it as part of a durability assessment, recent research has suggested that it has no advantage over (2) for British stone and conditions[10].
5. d_{10}	The maximum pore diameter still filled with water when 10% of the water from an initially saturated piece of stone has been removed by suction.	This is clearly related to (3). It forms part of the Belgian selection procedure. Stone with d_{10} less than 2.5 μm is considered susceptible to frost. Trials of this parameter under British conditions have not been undertaken.

have become known as AFNOR numbers. If the stone chosen is a French Limestone its AFNOR number may be sufficient indication of its workability.

Selection for plinth courses

Stone that has adequate durability for a plinth course will not necessarily have the desirable property of discouraging the upflow of soil water. Stone of very low porosity usually remains apparently dry, but so will some stone of very low suction. The capillarity test in the French Standard is useful for distinguishing such stone.

References

1. British Geological Survey, Keyworth, Nottingham NG12 5GG, England
2. Building Research Establishment, Garston, Watford, Herts WD2 7JR, England
3. Sedgwick Museum of Geology, Downing Street, Cambridge, England
4. Cathedral Works Organization, The Cathedral, Chichester, West Sussex, England
5. Anon, *The Natural Stone Directory*, 7th edn, Ealing Publications Limited, Maidenhead, 1987
6. *Building Research Establishment Digest No 269*, HMSO, London, January 1983
7. Honeyborne, D.B., *The Building Limestones of France*, Building Research Establishment Report, HMSO, London, 1982
8. Association Française de Normalisation, *Matériaux Pierres calcaires*, Paris, 1945
9. BS 680, *Roofing slates*, British Standards Institution, Milton Keynes, 1971
10. Leary, E.A., 'A preliminary assessment of capillary tests as indicators of the durability of British limestones' *Proc. Int. Symp. on Stone Conservation*, p.73, Bologna, 1981
11. Hochman, A. and Kessler, D.W., 'Thermal and moisture expansion studies of some domestic granites', *US Bureau of Standards, Journal of Research*, 44, 395–410, 1950

4

Mortars for stone buildings

John Ashurst

Introduction

The consideration of historic masonry must necessarily include the mortar on which its unity and stability, to a greater or lesser degree, depends. True, there are unmortared walls of all periods, from the spectacular polygonal masonry of Peru to the dry-stone walls of Europe, and others which were packed with earth; but for the most part masonry involves a mortar based on lime or gypsum. Generally speaking, gypsum mortars are most likely to occur in those countries where trees are scarce and sources of gypsum are plentiful. They are found in Mesopotamia, Egypt and other countries of the African continent and Greece. Gypsum for mortar and plaster is prepared by heating selenitic rock (composed of hydrated calcium sulphate) to temperatures in the 150–160°C range. The resultant hemi-hydrate ('plaster of Paris') sets rapidly when mixed with water. The set is accompanied by a slight expansion. In wet climates, even when raw materials are plentiful, gypsum is rarely used on external, exposed surfaces because of its slight solubility in water. There are, however surprising examples in the fifteenth and sixteenth centuries of external gypsum plastering in England, and combinations of lime and gypsum are not unknown. It is wise, therefore, to eliminate all assumptions in the investigation of historic mortar.

Materials

Lime (non-hydraulic)

Lime is the ubiquitous constituent of the greatest percentage of ancient mortars. Almost any source of calcium carbonate will provide lime, the most obvious being a very wide range of limestones; but lime produced from burning sea shells and coral and from marble is also common.

Richard Neve[1] and other writers of his time in England drew attention to differences in limes prepared from 'Chalk' and from 'Stone'. The 'Chalk' lime was considered suitable for internal use only, whilst the 'Stone' lime (that is lime burnt from limestone other than Chalk) was suitable for external mortar and plaster. Regional differences affecting the quality of the lime were also recognised to be important by these early observers, as were the firing techniques.

It is as well to remember the contexts in which lime was produced historically and to be careful about simple assumptions arising from, say, analysis of ancient mortars. We have as much to learn about production and preparation as about constituent parts; in particular we must remember that there are significant differences between a modern, commercially produced lime and a lime, full of impurities such as slag and ash, produced in a clamp in the fourteenth century.

Lime is produced by breaking the stone into lumps and heating the raw material in a kiln. Early kilns were sometimes very crude, being no more than simple clamps of alternate layers of stone and fuel, covered with a clay skin ventilated through stoke holes. Traditional kilns, however, are normally flare kilns, in which intermittent burning takes place, or draw kilns, in which loading and burning are continuous. Modern rotary kilns are fuelled by oil or gas, and burn the limestone at temperatures between 900°C and 1200°C (1650–2200°F). The minimum effective temperature for burning limestone for lime is 880°C (1616°F), but for this temperature to be reached in the centre of the stone lumps, an overall temperature at the surface of 1000°C (1800°F) is necessary.

During burning, carbon dioxide (and any water) is driven off. The chemical process consists in the dissociation by heat of calcium (and sometimes

78

magnesium) carbonate, in an atmosphere relatively free of carbon dioxide, to prevent recombination. The end product is calcium oxide, 'quicklime', sometimes described as 'unslaked lime' or, rather misleadingly, as 'lump lime'.

Slaking

Most lime is slaked as part of a production process and sold either as a dry powder (hydrated lime), or, rarely, as lime putty.

If calcium oxide (quicklime) is left exposed to the air, it will air-slake, or wind-slake. The calcined lumps will gradually reduce to powder, with an increase in volume. For site slaking, the lime should be delivered as fresh as possible and kept in dry conditions.

Slaking is the reaction of the quicklime with water. During the process, hydroxides of calcium (and magnesium) are formed by the action of water on the oxides. Traditionally, this process was carried out in pits and the slaked lime was left to mature for several months, or even years. Slaking on site for repair work is most conveniently carried out in a galvanized steel cold water storage cistern.

Clean, potable water is run into the tank to a depth of approximately 300 mm (12 in) and the quicklime is added by shovel. Because of the violent reaction which occurs between the water and the quicklime, which frequently raises the water temperature to boiling point, this operation must be carried out slowly and carefully. Eyes must be protected by goggles and hands by suitable gloves. Anyone who is unprotected must be kept away from the slaking tank. The initial slaking process may be carried out more quickly and safely by first breaking the lumps of quicklime down to a large aggregate size and then by using hot water in the tank. The slaking lime must be hoed and raked and stirred until the visible reaction has ceased. Enough water must be used to avoid the coagulation of particles together, which significantly reduces the plasticity of the lime. Experience will dictate the correct amount of water required, which can be adjusted as the process demands. It is always better to have an excess of water than not enough. The addition of water and quicklime continues until the desired quantity has been slaked. Using an excess of water without 'drowning' the lime results in the formation of a soft, rather greasy mass of material, described as lime putty. Sieving the putty through a 5 mm (0.2 in) screen will remove unburnt lumps and the larger coagulations. The screened putty should be left under a few centimetres of slaking water. This lime water may be siphoned off when required for use. It contains small quantities of calcium hydroxide (0.14 g in 100 ml of water at 15 °C)[2] which can be useful in hardening up lime plaster. A thin skin will form on the surface, which should be left unbroken until the insertion of a small siphon tube to remove the water.

The lime putty, with a shallow covering of water, should be kept for a minimum period of two weeks before use. It is better to keep it for two months if practicable and there is no upper limit of time. The minimum period is to ensure that the entire mass is thoroughly slaked. After this time, plasticity and workability go on increasing. Pliny's well known and much quoted view that '. . . the older the mortar . . . the better it is in quality . . .', supported by Vitruvius and Alberti and by rather more recent experience, is based on observations of this increasing plasticity. Old lime putty, which is protected from the air in a pit or bin, acquires a rigidity which is rather like that of gelatin. When the rigid mass is worked through and 'knocked up', it becomes workable and plastic again. This property is peculiar to non-hydraulic lime putty. Any material which has a hydraulic set (see below) must not be 'knocked up' after it begins to stiffen.

A variation on the slaking procedure, which has a long tradition behind it, is to slake the quicklime in a pit, already mixed with the sand with which it is to be combined as mortar, or plaster. This process requires time and space and is really only practicable in long programmes of repair or restoration, where it is intended to lay up quantities of lime putty and sand for a long time. The technique has, however, a distinct advantage over more familiar mixing procedures, in that this early marriage between binder material and aggregate encourages the covering of all the aggregate particles with a lime paste, in a way and to a degree which can never be matched by conventional modern mixing.

A recommended compromise between slaking the lime and sand mixture and turning over dry constituents later, is to mix the slaked putty with the sand and other aggregates and to store the constituents together, protected from the air, as wet 'coarse stuff', for as long as possible to mature. This 'coarse stuff' is the best possible base for mortar and lime plaster, whether or not it is to be gauged later with any pozzolanic additives. Storage is best arranged in plastic bins with an additional covering inside the bin, of wet underlay felt, or wet sacks. (Slaking must not, of course, be carried out in a plastic bin!) Another advantage of storing wet 'coarse stuff' is that all the mixing for a large job can be carried out in one or two operations and a consistent mortar, or plaster, will be available for use as required.

Mixing

Initial mixing of the 'coarse stuff' and final mixing, or 'knocking up', must be thorough. But mixing, in the familiar sense of turning over with a shovel, was not considered sufficient in ancient times, nor is it sufficient now, if the best possible performance is to be obtained from the lime mortar. The old practice of chopping, beating and ramming the mortar has largely been forgotten and seems to have acquired the status of a quaint superstition. It requires additional labour and is, therefore, unwelcome in terms of cost and effort. Therefore it can only be justified by proven returns. Recent field work has confirmed that 'coarse stuff', rammed and beaten with a simply made wooden rammer and paddle, interspersed with chopping with a shovel, does improve workability and performance. The value of impact is to increase the overall lime-aggregate contact and to remove surplus water by compaction of the mass.

Much of this labour can be avoided by making use of a mortar mill which blends and squeezes the lime putty and aggregates very efficiently. Although initially expensive, a mill soon pays for itself in terms of labour saved.

Hardening of lime mortar

When the coarse stuff is left exposed to air, it stiffens and hardens, with a contraction in volume. There is a much greater contraction in volume of the lime putty alone as it loses water. This is why it is always used with sand, except in very fine joints, where no more than a buttering of lime is used in the work. This hardening is not to be confused with the setting of hydraulic limes and cements. Hardening will only take place through contact with air, by reaction with atmospheric carbon dioxide and evaporation of water. Preliminary hardening takes place fairly rapidly, both as water in the mix is lost to the porous surface of the masonry and by evaporation. Water renders the mix plastic, but has no chemical effect on ordinary lime mortar, except as a carrier. Only the minimum additional water should be added to wet coarse stuff, to achieve the necessary workability, so that the volume changes during drying out can be kept to a minimum. Further evaporation takes place over a very long period of time and the carbonation process may continue for many years. Soft mortar, which is isolated in pockets of construction from contact with the air, will remain soft indefinitely.

Studies carried out by ICCROM[3] on mortar cubes showed that only a superficial external carbonation of a few millimetres occurred after standard curing periods (i.e. 60 days for lime:sand mortars and 28 days for cement-gauged lime:sand mortars). Evidence suggests that complete carbonation of 50 mm cubes could take place in three to six months. The carbonation process is, in practice, difficult to control or to predict since it is affected by temperature, moisture presence, pore structure (access of carbon dioxide) and bulk of material.

Various experiments have indicated that the carbonation process may be significantly accelerated by periodic wetting of the work. Rapid drying out, which sometimes takes place in hot weather on unprotected work, retards the carbonation process and results in poor ultimate strength. Direct heat and local draughts should be avoided and good general circulation of air encouraged. The periodic wetting is most conveniently carried out using a hand spray with a fine nozzle, sufficient to create a fine mist. (Jets of water will disrupt the surface of the mortar and cause staining of the masonry and must be avoided.) This process is a refinement which has rather a limited application, but it is simple enough to execute for a day or two after the mortar has been placed. Local conditions will dictate the frequency of wetting, but it may be as often as every hour initially, if drying-out of the face is likely to be rapid, and eventually decreasing to every three or four hours. Current experiments are comparing the effects of using water containing carbon dioxide (soda water), or lime water, with ordinary tap water.

A summary of procedures to obtain optimum performance from mortars based on non-hydraulic lime is as follows:

1. Slake freshly burnt lime on site with enough water to obtain a soft mass of putty. Continue stirring during the slaking process. Sieve to remove lumps. Keep the putty under a water layer for at least one week to ensure thorough slaking.
2. Mix putty thoroughly with chosen aggregates in the desired ratio (1:3 or similar) mechanically, or by hand, turning, beating and chopping the coarse stuff. Alternatively, blend the putty and aggregates in a mill.
3. Store wet coarse stuff under wet underlay felt, or wet sacks, preferably in bins with air-tight lids, for a minimum period of one week, but for as long as possible.
4. Remove the required quantity for one day's work on to a clean, boarded platform. Mix again, chopping, beating and ramming. If the coarse stuff is too crumbly, add a little water to increase plasticity, but keep additional water to an absolute minimum. Remember that chopping and beating coarse stuff based on lime putty will render it more plastic and workable without more water.
5. Keep the finished work protected from rain, strong heat and local draughts. Encourage good general air circulation. In special cases, where justified, carry out intermittent mist spraying of the mortar surfaces, to retard the drying out and to encourage carbonation.

Alternative sources of lime putty

If there is no supply of lime putty available and site slaking is impossible, use hydrated lime and soak it in enough clean water to produce a thick cream, for a minimum period of twenty-four hours. Proceed from stage 2 after soaking.

Another method is to buy ready-mixed lime and sand. Ready-mixed coarse stuff should be kept from drying out and used as soon as possible. It is better restricted to work where the mix is to be gauged with cement, and will always benefit from beating or milling.

Gauging with pozzolanic additives

Certain materials will react with lime in the presence of water, to enable a lime mortar, or rendering, to set hydraulically. This phenomenon seems to have been appreciated first in Mediterranean countries under Roman influence, where there was an abundance of natural materials ejected from volcanoes. These materials were in the form of rocks such as tuff, trachyte and pumice, or deposits of volcanic ash or earth, such as pozzolana or trass. Large deposits of ash in the region of Pozzuoli near Naples, used from early times with lime for mortar and Roman concrete and described as *pozzolana*, are still used extensively in Italian and other Mediterranean building industries. (Another well-known source, used by the Romans, was the great caldera of Thera (Santorini), situated on the southern periphery of the Cyclades. 'Therian Earth' is still quarried from this active volcanic site for the building industry.) *Pozzolana* has become a generic name for any additive which will react with lime to produce a hydraulic set; however, unless *pozzolana* is specifically meant, other similar materials should simply be described as 'pozzolanic additives'.

These volcanic materials contain reactive silicates, from the rapid cooling of bubbling, molten material. Their structure typically is vitreous, amorphous and unstable. Their reaction with lime and water produces calcium aluminate hydrate and calcium silicate hydrate. The process is observed as relatively rapid hardening of the material.[4]

One of the interesting pozzolanic additives used in Roman times, and again from the seventeenth century in Europe, is trass, variously described in historical texts as 'terrace', 'tarrace' or 'tarras'. The principal source appears to have been the region of Andernach on the Rhine. Trass was imported to England via Holland (hence the occasional reference to 'Dutch tarras') for engineering and dock works, mixed 1:2 or 1:1 with lime. Roman builders also used bricks, tiles and pottery crushed to dust and ground iron slag as pozzolanic additives.

Modern practice in Britain makes use of crushed brick dust, HTI powder (a ceramic material: high temperature insulation) and PFA (pulverized fuel ash) of low sulphate content as pozzolanic additives mixed with lime. Yellow brick dust, HTI powder and PFA in the form of light-coloured cenospheres do not significantly affect the colour of lime mortars, but red brick dust and grey fuel ash have somewhat limited applications. These materials are particularly useful where a strong set is not required. The most common practice is to gauge lime mortar with cement when a set is required.

Hydraulic limes and natural cements

Hydraulic limes

The technology of hydraulic mortars, developed during the Roman period, survived in texts, but seems to have almost completely disappeared from use until the seventeenth century.

The source of hydraulic limes is also limestone, but limestone which contains a proportion of clay, in addition to calcium and magnesium carbonates. Such limestones will yield 'hydraulic' lime after calcination, i.e. limes which will set by reaction of hydraulic compounds with water, even without the present of air. Other impurities, such as iron and sulphur, may also be present in these limestones.

Kilning procedures are the same as those for high calcium lime, but the chemical actions are much more complex during the calcination process. As the temperature reaches $900\,°C$ ($1650\,°F$), pozzolanic compounds are formed while decomposition of the carbonates and reaction with clay materials proceeds. Over $1000\,°C$ ($1800\,°F$), calcium aluminates and silicates are formed and sintering takes place. This produces a clinker which is somewhat inactive until finely ground. Changes in the firing temperature, as well as in the constituents, can produce hydraulic limes of very different characteristics. Although many famous hydraulic limes were produced in the UK until before World War II and the raw material is still plentiful, no hydraulic lime is now made there. Hydraulic lime is still imported from France, and is in use on many sites, including some as far north as Edinburgh. The only other available lime is the well known, feebly hydraulic Totternhoe, which still gives good services in mortar and rendering.

The French lime ranges in colour from grey to white to a light buff, and is delivered in sacks as a dry, ground hydrate. Sacks of hydraulic lime must be delivered sealed and must be kept dry. The lime must be mixed very thoroughly with the selected aggregates and with the minimum amount of water to make the coarse stuff workable. The mixed material should be able to take a 'polish' from the back of a shovel. Mixing should take place on a clean, boarded platform before any water is added and then again after watering. This coarse stuff must be used within four hours and must not be knocked up after stiffening has taken place. Correct judgement on the quantity required for each working phase is, therefore, important.

Natural ('Roman') cements

Natural cements are really eminently hyraulic limes. In the eighteenth century various experiments were taking place, mixing different limes with volcanic earths. John Smeaton found that Aberthaw (Glamorgan) lime gave better results than others and concluded that the best limes for mortar were those fired from limestones containing a considerable quantity of clayey matter. The discovery that a useful, quick-setting hydraulic cement could be made by calcining nodules of argillaceous limestone (septarian nodules) resulted in a patent being taken out in 1796 by James Parker of Northfleet. Similar, brown coloured natural cements were made from the septaria of Harwich and the Solent ('Sheppey' and 'Medina' cements) and Weymouth, Calderwood, Rugby and Whitby. At about the same time, similar natural cements were being used near Boulogne and at Rosendale and Louisville in America.

These cements were characterized by their colour and their quick set, which might be as little as half an hour. They were mixed with sand in a 1:1 proportion, sometimes 1:2 and sometimes, for fine moulded work, almost neat. The name 'Roman Cement' seems to have been acquired about 1800 and arose from the distinctive colour and hydraulic properties.

It is a strong durable material, and was welcomed as an external rendering. It is in this form that Roman Cement is usually found, lined out in the imitation of masonry, sometimes coloured with ('green') copperas in lime, sometimes painted, sometimes left uncoloured. Peter Nicholson[5] commented in 1823: '... when the works are finished, they should be frescoed, or coloured, with washes, composed of five ounces of copperas to every gallon of water, and as much fresh lime and cement as will produce the colours required ... these sorts of works ... are drawn and jointed to imitate well-bonded masonry, and the divisions promiscuously touched with rich tints of umber, and occasionally with vitriol ...'. Unfortunately, it was also used extensively for plastic repairs of masonry and for pointing, roles for which it is too impermeable and too strong. The removal of Roman Cement from mediaeval masonry, especially architectural detail and carving, is one of the most familiar and taxing jobs for the conservator.

A form of Roman Cement was available until the 1960s, but is no longer made. To imitate its colour pigmented cement, lime or, much better, a plasticized cement should be used for repairs. Carefully selected red and yellow sands must be used to provide the colour.

Portland cement

In 1811, James Frost took out a patent for an artificial cement obtained by lightly calcinating ground chalk and clay together, anticipating the principle which later led to the establishment of many similar artificial hydraulic cements. The most famous of these became known as Portland cement, from its supposed appearance and similarity to Portland limestone. The beginning of the nineteenth century saw much experiment and investigation into these materials.

The first Portland cement type in the UK was patented by Joseph Aspdin of Leeds, whose plant at Wakefield crushed and calcined a 'hard limestone', mixed the lime with clay and ground the mix into a fine slurry with water. The mixture was fired, broken into lumps and fired a second time, until the carbonic acid is expelled (*sic*). Because low temperatures were used, the quality of the cement cannot have been high. By 1838, however, Aspdin's son, William, was producing the cement at Gateshead and on the Thames. Brunel used it for his Thames Tunnel, in spite of the fact that the price was twice that of Roman Cement. Therefore it may be assumed that results were satisfactory and, perhaps, the calcination was taking place at higher temperatures. To Isaac Johnson belongs the credit, however, of observing that overburnt lumps in the old Aspdin kilns at Gateshead, which he had taken over, made a better final product and were slower setting. At Johnson's works at Rochester, the results of his observations were produced as Johnson's Cement. Along the Thames and Medway a number of cement works opened up, making use of the Chalk and the Thames mud and firing at a temperature high enough to produce vitrification.

The cements produced by the late 1850s were close to those produced by modern methods. They were made by grinding Chalk and clay together in a wet mill and firing the screened slurry at temperatures of 1300–1500 °C (2400–2700 °F). The Chalk is converted into quicklime, which unites chemically with the clay to form a clinker of Portland cement. After regrinding and firing, the white hot clinker is allowed to cool and a small amount of gypsum is added to lengthen the setting time.

Objections to the use of hydraulic limes, natural cements and especially Portland cement are based on their high strength, their rather impermeable character and the risk of transferring soluble salts, especially sodium salts, to vulnerable masonry materials.

Other modern cements

White Portland cement

This cement is produced from Chalk and china clay and is burnt, using oil fuel instead of coal. The strength of white cement is rather less than the strength of ordinary Portland cement (OPC). However, this factor is of no importance in the conservation context and may even be an advantage. White cement is useful in gauging white lime mortars and pale mortar repairs and, occasionally, in rendering, where the colour of OPC would be wrong. The cement should comply with the requirements of BS 12: 1971. It is about twice the cost of OPC. Some practitioners object to its use on the grounds that the surface is liable to craze. This problem can be overcome by keeping the water content low, using water-reducing agents, and avoiding overworking of surfaces.

Masonry cement

Masonry cements have the advantage over unplasticized OPC of greater plasticity and greater water retention. They are based on OPC, but have fine, inert fillers and plasticizers added, which do not present any additional hazards to porous masonry. However, properly slaked lime is preferable for historic building work. Their principal use is in rendering, where lime would kill the colour of natural aggregates, or in sandstone masonry repairs, especially 'plastic repairs', where lime has played a role in the decay of the sandstone. Masonry cements are useful in sites liable to be attacked by frost because of the air-entraining property of the plasticizer. The cement should comply with the requirements of BS 5224.

Sulphate-resisting cement

Some situations require the use of a cement which will resist sulphate attack. Industrial monuments, such as kilns and masonry associated with flue condensates or sulphate concentration in ground water, are common examples. Sulphate-resisting cement has a reduced tricalcium aluminate content (about 5% C_3A with 11% C_3A in OPC) and has good resistance to chemical attack from sulphates in these typical conditions. Mixes for mortars and renderings are the same as those based on OPC. Sulphate-resisting cement should comply with the requirements of BS 4027:1972.

High alumina cement

This cement (HAC) is produced by fusing limestone and bauxite together. It is grey-black in colour and has different properties to OPC. Setting is slow (up to six hours for the initial set, as against 45 minutes for OPC), workability is good and rapid heat evolution, coupled with early strength development at low temperatures, makes cold weather working less hazardous. Resistance to sulphate attack is good, but resistance to caustic alkalis is poor. The use of antifreeze additives, lime and waterproofers should be avoided. Crushed Chalk may be added in place of lime.

This cement is sometimes recommended for repairing Roman or Portland cement stuccos, because, it is claimed, such repairs can be painted at an early stage without the use of special primers, unlike repairs based on OPC, which require special alkali-resistant primers and a long period of waiting to avoid alkali attack on paint. However, it should be realized that the early alkalinity of HAC is not likely to be much less than the alkalinity of OPC (HAC pH12: OPC pH12−13), so that special primers are still recommended, if early painting is necessary.

The distinctive colour can be useful in matching black ash mortar. HAC should comply with the requirements of BS 915: 1972. HAC is about three times the cost of OPC. Loss of strength and increased porosity due to conversion of calcium aluminate hydrates in conditions of prolonged warmth and humidity, which are critical in concrete construction, are not relevant in the context of renderings and mortars.

Pozzolanic cements

Pozzolanic cements in Britain are principally mixtures of OPC and pulverized fuel ash. The PFA reacts with lime liberated during the hydration of OPC, to give a slow hardening, low heat cement, with good resistance to sulphates.

Additives

One of the most interesting aspects of the study of old mortars is the identification of additives included to improve the workability or to induce hardening of lime:sand mixtures. Lauren-Brook Sickels[6] has carried out work on organic additives and on possible synthetic substitutes in mortars for conservation work, which provides a useful reference.

Typical of organic additives are materials such as urine, beer, milk, egg white, animal fats and beeswax. Not all these materials are readily identifiable, but a current programme of investigation by English Heritage and ICCROM is seeking to establish patterns of use in historic mortars. Nicola Ashurst, in an unpublished work, has identified animal fats and beeswax in mortars where waterproofing and/or adhesion to impermeable meterial such as flint was necessary. The English Heritage/ICCROM programme is re-creating Roman mortars incorporating pozzolanic additives and fats as a contribution to the correct on-going maintenance of historic sites.

Antifreeze additives

Although cold weather working should be discouraged, because of the hazard of exposing fresh mortar and rendering to freezing, there are situations when work must continue in undesirable conditions. The principle of the antifreeze additive is to increase the rate of heat evolution by accelerating the set. In most proprietary products the accelerator is calcium chloride; this should be specified as 1.5% anhydrous calcium chloride, dissolved in the gauging water. The introduction of chlorides into porous masonry is obviously undesirable. This practice must be kept to an absolute minimum generally and never extended to work of high intrinsic value.

'Waterproofers'

'Waterproofed' Portland cement is OPC mixed with small percentages of calcium stearate, or mineral oil, with the object of either preventing water movement or reducing permeability. The term 'waterproof', in the present context, is very misleading. 'Waterproof' should not be relied upon for rendering historic buildings. A thick, porous rendering, for instance, is usually likely to be much more efficient in keeping water out than a thin, 'waterproofed' one.

Air-entraining agents

A macro-porous mortar or rendering will tend to be resistant to frost and to stresses caused by the cystallization of soluble salts. Air-entrained OPC contains agents, such as calcium lignosulphate, which entrain 4–5% minute, discontinuous, uniformly distributed air bubbles. The density reduction may mean a decrease in strength of up to 15%. Experiments carried out in North America and in the UK have shown that up to 16–18% entrained air is a desirable percentage for aggressive freeze-thaw conditions.

Surfactants (surface active agents) improve the workability of mixes, by entraining small air bubbles and by reducing the surface tension of water, so that surfaces are wetted more easily. Experiments are in hand to determine how well air-entrained, thick renderings are able to withstand the problems associated with rising damp.

Water-reducing agents

The mechanical properties of mortars are significantly improved by water-reducing agents such as those based on naphto-sulphonates or sodium gluconate. The quantification of the effects is part of the current English Heritage/ICCROM study.

Pigments

Wherever possible, aggregates should be chosen to provide the necessary colour for a joint or rendering repair, in preference to colouring the cement or lime with pigments. However, it is not always easy to find the right constituents.

Where pigments are to be employed, they should be specified to conform to BS 1014:1961 and should ideally be incorporated in ready-mixed lime:sand coarse stuff. Controlled mixing is essential for consistency and site conditions are often against careful batching of the small quantities of pigment powder necessary to avoid colour changes.

PFA

To produce PFA, pulverized coal is blown into combustion in a stream of air and burnt. A high percentage of the resultant ash is in the form of minute, separate spheres. Seventy-five per cent of this ash is carried away in fine gases and is extracted as pulverized fuel ash ('fly ash' or PFA). Some PFA will react with lime in the presence of water, to form a cement-like material (pozzolanic PFA). Mixed with cement, PFA will react with the lime liberated during hydration. Colour, grading and pozzolanicity vary between power stations producing ash. Even the same station will produce different ash from time to time. Some of the ash is mixed with cement, or lime, with various other additives for grouting. Always specify what the ash is to be used for and ensure that a low sulphate ash is supplied. A typical sulphate content (as SO_3) is 1.2%, but the amount can be as low as 0.5%.

HTI powder and other brick powders

Fireclays are used in the production of ceramic products which are required to withstand high temperatures (refractories), such as furnace and flue linings. Finely ground material of this kind can be obtained which will react with lime (as will finely ground brick dust or pozzolanic PFA) to produce hydraulic properties in mortars. The HTI (high temperature insulation) is most conveniently purchased as a fine powder, rather than as a coarse granular material, which must be crushed on site. One of the most important recent observations is that all brick powders improve the frost resistance of both lime:sand and cement:lime:sand mortars.

Aggregates

Materials

Limes and cements are used with fillers in the form of aggregates to make mortars and renderings. The proportion of binder to filler is normally 1:3. The binder paste occupies the 30% void likely to be present in the volume of aggregate.

Aggregates are commonly sand or grit, and may be rounded or angular. Old mortars may contain a wide variety of other materials, such as crushed brick, small lumps of old mortar, chalk, sea shell, kiln slag and ash. The performance of a mortar, plaster or rendering is affected by the size and condition of these fillers, as well as the quantity.

Washing

In general, a selection of clean, well-washed aggregate, which shows as small a volume of voids as possible and is well graded, will give the best service.

Washing is necessary to remove silt, sea salt and organic matter, which will weaken the mix, affect porous masonry and cause efflorescence. A useful on-site test for silt and clay is to add some salt solution (one teaspoonful of table salt to one half litre of cold tap water) to a sample of the aggregate in a clean jam jar. The contents should be shaken up together and left to stand for half an hour. The layer of silt which will settle on top of the sand should not exceed one tenth of the depth of sand in the jar. If it does, it is too dirty to use. Sand which stains excessively, or balls up in the fingers when rubbed, should also be avoided.

Grading

Uniform aggregate size creates problems in mixing and in performance. If a uniform coarse sand is used, the large voids between the grains will not be filled if the right proportion of binder paste is used. As a result the mix will be very harsh to work and will produce a weak, porous material. A uniform, fine sand is difficult to distribute evenly in a binder paste and is liable to produce a mortar or rendering which shrinks and cracks as it dries out and is of low strength. In particular, large percentages of limestone dust should be avoided, as these will always cause shrinkage cracking, with weakness and poor adhesion.

Allowance for 'bulking' should be made when gauging with damp sand. When dry sand is moistened, an expansion takes place, which Schaffer[7] suggests is due to the entrance of water into capillaries. This bulking reaches a maximum point, after which, as the sand becomes very wet, shrinkage back to the original volume occurs. The phenomenon of bulking is most apparent in very fine sands.

Poor workability, due to the use of a uniform, coarse sand, will sometimes lead to the use of increased amounts of water to try to counter the harsh working. However, high water contents cause excessive drying shrinkage. Additional water must not be used to achieve plasticity and wet, sloppy mixes must be avoided.

Summary of requirements for aggregates

1. Select a well graded sand, ranging from fine to coarse.
2. Avoid high percentages of clay and limestone.
3. Wash the aggregates thoroughly with clean water.
4. Keep the water:binder ratio low. Use only enough water to achieve stiff working.

To obtain a well graded sand, it may be necessary to mix aggregates from different sources together. Adding rounded grains to a predominantly angular grained sand improves workability.

Maintenance and repair

Mortar joints

Pointing

If the surface of mortar joints has weathered out to the extent that the face of the stones is vulnerable to damage, so that water can lodge and penetrate and support is inadequate, then a matching mortar must be introduced. The process of filling the joints from the face is known as pointing. In general, the original mortar joints of historic work were not bedded and pointed in separate operations (with notable decorative exceptions) but were filled full and struck off flush as the work was raised. If the stones have retained their sharp arrises, then the joints should be filled flush again, unless there is specific evidence that the joint face was profiled in some other way. Long years of weathering, however, will normally have blunted these arrises and, sometimes, all the original face of some stones will have spalled off. Flush filling in such a situation will greatly increase the apparent width of the joint, and therefore great care must be taken to keep the face of the new mortar within the original width, however far back that may be.

The correct procedure of cleaning out and refilling is well known, but, unfortunately, not widely practised. As a general rule, joints should be cleaned out to a minimum depth of 25 mm (1 in) and never to a depth less than their width. However, wide joints, especially those liable to exposure to extreme weathering, should be cut out to a minimum 38 mm (1.5 in), or even 50 mm (2 in). Sometimes the mortar has disintegrated to such an extent that the joints are largely empty. In this case they must first be deep tamped and, if necessary, hand grouted to fill the joint to the required depth for pointing. If tamped or grouted mortar comes closer to the face than 25–38 mm (1–1.5 in), it must be cut back to the proper depth and to a square face before pointing.

Raking out may be a simple operation, without risk to the fabric, where mortar is substantially decayed, but it is over-simplifying the situation to say that the joint does not need attention if it requires cutting out. Not infrequently, the face of a lime joint has been lost early in its lifetime, before sufficient drying out and carbonation had taken place to enable it to resist the winter. Meanwhile the more protected mortar has survived to become extremely hard. The empty joint at the face may be too much of a risk to leave alone, and additional cutting out may be necessary to achieve enough depth for pointing. More commonly, cutting out (as distinct from raking out with a knife blade or bent spike) is necessary to remove dense repointing of an earlier period, expecially where this mortar (fortunately usually shallow in depth) is causing problems because of its high strength, impermeability and tendency to trap water behind it and accelerate the decay of the stones.

Cutting out should be carried out using plugging chisels, long-necked jointing chisels and toothed masonry chisels with a 2½lb club hammer. Cold chisels should never be used because they may tend to wedge the joints and cause spalling. Impact should be at an oblique angle to the joint face, not directly into it. Drilling with masonry drills is a useful way of creating an initial breach into a strong mortar. In exceptional cases, small carborundum disks may be used in cutting out, but usually only on regularly coursed work, with level beds, where running rules can be fixed to the wall as guides for the power tool. The risks of over-running are obvious, and extreme caution must be used in order not to cut into the masonry or increase the width of the joint.

All cutting out should leave a clean, square face at the back of the joint to provide maximum contact with the new mortar. Time for cutting out, which may be considerable, must be properly programmed.

Cleaning the joint

The prepared face should be carefully cleaned out with a soft or stiff bristle brush and flushed out with clean water, avoiding unnecessary saturation. All dust and loose material must be removed, working from top to bottom of the wall. If old, weathered-out joints have been colonized with algae or lichens, a biocide must be used on the dry surface as part of the cleaning out.

Filling the joint

If the joints have dried out after cleaning, they must be re-wetted before placing the new mortar, to avoid undue suction taking too much water too soon from the mortar. The mortar should be pushed into the joint from a board and ironed in with the maximum possible pressure. Pointing trowels are in common use, but it is regrettably unusual to see pointing irons, which can be improvised to suit the particular work in hand. These may be made of cranked iron, steel, flat or beaten out rod, or even wood. The function of these simple tools is to push the mortar evenly into the joint for the full joint width. They can do this because they fit into the joint and do not try to achieve compaction from the surface alone. In irregular work, this is particularly important.

The mortar face should be fitted flush, or slightly recessed, to avoid spreading the mortar over the face of the masonry. It should be struck and lined out as required.

If a weathered appearance is desired to match existing surviving work, a roughened texture can be produced after the initial set of the mortar has taken place, by light spraying, stiff bristle stippling, or rubbing with coarse sacking. Experience, but above all an understanding of what is required, on the part of the mason is essential. Of the above techniques, stippling with the ends of the stiff bristles in the brush is probably the most universally successful. The bristles should not be dragged across the face, but tapped against it. Timing is critical and no specification can substitute for experience. If this technique is applied too soon, mortar will be removed too easily and the bond forming between mortar and stone will be disrupted. If it is done too late, it will be difficult to make an impression and too vigorous efforts may be made with wire brushes, or masons' drags, to achieve the effect.

Apart from leaving a pleasant, weathered appearance, the rough textured joint tends to assist the wall to dry out and to concentrate wetting and drying activity in the joints, provided the right mortar is used.

There is a danger with this type of weathered finish that the joints may take on too distinctive a character. The old style of washed grit pointing, which used to be carried out by the Ministry of Public Building and Works (UK) on ancient monuments, was often a work of art, but tended to become an end in itself.

Over-pretty work, with mortar kept back to emphasize the outline of every stone, can look very self-conscious and rather odd in an area where the tradition is to slurry over joints in rough rubble masonry, to produce a flush face. A study should be made of surviving masonry to avoid the worst mistakes of this kind. More serious and more common is the error at the opposite end of the scale. Thick, strap pointing, raised proud of the wall, will positively shorten the life of much masonry, especially when the surface is already weakened with decay.

Cleaning off

Keeping the work clean is part of the skill of the mason, but occasionally staining from mortar is an inevitable hazard. Sometimes washing and brushing down is sufficient to remove recent material. However, if the traditional 10% concentration of hydrochloric acid is used (or a proprietary product based on this acid and a surfactant), the masonry surfaces must be pre-wetted to limit absorption and the acid must be thoroughly washed off afterwards. The biggest problem is keeping gauged brickwork clean. Every effort must be made to protect the vulnerable surface of these bricks from mortar spread and droppings when filling the joints.

Special joint treatment

Common historic variations on the flush joint were the beak, or double struck, joint and, later, in the eighteenth century especially, 'joints jointed' and

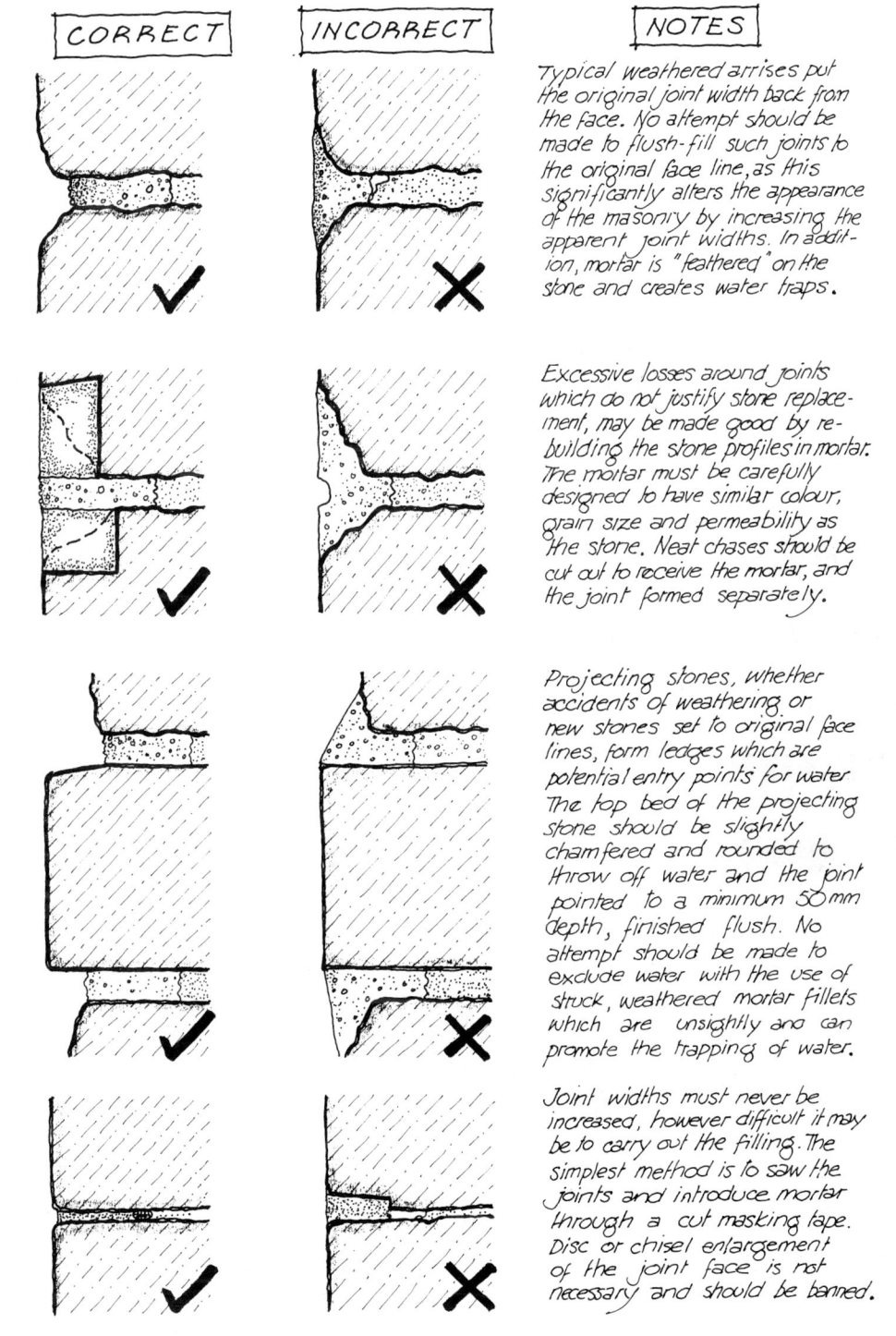

CORRECT	INCORRECT	NOTES

Typical weathered arrises put the original joint width back from the face. No attempt should be made to flush-fill such joints to the original face line, as this significantly alters the appearance of the masonry by increasing the apparent joint widths. In addition, mortar is "feathered" on the stone and creates water traps.

Excessive losses around joints which do not justify stone replacement, may be made good by rebuilding the stone profiles in mortar. The mortar must be carefully designed to have similar colour, grain size and permeability as the stone. Neat chases should be cut out to receive the mortar, and the joint formed separately.

Projecting stones, whether accidents of weathering or new stones set to original face lines, form ledges which are potential entry points for water. The top bed of the projecting stone should be slightly chamfered and rounded to throw off water and the joint pointed to a minimum 50mm depth, finished flush. No attempt should be made to exclude water with the use of struck, weathered mortar fillets which are unsightly and can promote the trapping of water.

Joint widths must never be increased, however difficult it may be to carry out the filling. The simplest method is to saw the joints and introduce mortar through a cut masking tape. Disc or chisel enlargement of the joint face is not necessary and should be banned.

REMEDIAL TREATMENT OF JOINTS

tuck pointing. Where evidence of these survives it should be the pattern for the remedial work, unless the face of the masonry has decayed to the extent of making a finished joint of this kind appear nonsensical. Page 87 shows a method of filling very fine joints.

Damage to joints by 'masonry bees'

Some wild bees species (notably *Osmia rufa*) will burrow into soft mortar joints and even into some weak stones, in lieu of their normal habitat of easily eroded rock and earth banks. Raking out and filling of joints destroyed by these solitary bees may need to be accompanied by spraying or hole injection with a suitable insecticide (general-purpose sprays for garden pests approved under the Pesticide Safety Precautions Scheme). One of the most effective means of control, established by the Research, Technical and Advisory Service of English Heritage, is to place a plug of paste made up from water and the synthetic pyrethroid Permethrin in the hole and then to seal it over with lime:sand mortar. If many bees are present, the safest period for working is late summer or autumn.

Mortar mixes

Table 4.1 shows a range of mixes widely used in joint filling, but reference should also be made to the standard recommendations and codes, especially BS 6270: Part 1 1982, *Cleaning and Surface Repair of Buildings.*

Mortar analysis

Limitations

The choice of a mortar must relate firstly to the type and condition of the masonry and secondly to the degree of exposure. This choice is primarily based on a knowledge of the properties of various mortars and is not arrived at by analysis of the existing mortar alone. There may be good archaeological reasons for wanting to establish the identity and proportions of constituents in an old mortar, and simple separation of aggregates may be useful in identifying likely sources of aggregates for matching purposes. There are, however, limitations which should be understood and mortar specifications should not be based on the simple breakdown analysis of a sample. Analysis requires interpretation and there are important factors which affected the condition and performance of the mortar that is being sampled which analysis will not reveal. Examples of such factors are the original water:binder ratio, the rate of drying out, the method of mixing and placing, and the cleanliness and conditions of the aggregates.

There are also practical difficulties in isolating and identifying constituents. For instance, calcareous aggregates will be digested with the calcareous binder material in acid and present a misleading binder:aggregate proportion. The occurrence of old mortar crushed down and re-used as aggregate is a notorious problem of this kind. Clay minerals, present as impurities, may not be readily distinguishable from the silicates present in an hydraulic cement. An additional difficulty is accurate matching of an old clamp-fired lime, well mixed with fuel and kiln slag, with a modern lime produced in closely controlled conditions and delivered as a very pure hydrate.

The method of mortar analysis selected depends on the information required. Sufficient data may be provided by *in situ* visual analysis or simple on-site visual, physical and/or chemical testing. Laboratory analysis can provide additional information which may not be necessary for the task at hand.

The analysis of mortars is a specialized field. Even for the simplest method, experience is required for the identification of materials and the correct interpretation of evidence.

Mortar analysis and dating of structures

The analysis of old mortar is the analysis of changing technology. Only rarely can it be used to provide a specific date of construction. Laboratory analysis and expert interpretation will provide the most detailed and accurate results, but by themselves they are unlikely to give much indication of the dates when a mortar was prepared. The dating of masonry walls should not be attempted or expected from mortar analysis alone. A combination of evidence is necessary. A thorough examination of documentary sources relating to a structure and its site should be carried out by an experienced person with training in historical research. This should be correlated with analysis of the fabric, one aspect of which is mortar analysis. Further examination of the fabric should include interpretation of the method of construction and the manufacturer of its bricks and/or preparation of its stone.

Methods of analysis

On-site analysis

On-site visual analysis by an experienced person will provide a good indication of the general components of a mortar, particularly where a hand-held ×10 magnifying glass is used. The binder, aggregate and other large particle inclusions can usually be identified. Gentle scraping of a weathered surface may be necessary to reveal the unweathered mortar. This

Table 4.1 Mortars for remedial work on historic buildings

Mortar desig-nation	Mortar mixes							Recommended uses (In selecting a suitable mortar the first consideration must be the condition and type of masonry unit; mortar function and degree of exposure are the next considerations)
	Cement	Brick dust	Lime	'Sharp sand'	'Soft sand'	'Stone dust'	Air en-trainer	
A1	1	1	1	5–6	–	–	√	Dense, impermeable, durable material such as granite, basalt, flint or well-vitrified brick. Severe exposure situations such as sea and river walls, retaining walls, and demanding locations such as paving, plinths and copings. **1**
A2	1	1	1	4	1–2	–	√	
A3	1	1	1	3	2–3	1	√	
A4	1	1	1	5–6	–	–	–	
A5	1	–	1	5–6	–	–	–	
A6	1	–	1	4	1–2	–	–	
A7	1	–	1	3	1–2	1	–	
B1	1	1	2	8–9	–	–	√	Durable, moderately permeable material such as many compact limestones and sandstones or semi-vitrified brick. All exposures and demanding situations such as cornices, quoins and other weatherings. Also recommended for Group 1 material in less severe situations. **2**
B2	1	1	2	6	2–3	–	√	
B3	1	1	2	4	3	1–2	√	
B4	1	1	2	8–9	–	–	–	
B5	1	–	2	8–9	–	–	–	
B6	1	–	2	6	2–3	–	–	
B7	1	–	2	4	3–4	1	–	
C1	1	1	3	10–12	–	–	√	Weathered examples of Groups 1 and 2 which are tending to scale and powder, in all exposures and locations. Also recommended for less durable limestones, sandstones and bricks in all locations. Designations C1, C2, C3 recommended for more severe exposures. **3**
C2	1	1	3	7	3–5	–	√	
C3	1	1	3	7	2–4	1	√	
C4	1	1	3	10–12	–	–	–	
C5	1	–	3	10–12	–	–	–	
C6	1	–	3	8–10	2	–	–	
C7	1	–	3	7–9	2	1	–	
D1	–	1	1	2½–3	–	–	√	Poorly durable material such as some calcareous sandstones, microporous limestones or gauged 'rubbing' bricks. Also recommended for Groups 2 and 3 in sheltered environments and locations other than paving and major weatherings. Reduced aggregate loadings on D7 suitable for fine joints. **4**
D2	–	1	1	2	½–1	–	√	
D3	–	1	1	1	1	½–1	√	
D4	–	1	1	2½–3	–	–	–	
D5	–	–	1	2½–3	–	–	–	
D6	–	–	1	2	½–1	–	–	
D7	–	–	1	1	1	½–1	–	

Left margin, bottom-to-top: Increase in strength and resistance to frost and salt damage

Right margin, bottom-to-top: Increase in workability and ability to accommodate movement

Cement	In this table 'cement' refers to white cement. Cement to be slurried before adding to wet lime:sand mixes.
Brick dust	To be ground dust <150 μm.
Lime	To be non-hydraulic white lime—high calcium or dolomitic.
'Sharp sand'	To consist of angular, well graded sand, ranging evenly from 2.36 mm to 150 μm.
'Soft sand'	To consist of rounded aggregate with some silt but not more than 15% below 150 μm.
'Stone dust'	To consist of limestone powder graded between 600 μm and 150 μm.
Air entrainer	To be proprietary entrainer added to achieve 15% entrapped air.

inspection will also provide useful information about the construction of the masonry, such as the original joint profile, the condition of the original mortar and whether the joints have been repointed. It is usually advisable to remove a representative unweathered sample of mortar and inspect it with a × 10 magnifying glass in good lighting conditions. This sample should be inspected further after it has been disaggregated (crushed, but not ground).

At the completion of these inspections it should be possible to know whether the binder is predominantly lime-based or cement-based (Roman or Portland) or whether it contains a substantial proportion of clay or loam. The type and general characteristics of the aggregate as, for example, rounded or angular sand grains, crushed stone and brick dust should be revealed. Larger inclusions such as gravel, unburnt shell lime, shell aggregate and kiln slag will also be identified. The ease with which the mortar is scored with a fingernail and knife and the removed sample broken will help to identify the presence of any hydraulic constituent.

Simple chemical analysis

Chemical analysis is usually required to determine the proportions of mortar constituents. Several professional mortar analysis services are available in the UK. The basic principle of this analysis is first to dissolve the lime binder in acid, then to separate the aggregate (sand, brick dust, crushed stone) and the fines (cements, fine brick dust and crushed stone), and thereby determine their proportions. Only simple laboratory facilities are required to undertake the procedure which is as follows:

Examination and dissolution of the binder

1. Collect a sample of about 40–50 grams (2 oz). Examine it and record characteristics such as colour, texture, aggregates, inclusions and hardness (scratch resistance).
2. Powder half the sample with a mortar and pestle. Dry at 110 °C for 24 hours and then weigh it with a balance (to an accuracy of 0.1 g).
3. Place the sample in a glass beaker and moisten it with deionized water. Then immerse the moistened sample in a 10% solution of hydrochloric acid to dissolve the binder. The mixture will effervesce as CO_2 is given off (safety glasses should be worn). The mixture should then be stirred with a glass rod to make sure the reaction is complete.

Separation, filtration and sieving

4. Weigh a piece of filter paper, place it in a funnel positioned over a large flask.
5. Add a few drops of hydrochloric acid to the sample to ensure complete acid digestion of the binder and stir. Add water to it slowly and swirl with a glass rod to suspend the fines.
6. Pour the liquid with the suspended material through the filter, being careful to keep the solid particles at the bottom of the beaker. Add more water and repeat the swirling and pouring until the water added to the beaker remains clear.
7. Dry the fines collected on the filter paper and weigh. Determine the weight of the fines.
8. Wash the sand with water several times and leave to dry for 24 hours. Weigh the dry sand.
9. Express the amounts of sand and fines as a percentage of the whole sample. The amount of dissolved binder is calculated by subtracting the

sand and fines weights from the weight of the original sample. The weights determined will give the proportions of binder, fines and aggregate of the original mix. Allowances must be made for the loss of any calcareous aggregates dissolved with the binder. The results of the analysis can be recorded on a sheet such as the one on pages 91–92.

Further sand and fines analysis

10. Inspect the colour of the dried fines. Simple inspection of this kind is normally sufficient to identify clay (yellow, plastic when wetted), brick (red/brown), cement (grey), sand (almost any colour, gritty to touch).
11. More accurate examination must be made with a binocular microscope to determine colour, particle shape and material types. Sieve through standard sieves to determine particle size distribution, expressing the amount of each particle size as a percentage of the whole. Note that the acid may have changed the colours of the sand.

X-ray diffraction

Sometimes more sophisticated techniques are needed, mainly for historic mortars research to provide more specific information than separation and sieving of constituents. In this case a sample is submitted to a laboratory where a portion of it is ground to a homogeneous powder and a mineral analysis conducted by X-ray diffraction (XRD). The sample is irradiated and the crystal planes of the material in it reflect the rays.

Lime, sand, Roman Cement, Portland cement and pozzolanic additives such as trass are all clearly identified by this method of analysis because each has a different crystal diffraction pattern. Most importantly, XRD provides conclusive evidence of clay in a mortar and is able to identify the type of clay present.

The XRD results can be expressed in the form of a graph with several prominent peaks. The position of these peaks on the scale indicates the type of material present. To positively identify a material it is usually sufficient to match its three most intense peaks. The approximate proportions of the constituent materials can be gauged from the height of the major peak of each mineral.

Sampling procedure

Particularly where mortar analysis is part of a programme of archaeological and historical research, a thorough sampling procedure is required. The objectives of the sampling should be defined well in advance. The number and size of the samples should

MORTAR ANALYSIS SHEET

SITE:	SAMPLE LOCATION:
Cardray Castle	South Wall

VISUAL DESCRIPTION:

A soft white mortar which is easy to crumble by hand.

WEIGHT OF SAMPLE: 96.91g   WEIGHT AFTER DRYING: 95.74g   LOSS ON DRYING %: 1.2%

BS SIEVE REFERENCE	WEIGHT OF SAMPLE RETAINED	PERCENTAGE %	RATIO	REMARKS
A 5.0 mm	0.21g	0.2)		Single large aggregate
B 2.36 mm	0.10g	0.1)		Mixed aggregate plus burnt wood.
C 1.18 mm	0.13g	0.1)	½	As above. Ratio total of A, B, C.
D 600 μm	1.17g	1.2	1	Silvery sand mixed aggregate.
E 300 μm	25.11g	26.2	21 3/4	As above.
F 150 μm	18.89g	19.7	16½	As above.
G finer than F	6.54g	6.8	5½	As above.
H other				
Lime by difference	43.59g	45.5	1:1	Strongish mix.
TOTAL	95.74g	99.8		

92

COMMENTS ON ANALYSIS:

The sample was quite dry at 1.2%. The lime to aggregate ratio is 1 of lime to 1 of aggregate producing an original strongish mix. Sieves A, B and C where added to produce a ratio of ½.

CHEMICAL ANALYSIS	PERCENT BY WEIGHT	REMARKS
TOTAL IRON:		
CALCIUM:		
MAGNESIUM:		
SULPHATE:		
NITRATE:		
CHLORIDE:		
OTHERS:		

RARELY REQUIRED

FURTHER COMMENTS:

REPORT PREPARED BY:　　　　　　　　SIGNED:

　　　　　　　　　　　　　　　　　　DATED:

be the minimum necessary to gain the required information without doing damage to the historic structure. The sampling procedure should include the following guidelines:

1. Sampling should be done by persons well acquainted with a building or its remains, to ensure that a proper programme of sampling is prepared and the samples receive proper interpretation. It is essential to involve the analyst in the sampling operations.
2. The sample should preferably be in the form of lumps, not crumbled or powdered. The quantity usually required for comparative analysis and for reference material is about 40–50 g (2 oz), preferably in one or a few compact fragments (half for analysis, half for reference).
3. The exact position (not just the location) from which the sample was taken must be accurately recorded.
4. To make certain that a particular kind of mortar is typical for a certain wall, at least three samples should be taken from different parts of that wall and analysed separately. If they prove to be identical within limits of practical deviations, their composition and properties can be considered as typical.
5. The sample must be clearly and thoroughly labelled.

Recording

Pages 91–92 show a typical mortar analysis sheet on which the analysis of a lime render sample has been recorded. The sheet shows the kind of information which would be received from a laboratory after examining a mortar by chemical analysis and grading of aggregates. In this case the most useful contribution made by the analysis to work on site was the identification of aggregates which enabled them to be matched with some accuracy. Five per cent HTI powder was added to the repair mix because the wall surface, which was originally internal, was to remain exposed.

References

1. Neve, R., *The City and Country Purchaser and Builder's Dictionary*, 1726, reprinted 1969 by David and Charles, Newton Abbot, England
2. Peterson, S., 'Lime water consolidation', in *Mortars, Cements and Grouts used in the Conservation of Historic Buildings*, Proceedings of ICCROM Symposium, November 1981
3. Peroni, S. *et al.*, 'Lime-based mortars for the repair of ancient masonry and possible substitutes', in *Mortars, Cements and Grouts used in the Conservation of Historic Buildings*, Proceedings of ICCROM Symposium, November 1981
4. Torraca, G., *Porous Building Materials—Materials Science for Architectural Conservation*, ICCROM, 1982
5. Nicholson, P., *The New Practical Builder and Workman's Companion*, 1823
6. Sickels, Lauren-Brook, 'Organics vs. synthetics: their use as additives in mortars', in *Mortars, Cements and Grouts used in the Conservation of Historic Buildings*, Proceedings of ICCROM Symposium, November 1981
7. Schaffer, R.J., *The Weathering of Natural Building Stones*, Department of Scientific and Industrial Research Special Report 18, HMSO, London, 1932 (available from Building Research Establishment, Watford WD2 7JR, England)

Figure 4.1 The pointing key, a cranked bar or flat rod designed to fit into the width of the joint, is essential to the efficient packing of mortar from the back of the joint. Packing cannot effectively be carried out using a trowel

Figure 4.4 Below 5 mm thickness joints need to be sawn out with hacksaw blades set in purpose-made two-piece handles. Impact tools should not be used

Figure 4.2 Tamping the packed joint with the ends of a flat bristle brush raises the joint texture and provides a good evaporation face. The textured mortar also matches old, weathered mortar. The brush should not be dragged on the surface or leave any marks

Figure 4.5 To place mortar in fine joints effectively, a heavy-duty canvas-backed adhesive tape is placed over the centre-line of the cut joint, and pressed firmly onto the surface. A sharp knife is used to slit the tape through to the joint, and the edges of the tape are pressed down

Figure 4.3 Joints should be cut out with sharp, flat-bladed quirks and a light hammer, as shown in this illustration. Quirks are satisfactory for joints down to 5 mm thickness

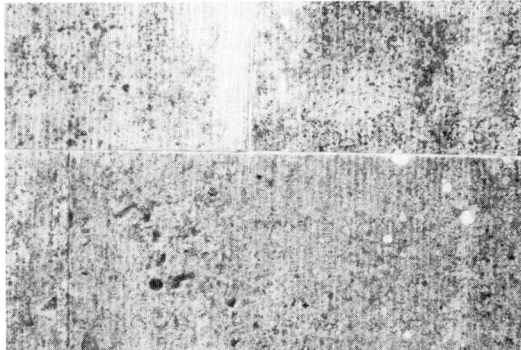

Figure 4.6 The open joint is flushed out with a fine water jet. In the final stage, a lime putty:stone dust mortar (1:1) is firmly pressed into the joint using a filling knife

Figure 4.7 The tape is removed and any further packing of the mortar face takes place with a small iron or copper flat. The mortar is contained neatly in the joint and is well compacted, and the joint has not been widened to achieve success

Figure 4.8 Dense, impermeable walling stones such as granite provide good resistance to weather but make great demands on the mortar in the joints. Traditionally, quite strong mortars have been used with granite; Lutyens' mortar at Castle Drogo is 1:1:6, cement:lime:sand. Unfortunately, such mortars often exhibit shrinkage cracking at the mortar:stone interface. When water is consistently allowed access the inevitable result is wet conditions internally and lime leaching out onto the surface

Figure 4.9 Superficial repointing in similar strength mortar gauged with a PVA bonding agent has only exacerbated the problem in this early repointing, exhibiting substantial shrinkage cracking

Figure 4.10 There are no short cuts to resolving the problem. This illustration shows joints cut out to 50 mm depth, carefully removing all old mortar with plugging chisels. To the left and right is new mortar consisting of a 1:1:6 mortar which has been firmly packed to the full depth of cut and allowed to cure slowly. Success depends on a low water ratio in the fresh mortar and on slow drying

Figure 4.13 The mastic plug is firmly ironed into place using a spatula dipped into white spirit

Figure 4.11 Joints which are particularly vulnerable to penetration may receive a different treatment. Such joints may be ledges, copings or the top bed joint of weatherings. Into a 50 mm cut a foam backing rod is inserted to the back of the joint

Figure 4.14 A 40 mm depth of 1:1:6 mortar masks the plug

Figure 4.12 A two-part polysulphide mastic plug is placed against the backing rod, using a mastic gun with an extended nozzle

5

Traditional handworking of stone: methods and recognition

Peter Hill

Introduction

The faces of stones which bear the weathered marks of the tools used by the masons in their preparation are always of considerable interest to archaeologists and conservators and well worth study. How much may be safely deduced from such evidence, however, is a subject fraught with pitfalls. It seems reasonable that opinions on technical subjects should be based on a sound working knowledge of the principles involved. Some scholars, however, seem to have no inhibitions when discussing stonework in archaeological contexts, whether it be a discussion of excavated masonry, or papers and books on the techniques of the mason. A few examples will serve to illustrate the dangers involved. By one authority we are told that 'to cut long straight lines over a metre in length by means of a chisel alone is an almost impossible task'. This is a denial of the basic training of a mason in any age, the ability to dress stone against a straight edge being one of the more important indicators separating the skilled workman from the amateur. A deviation from the mean of under 1 mm can readily be achieved without recourse to any secondary work with abrasives.

Elsewhere, the gouge is variously referred to as 'unsuitable for stonework' and 'useless for working stone', statements readily refuted by a visit to the nearest mason's workshop, where any number of these tools may be found in use on both hard and soft stones.

A discussion of the 'drove', more properly called a 'boaster', contains the assertion that 'its size would have made it difficult to push evenly along the stone and, anyway, if this had been done, the resulting surface would have been very patchy and unpleasant'. It need only be said that it is used in precisely this way with excellent results and is, in

fact, the basic tool used in finishing a clean, flat surface.

These few examples from a very rich field are of necessity selective in a partial approach and are perhaps somewhat extreme, yet it remains true that almost all writers on this subject perpetrate similar inaccuracies and tend to rely too heavily on work of other authors who are themselves working at second-hand. The Latin scholar will as a matter of course recognize gaps in his experience and consult an epigraphist about an unusual inscription, yet is quite prepared to perpetuate this almost circular transfer of what is, in some cases, little better than a collation of imperfectly grasped hearsay evidence.

The purpose of this chapter is to give sufficient, accurate information to enable the archaeologist or conservator to identify the tools used in the production of masonry on sites of any period and to assess the quality of the work on a common basis.

Identification of stone types

The starting point in any examination of masonry must be to identify the type and, as closely as possible, the source of the stone. (All excavated worked stone should be fully reported.) It is not sufficient, for example, to refer to limestone, or even oolitic limestone. The distance the stone has travelled has an obvious bearing on the difficulty and cost of the construction. For example, when Tutbury Castle was repaired in 1314 the cost of transport over 5–6 miles (8–9 km) came to nearly twice the cost of the quarried stone.[1] Information on the nature of the stone gives some guidance on the degree of labour expended to achieve a given finish. It should be the aim where possible to give at least a narrow geographical area, if not the precise quarry of origin. To this end, a petrographical analysis is clearly desirable, although a local stonemason may be able to give an accurate indication. As a general rule, sandstones tend to be uniform within a given quarry, whereas limestones may vary markedly in colour, texture and hardness within a 300 mm cube (approximately 65 kg or 150 lb).

Once the stone is known, some indication of its hardness and ease of working (not always the same thing) should be attempted. To determine this, a banker-mason trying a chisel on an unimportant part of the work is indispensable. It will be very difficult to relate the nature of the stone to a fixed standard, but an experienced subjective opinion should have some value.

A common misconception is that limestone is 'softer' (i.e. easier to work) than sandstone. However, the proportion of 'hard' to 'soft' stones commonly used in building is probably about equal between the two types, and apart from the problems of silicosis many sandstones are much more pleasant to work than limestones.

Types and descriptions of masonry

Stones appearing on the face of a wall should be referred to in general terms as facing stones. A more detailed description of stonework should be on the lines of the categories set out below. The term 'ashlar' must never, contrary to popular practice, be used as a synonym for 'facing stone', unless it is strictly appropriate.

The following categories are given in descending order of the degree of labour required.

1. *Ashlar.* This term should be confined to masonry that meets the following criteria. The stones should have carefully worked beds and joints, and be finely jointed (generally under 6 mm (0.2 in)) and set in horizontal courses. Stones within each course should be of the same height, although successive courses may be of different heights. Where the centre of the face, however it is finished, intentionally projects beyond the wall line, it should be bounded by a well chiselled margin, 20–25 mm (0.8–1 in) wide, worked straight and square to the beds. This allows accurate setting both to adjacent stones and to the general line of the wall. These drafts (strips of surface worked to the width of the chisel) should twist in reasonably well and, ideally, the stone should be perfectly rectangular in elevation. Ashlar should be described according to the surface finish. The more common finishes are listed below.

(a) *Plain or rubbed ashlar* is ashlar where the surface has been rubbed, usually with a piece of sandstone or carborundum, to remove all tool-marks, leaving a perfectly smooth surface.

(b) *Boasted or axed ashlar* is left finished with toolmarks visible. The regularity and form of the toolmarks will vary according to the style of the mason. They will in general show a row of diagonal grooves set in a series of drafts, although the individual drafts may not be distinguishable.

(c) *Punched ashlar.* The surface is left from the punch after the marginal drafts have been worked. The marks may be random or regular, the latter being the most likely on stone worked carefully enough to be called ashlar. A very finely worked surface, with very small and even indentations, is referred to as being *pecked.*

(d) *Rock-faced ashlar.* The centre of the stone is left boldly projecting in its natural state, or with a little assistance from a pitching tool within the chiselled margins.

(e) *Tooled or batted ashlar.* This is left with regularly spaced chisel marks set vertically on a rubbed surface. It represents not so much a stage of work, but rather a deliberately applied design introduced within the last 150 years or so. It is thus one of the few surface finishes to give any definite indication of date. It is sometimes seen today, often with diagonal toolmarks on a sawn surface, in a vain attempt to simulate non-mechanical work.

(f) *Rusticated ashlar.* The face projects from the wall line in a distinct step. The simplest indication is that the joints are set in a rebate behind the marginal drafts around the face, which may be finished in any fashion. The term is not a synonym for rock-faced work.

2. *Block-in-course.* This is a class of masonry, nowadays seen largely in railway and dock engineering, in which the stones are squared and brought to fair joints. The faces are usually dressed with the walling hammer or punch. It may resemble ashlar or coursed rubble according to the degree and quality of work applied to it, although the stones will usually be larger than coursed rubble. The distinction may be difficult at times, but measurement of the dressed stonework should assist. Joints may be wider than in ashlar work, and there will not necessarily be a good chiselled margin. The tools used for dressing the face should be specified where possible.

3. *Coursed rubble.* The term rubble is not a derogatory term. The majority of ancient stone buildings in Britain are in coursed or random rubble. Many have stood for centuries without any regular maintenance. Rubble is more cost effective than ashlar. In coursed rubble the stones are squared up, more or less roughly according to the quality, to about the same height within each course, usually not above 250–300 mm (8–12 in). The faces may be left rough, or dressed with walling hammer or punch. The joints and beds will tend to be in excess of 15 mm (0.6 in) and, on elevation, the corners of the

stones will tend to exhibit roundness rather than angularity. It is normal for the joints to be worked to something of a taper. This increases the hold of the mortar and makes accuracy in working (and thus cost) less important. Where the stones, although often small, appear to be particularly uniform in height and rectangularity, the style may be referred to as *coursed squared rubble*.

4. *Random rubble*. This is walling in which the stones have received little attention beyond knocking off the sharpest angles. Only minimum attention is paid to coursing, although the stones are laid horizontally as far as possible. Generally, this work occurs where stone of a highly stratified or fissile nature is available, because the resultant thin flat slabs, usually 100–200 mm (4–8 in) thick, are easily broken into a suitable size and can be bedded with a minimum of labour. When the stones are placed so as to level up to a horizontal course at intervals, the work is known as *random rubble built to courses*.

5. *Polygonal or rag walling*. In this work, the stones are of any shape as they come from the quarry. They are placed so as to fit best with their neighbours after a minimum of hammer-dressing. The effect is similar to that of crazy paving set vertically.

An approach to the measurement of dressed stonework

This section is relevant largely to the assessment of ashlar and block-in-course work. The principal indicators of the quality of work are the truth of the surface against a straight edge and the squareness of the stone on both elevation and plan. It is essential that physical checks of these factors be taken; the eye alone will not give the necessary objective evaluation. These indicators are not new. The ancient Egyptians also used these to check the quality of their stonework.[2]

To test the straightness, an edge is held so that it lies parallel to the notional face of the stone. Where the distance at point 'a' in *Figure 5.1(a)* is no more than 2 mm in 300 mm, the surface may in general be regarded as straight. Greater deviations should be recorded in steps as suggested in *Table 5.1*, to assist in comparative studies. The amount of acceptable deviation will depend to an extent on the nature of the work and the type of surface finish. On good, finely chiselled or rubbed ashlar or mouldings, the deviation should be not more than 1 mm. On run-of-the-mill ashlar walling, up to 3 mm in 300 mm would not necessarily be out of place, depending on the date and class of building.

The same test should, where possible, be applied to the beds and joints. The joints are relatively

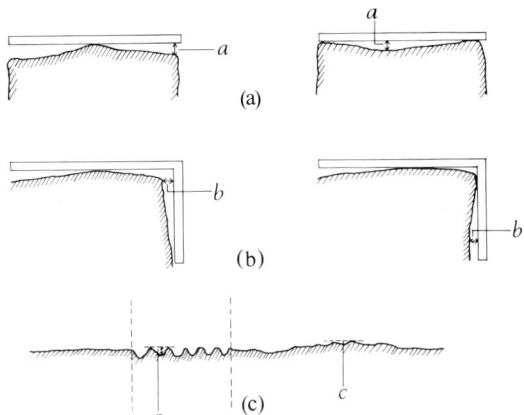

Figure 5.1 Measurement of dressed stonework (see text)

unimportant and need only to be examined closely to confirm the excellence of first-class work. For both ashlar and block-in-course work, they should be reasonably parallel as they run back into the wall. Bedding surfaces should be checked with some care. Although they will often not be worked particularly cleanly, the deviation should not exceed 2 mm. The principle to follow is that the stones should rest on one another with minimum use of mortar to give stability. On the other hand, beds should never be worked concave, as this causes pressure to fall on the arrises, with consequent spalling of the face.

It is an axiom in masonry that mortar is used to keep the stones apart rather than to hold them together. Structures in ashlar and block-in-course depend for their stability on the large size of the stones, the well fitting beds and joints and the arrangement of the bonding. Where the strength depends largely on the mortar, the classification is more appropriately some type of rubble work.

To test for squareness, the square should be held with one arm parallel to the notional line of one face and any discrepancy measured on the other arm (*Figure 5.1(b)*). Anything under 2 mm in 300 mm may be regarded as square. As before, any greater deviations should be recorded as in *Table 5.1*.

Table 5.1 Recording data

Deviation per 300 mm (mm)			Possible description
(a) *Straight*	(b) *Square*	(c) *Range*	
under 2	under 2	under 1	Ashlar
2–4	2–4	1–2	
5–12	5–6	3–5	
over 12	7–12	7–12	Block-in-course

The angles to be checked are the quoins, the corners on the elevation of the faces and, where possible, the beds and joints against the face. The beds should always be square to the face, but the joints are not as important and up to 6 mm in 300 mm under square is not out of place in good work.

Note should be taken next of the surface finish, which should be accurately described according to the tools used and the regularity of the tooling. The profile of typical portions of the surface should be taken, especially on the better finishes, as an aid to identifying the general standard of the work. On good, straight, finely chiselled work, the range may well be less than 0.5 mm, although this will vary according to the heaviness of the chiselling. The key lies largely in the regularity of the surface. Punched work in which the peaks and troughs are all at similar levels will clearly have been worked with more care, or ability, than roughly chiselled work in which the range is perhaps less, but where much unevenness is apparent, although the labour on the punched work is likely to have been less. Examples are given in *Figure 5.1(c)*.

Where the maximum of more than one column of *Table 5.1* is exceeded, the work is tending towards coursed rubble. Measurements taken on the margins are the best guides to nomenclature, especially where (c) approaches the maximum when measured across the face. Isolated holes in an otherwise good face may be disregarded for measurement, but should be noted as detracting from the quality. It is important to remember that, in any period from Roman to modern, the *skilled* mason can achieve a deviation from both straight and square of under 0.5 mm, without excessive lack of skill, or a relatively low specification. The figures shown in *Table 5.1* reflect human frailty, rather than the achievable.

An indication of the size of stones used should be given. The dimensions should always be quoted in the order length of face, depth into the wall and bed height.

The overall assessment of stonework must be based on a combination of the above factors. Because of the infinite variety possible in stone dressing, it is difficult to establish a coherent system of grading. An experienced eye must take precedence over rigid rules, but it must be backed by physical measurement. Some of the standards given may seem over exacting, but they are no more than may readily be achieved, as required, by a skilled mason. It is only by using the best as a base that a common standard of appreciation, which is lacking at present, may be established.

It is worth noting in passing that, especially in regard to medieval work, the final position of a stone in the building should have relatively little bearing on the quality of workmanship. When the stone is being worked, it is only a few inches from the eye of the mason, who will be satisfying a fixed standard with small regard to its destination.

To assist the archaeologist with stonework, it may be well at times to take direct advice from a stonemason, but care is necessary here. 'Stonemason' can cover a number of different trades. The one to choose is the person who has been trained as a banker-mason and who spends the greater part of his time dressing stone with a mallet and chisel to a high standard. It is important to appreciate the distinction. Someone who has spent his life pointing or building rubble walls is no more competent to judge the dressing of ashlar than a banker-mason is to assess a dry-stone wall. An attempt may be made in each case, but this is hardly the approach for the professional archaeologist. No matter who finally judges the work, it must be within the framework of this or some other common standard of approach.

Tools, toolmarks and methods

The tools discussed below are, with a few specified exceptions, known to have been in use in one form or another from Roman times to the present day. When considering dating of stonework, it is of prime importance to bear in mind that the majority of modern masons' handtools are very similar in number, style and use to those of the medieval and Roman mason. Tomb drawings dating from *c.* 2600 BC to *c* 1100 BC found at Saqqara and Thebes[3] show tools indistinguishable from those in daily use today.

The marks left from the use of the tools are described and differentiated as far as possible below. However, in some cases it is quite impossible to differentiate between work done by different tools. This may be disappointing for the archaeologist, but it is a matter of simple fact which can be demonstrated by any competent banker-mason. Also, it is often the case that there will be a greater difference between the work of two contemporary masons than between works of two different millennia. As a general principle, it is not possible to use toolmarks to provide absolute dating evidence; even relative dating can be extremely hazardous and is best avoided.

The illustrations do not relate to any specific period. They are representative types showing the general form of the tools. They are described in approximate sequence of use.

Axe/adze (Figure 5.2a,b). These tools occur in a number of variations, including both tools combined in one.[4] They may, in their different forms, be used for either initial roughing out, or in final dressing. For rough dressing of rubble, an acceptable result can readily be achieved, particularly where the tool

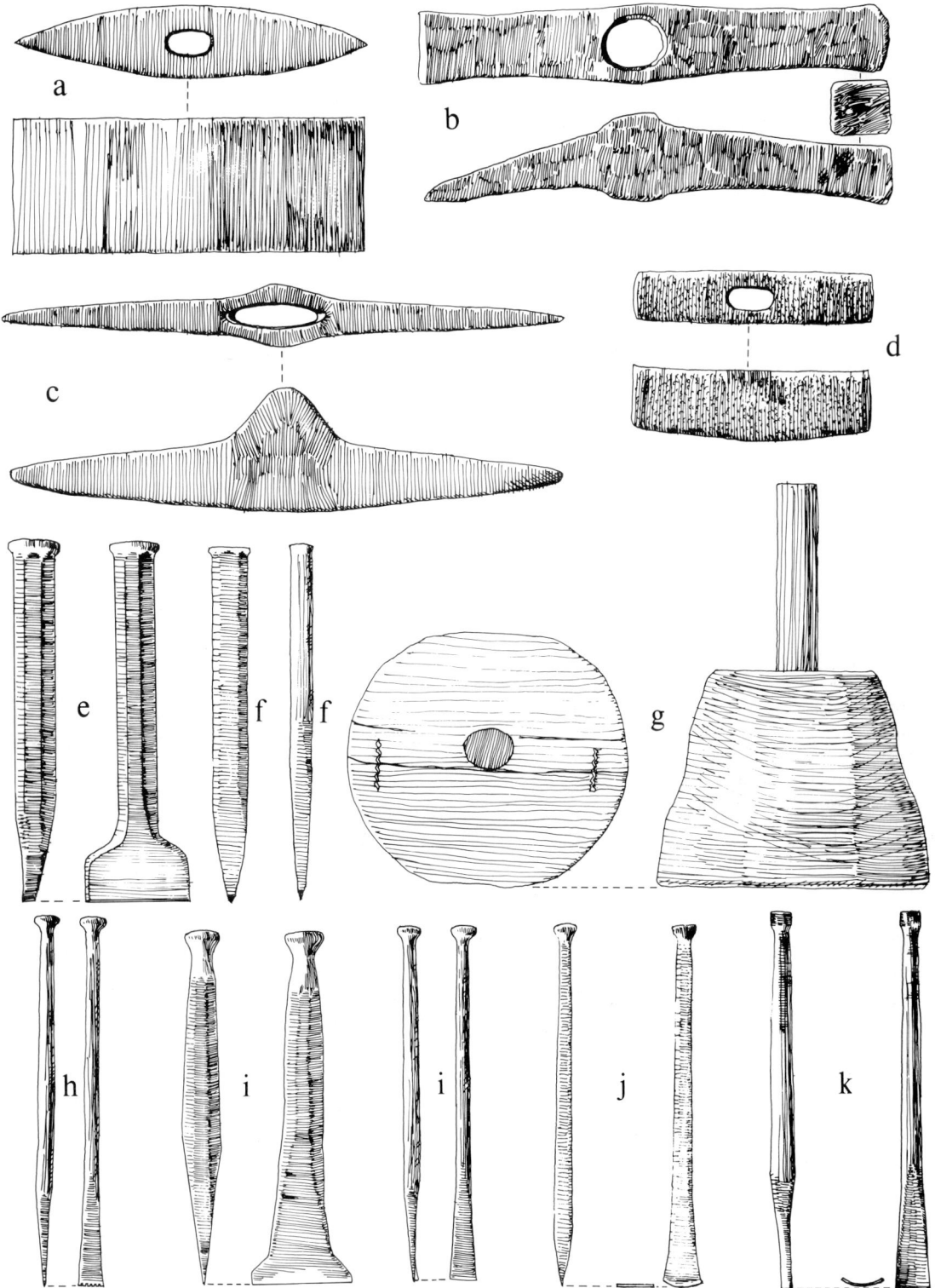

Figure 5.2 Representative types of stoneworking tools (see text)

consists of a vertical axe blade, and a hammer head,[5] which resembles one type of modern walling hammer. Other versions of the axe have two vertical blades. The adze has a horizontal blade, which may be combined with a hammer head,[6] pick[7] or axe.[4] The adze does not seem to figure in medieval records, but it may not have been distinguished by name from the varieties of axe. Neither of these tools is in general use today in England.

Pick (Figure 5.2c). This tool may have a point at each end, or it may have a hammer head at one end. It may also have an axe or adze blade—indeed axe, adze and pick may on occasions be the same tool. They are all referred to here according to which working surface is being used; in this form it is in effect a scappling hammer, which is a quarryman's tool.

The pick is mainly used for rough working of the stone, either for rubble work or in the early stages of ashlar. Use of a heavy pick, especially the type weighted with the hammer head on the back, will show a relatively long striation according to the softness of the stone. This may be V-shaped or U-shaped in section, depending on the form to which the tool has been sharpened and how blunt the edge has become. A small pick will leave marks largely indistinguishable from the use of a punch struck by a hammer. However, the finer dressed or smaller work will be more likely to have involved the punch. The effects of both will be treated together.

Hammer (Figure 5.2d). This tool is for driving other cutting tools. It is generally several centimetres long, hafted centrally and weighs 1–3 kg with a relatively small striking face. (Roman examples may be seen in the museum in Chester, England.) Tools designed to be used with the hammer have the struck end of about the same diameter as the shank.

Pitcher or pitching tool (Figure 5.2c). The antiquity of this tool is uncertain. It has never been positively identified in an archaeological context and its use leaves no trace. It is included for the sake of completeness. It resembles a very heavy chisel, with a blade from 40 mm to 75 mm (1.5–3 in) wide. Instead of a cutting edge, the end is up to 8 mm (0.3 in) thick and almost flat. It is used with a heavy hammer blow to remove surplus stone by fracture. One good blow may detach a piece weighing 2–3 kg. The only trace of its use is a slight bruising where the blade has been in contact. This mark is usually removed by further working and will, in any case, disappear after only slight weathering.

Punch (Figure 5.2d). This is an extremely versatile tool which is normally used with a hammer for removing either large or small amounts of waste. The amounts removed depend on the size of the punch, the hammer and the weight of the blow. The softer stones are not always quicker to rough-off with a punch than are the harder stones. Soft stone will often largely absorb the blow with only small effect and it may be easier to dispense with this tool in favour of a claw-tool or chisel. A good example of the variety of punched work is afforded by the east-central pier of the east gate of Chester Fort. There the upper right-hand side has been roughly worked-off with a punch to give a very irregular surface. The lower-right hand side has been more neatly worked over with the same tool to give a rather flatter finish. The left-hand side has been punched (or picked) to give an intermittently furrowed effect.

With both the pick and the punch, a single heavy blow in the right place will detach a large flake of stone, perhaps as big as a fist, by fracture alone, with only slight trace of abrasion at the point of contact. Repeated use of the tool over the surface will show as a number of pock-marks, whilst repeated blows of the hammer without removing the punch from the stone between each blow will result in furrows which may be a few millimetres long, or may extend across the face of the stone. Careful use of the pick can give the latter effect, but more irregularity will be likely. The variety of different effects to be obtained from the punch is almost infinite and the quality of finish depends largely on the skill and effort put into the work.

The cutting edge of a punch may be around 6 mm (0.2 in) wide for use on softer stones, but is normally drawn out to a point for harder stone. Where the tool has a head suitable for use with a mallet it is generally known as a point, as is the more delicate, hammer-headed tool of the carver.

Mallet (Figure 5.2g). A modern mason's mallet is circular or oval in plan, about 150 mm (6 in) across, and tapering in towards the handle. This is precisely the shape shown in Egyptian tomb drawings. However, medieval illustrations show a type more akin to a joiner's mallet, which is rectangular in plan and elevation. The Roman mallet is shown on tombstones, but its precise form is not discernible.

Chisels intended for use with a mallet nowadays have their heads mushroomed out above a narrow neck to present a large area to the mallet. The previous practice is not known, because no chisels have survived in this form and contemporary illustrations are not clear on the point.

Claw-tool (Figure 5.2h). This is basically a chisel, for use either as a finish in itself, or to bring the stone to within 2–3 mm of the finished surface prior to chiselling. Its use is optional on the softer stones, but it is of great value on the harder stones and on those stones which have a tendency to pluck into holes when equivalent amounts are removed with an ordinary chisel of the same width. Because of the reduced length of the working edge, it requires less effort to drive than the equivalent full-bladed chisel.

The effect of the claw-tool is to leave an irregularly 'combed' surface in which the tooth marks may easily be seen. Where the stone has been further chiselled or rubbed, the indentations may be very short and shallow, looking more like pin-pricks. The variety of claw-tools is endless. The teeth of the tool may have been close set, 2–3 mm long and sharply pointed, or the tool may have more nearly resembled a plain chisel, with the cutting edge interrupted by a series of nicks, 3–4 mm apart. The effect should be closely observed. No examples of the claw-tool are known to have survived in archaeological contexts in Britain, but its use is known at many Roman sites and on the majority of medieval churches. The date of the re-introduction of this tool some time in the early medieval period is uncertain, but it would be very surprising if such a useful tool, used by the Ancient Greeks and perhaps earlier, went completely out of use for a period of several centuries.

Chisels (Figure 5.2i). The term is used to cover all cutting tools driven by mallet or hammer, whose edge forms a straight line when viewed from the cutting end. Chisels are generally classified according to the width of the cutting edge, those of over 50 mm (2 in) also being referred to as boasters and used for final dressing of the stone to give a true surface. When the tool has, in elevation, a rounded edge, it is known as a bull-nose chisel *(Figure 5.2j)* and is used for working concave surfaces. The gouge, with a cutting edge curved on end view *(Figure 5.2k)*, is used for largely the same purposes as the bull-nose.

The smaller chisels, from 20 mm down to 3 mm (0.8–0.1 in), tend to be used for working mouldings and for carving. As Blagg[8] points out, small chisels can be as finely drawn out as wood-chisels, making recognition difficult after years in the ground. A chisel of about 25 mm (1 in) is usually used for cutting-in marginal drafts, but this may vary according to the type of stone and the whim of the mason. No two masons today work in exactly the same way and there is no reason to suppose that they have ever done so. The chisel is also often used, especially on the harder stones, in sequence after the claw-tool to clear successive parallel drafts across the face which may then be left or finished off with a boaster, according to the quality of the work in hand.

The most commonly used chisels for work not going beyond simple, bold mouldings are probably 12 mm, 25 mm and 50 mm (0.5, 1 and 2 in) wide. With these three, plus appropriate roughing-out tools, a surprising variety of work can be undertaken.

The identification of marks left by the chisel is not always easy, owing to weathering, further finishing by abrasion and interference with the surface due to careless roughing out. A plain chisel, used with a little vigour on a hard, close-grained stone, will leave a series of contiguous, straight grooves.

The length of the grooves will correspond to the size of the chisel, except where successive drafts have overlapped (which is the norm). On coarse-grained or soft stone there may be no clear evidence of the tools used, even immediately after working. Where flat surfaces are being cleared, the grooves are at an angle to the line of approach, which is normally across the body of the mason. The right-handed mason holds the chisel in the left hand and works from right to left. If the mason stands square to the job, the chisel marks will slope from bottom left to top right, at an angle of about 60°–70° to the lower edge of the stone. The opposite slope will result from left-handed work. Holding the chisel at an angle is not done for any particular effect, but because it is the easier and most natural way to dress ashlar, whether chisel or axe is being used. The belief that diagonal tooling is a mark of axed work does not stand the test of close examination. Comparative studies have shown that, providing all the work is carried out to the same standard, it can be impossible to tell which portions of a surface have been worked with a boaster and which with an axe of similar-sized cutting edge. Even on occasions where differences were apparent, it was not possible to say which tool had worked which part.

The use of the adze can also be difficult to distinguish because it does its work with a paring action, cutting the stone in precisely the same way as a chisel used with a good swing of the mallet. Moreover, marks from the boaster may, depending on the coarseness of the surface, be as much as 5–6 mm (0.2–0.24 in) apart and 3–4 mm (0.12–0.16 in) deep. In contrast, the axe or adze can be used, as can the boaster if desired, to give a finer, shallower effect. Like the axe/adze, in heavily boasted work one corner of the chisel tends to dig in with depressing ease and frequency. The slightly radiating marks sometimes claimed as axed work can also readily be achieved in boasted work with only minimum carelessness.

The problem of differentiating the different tools applied equally to the work of all periods. All edged tools used on stone tend to wear first at the corners, both by abrasion in use and by the action of sharpening. This can lead to some confusion; for example, a pick which has suffered heavy use can leave a mark not dissimilar to that made by some indeterminate type of curved chisel.

Given the survival of individual marks, the work of the bull-nose chisel is readily identified and distinguished from that of the gouge. Although the grooves from both tools are curved on plan, those of the bull-nose chisel have the centre of the curve ahead of the sides. The opposite effects shown by the gouge. The direction of movement is usually easily determined, as the groove tends to show a slow descent and a sharper step up in a forward movement.

On the general question of toolmarks, it should be noted that on all but the hardest stones they are easily removed, or at least softened, by rubbing with a piece of sandstone or other abrasive. This is particularly true following use of the smaller chisels, whch tend to be used with a light blow and where, in careful finishing with the larger chisels, the tool is not removed from the job between strokes. this technique may leave a surface devoid of all but the faintest of marks.

Basic stone dressing

In both the initial reduction of the surface with the punch and in the final dressing of the plane surface,

the archaeologist may care to substitute the use of an axe or adze. Whatever tool is used, the basic principle is the same.

To produce a piece of ashlar from the quarried block, a 25 mm (1 in) chisel is used in conjunction with a straight-edge to cut two rebates at opposite sides of the stone. These are checked for twist (the failure of a surface to lie in a straight plane) and adjusted as required. They are joined by similar rebates on the two remaining sides. These marginal drafts (drafts worked along the edge of a stone) should now be straight and lie in the same plane. The quality of the finished work depends to a large extent on their completeness and accuracy.

For rock-faced ashlar, the stone in the centre is left standing or perhaps reduced a little with the walling hammer. For better class work, the waste is removed with the axe/adze, pick or punch followed by the claw-tool, 25 mm (1 in) chisel or boaster according

Figure 5.3 Examples of toolmarks on newly dressed stone: (a) Variations in axed work

(b) Pitched face with random punch marks

to the nature of the stone. These three tools are all used in a similar manner: successive drafts are worked across the face, moving away from the mason, the accuracy is judged by laying the straight edge between the marginal drafts. The other four surfaces (the back is normally left rough) are squared off from the marginal drafts, and are worked with a care appropriate to their function.

Where convex profiles are required, the surface is normally worked in a series of successively smaller drafts at a tangent to the curve, using whichever tool best suits the nature of the job. Curved work is normally finished by chiselling around the circumference, with the chisel held parallel to the axis.

Since at least the early medieval period the profiles of mouldings have been transferred to the stone with the aid of a wooden templet, or profile of the design. Surprisingly, the Roman masons seem not to have used the technique, as examination of the West Range of Site XI at Corbridge, England, makes clear. The stones there seem to have been cut roughly to size in the workshop and finally dressed when set in position. This method is exceedingly laborious and time consuming. This may account for the generally poor finish of the work, but it is certainly remarkable that so simple a device was not developed by such practical engineers.

The basic method of using templets is first to square the stone to the overall size demanded by the mouldings and then to apply the templet to each end of the stone in turn. The profile is marked on with a sharp point and the shape is worked through between the two ends, using a straight edge for straight mouldings and an edge cut to the correct radius for voussoirs, tracery and other curved work.

Columns, other than those cut on a lathe, are produced by the application of the same principle. If one long side is dressed flat and the two ends

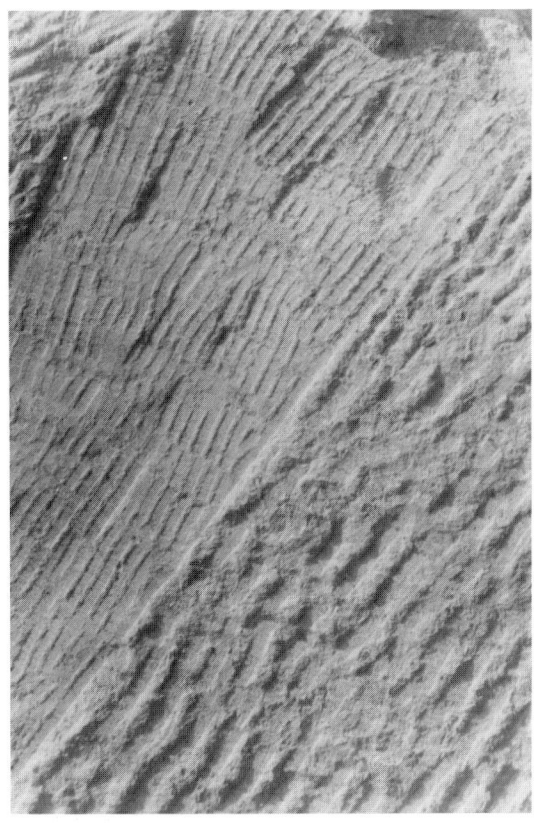

(c) Fine and coarse claw tooling

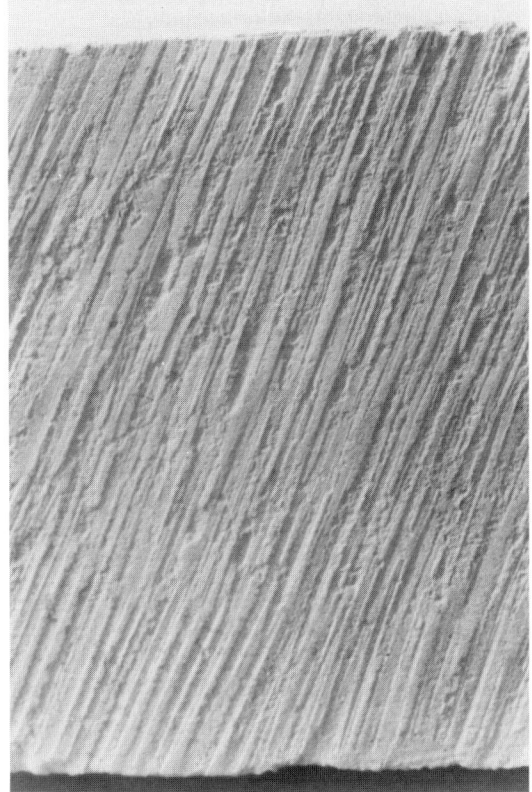

(d) Boasted ashlar

squared off from it and made parallel to each other, the centre point of the column may be marked on at each end. Circles of an appropriate size, depending on whether the column is to be a true cylinder or is to have an entasis, are scribed and the stone is worked in the manner described above.

If complex, stepped circular mouldings are to be worked, the basic method is the same, but the successive diameters are marked on the top bed of the stone, transferred to the appropriate point by squaring and worked in a series of sinkings.

Conclusion

There is much relevant information to be gained from close examination of the method of construction and the method of working and finishing the surfaces of building stones. However, unless the evidence is correctly understood and interpreted and unless it is accurately recorded and described, gross errors can be made and perpetuated by constant reference to the original mistake.

An appreciation of the methods of working stone will do much to avoid the use of meaningless generalizations and the over-confident assumptions sometimes made through ignorance and misconceptions.

Acknowledgements

Grateful thanks are due to Dr B. Dobson and Dr D.J. Breeze for their advice and encouragement over a long period. Chief amongst others who read early drafts, Mr A.D. Phillips and Dr B. Heywood made a number of valuable suggestions. Two colleagues, Messrs G. Butler and M.C. O'Connor, gave invaluable advice on certain technical aspects. The drawings were prepared by Mr P. Schofield of the York Minster Archaeology Office. Much of this chapter was first published in *Archaeologia Aeliana,*[9] hence the emphasis on Roman examples. All opinions are the author's and are not necessarily shared by those mentioned above.

References

1. Salzman, L.F., *Building in England*, p. 119, Oxford, 1952
2. Petrie, W.F.M., *Ancient Egypt*, pt. 2, pp. 33–39, 1930
3. Richter, G.M.A., *AJA*, xlvii, figure 8, 1943
4. Proceedings of the Society of Antiquaries of Scotland, 1952–1953 fig 6 E16
5. Bushe-Fox *Richborough iv*, plate lxi, no. 341, Oxford 1949
6. *Archaeologia*, lxxviii, Plate xxxii no. 50.
7. Collingwood, R.G. and Richmond, I.A., *Archaeology of Roman Britain*, Plate xx(u), Methuen, 1969
8. Blagg, T.F.C., 'The Roman stonemason', Britannia, **X**, 109–120
9. Hill, P.R., 'Stonework and the Archaeologist', *Archaeologia Aeliana*, **51X**

6

Earthquake damage to historic masonry structures

Alejandro Alva Balderrama

Introduction

It would be pretentious to try to summarize in a few pages the vast and complex problems created by earthquake damage to historic buildings. This chapter, therefore, will deal only with the broad aspects of these problems and with the concerns of the experts who are responsible for the protection of the built architectural heritage. It is hoped that the following considerations will be helpful in identifying current lines of action and research in soil dynamics and earthquake engineering, which are specifically related to the problems of earthquake damage to historic buildings.

Earthquakes

During earthquakes rocks will suddenly rupture and move, often violently, when stressed. Frequently rocks on one side of the rupture move relative to the rocks on the other side. As the rocks move the earth is shaken. Slight movements may give rise to disastrous earthquakes.

If the seismically active regions of the world are considered, it can be seen that much of the property susceptible to earthquake damage, or that which has already suffered damage, is of historic importance. The disasters of Buyin-Zava (Iran) 1962, Skopje (Yugoslavia) 1963, Varto (Turkey) and Lima (Peru) 1966, Mudurnu (Turkey) and Koyna (India) 1967, Dasht-e Bayaz (Iran) 1968, Banja Luka (Yugoslavia) 1969, Gediz (Turkey), Luzon (Philippines), Ancash (Peru) and Karnaveh (Iran) 1970, Ghir (Iran) and Managua (Nicaragua) 1972, Pattan (Pakistan) 1974, Friuli (Italy) and Antigua (Guatemala) 1976, Montenegro (Yugoslavia) 1979, Alta Irpinia (Italy) 1980 and El Asnam (Algeria) 1981, all affected historic structures.

Earthquake risk and historic buildings

In the conservation field, earthquake risk is one of the many decay factors encountered. It is, however, one of the least understood, perhaps because most of the related research is carried out on the performance of current or future construction, neglecting the world-wide problem of the existing building stock, which includes millions of historic properties in which people live and work.[1] The efforts put into the study and improvement of masonry construction are very limited, since this method of building tends to be regarded as out of date. Such an attitude, however, fails to consider the existing building stock and the very large number of structures which continue to be build of adobe, brick, or stone masonry. As little dynamic testing of masonry has been carried out so far, knowledge of the seismic response of this form of construction is based largely on field observations made after earthquakes. Such information does not provide satisfactory guidelines for strengthening unframed existing buildings (historic buildings are predominantly of this type), especially since so many different types of masonry exist. Much more dynamic testing is needed, in order to establish the principles of the seismic response of masonry structures in their various forms.[2]

Structural characteristics of historic buildings

The structural characteristics of historic buildings have great significance when considering their response to earthquake excitation. A primary and serious drawback in identifying the distinctive structural characteristics of historic buildings is the extremely variable quality of the materials and construction methods used. Except for timber, or timber-framed, buildings, most historic structures are in unframed masonry. They are built of a very wide range of materials including unburnt earths, bricks and stones, which are assembled with mud, or set in lime mortar or gypsum. Each of these materials varies widely in form and physical properties and is often used in combination with other materials, or in composite assemblies.

Masonry is brittle. It has a high mass and, therefore, a high inertial response to earthquakes. It is rigid and has low tensile and shear strengths, little ductility and a low capacity for bearing reversal loads and the redistribution of stresses.[2,3] In general, masonry structures are designed for static conditions and do not conform to the elastic theory.

From a limited viewpoint, the characteristics of historic buildings are disadvantageous to earthquake resistance. The poor performance of some forms of masonry has resulted in cautious attitudes that presume the inferiority of masonry materials and forms of construction. There are, however, several observations that contradict such a presumption.

Firstly, very little research has been done into the seismic response of masonry structures, whether reinforced or unreinforced, with or without a built-in frame. Most of the available knowledge is based largely on inferences from static loading tests.[2]

Secondly, field observations seldom mention the relationship between construction quality and the seismic structural performance of masonry buildings. Evidence has shown that there is a direct link between good quality construction and minimum damage. If properly used, masonry construction can have a reasonable resistance to earthquake movements. A common fallacy in field observations after earthquakes is the assumption that the performance of materials and structures is due to their inherent qualities.[4] It is often assumed that certain materials are, in themselves, either good or bad, durable or non-durable, resistant or non-resistant, strong or weak. In reality, these properties are relative and vary according to the conditions of exposure of the structure, the level of its loading and its capacity to re-distribute stresses, amongst other factors.

Historic buildings are not necessarily weak because they are old, or have been built with masonry. Some historic buildings, like some modern buildings, are weak because they are poorly constructed, or are subjected to abnormal stresses. From the engineering viewpoint, historic buildings have the useful characteristic of demonstrating all the inaccuracies in their construction, the possible mistakes made in assuming tolerances, and the unknown differences between the strengths of materials and structures.[5] All of these adverse factors can be identified and eliminated, one by one.

Strenghening historic buildings in earthquake areas

There are two main reasons for strengthening historic buildings in earthquake areas. The first and most important reason is the thousands of human lives at risk in these areas. The second reason is based on the recognition that architectural heritage is one of mankind's priceless and irreplaceable possessions and that its loss, through deterioration or disappearance, impoverishes the heritage of all the people of the world.[6] The first reason is incontestable. Fortunately the need to safeguard the world's architectural heritage is also becoming more and more widely recognized.[7]

For the strengthening of earthquake-damaged structures, however, new forms of earthquake engineering must still be developed. Buildings of this type have so rarely been strengthened after an earthquake that very few engineers, architects, or builders have any experience of how, or where, to begin.[1] As a consequence, strengthening is often carried out by using large masses of material and overdesigned structural members, which are, in most cases, incompatible with the character of the existing building. An historic building, as opposed to any other building, has values which go beyond the accommodation and facilities which it provides. In many cases these values derive from the physical characteristics of the historic building, including those of its structure. It is unfortunate that so often these structural characteristics are altered, destroying part of the value of the building.

Based on the previous considerations, certain conclusions can be drawn relating to the strengthening and repair of earthquake-damaged historic structures. These are:

1. The problems of strengthening, or repairing, historic buildings which have been damaged by earthquakes differ from those of new seismic design.
2. A plan for the strengthening or repair of this type of building should aim to alter the existing structure as little as possible, whilst enabling it to respond satisfactorily to seismic excitation. Satisfactory response does *not* go beyond obtaining reasonable security against damage in the event of an intense earthquake. The plan should consider traditional materials and techniques, as well as compatible modern technology.
3. There is an important body of reliable, observational data[8–10] concerning earthquake damaged masonry structures, making it possible, by informed comparisons of damage in various locations, to reach simple and logical generalizations about the causes and types of earthquake damage and to choose rational courses of action.

Figure 6.1 Kotor, Yugoslavia. Two historic masonry structures on the same site; one seriously damaged, the other virtually unaltered after the earthquake of 1979. Differing performance is related to the construction quality of each building

Figure 6.3 Ancona, Italy. A house in the historic centre of the city where reinforcement has been carried out by encasing the structure in a metal grid and spraying it with cement

Figure 6.2 Budva, Yugoslavia. A basically sound building which shows damage in one of its weakest points: a curved surface, insufficiently bonded and punctured by the apse window

4. Experience of earthquakes has shown that there is a direct relationship between the extent of the damage and the condition of the structural components and the quality of the construction of the damaged building.[11]

The building's original capacity to absorb seismic stresses is related to the condition of its structural components. This should be established. The quality of the construction of the damaged building is an important factor. Records of earthquake damage[8] provide evidence relating the extent of damage to such construction factors as the quality of the building's masonry units, the proportions of the single units, the bond between assembly elements, the connection of orthogonal walls, the quality of workmanship in the laying of the masonry courses, the ratio of height to base of the structure, the distribution and position of openings in the masonry walls, the connection between structural elements which should function as a complete unit, the characteristics of embedded structural elements, the appropriate use of partition walls, the characteristics

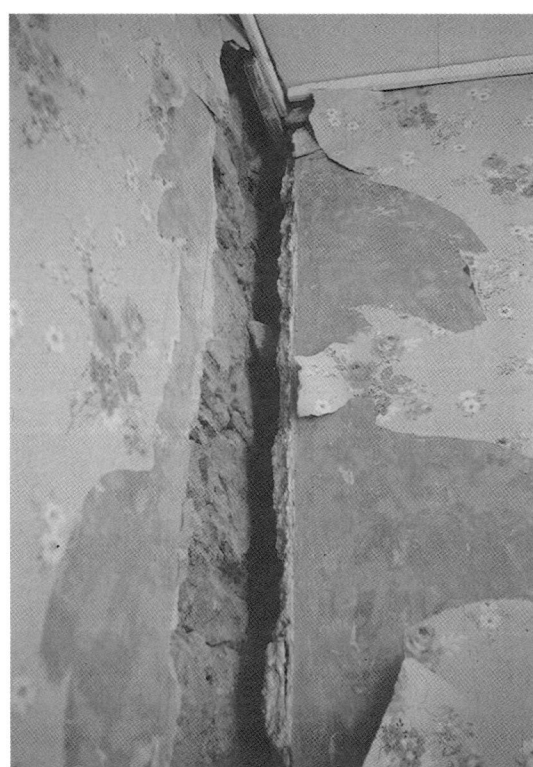

Figure 6.4 Kotor, Yugoslavia. Details of the masonry structures illustrated in Figure 6.1 showing the relationship between quality of construction and earthquake damage

Figure 6.5 Tito, Southern Italy. Interior and exterior view of a stone masonry house where poor connection between orthogonal walls has led to the damage illustrated

Figure 6.6 Budva, Yugoslavia. A situation in which the placements of apertures combined with the complete lack of lintels has led to collapse

Figure 6.7 Tito, Southern Italy. A situation in which a properly embedded lintel of adequate length has prevented earthquake damage

Figure 6.8 Tito, Southern Italy. A section of a damaged wall where collapse has resulted from the poor quality of the mortar

and condition of foundations, the soil–structure interaction, the quality of the mortar used, the quality of past repair works and the effects of these factors upon each other. The observation of inaccuracies in any of these factors can lead to the identification of potentially weak points in the structure, or, where some failure has occurred, to a reliable interpretation of the exposed earthquake damage. The progressive and careful elimination of the identified weaknesses, without elaborate strengthening procedures, will certainly provide the structure with an improved capacity to withstand future seismic events.

The approach proposed to repairs or strengthening is not a new one. Traditional principles of analysis are frequently overlooked by those seeking new techniques in the repair of earthquake-damaged historic structures. However, such an oversight seriously limits the validity of any diagnosis and any solution proposed

Figure 6.9 Kotor, Yugoslavia. Failure resulting from the quality of past repair and modifications, in this case the introduction of a large opening on the second floor

Figure 6.10 Arequipa, Peru. Buildings of traditional technique and materials which respond, in their architectural form and structure, to an understanding of seismic disturbance (lowered bell towers, self-buttressed walls, small and limited apertures, solid masonry assembly)

Figure 6.11 Tito, Southern Italy. The demolition of the Cathedral after the earthquake of 1980

Conclusions

In recent years historic monuments, or whole groups of old houses, have been completely and systematically demolished, or seriously altered, after earthquake. This destruction of the architectural heritage could be avoided with a better understanding of the performance of historic structures by those who are responsible for them.

Decisions regarding the strengthening or repair of historic structures should result from an informed analysis of earthquake risk and damage. Each type of damage should determine the selection of repair methods, based on the consideration of the condition of the building, the resources available (funds, materials and craft skills, for example), the value of the building and the prevailing conservation philosophy.

Completed repair work should be monitored, to assess its performance under any further seismic stresses. It is equally important to co-ordinate all the available experience and observational data concerning earthquake damage to historic structures.

Priority should be given to special research on aspects of the design and construction of existing buildings, related to their pre-earthquake and post-earthquake condition. In the same way, efforts should be made to promote special research in related fields, such as soil dynamics and earthquake engineering, which is specifically relevant to the problems of earthquake damage to historic structures.

Acknowledgements

The author wishes to thank Professor Eiichi Kuribayashi (Toyohashi University of Technology), and Professor Eng. Fabio Casciati (University of Pavia). He is also indebted to his colleagues Ms Cathleen Malmström and Ms Jeanne Marie Teutonico for their suggestions and criticism, and most grateful for the invaluable help of Mme Marie Christine Uginet, Head of the Documentation Centre of the ICCROM.

References

1. Moran, T. 'Strengthening earthquake-damaged structures', p. 234, in *The assessment and mitigation of earthquake risk*, Unesco, Paris, 1978
2. Dowrick, D.J., *Earthquake resistant design. A manual for engineers and architects*, p. 253, Wiley, London, 1977
3. Sachanski, S., 'Buildings: codes, materials, design', p. 158, in *The assessment and mitigation of earthquake risk*. Unesco, Paris, 1978
4. Baker, M.C., 'Introduction to the problem of cracks, movements and joints in buildings', p. 1, in *Cracks, Movements and Joints in Buildings*, Record of the DBR Building Science Seminar, National Research Council of Canada, Ottawa, 1972
5. Beckmann, P., *Third Mission to Kotor, Montenegro (YU)*, p.2, ICCROM/Unesco, Rome, 1982
6. Unesco, *Operational Guidelines for the Implementation of the World Heritage Convention*, p.1, Unesco-Intergovernmental Committee for the Protection of the World Cultural and Natural Heritage, Paris, 1977
7. Unesco, 'The Cultural Heritage and Natural Disasters', in *World Cultural Heritage Information Bulletin*, **15**, 5, Division of Cultural Heritage, Paris, 1980
8. CRYRZA, 'Peru: practical adobe construction with emphasis on earthquake resistant techniques', in *Adobe News*, **12**, 5–11; **13**, 10–11; **15**, 10–13, 1977
9. Benedetti, D., 'Riparazione e consolidamento degli edifici in muratura', in *Costruzioni in Zona Sismica*, Masson Italia, Milano, 1981
10. University of New Mexico (ed.), *Proceedings of the International Workshop, Earthen Buildings in Seismic Areas*, The National Science Foundation, New Mexico, 1981
11. Ambraseys, N.N., *Engineering Seismology*, p. 59, Imperial College of Science and Technology, London, 1975
12. Feilden, B.M., *Conservation of Historic Buildings*, Ch. 8, Butterworths, London, 1982

7

The repair and remedial treatment of the East Block Parliament Buildings, Ottawa, Canada

Keith Blades and John Stewart

Introduction

The East Block of the Parliament Buildings occupies a unique position in Canada's history. Built between 1859 and 1867, it has housed the offices of the Governor General and fifteen of seventeen Prime Ministers. Until recently, the Privy Council and Cabinet met periodically in the building. In 1974, the East Block was vacated to allow the Department of Public Works to start an ambitious programme of repair and restoration to the building. In April 1982, with the interior work completed, Her Majesty Queen Elizabeth II re-opened the building to serve once again as offices for Parliamentarians from the House of Commons and the Senate.

Following the Act of Union of 1840, Kingston, on Lake Ontario, was named the capital of Upper and Lower Canada. However, within three years, the capital had moved to Montreal. After riots and burning of the legislative buildings in 1849, the government resorted to a system of rotation, whereby the capital alternated every four years between Toronto and Quebec City. When Queen Victoria announced in 1858 that Ottawa was to be the permanent seat of government for the Province of Canada, the decision was met with considerable surprise because at that time Ottawa was little more than a frontier lumber town.

The Department of Public Works moved quickly to announce a competition, with designs to be submitted by architects for three public buildings: a parliamentary building, where the Provincial Parliament would sit, a library and two departmental buildings, to house various principal offices and all the civil service of the time, consisting of fifteen government departments.

The buildings were constructed between 1859 and 1867, in accordance with the competition requirements, 'in a plain, substantial style of architecture, the masonry to be coursed hammer dressed, with neatly pointed joints, cut stone quoins, window dressings and entablatures'[1], in a style referred to as 'Civil gothic' by Augustus Stent and Thomas Laver, the architects whose design was selected for the Departmental Buildings.

Of the three parliamental buildings, only the East Block remains in a form similar to that of the 1870s. The Centre Block, the Houses of Parliament, was destroyed by fire in 1916. It was subsequently rebuilt, although the octagonal library to the rear of the building was saved. The West Block was damaged by fire in 1899 and, while the original fabric remains, the interior has undergone extensive modernization. The East Block programme, begun in 1974, has restored the interior of the building as it was in 1880. Externally the consolidation and repair of the masonry is being carried out under a phased programme. This chapter deals with the first phase of that masonry programme, which was completed as part of the overall restoration project.

Construction

The construction of the East Block reflects the changing technology and materials available at the time. The building incorporated a trussed roof of heavy timbers, under a slate covering, with iron cresting. The present copper roof was installed in 1948. 'Fox and Barret' fireproof floors, consisting of wrought iron joists with a lightweight concrete infill, replaced the log floors of the original design and bear on solid masonry walls. Foundation walls 1200 mm (4 ft) thick, formed of an inner and outer skin of squared rubble masonry, with a rubble filled core, bear directly on bedrock. Above basement level, the external masonry, approximately 525 mm (20 in) thick, is tied through a dry, ventilated cavity to a one brick thick inner skin with iron straps and bond-stones.

Exterior stonework is a combination of rock-faced, squared rubble walling, known locally as 'Scotch work' because many of the stonemasons had emigrated from Scotland. Dressed ashlar was selected for the quoins, surrounds to openings and decorative features. The rubble stone is a local sandstone and the ashlar is a fine to medium grained siliceous sandstone from the Berea Formation in Ohio, USA. Interior walls and the core material of the basement walls are a compact, crystalline limestone, local to the Ottawa area.

Programme of repairs

Initial surveys indicated that there were three areas of concern which would require more detailed study: the third floor roof space, where many truss members were missing; the basement walls, which appeared in poor condition because of deteriorated or missing pointing; and the southwest tower, where large cracks and movement of the stonework suggested a serious problem might exist.

Repairs at roof level

In the 1890s previously unoccupied space was converted to offices, in response to the demand for accommodation for the ever expanding civil service. Dormer windows were inserted in the roof and numerous roof truss diagonals, columns and bottom chord members were cut, or removed, from the mansard roof trusses, resulting in fractures through the eaves masonry caused by thrust from the spreading roof. Selected replacements and reinforcement of members has restored the integrity of the structural system, which is now tied into a reinforced concrete ring beam, dowelled into the eaves masonry.

Masonry repairs

A detailed examination of the fabric of the East Block revealed that, at ground level, the exposed foundation walls below the plinth course were in poor condition. Open joints could be seen in many areas where the hard, cement-rich, projecting ribbon pointing had either failed through shrinkage, or had been lost through frost action after moisture had penetrated the joint. It was found that maintenance of the pointing had been a constant problem since completion of the building. John Page, Chief

Engineer for the Department of Public Works, wrote in 1867 in his report on the buildings, 'the roof projections are so small, and there being no eaves-troughs, the water falls directly on the basement walls, and the alternate action of wet and frost takes out the pointing, which must be renewed from time to time'. Ottawa winter temperatures often dip below $-20\,^{\circ}$C ($-4\,^{\circ}$F) and sometimes reach $-30\,^{\circ}$C ($-22\,^{\circ}$F). Many winter days are clear with bright sun and on such occasions many freeze/thaw cycles occur, particularly in south and west facing masonry walls.

Internally, moisture staining and rusting of the iron floor joists where they bear into the foundation wall suggested that water was passing through the full thickness of the walls. Trial opening up revealed that the rubble core was a poorly consolidated mixture of stone rubble and a weak lime:sand grout. As a result, voids were present from the time of construction. Water penetrating the wall through defective pointing had leached out some of the grout, and in certain places settlements of the core material, in conjunction with frost action, had caused bulging of the outer skin of stonework. In many areas the facework was found to be bedded in wet sand, indicating that repointing contracts over the years had specified only replacement of a superficial bead of pointing, without any attention to the consolidation of the bedding material (*Figure 7.1*).

Trial excavations revealed a stable foundation below ground level, with stepped footings bearing directly on bedrock, but confirmed the absence of a drainage system. In periods of heavy rain and particularly during the spring thaw, a build-up of ground water against the foundation walls led to a rising damp problem in basement rooms.

It was proposed that the foundation walls should be grouted to fill the voids in the core material and to restore the structural integrity of the walls. This involved completing the repairs and the repointing before starting the grouting operation. It was also proposed to install a drainage system at the level of the footings. The excavation necessary for the installation of weeping tiles meant that the foundation walls were to be exposed right down to the bedrock. With the walls accessible externally, the difficulty of having to grout down to the footings from inside the building was removed. Accordingly, contracts for the masonry repairs and grouting ran concurrently with the installation of the drainage system, enabling grouting of the footings to take place from the exterior (*Figure 7.2*).

The mix found to have the best flow characteristics, a cement:pulverized fuel ash (PFA):expansive admixture combination, was injected through plastic tubing set in 25 mm (1 in) diameter holes, drilled approximately 750 mm (30 in) into the 1200 mm (4 ft) thick wall on a 450 mm (18 in) staggered grid.

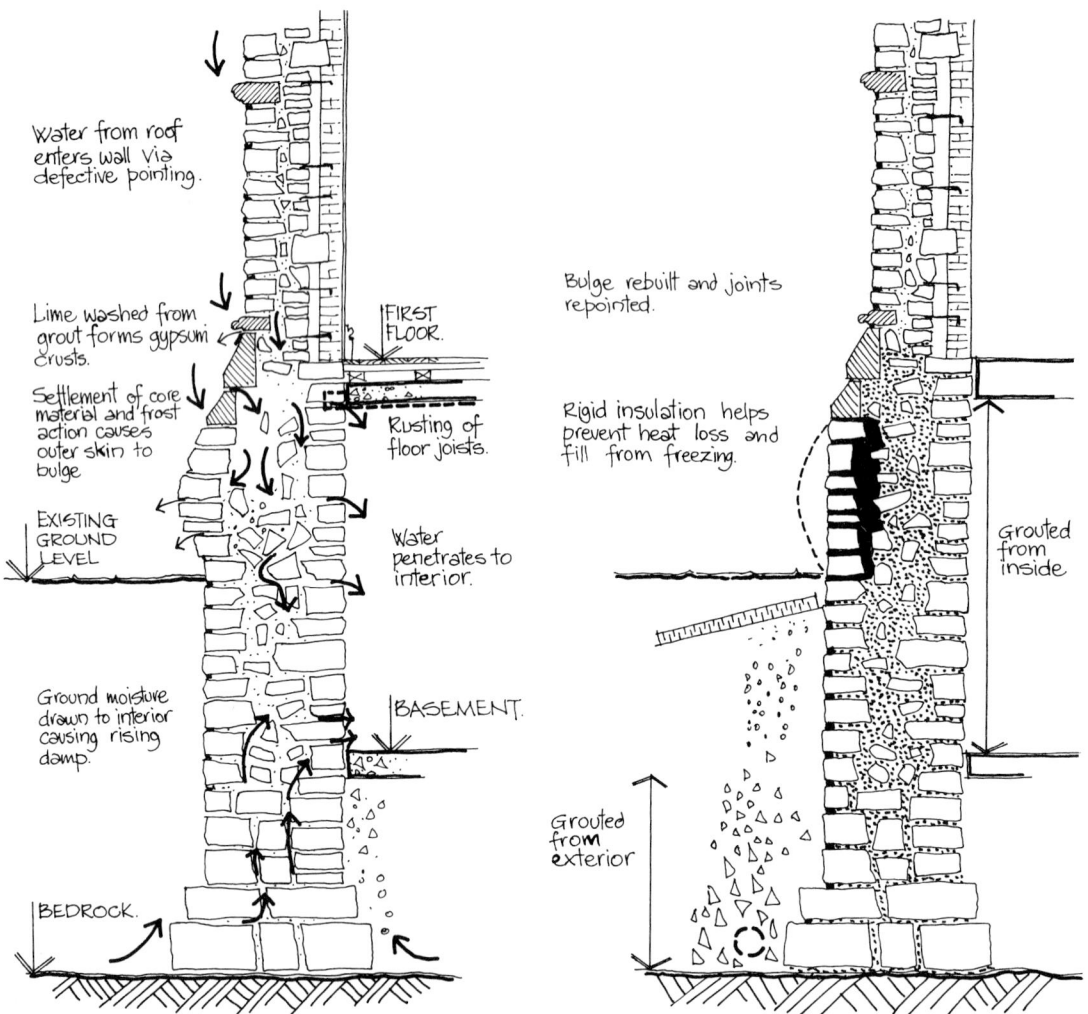

Figure 7.1 Typical section through basement walls before repair

Figure 7.2 Section through basement walls following repair

The initial pumping pressure was quite low (69 kPa), but following careful monitoring this was increased to 276 kPa without any problem and was adopted for the whole programme. In total, some 30 cubic metres (39 cubic yards) of grout was placed in the foundation walls, representing an actual grout take of 8% compared to the initial estimate of 10%. For sample cores taken, it is estimated that only 0.5% voiding remains in the walls.

The areas scheduled for rebuilding were carefully taken down, the position of all stones recorded on survey drawings and the rear face of each block identified with a water-based paint, to ensure the same pattern of bonding on rebuilding. The core material was raked back until sound mortar was encountered. It was filled solid in the traditional manner on rebuilding, with the addition of 12 mm (0.5 in) diameter brass dowels, randomly placed.

All the joints to the exposed foundation wall were raked out to a minimum of 50 mm (2 in) and repointed with a 1:1:6 cement:lime:sand mix, with the addition of a small amount of latex to the mixing water, to provide additional frost resistance. Where the bedding material was found to be in poor condition, deep tamping was carried out or individual blocks were reset.

The replacement of damaged stone was limited, because of the difficulty in obtaining suitable material at the time. The Ohio quarries are still operative, but only small quantities of the sandstone could be

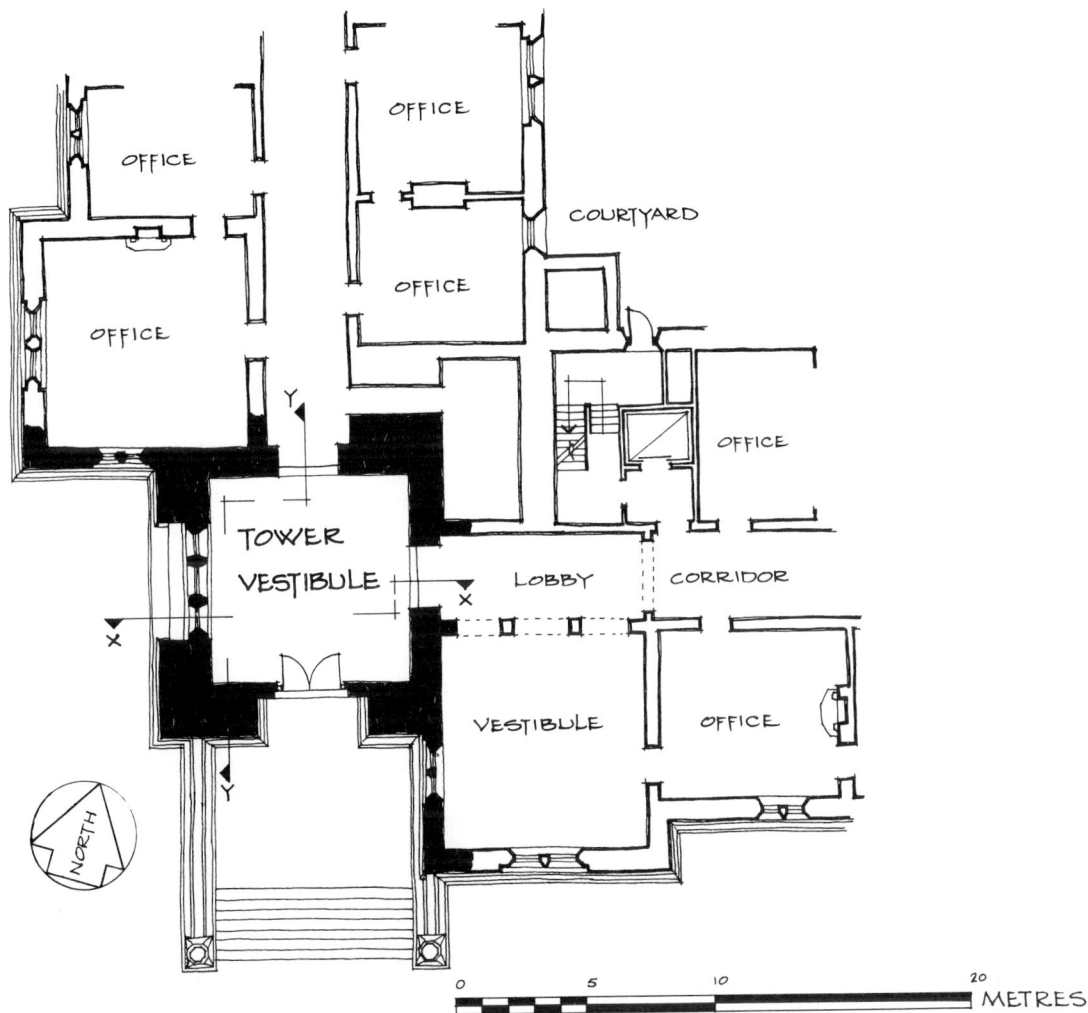

Figure 7.3 Part first floor plan at south-west corner of East Block Parliment Buildings, Ottawa

obtained for repairs to the window surrounds. The local Nepean sandstone quarries, which have supplied stone for many public buildings in the Ottawa area, have been inoperative for many years. It is hoped to re-open some faces in order to obtain the bed depths required for repairs to the plinth courses.

The south-west tower

The south-west tower is the dominant architectural feature of the East Block and, until the completion of the Centre Block in the 1920s, was the tallest structure on Parliament Hill. Movement, large crack patterns and spalling of stonework, not apparent

elsewhere on the building, gave rise to some concern. A separate study was therefore commissioned to determine the causes and effects of the damage to the tower masonry.

Construction

The tower is constructed of massive load-bearing masonry walls, which support a first floor entrance vestibule, a balcony at the second floor level, a masonry vaulted ceiling, three intermediate floors, a copper-clad timber roof and decorative wrought-iron cresting (*Figures 7.3, 7.4* and *7.5*). The masonry rises some 50 metres (160 ft) above ground and it is a further 20 metres (65 ft) to the top of the

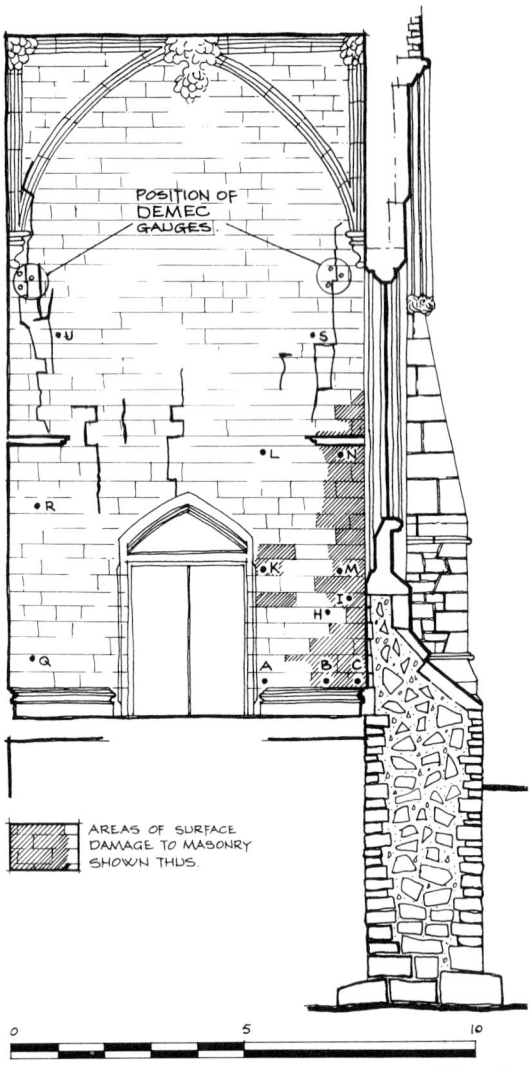

POSITION OF
DEMEC
GAUGES.

•U

•S

•L   •N

•R

•K   •M
                I•
        H•
        H•

•Q   A   B C

AREAS OF SURFACE
DAMAGE TO MASONRY
SHOWN THUS.

0   5   10

METRES

Figure 7.4 Section on X–X in Figure 7.3: elevation of south wall

decorative cresting. The foundation walls are 2.4 metres (8 ft) thick and bear directly on bedrock. The total weight of the tower is estimated to exceed 5500 tonnes.

Externally on the west and south faces, between the first and third floor levels, arches spring from buttresses, tapering from 2.4 to 1.5 metres (8–5 ft) thick, to enclose infill panels 750 mm (30 in) thick. Window and door openings, framed with secondary arches, penetrate these panels. The interior ashlar is Ohio sandstone, varying in thickness from 150 to 300 mm (6–12 in).

Structural problems

Surveys of the tower masonry identified movement and cracking in the large blocks of the raking buttresses externally, and extensive cracking to the interior walls between the second floor balcony and the top of the vaulted ceiling. These internal crack patterns to both the south and west walls closely followed the lines of the junctions between the exterior buttresses and the infill panels. To record movements, a two stage programme of monitoring was set up, using glass tell-tales to act as a visual indication of movement and 'Demec' studs to provide accurate measurements. Recordings were taken over an eighteen month period to ensure that seasonal variations were covered.

Results from the monitoring showed that the cracks were continuing to open at a rate of 0.25 mm (0.01 in) per annum. Comparing this rate of movement to the total widths of cracks suggests that movement had been taking place for at least 20 years. Due to the construction of the tower, differential settlement was to be expected since stress levels from concentrations of loading in the tower buttresses and infill panels varied considerably. It was assumed that voiding and settlement of the core material had also occurred and that this, coupled with moisture penetration and freeze-thaw action, was the primary factor responsible for the movement of the blocks. As for the remainder of the building, repointing of external masonry and grouting of the interior of the wall was recommended to stabilize the tower, with a note of caution that the condition would be improved, but not eliminated. Grouting of the two outer buttresses was carried out from within the adjacent offices, but for the central buttress it was necessary to core the ashlar wall to provide grouting points.

When the structural repairs were completed, attention was turned to the spalling ashlar of the internal masonry of the tower. Earlier analysis work had identified the presence of soluble salts on the building. Under protective mouldings (that is, areas not regularly washed by rain) gypsum crusts had formed on the surface of the sandstone and eventually caused spalling as crystallization and ice lensing detached the crust. These salts most likely were formed from leached calcium carbonate from the lime:sand mortar, in reaction with dilute sulphuric acid carried in rain and snow. For many years, Ottawa suffered from sulphate pollution from a pulp mill situated within one kilometre of Parliament Hill.

In the south-west tower the pattern of spalling was different. The decay of blocks around the entrance could be attributed to the practice of heavy winter salting, but not the efflorescence on the walls above the second floor balcony. The original intention was to repaint the interior of the south-west tower, in

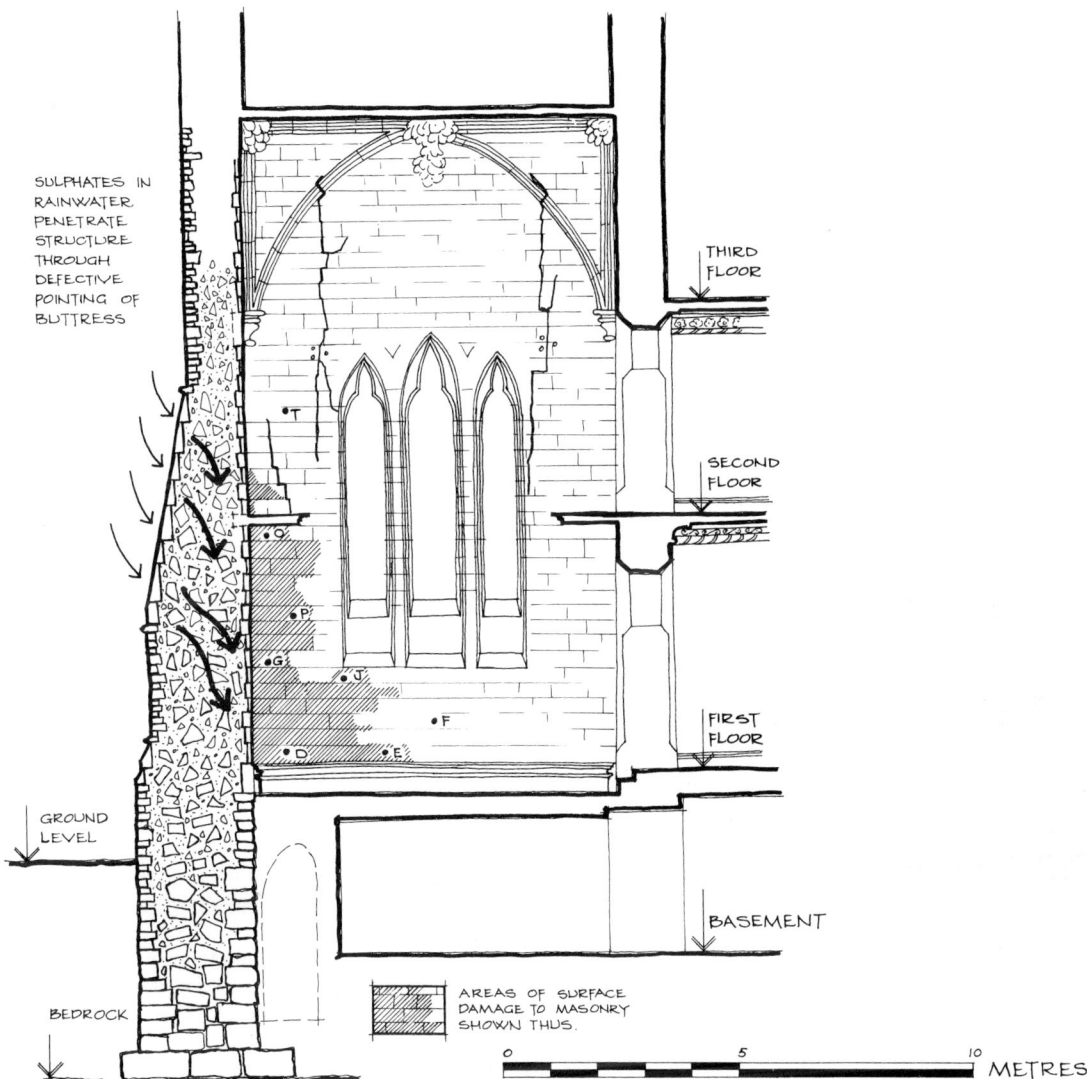

SULPHATES IN
RAINWATER
PENETRATE
STRUCTURE
THROUGH
DEFECTIVE
POINTING OF
BUTTRESS

THIRD
FLOOR

SECOND
FLOOR

FIRST
FLOOR

GROUND
LEVEL

BASEMENT

BEDROCK

AREAS OF SURFACE
DAMAGE TO MASONRY
SHOWN THUS.

0   5   10
METRES

Figure 7.5 Section on Y–Y in Figure 7.3: elevation of west wall

order to link the colour schemes of the adjoining corridors. However, the continuous spalling and efflorescence determined that the original ashlar and ribbed vaulting should be exposed while a more detailed study of the nature and extent of the problem and methods for removing the salts was undertaken.

This involved a general examination of the structure to see if the damage was related to any specific architectural feature; the sampling and identification of the efflorescence and subflorescence to determine the salt responsible for the damage; the core sampling of the walls and the analysis of the cores to find the depth and location of the salt in the walls; and the monitoring of the relative humidity in the walls to determine their dampness. This study provided information on the cause of the damage and should now allow a rational restoration scheme to be planned.

General examination

Internally, the damaged stone (*Figure 7.6*) was spalled and covered with efflorescence. As much as 25 mm (1 in) of surface had been lost, and in general the surface was weak and friable. This was consistent

Figure 7.6 Area of damage inside south-west tower

with salt damage resulting from subflorescence. The damaged areas were localized on the two walls of the south-west corner (*Figures 7.4* and *7.5*). In all other areas, the ashlar appeared to be in good condition.

Examination of the outside of the tower revealed only a minor amount of salt damage to the stone, with some black crust and efflorescence evident. There was, however, obvious physical damage due to cracking of the stone and missing pointing. This was particularly apparent on the sloping portion of the buttress at the south-west corner. These open joints in the masonry allowed direct penetration of water into areas of wall associated with internal damage.

The general examination indicated that the internal ashlar had been damaged by salt and that this was localized in areas associated with the easy ingress of water through open joints and cracks in the external masonry (*Figures 7.4* and *7.5*). The association of these two factors indicated that deterioration of the interior resulted from the exterior conditions. The localization of the problem in one corner also tended to rule out rising damp as the source of damage.

Identification of salt

Samples of efflorescence adhering to the surface of the stone were taken from several locations inside the tower. These were examined with the micro-analyser of a scanning electron microscope (SEMEDX). This showed the presence of the elements silicon (from the sandstone), sodium and sulphur. Elements such as oxygen, with an atomic number less than eleven, are not detected by this technique. No chlorine was detected, indicating that the damage was not caused by either sodium or calcium chloride from de-icing salt.

The efflorescence was characterized further by X-ray powder diffraction. This identified the efflorescence as anhydrous sodium sulphate (Na_2SO_4). This agreed with the microprobe results, which showed the presence of both sodium and sulphur.

Samples of spalling stone were removed from the damaged area inside the tower. These were broken in cross section and examined by SEMEDX. *Figure 7.7* shows a good example of the type of subflorescence found. The large crystals show the presence of silicon and are the quartz grains from the sandstone. The small crystals filling the pore in the centre of the field show the presence of sodium and sulphur and are sodium sulphate crystals. Thus sodium sulphate is being deposited in the pores of the sandstone.

Core analysis

The presence of sodium sulphate at the surface of the stone was a strong indication that the walls contained reservoirs of this salt in their cores. This, however, was not a firm conclusion; the sulphate may only be a surface phenomenon. If it is, then the problem of its removal is much simpler than if the sulphate is distributed throughout the walls. To determine the distribution within the walls and to help to identify the source of the sulphate, twenty-one core samples were taken with dry diamond drills from the points indicated in *Figures 7.4* and *7.5*. Wet drilling would have removed soluble salts. These cores were analysed along their lengths, to determine their sulphate and chloride content (*see Annex*).

The mean soluble sulphate content of the two walls was 0.07%, compared with a mean soluble chloride content of 0.007%. This reinforced the conclusion, reached from the study of efflorescence, that chloride de-icing salts were not a source of damage. Calculating the mean value for the sulphate concentrations of the cores from damaged and undamaged areas showed that the damaged areas had a higher average sulphate concentration than the undamaged areas. A plot of the mean level of soluble sulphate for these two groups is shown in *Figure 7.8*.

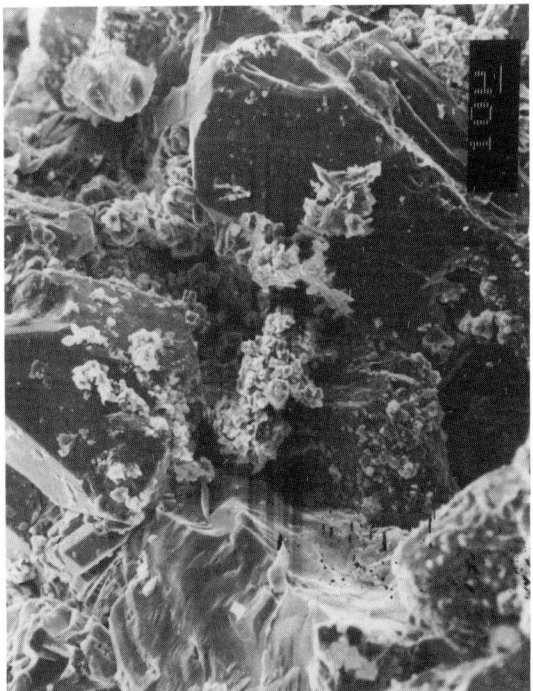

Figure 7.7 Scanning electron micrograph of fresh break surface of damaged ashlar (× 350)

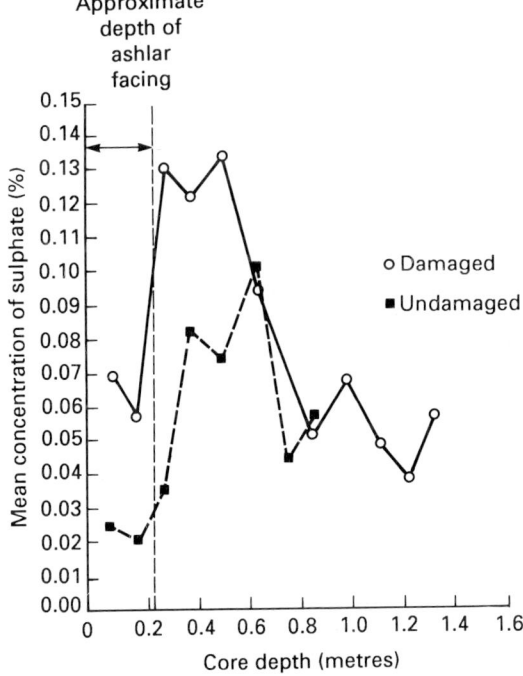

Figure 7.8 Mean levels of sulphate in cores

Dampness in walls

One method for measuring the dampness in a wall tried was the drilling and gravimetric technique.[2] Due to the heat generated by the coring operation in this method, samples were removed from the wall hot and steaming. Such samples were not suitable for any reliable gravimetric analysis of water. Conductivity measurements on the surface suffered from interference from the salts acting as electrolytes. Impedance measurements and thermal cooling techniques were not practicable due to lack of equipment.

As an alternative, three relative humidity probes were placed in the core holes at 250 mm (10 in) depth. This method does not tell the absolute water content of the wall, but it does give an indication of the relative humidity found within the walls.

These probes were left in place and monitored daily for a period of eighteen months. The results are shown for the two overlapping winter periods in *Figure 7.9*. Also shown is the relative humidity of the foyer air if it were cooled to the wall temperature found at the 250 mm (10 in) depth. The last number, RH_1, is derived from:

$$\% \ RH_1 = \% \ RH \times \frac{p_1}{p_2}$$

where %RH = relative humidity of foyer

p_1 = equilibrium vapour pressure of water at temperature of foyer

p_2 = equilibrium vapour pressure of water at temperature of wall

Figure 7.9 shows that the wall still has a moisture content higher than would be expected if it were in equilibrium with the foyer and, hence, is still damp. Furthermore, natural drying for an eighteen month period has done little to reduce the relative humidity in the walls.

Discussion of the wall study

To design a rational restoration plan, the examination of the walls was undertaken to answer three questions:

1. What is the nature of the damage to the stone?
2. What is its cause and source?
3. What factors influence the damage?

The spalling of the ashlar is a typical case of salt damage due to the crystallization and hydration of salt. The salt that is causing the damage is sodium sulphate. This conclusion is based on the fact that large quantities of sodium sulphate efflorescence and subflorescence were found in the walls and the damaged areas have a higher concentration of soluble sulphate than the undamaged areas. The

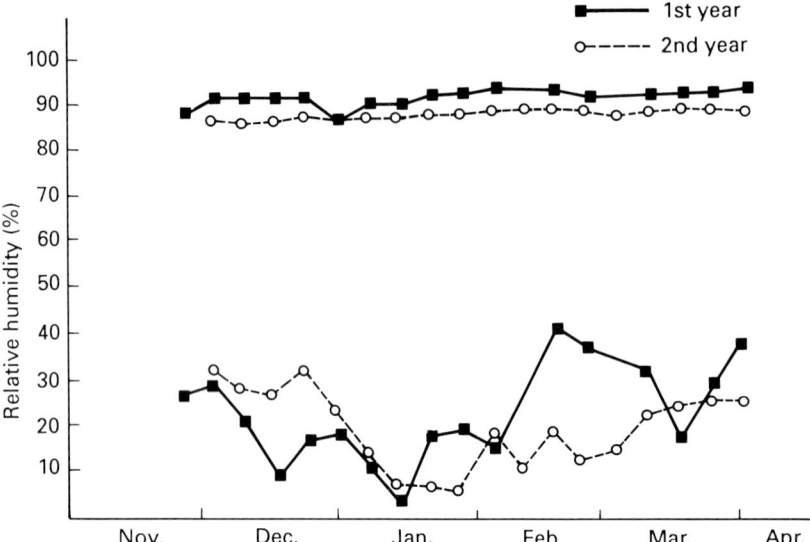

Figure 7.9 Top: Weekly averages of relative humidities at
250 mm depth within the walls. Bottom: Weekly averages
of relative humidities in the foyer, adjusted to the wall
temperature at 250 mm depth

problem is made more serious as the salt contamination is not localized on the surface. Instead, it is distributed throughout the wall, with a large reservoir of soluble sulphate at a depth of 200–750 mm (8–30 in) in both the damaged and undamaged areas (*Figure 7.8*). This means that, while the spalling is a surface phenomenon, the salt causing it is located deep with the walls.

The damaged ashlar inside the tower is associated with two factors:

1. A source of moisture from deteriorated external pointing.
2. A higher soluble sulphate concentration than found in the rest of the wall.

From these two facts, several sequences to explain the damage are possible. One such sequence would be the following: rain-water enters the masonry on the buttress and, as the presence of gypsum crusts on the exterior facade would suggest, this rain-water is polluted with sulphur oxides. The water leaches sulphate from the mortar in the masonry. This sulphate and the sulphate already in the rain-water travel in combination with sodium ions from the masonry and form sodium sulphate on the internal surfaces associated with the buttress. This sequence is sufficient to explain the association of the damage with both the damaged pointing and the higher than average sulphate content. However, the main facts are that the pointing has deteriorated and must be

repaired; that the internal walls are suffering from spalling caused by salt damage; and that this salt is located throughout the depth of the wall.

The process by which sodium sulphate damages stones involves the formation of subflorescence. Sodium sulphate forms two hydrates,[3] the metastable heptahydrate ($Na_2SO_4 \cdot 7H_2O$) and the decahydrate ($Na_2SO_4 \cdot 10H_2O$). Of these two, only the decahydrate is stable and so is most probably the one that forms in the walls. Under sufficiently damp conditions, the sodium sulphate in the interior of the walls picks up moisture and forms a solution of sodium sulphate. If the moisture content of the walls exceeds the critical level (the level above which liquid water will move in the pores of the stone), the salt solution will migrate in all directions until it reaches a barrier. When it reaches the surface, the solution can travel no further and will start to evaporate and deposit salt as efflorescence. This, while unsightly, will do little damage to the stone, because the salt forms on the surface. However, when evaporation takes place a few millimetres behind the surface, subflorescence occurs.

Subflorescence is the growth of crystals in the stone pores. Initially, tiny crystals form, which then draw more salt from the solution and grow until they reach the pore walls. At this stage, the crystals still have a tendency to grow and exert pressure on the stone. When this pressure is greater than the mechanical strength of the stone, it will spall.

Crystallization pressure by sodium sulphate is one means by which stone is destroyed. The other is hydration pressure. The subflorescence found in the walls was anhydrous sodium sulphate, which is formed from the drying out of the decahydrate crystals and from the evaporation of the salt solution. As long as the salt stays as the anhydride, it should do no further damage to the stone. However, above a certain relative humidity, the anhydrous salt transforms into the decahydrate. The decahydrate has a volume 200% greater than the anhydride (reference 4, p.B-140) and, as such, the conversion to the hydrate exerts a hydration pressure on the stone pores, with subsequent spalling. When the relative humidity is over 93% at 20 °C (reference 4, p.E-40), the decahydrate absorbs water from the air and goes into solution. Thus, even without liquid water present, a salt solution forms in the pores. As the relative humidity drops below 93%, recrystallization occurs, with more spalling. Thus, three factors are involved in the destruction of stone by sodium sulphate:

1. Deposition of sodium sulphate subflorescence from liquid water.
2. Conversion of the decahydrate to the anhydrate and back again, as the relative humidity cycles around the conversion point.
3. Deliquescence of the decahydrate at 93% relative humidity, with subsequent recrystallization when the relative humidity drops again.

The first factor should stop after the source of liquid water, i.e. the damaged pointing, is eliminated. The second, that of hydration–dehydration, will stop when the relative humidity in the first few centimetres drops below the relative humidity at which conversion occurs.

This relative humidity is dependent on temperature and can be calculated from equilibrium vapour pressure data,[5] using the Clausius–Clapeyron equation. The calculated values are shown in *Table 7.1*. Damage will continue to occur until the relative humidity in the wall drops below the 70–80% range. However, the data from wall relative humidity monitoring (*Figure 7.9*) shows this is not likely to happen in the near future.

The study of the walls has indicated that the spalling is due to the action of sodium sulphate. This has been transported to the damaged area by water entering from deteriorated pointing on the outside buttress. This water is also responsible for the high level of sulphate in the damaged area, because it is polluted with sulphur oxides. The salt is located throughout the walls and is not just a surface deposit. The spalling will continue to occur for as long as the walls remain damp enough to have a relative humidity greater than the conversion point of sodium sulphate to its hydrate.

Table 7.1 Relative humidities at which the reaction $Na_2SO_4 \cdot 10H_2O \rightarrow Na_2SO_4 + 10H_2O$ occurs at selected temperatures.*

Temp. (°C)	RH (%)
24	85
23	84
22	83
21	82
20	80
19	79
18	78
17	77
16	76
15	75
14	74
13	73
12	72
11	71
10	70

*Derived from equilibrium vapour pressure data using the Clausius–Clapeyron equation:

$$\log P = \frac{-\Delta H_{vap}}{2.303\, RT} + \text{constant}$$

where P is the equilibrium vapour pressure at temperature T, ΔH_{vap} is the heat of vaporization, and R is the gas constant.

Conclusions

At the time that the analysis work was undertaken, it was felt that the tower masonry could be restored and stabilized through a programme of poulticing to remove, or to appreciably lower the level of, the salts in the wall, coupled with replacement of some of the more damaged blocks. However, the results have shown that the situation is more complex and not so easily resolved. It is recognized that grouting the tower walls may well have compounded the situation by activating dormant salts deep in the wall, and has probably increased the time necessary for the masonry to dry out completely. Because the tower vestibule is the principal entrance to the building, it is still desirable to consider a programme of repair and replacement of the internal masonry.

Whilst replacement would be feasible, new stone blocks would quickly become contaminated by the salts behind the ashlar face. Coating the backs of new stones to prevent the transfer of salts would drive salt-laden moisture to seek other surfaces in the currently undamaged areas of the tower from which to evaporate and crystallize. Poulticing most probably would reduce salt levels in the surface layers, but could not hope to pull salts from deep within the walls.

For poulticing to be effective, thorough saturation of the wall with water is essential to ensure that all of the salts are put into solution. This, however, seems contrary to the overall desire to stabilize conditions by drying out the wall.

A more appropriate solution then would be to consider a longer-term poultice or render designed to act sacrificially, but avoiding the repetious saturation necessary with a series of poultice applications. This could be achieved by the use of a traditional lime:sand render with selective screening of the aggregate from 600 μm and below, in order to produce a micro-porous mix, which will more readily absorb moisture from the wall. Supporting this render with an alkali-resistant fibre mesh reinforcing will help retain it in place until saturated with salts. It is expected that this treatment will need to be replaced intially within a few months but subsequent applications may last up to a year. It is hoped that within four or five years conditions will be stable enough to contemplate repairs to the stonework.

Clearly the use of a sacrificial render in this situation has a number of advantages; it is a very simple approach, easily reversible, using traditional materials and techniques. It offers the least disruption to the building occupants and of all the options is truly a minimum intervention.

Annex: Analytical scheme for cores

1. The cores were taken using a diamond-tipped coring drill, without water as a coolant, i.e. dry.
2. The depth of the sample from the core was noted and the sample was put in a plastic bag. Generally, only the chunks were retained for analysis and the powder was discarded.
3. In the laboratory, the more friable chunks (sandstone and cement) were ground up in a mortar and pestle. No sieving was done. The limestone pieces were first crushed in a steel mortar, to a coarse size, and then pulverized in a spex grinder mill to pass a 30-mesh sieve (ASTM).
4. The total sample was weighed, put in an oven at 110°C for 24 hours and then weighed again. The per cent moisture content was calculated as follows:

$$\frac{\text{wt. sample before drying} - \text{dry sample wt.}}{\text{dry sample wt.}} \times 100\%$$

5. Approximately 10 g of each dry sample was exactly weighed into a 50 ml disposable beaker. Twenty ml of distilled water was added to each sample, using an Oxford Pipettor, and the beaker was covered. It was agitated periodically over the next 24 hours.

6. The resulting slurry was filtered through Whatman No. 40 ashless filter paper into another set of 50 ml disposable beakers.
7. For the $SO_4^=$ analysis, 5 ml of sample solution was measured using a calibrated Oxford Macroset pipette into a 100 ml volumetric flask. To this was added 10 ml of sodium chloride/hydrochloric acid reagent and 20 ml of glycerol alcohol solution, and then it was made up to volume with distilled water (after reference 6). In the analysis, 0.3 g of $BaCl_2$ (Fisher, Cert. ACS, (Crystal)) was added to the volumetric, then sealed and inverted once every 2 seconds for 1 minute. It was allowed to stand at least 3 minutes (up to 10 minutes). Light transmission measurements were taken using a Perkin-Elmer UV-Visible spectrophotometer (Hitachi 200). All measurements were taken at 600 nm with a slit width of 2.0 nm using a tungsten lamp. One cm cuvets were used and readings were taken in per cent T. The instrument was set to read 100% T on blank, and 0% T with the shutter in. It was found that a linear correlation existed between per cent T and the concentration of sulphate below 3.0 mg $SO_4^=/100$ ml. Standard solutions of sulphate were made ranging from 0–3 mg $SO_4^=/100$ ml and run with the samples. In cases where the amount of sulphates exceeded 3 mg/100 ml, the analysis was repeated, using only 1 ml of filtrate.
8. For the chloride analysis, a Buchler Digital Chloridometer was used. It was run using the small sample cup on the hi range. Two ml of sample (using 2 × 1.0 ml delivery from an Eppendorf pipette) was added to 4.0 ml of acid solution and 4 drops of gelatin/indicator solution.

References

1. *Canada Sessional Papers* 1863, No.3, p.3
2. Morton, W.B., 'Field procedures for examining humidity in masonry buildings', *Bulletin of the Association for Preservation Technology*, **8**, 3–19, 1976
3. Hougen, O.A., Watson, K.M., Ragatz, A.R., *Chemical Process Principals. Part I Material and Energy Balances*, p.142, Wiley, New York, 1967
4. Weast, R.C., *Handbook of Chemistry and Physics*, 52nd edn. p.B-140 and E-40, The Chemical Rubber Company, Cleveland, 1971
5. Hamad, S. El D., 'A study of the reaction $Na_2SO_4 \cdot 10H_2O$ $Na_2SO_4 + 10H_2O$ in the temperature range 0 to 25°C', *Thermochimica Acta*, **17**, 85–96, 1976
6. Vogel, A.I., *A Text Book of Quantitative Inorganic Analysis*, 3rd edn. p. 850–851, Longman, London, 1961

8

Cleaning masonry buildings

John Ashurst

Introduction

The Crafts Council *Science for Conservators* series defines dirt as 'material which is in the wrong place' and goes on to classify it in two categories:

1. *Foreign matter*, not part of the original object, such as soot, grease and stains, but which has become fixed with it.
2. *Products of alteration* of the original material, such as calcium sulphate on the surface of a limestone. A product of alteration forms through the chemical combination of the original material with chemicals from the environment.

It is apparent from these classification definitions that the removal of dirt which is a 'product of alteration' involves the removal of some of the surface. Even the removal of 'foreign matter', if pursued too far, may cause losses when, for example, dirt fills very fine cracks in a weathered surface. All cleaning of masonry buildings must, therefore, involve consideration of any immediate or induced possible losses which may be caused by cleaning, against the possible long-term losses associated with leaving the dirt alone.

Until the Clean Air Acts of 1956 and 1968 in the UK, smoke emissions from coal burning were seen as primarily responsible for the soiling of buildings. However, it is abundantly apparent that re-soiling of buildings cleaned since that time is quite significant, especially in urban environments. Vehicle emissions, especially diesel engine emissions, are seen as largely responsible for this rapid re-soiling with sticky particulate carbon deposits.[1] A survey carried out by the Urban Pollution Research Centre at the Middlesex Polytechnic[2] recently explored the relationship between the properties of these airborne particulates and the soiling of facades as a basis for the cost-

benefit assessment of building cleaning. The indication was that there were benefits in maintenance cleaning in towns at 5–10 year intervals. The implications for building are considerable.

To clean or not to clean?

The motivation for cleaning a building is usually aesthetic. Although this is a very subjective issue, it is probably true that, as cleaning techniques have improved and the cleaned surfaces of buildings have become more familiar, there is less opposition to cleaning, at least in the United Kingdom, than there was ten or fifteen years ago. But there are often good, practical reasons for cleaning heavily soiled masonry buildings as part of a general maintenance and repair programme. Dirt fills cracks and open joints, obscuring pockets of decay; heavy encrustations on sheltered limestone or marble alter the surfaces on which they form and encourage their deterioration. If for aesthetic or maintenance reasons, it is decided that cleaning is desirable, what are the practical risks involved?

Ideally historic buildings should be cleaned with the same amount of care and attention to detail which is given to the cleaning of sculptures. However, the stone cleaning which has become a firmly established part of the building industry is not sculpture conservation and is not generally carried out by conservators. There is a very considerable wealth of stone cleaning knowledge and expertise in the building industry, which produces excellent results. Perhaps the important difference between the cleaning carried out by a sculpture conservator and a stone cleaner is that the conservator has been especially trained and has a personal reputation to protect, while the stone cleaner is not necessarily trained and will often be anonymous. It is his company's reputation, rather than his own, which will be enhanced or damaged by the quality of his work. There are incompetent practitioners in both fields, but the incompetent conservator can be more readily recognized and more quickly known. The practical risks in employing stone cleaning contractors will certainly be kept to a minimum if reputable companies are involved. These companies see the cleaning activity as inseparable from the maintenance and surface repair of the whole facade and are able to offer a range of cleaning techniques.

The selection and specifiction of a method is not all that needs to be considered. When any building surface is at stake, but especially the surface of any historic building, the level of expertise available must also be known. Regrettably this is not always high, and in some situations competitive tendering for cleaning work, with an obligation for the lowest price to be accepted, can work against the conscientious contractor who is not prepared to take short cuts or to accept low standards. A welcome development in the United Kingdom is the formation of the Stone Cleaning section of the Stone Federation, whose members are frequently in competition, but who share a common interest in the maintenance of high work standards. Members cooperate with the British Standards Institution in the production of the BS Codes, produce their own Code of Practice, and meet architects and other specifiers in the Standing Joint Committee on Natural Stones.

Cleaning methods

Whilst it is obviously better not to clean a building at all than to cause damage which will reduce its life expectancy, or adversely affect its appearance, in almost every case some cleaning is possible without significant risks, provided the right level of expertise is available. There is no cleaning category currently in use which should not be used in any circumstances. The wide range of results which has been obtained over the last two decades of cleaning accounts for the wide range of reaction which any discussion on the cleaning of buildings is likely to provide. It is quite common to hear architects refusing to have anything to do with chemical cleaning, or with sand-blasting, and some authorities have banned such techniques. In most such cases, these adverse reactions are based on first-hand experience of an inappropriate specification or incompetent work and supervision on site, or, alternatively, on misconception caused by ignorance.

Methods which will be described in this chapter include:

- *Washing*, used principally for limestone and marble
- *Mechanical*, used principally for sandstones, but also for some limestones and marble
- *Chemical*, used principally for sandstones and granites
- *Special cleaning techniques*, including cavitation, lasers and special poultices

The survey

Any proposal to clean the facades of a building must be preceded by a careful survey. Three levels of survey may be appropriate:

1. A relatively superficial inspection from existing vantage points. This survey will identify the general type and condition of the fabric and the degree of soiling. It should also look at the condition of adjacent buildings. Such a survey is appropriate in determining the desirability of cleaning at all. Some idea of how the cleaned building would look should also be formed.
2. A preliminary survey, designed to determine the best method of cleaning and to assess with some accuracy the extent of stone repair and replacement which will be involved and how the building will appear after cleaning. Problems which might be created by alternative methods and how access and programming can be planned to suit the occupants and public should be discussed and evaluated.
3. A detailed survey, possibly involving some trial cleaning, should be carried out to finalize the specification and to ensure that as many problems as possible involved in preparing the building and occupants for the cleaning contract are anticipated. Trial cleaning sites should not be on the most prominent part of the building, of course, but chosen to include as many typical problems as possible. Such problems may be experienced at openings, open joints, under overhangs and in the vicinity of old repairs and suspected staining. Cleaning contractors should not be expected to provide trial cleaning samples as demonstrations for no charge. Trial cleaning is a fact-finding exercise, which should have its own clear specification and be paid for separately from the main contract. The trial clean should also establish an 'acceptable standard' reference for the contract.

At the end of the survey, the following important questions should have been asked and answered:

1. Is the building dirty and, if so, is the presence of dirt damaging or only disfiguring?
2. What are the stones and other materials of the building?

3. What is the nature of the soiling? Are there evidences of previous treatments, such as oil or paint?

4. How much cleaning is desirable? How much dirt can be removed safely? How will the removal of dirt affect the appearance of the building now and in future years?

5. How will cleaning affect the weathering properties of the stones?

6. What method, or combination of methods, could be used to remove the dirt? How will these methods work and what hazards may be involved for the operatives and the public, as well as for the building?

7. How often is the building likely to need cleaning? Should some cleaning maintenance programme be established?

8. What remedial work, in the form of repairs to the stones and joints, should be included in the cleaning contract?

9. What surface treatments, if any, such as biocides, water repellants or consolidants, should be applied after cleaning, and to what areas?

10. What needs to be provided in the form of protection for windows and other openings, or for polished and painted surfaces?

11. What form of scaffold and what sheeting are required?

12. What water and electricity supplies are needed? What provision must be made for plant access, acoustic shelters, storage of materials and waste disposal?

13. Have the building owner and occupants been fully informed about the possible inconvenience, such as the nuisance from water, dust and noise which may be experienced? Have the necessary authorities been informed and all relevant permissions been obtained, especially if listed buildings are involved?

14. Having answered all the above, are the necessary skills available to carry out the cleaning to the required standard?

Note: Cleaning, like any other building craft, is a skill that is acquired to differing degrees by different individuals. Cleaning operatives must be able to demonstrate that they can clean to the 'acceptable standard' established during the trial clean. They should be named. Substitute operatives should not be accepted during the work unless they too can demonstrate their ability and experience.

The specification which is produced at the end of this preparatory work should cover all the foreseeable problems and be sufficiently comprehensive to make an accurate estimate possible. It may be advisable to write in a requirement that one of the cleaning team is to be stationed inside the building to maintain regular liaison with the team out on the scaffold, especially on a large and complicated building. In addition, regardless of the size of job, washing must never be left unattended and proper site security must be maintained. Regular site visits must be made at least weekly by the architect or professional supervisor.

Washing

Any soiled limestone building will exhibit the effects of regular rain washing on its exposed surfaces. Unlike sandstone, washing by rain inhibits the formation of dirt on limestone. The dirt which forms on limestone and marble tends to be soluble in water. Washing, whether by bucket and brush, multiple sprays, water lances or wet packs, is therefore a well established method of cleaning these surfaces.

Washing is a very simple process in principle. It requires only some sensible means of putting enough water in contact with the dirt deposits to wash them away directly or to soften them sufficiently to allow their release by brushing. Most problems associated with washing have to do with saturation. Unfortunately, most spray cleaning systems are insufficiently versatile to deal effectively with the different degrees of soiling usually found on a building with openings, projections and enrichments. A row of jets placed along a horizontal boom, or with their hoses looped along a scaffold ledger pole, may clean a flat surface within two hours, but a piece of carved cornice with encrusted dirt may well require two or three days of spraying before the stone is clean. Unless there is provision to modify the washing programme to avoid unnecessary general saturation, there may be a number of consequences such as:

1. Light to dark brown staining will take place as dirty water dries out from the stones and joints.

2. Staining, usually brown, and white efflorescences may appear as a result of salt migration to the surface.

3. The release of small flakes of stone, especially on small-scale and undercut detail, may occur as a result of the dissolution of salts. Such flakes may sometimes be attached to the surface only by water-soluble material present as the result of the activity of a polluted environment on the stone surfaces. Surface losses will also be incurred when the stone is powdery.

4. Weak jointing material may be washed out.

5. Water penetration through defective joints, or through cracks and contact with iron fixings, plaster, beam ends, bond timbers, panelling, electrical fittings and furnishings may take place. There is also the risk of water entering unsuspected reservoirs above vaults, in floor spaces or

in basements, which may result in direct damage or future problems with dry rot (*Serpula lacrymans*). In old walls, especially those of double skin and rubble fill construction, water from the outside may travel considerable distances before emerging in other parts of the building.

6. The development of disfiguring green, red or orange algae on recently washed surfaces, especially flat or inclined catchment areas, may be noticed.

7. In wintry conditions, considerable damage can result from the freezing of water trapped in the joints or in the pores of the stones. Ideally, no washing should take place during months likely to be frosty. If washing must continue, the work must be halted before sunset and be fully covered up. In exceptional circumstances, background heating on the scaffold will be necessary.

Washing with minimum risk

Successful washing programmes are those which put the minimum amount of water for the minimum time exactly where it is required and nowhere else. This may be achieved in different ways. Traditionally, water jets tied to the scaffold have been turned on and shut down as the surface response dictates, but this is difficult to control in practice and groups of sprays tend to be left on for as long as dirt remains in the most stubborn area. An experienced cleaner will get to work with small brushes of bristle, phosphor bronze or brass wire as soon as possible to cut down the saturation period. Steel wire brushes should never be used, because of their harsh action. Their design is usually inappropriate and there is a risk of leaving steel fragments on the building, which will later produce small, but vivid, rust stains.

The ideal condition for washing is a persistent wet mist over the soiled face of the building. This technique avoids the impact effect which large water droplets have when delivered by coarse sprays and the subsequent cascading which, when prolonged, can cause damage. To achieve the mist, or 'fogging', the sprays must be from fine nozzles situated at least 300 mm away from the masonry face. Enough water pressure and small enough orifices are required to atomize the water. In practice, this is rarely easy because, even on a tightly sheeted scaffold, draughts of air can carry the water mist away from the building. The effectiveness of the system therefore depends on how successfully the mist can be contained.

A more dependable system of washing was devised by R.H. Bennett in 1970 to reduce saturation and has since developed into an established method. It makes use of readily achieved fine sprays of water playing intermittently on the building surface. The water is controlled electronically by means of sensor heads or a pre-set clock. The sensor heads comprise twin carbon rods set in a non-conductive plastic body linked to an electrical control box. The sensors, about 20 mm (0.75 in) long, are pinned at intervals into the masonry joints with stainless steel staples. When a water bridge forms on the sensor head, the water is automatically cut off. When the water bridge is broken by drying out, the sprays are automatically switched on again. In most cases the clock control is preferred because it is more positive. With clock control a washing interval is established by preliminary trial and error. The clock is set to control a spraying time of, say, eight seconds, followed by a four-minute shut-down. The aim with either system is to supply just enough water to progressively soften the dirt without causing saturation and risking penetration through vulnerable areas. The system is usually referred to as intermittent or pulse washing. Close attention is still required to commence scrubbing as soon as the dirt becomes responsive to brushing.

A more recent development in washing is the use of flexible bars to position the nozzles exactly where they are required. Because of the difference in soiling conditions and variations in response times, the cleaner must constantly re-position the spray heads as the situation changes on the building face during cleaning. Because the fixed scaffold and any short battens secured to it are the only means of support for the sprays, it is very difficult to direct the water exactly where it is needed. Plastic-sleeved flexible bars are fixed to the scaffold with brackets and swivel mountings. These bars provide support for the nozzles and in this way a true three-dimensional flexibility in positioning water sprays is achieved. This enables the underside of a moulding or soffit of a niche to be cleaned as easily as a straight run of ashlar.

Brushes have also been the subject of some development and the variety in design has increased. Several sizes of scrubbing and stencil-type brushes are needed for all but the simplest facade. A light formation of phosphor bronze crinkle wire and synthetic bristle combination designed by Picreator is particularly useful. Small blocks of rubbing or abrasive sandstones can also be used to remove stubborn staining and encrustation from flat surfaces.

Water penetration risks may further be reduced, especially on high buildings, by the construction of splash or slurry boards of resin-bonded plywood, sheathed in polyethylene sheet, at intervals to form horizontal catchment to collect and carry off the water flowing down the building face. The water from these boards is collected in plastic gutters fixed at their outer edge and carried off in plastic downpipes. Similar constructions may be built over large openings which remain in use during the cleaning.

Cold water direct from the mains is normally used for cleaning facades of buildings. Hot water may be justified for particular situations, especially where detergents or de-greasing chemicals are used.

Water lances

Light soiling, especially where a high proportion is organic, may sometimes be removed by water lances without any preliminary softening by water spraying. Alternatively, they may be used in combination with water sprays, mechanical or chemical cleaning. Pressures are often in the 800–1200 psi range, and the lance is usually low volume, high pressure. Water at these pressures has a cutting action, however, and the design of the outlet and the technique of the operative both significantly affect the economy and the safety of the cleaning. Much higher pressures can be obtained enabling water jets to cut through concrete, so potential damage from indiscreet or careless lancing is a factor that must be taken into consideration.

A technique introduced approximately ten years ago mixes fine sand and water together at source for delivery through a lance at comparatively low pressures of between 18 and 30 psi. The water carrying the abrasive has a light scouring action. The abrasive can then be cut out to permit flushing with water alone. This system was used to clean the principal facades of the British Museum in London from a hydraulic platform, avoiding the need to scaffold. In common with conventional wet sand blasting, it will also clean sandstone.

Mechanical

Mechanical cleaning removes dirt by abrading the surface. The simplest form is dry brushing. This technique will remove loosely bound dirt and organic growth but little else. Sometimes it is practicable to use hand-held sandstone or carborundum blocks lubricated with water to improve the appearance of simple, flat surfaces, but only on resistant, tough materials that will not be scoured by the abrasive action. A harsher method is scraping the surface down with a suitable tool such as a mason's drag which is sometimes used to remove paint from flat surfaces. The most damaging cleaning in this category in the past has undoubtedly been 'spinning off', normally entailing the use of a power tool with an interchangeable set of heads including soft wire brushes, carborundum heads and discs. Flexible carborundum discs are also available. Unfortunately this technique removes some of the surface to achieve cleaning. It is also notoriously difficult even for an experienced operative to avoid scouring flat surfaces with shallow depressions and leaving wavy arrises on external angles. Good quality work is usually finished by hand. The surface is rubbed to remove the imperfections and is, in effect, re-dressed. In most situations it is a technique to avoid, unless there has been deep staining of a surface or a paint which will not yield to solvents must be removed.

Spinning-off has been largely superseded by the use of compressed air and abrasives. Wet or dry sand-blasting or grit-blasting have become very familiar methods of cleaning building facades. These systems were often used to descale large surface areas of iron and steel sheet. Their appearance in the field of building cleaning dates from the 1950s. In the United Kingdom these systems were very much in evidence during the decade 1965–1975. They were often used indiscriminately, unfortunately stimulated at the time by a government environmental improvement grant scheme.

A blasting system projects abrasive through a nozzle in a stream of compressed air. The basic equipment consists of a compressor, a pot for the abrasive and air and abrasive delivery lines. Some types of system introduce water by running a twin hose to carry water to the end of the abrasive delivery line and discharging several small jets of water through a ring adaptor into the air and abrasive stream. Other types mix the water, air and abrasive at source. Air pressures at the nozzle vary in practice from 15 to 80 psi and there are different orifice sizes and nozzle patterns available.

Abrasives are selected according to the toughness of the dirt to be removed, but cost and safety factors also have an influence. Sand is the cheapest abrasive, but the most hazardous, and is now banned in several countries. Harmful dust is always generated by dry blasting of sandstone, and the operatives must have the protection of helmets supplied with filtered air and should wear full protective clothing. Other tough abrasives are non-siliceous grits, such as copper or iron slag, carborundum and aluminium oxide powders. For less demanding or more fragile surfaces, olivine, dolomite, crushed egg or nut shells, minute glass beads or even talc may be used as the abrasive.

Factors which must be considered when the use of such a cleaning system is contemplated are:

1. The relative hardness of the abrasive and the surface and the likely risk of damage.
2. The size of the particles of abrasive. Coarse particles should be used for the preliminary cutting and fine for finishing.
3. The need for water to lubricate and cushion the impact effect of the abrasive and to reduce dust.

4. The risks of dust to the public and of penetration to sensitive areas of the building.
5. The available operative skills (see Appendix 3).

Problems associated with the air abrasive technique include:

1. The surfaces being cleaned and even the abrasive used can vary in hardness. Less resistant stones, or areas of the same stone, may be attacked by the air pressure and abrasive which cleaned a trial patch without damage.
2. Grits of sand and flint contain free silica, as do sandstone and granite. Dusts generated during cleaning which involves these materials can cause long-term, irreversible lung damage to inadequately protected operatives.
3. The vision of an operative wearing a protective helmet can be obscured by dust when large nozzles are used.
4. Dust can penetrate even small openings and damage furniture, fittings and machinery.
5. Compressor and air delivery noise can be a considerable nuisance to the occupants of a building which is being cleaned and may become intolerable in the immediate vicinity of cleaning.
6. Residual dust and spent abrasive will remain on the building, giving an unnatural appearance, unless the cleaning is completed by washing down. This is most conveniently carried out by using a high pressure, low volume water lance, which does not involve any soaking of the building.
7. Cheap, soft sands which are sometimes used can cause staining.

Advantages of the air abrasive technique, on the other hand, may be listed as follows:

1. Saturation of the building is avoided, even with wet-head blast cleaning and lancing off, so that cleaning can usually proceed through the winter, even in cold climates.
2. There are few risks of water penetration and staining or efflorescence, although wet-head blasting involves some risks.
3. On simple facades, the method is probably the fastest way to clean safely, assuming the necessary skills are available.
4. On small-scale, fragile detail, especially where there is a history of salt crystallization damage, small-scale air abrasive cleaning, if used skilfully, is safer than water cleaning or poulticing.

A range of equipment is now available which enables experienced operatives to clean a variety of surfaces safely, avoiding most of the mistakes of the past. The drawing shows some of the equipment currently in use. Of particular interest is the safety-conscious water injection system, which can largely avoid hazardous dust during large-scale cleaning. Small air abrasive pistols and pencils, using 50 mm, 100 mm or finer dusts, can be used very effectively as supplementary tools to cleaning with water or chemicals sometimes after the initial softening up.

Compressed air and abrasive may be used to clean in a vacuum chamber on site. Many buildings in Paris, for instance, have been cleaned in this way from a mobile platform.

The operators must be experienced and alert to changes in the surface on which they are working. Adjustments in pressure or abrasive or a change of method may be necessary. Work may have to be abandoned altogether if damage appears likely to a valuable surface. Work must never be hurried. Rushed air abrasive work, especially on flat surfaces, can result in a mottled 'gun-shading', which becomes apparent with subsequent weathering. Whether air abrasive cleaning is used wet or dry, the surface should always be finished with a water lance in order to remove all dust and spent abrasive. On small-scale detail, hand sprays or air jets may be used.

Cleaning with hydrofluoric acid

Hydrofluoric acid (HF) is the chemical cleaning agent normally selected for cleaning sandstone and unpolished granite. It is the traditional method which has been in use for over fifty years, although improvements in abrasive systems have introduced some competition during the last twenty years. Even so, because HF cleaning is quiet, generally efficient and avoids the risk of damage associated with abrasive discs, or unskilled compressed air and abrasive cleaning, it has held its position. Although HF is a particularly dangerous acid to personnel and will etch glass and polished surfaces, it hs the distinct advantage over other chemicals that it will not leave behind potentially damaging soluble salts.

Hydrofluoric acid cleans sandstones by reacting with the silica which forms the main constituent of the stone. As the silica dissolves, the surface dirt bound to it is loosened and may be washed away. If there is a delay in washing off, some of the dissolved silica may be redeposited and it will show as a white bloom or as white streaks from the joints. This redeposited silica is very difficult to remove. Although weathering generally improves the appearance, it is of little help if the disfigurement is excessive. These deposits can only be removed by mechanical means, i.e. by an abrasive disc or airbrasive unit, by water cutting, or by a further application of the acid, all of which make nonsense of the original intention to clean by chemical means.

Sandstones which contain iron compounds present another problem. Generally stones of this kind

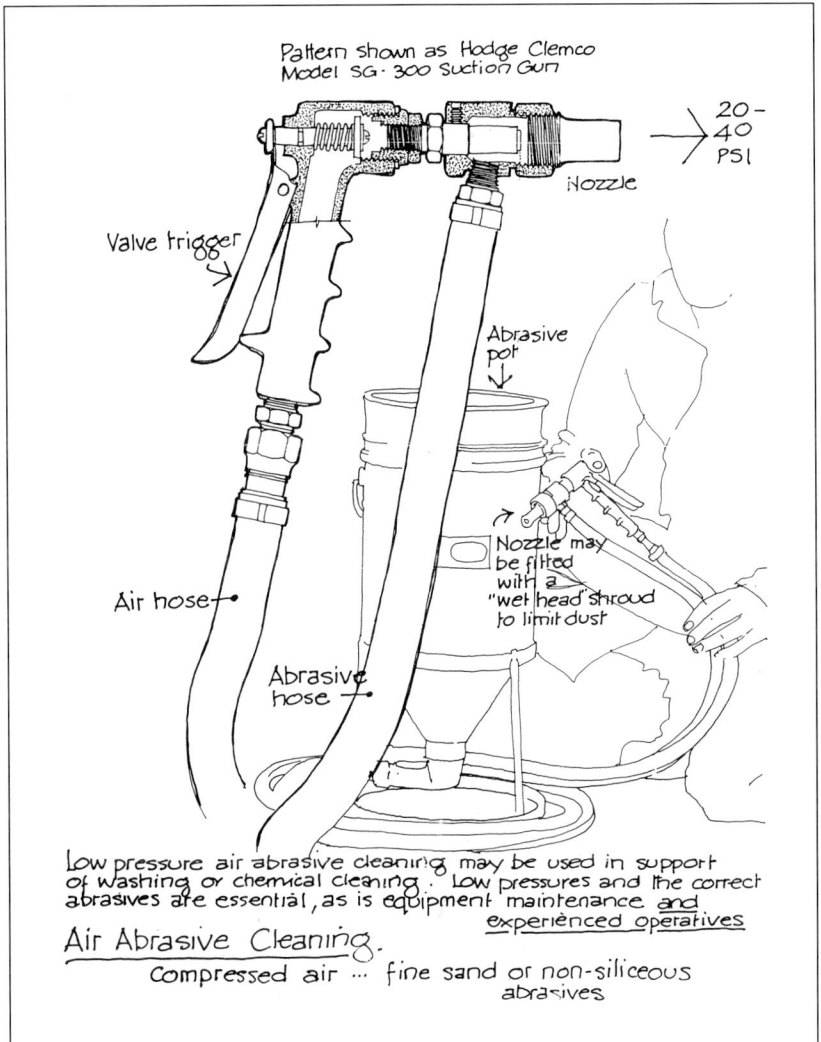

Pattern shown as Hodge Clemco
Model SG·300 Suction Gun

20 - 40 PSI

Nozzle

Valve trigger

Abrasive pot

Nozzle may be fitted with a "wet head" shroud to limit dust

Air hose

Abrasive hose

Low pressure air abrasive cleaning may be used in support of washing or chemical cleaning. Low pressures and the correct abrasives are essential, as is equipment maintenance and experienced operatives

Air Abrasive Cleaning.
Compressed air ... fine sand or non-siliceous abrasives

show the presence of iron in the form of light to deep brown staining in areas which have been subject to water percolation over a long period. Hydrated iron oxides appear as brown specks on the surface of the stone, even if staining is not apparent. Hydrofluoric acid will attack the iron and form soluble compounds, which then migrate to the surface and create deep brown stains. The risk of staining can be considerably reduced, but not eliminated, by adding phosphoric acid to the hydrofluoric acid. The phosphoric acid forms insoluble iron phosphates, which are unable to migrate to the surface. Before cleaning is undertaken, it is in everyone's interest to study the appearance of an iron-rich sandstone building, in order to assess the existing staining due

to weathering. In this way, the building owner will be prepared, the contractor will not be unfairly blamed and the architect will be spared the unnecessary time and expense of investigation, reporting and arbitration, should further staining result from the cleaning. Although attempts have been made to remove iron staining with subsequent applications of phosphoric acid and mixtures of phosphoric and hydrofluoric acids, the results have been disappointing. It must be said that there is increasing concern and dissatisfaction with the colour changes brought about by ill-considered acid cleaning of sandstone.

Two further types of sandstones which are particularly susceptible to decay in polluted environments, are calcareous sandstones and dolomitic sandstones, in which the siliceous grains are cemented principally by calcite and dolomite respectively. Both calcite (calcium carbonate) and dolomite (magnesium calcium carbonate) are attacked by hydrofluoric acid and there will, in theory, be greater losses when these stones are cleaned with hydrofluoric acid, than when a sandstone with a siliceous matrix is cleaned. In practice, however, it seems that the commonly powdery surfaces of these stones are likely to lose as much from the washing-off process as from the acid application, unless the acid treatment is particularly prolonged or concentrated.

Sandstone with a largely siliceous matrix may still contain calcite or dolomite, but in this case hydrofluoric acid is no threat to the binding constituent of the stone. However, fears are expressed from time to time that a change in pore structure may result from the formation of calcium fluoride (an insoluble product formed by the reaction of hydrofluoric acid with calcite) and/or calcium fluoride and magnesium fluoride (formed by the reaction of hydrofluoric acid with dolomite). Modification of the pore structure might well affect the long-term durability of a sandstone cleaned in this way, but an examination by the Building Research Establishment, carried out on a sandstone building where claims of positive damage from hydrofluoric acid cleaning had been made, showed no evidence to support the claims. Microscopic examination of petrological thin sections, prepared from cores taken through the cleaned surface, was made and a piece of each sample was analysed by X-ray diffraction. The sandstone was composed of silica, with small amounts of mica, feldspar, dolomite and hydrated iron oxides. No calcium fluoride was detected and there were no signs of chemical attack on grains of dolomite at the surface. The opinion of the Building Research Establishment in this case was that no short-term damage from acid attack on the matrix, or long-term damage from pore blocking, had been caused. It would be foolish to say that, from this, hydrofluoric acid will not cause damage in any circumstances. Consideration must always be given to the constituents of the stone, and a sensible assessment must be made of the vulnerability of the stone to this type of cleaning.

Procedures for the commercial cleaning of a sandstone or unpolished granite building with hydrofluoric acid are described below. All personnel must be experienced in the use of the acid and equipped with full face and head protection, heavy duty gauntlets, and waterproof boots and clothing. They should be familiar with the appropriate first-aid procedures and the local hospital should be informed.

1. General procedures for protecting the building and sheeting the scaffolding apply, but particular care must be taken to protect contract personnel and the public from spillages or drift. First-aid boxes must be kept on site. All scaffold tubes must be securely capped to avoid the trapping of acid or acid vapour. Glass should be coated with two applications of a latex masking paint (remember that some solvents are effective paint strippers!). If the window glass is particularly valuable, it should be covered with a polyethylene membrane and resin bonded ply templates. Templates alone, without the latex, should not be used.

2. Use a proprietary, pre-diluted form of hydrofluoric acid; the concentration must be known and displayed on the container (between 2% and 15%). Do not store the industrial concentrate (which may be over 70%) on site, or permit on-site dilution. Keep the acid in a secure store, adequately labelled.

3. Pre-wet the area to be cleaned with clean water. A convenient way of achieving this is to use a low-volume, high-pressure water lance. The objective is to provide a damp surface, on which the chemical will spread. If the surface is dry, or only superficially wet, the chemical will be absorbed, especially at mortar joints. Thorough wetting will limit the activity of the chemical to the soiled face.

4. Apply the acid by brush to the damp surface, or by using a low-pressure garden spray. The application should be even and planned between architectural features, e.g. cornice to plinth or between internal angles of buttresses. The coverage rate should be in the order of 1 litre per 3.7 square metres of surface area (1 imperial gallon per 12–15 square yards). The contact period with the stone surface will vary depending on the amount and type of soiling and on the ambient temperature. Proprietary hydrofluoric acid cleaners which carry an Agrément Board certificate (pH 1–1.5 and pH 3.5–3.8) are recommended to be left between 20 minutes (Agrément Board), 30 minutes on a warm day (Neolith) and up to 1 hour on a cold day (Neolith). Repeated applications may be necessary. The cleaning material must never be allowed to dry on the surface.

5. The acid should be thoroughly washed off at the correct time. This can be achieved most efficiently with a low-volume, high-pressure water lance — a pump producing, say, 1000 psi at 4 imperial gallons per minute. It must be recognized, however, that even 1000 psi may be too strong for many surfaces, and the temptation to use the lance to 'cut' may be a hazard. 'Safe' pressures are below 500 psi, and it is generally wise to specify this limit. The technique recommended by Neolith is to hold the nozzle approximately 760 mm (30 in) away from the surface, while passing the lance to and fro, in sweeps of

760 mm (30 in). Rinsing for four minutes per square metre (1 square yard) is recommended as a minimum time, with extra attention paid to water traps, such as sills and strings, or weathered joints. The rinsing water must not be allowed to accumulate on such traps. At one site in London, dribble staining resulted from rinsing water left in recessed joints. As the water evaporated, the acid concentration increased and white streaks of silica were left behind.

6. The scaffolding boards must also be washed off thoroughly after each rinsing of the building and the scaffold tube capping checked.
7. Subsequent applications of the chemical must follow stages 3 to 6. At least half an hour should elapse before a second application.

Burns must be washed immediately with copious amounts of clean water for at least one minute, followed by rubbing calcium gluconate gel into and around the burned area, with clean fingers. The gel should be rubbed in continuously for 15 minutes after the pain has subsided and hospital treatment must follow. If gel is not available, washing must continue until it is. Eyes which have been affected should be irrigated with isotonic saline or clean water for at least 10 minutes. Hospital treatment may involve injections of calcium gluconate into and under the burn and further treatment in the case of large or severe burns.

The problems associated with this kind of cleaning may be summarized by saying that they are caused by little or no analysis of the surface to be cleaned, quite inadequate specifications and supervision, and too concentrated acid solutions.

Other chemical cleaning agents

An increasingly wide range of other acid or alkali cleaning agents is available, but they all involve some risk of soluble salt residues. The most common alkaline cleaning agents are based on sodium hydroxide (caustic soda) or potassium hydroxide (caustic potash). Some may contain surfactants and detergents to degrease a severely soiled surface before cleaning with hydrofluoric acid, in which case there is not likely to be a problem with residues. The same general procedures and safeguards as for cleaning with hydrofluoric acid should be followed, even though some hazards are less. In particular, pre-wetting and thorough washing off are vital if staining and damage are to be avoided. Unfortunately, examples of such damage can easily be found, especially on the underside of window and door heads. Caustic alkali cleaning of limestone should really be considered only as a last resort, when cleaning by other means is not possible.

Proprietary pastes are available containing ammonium hydroxides as a degreasing agent. Other proprietary pastes containing sodium hydroxide may also contain organic amines such as diethylene-triamine which make calcium sulphate skins more readily soluble. Methyl cellulose is a common thickener for these pastes.

In paste form, sodium hydroxide or potassium hydroxide have been used to break down multiple layers of unwanted paint, but these pastes must be covered by thin polyethylene film and lifted off dry, before thorough washing with clean water.

In a typical test using sodium-hydroxide-based paste on Bath limestone, samples analysed for the presence of water soluble sodium compounds showed that the sodium content of the outer 3 mm was increased by a factor of more than eighty. This would be quite unacceptable in terms of a residue on a building facade.

In one case application of sodium hydroxide paste was followed by washing and the application of a clean Attapulgite clay poultice, in order to encourage any harmful residues to dry out into the clay. This procedure produces a very good result, but is very labour intensive, especially if undercut detail is involved.

Another acid in common use for the removal of cementitious stains and deposits is hydrochloric acid. Ten per cent acid applied to a pre-wetted surface will remove calcium carbonate. It is more likely to be used on brickwork and limestone than on sandstone. Citric and acetic acids are used in 'neutralizing' washes after alkali cleaning.

First-aid treatment for potassium hydroxide ('caustic potash'), sodium hydroxide ('caustic soda') and hydrochloric acid ('spirits of salts') is washing with copious amounts of clean water. Severe burns must be treated in hospital as soon as possible. When burns from hydrochloric acid have occurred, a magnesium oxide paste should be applied.

Reputable manufacturers of proprietary cleaning materials produce full product data, dealing with all associated hazards, waste disposal methods, protective clothing, face and eye protection, handling and storage. It is imperative that such information is made available, read and acted upon.

There is little doubt that the chemical cleaning of buildings, at its best, shows an increasing versatility based on a proper assessment of the surfaces to be cleaned and the nature of the soiling present. In particular, improvements associated with dilute acid and alkali cleaning materials held in poultices of clay or carboxymethylcellulose (CMC) against the surface of the stone are extremely encouraging; so is the recognition that safe and efficient cleaning is (and perhaps should be) more expensive than hasty and ill-considered gambling with unsuitably concentrated materials and high-pressure jetting.

Special cleaning systems

The Hempel 'biological pack'

Certain clays, such as attapulgite or sepiolite, are very useful poultice media. The structure of the clays enables them to contain considerable amounts of moisture and to produce a sucking effect as they dry out. To prepare the poultice a 50 μm clay powder is added to enough clean water to produce a thick, sticky cream. The water should not be added to the clay, because a lumpy paste will result. This mixture may be applied to the surface of soiled limestone or marble without a solvent, and covered with a thin polyethylene film. The poultice may be effective within a few days, but it may need to be left for several weeks. The contact period can only be determined by lifting the edge of the poultice and testing the tenacity of the surface dirt by gentle scrubbing. When a promising result is obtained, the complete poultice can be removed with a spatula and the surface scrubbed clean with bristle or soft, non-ferrous wire brushes. Used in this way, such poultices are a development of the more traditional wet-packs composed of whiting, paper pulp or even bread. They may be mixed with various solvents to lift stains.

Hempel developed the idea of a 'biological pack', based on these clay bodies, which claims to assist the breakdown of sulphate crusts on marble and limestone by the presence and activity of micro-organisms. These packs include 25 g urea and 10 ml glycerol in 500 ml of water. Enough sepiolite or attapulgite clay must be added to form a thixotropic paste. In common with all poultice packs, the paste must be applied to have good contact with all the surfaces to be cleaned. Spray wetting of the surfaces should precede the application, and again thin polyethylene film should be used to prevent air reaching the surface of the pack. This biological pack may remain on the surface for several weeks (perhaps for up to two months) before it is lifted and brushing and rinsing takes place.

This technique is primarily suited to the cleaning of sculpture and small-scale detail on, for instance, church monuments.

The Mora poultice

An interesting system for cleaning limestone and marble based on a chelating agent was developed by Mora. The chelating agent is ethylene diaminotetra-acetic acid (EDTA). This weak acid facilitates the dissolution of calcium salts by complex formation. Complexing or sequestering agents separate or are cut off. The Mora poultice has been used with considerable success on marble and travertine which have had moderate soiling. The poultice contains 60 g ammonium bicarbonate, 60 g sodium bicarbonate, 25 g EDTA, 10 g surfactant disinfectant and 60 g carboxymethylcellulose in 1000 ml of water. The ammonium and sodium bicarbonate give a slightly basic mixture of pH 7.5 and facilitate the dissolution of some salts.

The poultice, in the form of a clear jelly, is applied to a pre-wetted surface by spatula or by brush to a thickness of 3–4 mm, and is covered at once with a thin polyethylene film to prevent drying out. The film is of utmost importance as the cellulose body of the poultice is very difficult to remove if it dries and hardens. The contact period may be twenty-four hours, and intermediate lifting and reapplication may be necessary. After cleaning and removal of all poultice material by the use of small trowels or spatulas the surface should be washed thoroughly with clean water.

The advantages and attractions of this system are principally that it is safe chemically and avoids any excessive use of abrasion or water. It cannot, however, be applied to friable or flaking surfaces (any more than any other poultice) without removing surface material. Surprisingly large areas can be cleaned relatively economically when the surface is not too detailed.

The Baker or lime method

The cleaning of limestone surfaces by lime poulticing as part of a total consolidation and protection programme was pioneered and developed by Professor Robert Baker (UK). The system is fully described in Chapter 9.

Soaps

Grease, oil, tar and pitch will frequently respond well to scrubbing with warm water and a suitable soap, especially on marble or limestone. Slate, granite and even sandstone may sometimes be cleaned, or partially cleaned, by this method as well. Any of the deposit which can be lifted by a scraper or spatula should be removed first. Powdered detergents must be avoided, because of the cumulative deposits of sodium salts which build up, particularly in joints, after repeated applications (maintenance cleaning, for example).

Experience has shown that a proprietary methyl cyclohexyloleate (pH 10.5–11.5) which is soluble in water and spirit, such as white spirit or trichlorethylene, is able to remove a wide range of soiling and has good penetrating effects into fine crazing and small cracks. This soap blend is non-foaming and remains active while it is on the surface, usually about 5 minutes. Thick deposits of greasy or oily dirt need to be worked on with bristle, synthetic fibre or soft brass wire brushes. Hand-warm water produces the optimum effect. After cleaning, all the soap should be rinsed away.

Suitable, economic proportions are between 3–9 parts water/spirit to 1 part of soap. No particular safety precautions are needed, but the efficient degreasing effect of the solution makes it advisable to wear protection gloves.

Alabaster, the surface of which is dissolved by washing with water, may be cleaned with the soap and white spirit and finished with white spirit alone on cotton swabs.

Iron and cuprous stain removal

Iron gutters and hoppers, roofing fixings and long-term scaffolding all can produce disfiguring rusty stains on masonry. Copper roofing and bronze statuary and plaques produce an unsightly green staining. These stains may be lightened and sometimes removed altogether by the poultices described below. In all cases, the surfaces must be pre-wetted and all poultice material must be lifted off with plastic spatulas and placed directly into disposal bins or sacks, before thorough rinsing off with clean water. The longer a stain is left untreated, the more difficult complete removal becomes. Before cleaning, means to avoid re-staining should be decided upon. This may involve, for instance, the painting or removal of iron, or the regular treatment of bronze with lanolin and wax.

Removal of iron stains

To remove or lighten iron stains (principally from limestone and marble), the following method should be used:

1. Add a solution of one part sodium citrate and six parts water to an equal volume of glycerin.
2. Add attapulgite clay to the solution until a smooth paste is formed.
3. Apply the paste to the stained surface and leave until dry.
4. Remove the paste with a wooden or other non-metallic spatula.
5. Reapply and remove the paste as often as required to lift or satisfactorily lighten the stain.

Very stubborn stains may require the following alternative treatment:

1. Wet the surface with a solution of one part sodium citrate and six parts water.
2. Apply an attapulgite wet clay pack, containing sodium dithionite.
3. Lift off and follow by washing the surface with copious amounts of clean water.

Removal of cuprous stains

To remove or lighten cuprous metal stains (principally from limestone and marble), the following method should be used:

1. Mix dry one part of ammonium chloride with four parts powdered talc or attapulgite or sepiolite clay. Add a 10% solution of ammonia water.
2. Pre-wet the surface with clean water, apply the paste and leave until dry.
3. Remove the paste with a wooden or other non-metallic spatula.
4. Rinse thoroughly with clean water.
5. Reapply, remove and rinse off the paste as often as required to lift or satisfactorily lighten the stain.

Ultrasonic cleaning

Ultrasonic cleaning uses vibration to achieve its effect. It is primarily a museum technique, applicable to relatively small objects. Electrically produced vibration is transmitted through metal plates to a liquid in a cleaning bath. Sound waves are carried by the alternate compression and expansion of the liquid. If this alternation is rapid enough, the intense waves of vibration travelling through the water 'tear holes' in it. Vapour cavities appear and collapse at an ultrasonic frequency, a phenomenon known as *cavitation*. The 'ultrasonic bubbles' have a brushing action on the surfaces of an object placed in the tank because, as the bubbles collapse, the liquid, locally, moves very fast. The process can be thought of as abrasion with molecule-sized grit.

The equipment used by dentists to descale teeth, developed some 25 years ago, is also used in conservation work. The tool has an ultrasonic vibrating head immersed in a spray of water, which flows around and through it. The vibration is transmitted into the water layer, creating movement, vibration and cavitation which cleans the surface. This technique is used in a similar manner principally by museum conservators in the workshop.

Laser cleaning

The first laser (Light Amplification by Stimulated Emission of Radiation) was built in July 1960, by the American physicist Maiman. Since then, the exploration of the potential of lasers in the fields of surgery, industry and warfare has been taking place. Since 1972,[3] laser radiation has been under investigation as a means of stone cleaning, specifically in the field of sculpture conservation. The attraction of the principle lies in the relative ease with which even encrusted dirt can be removed from the most fragile surfaces as a result of laser irradiation. Under the sponsorship of the International Fund for Monuments, a portable laser system was fabricated for use in Venice. Using Neodymium YAG as the active laser material and a 2 kV power supply yielding an output of one pulse per second, a heavily soiled small marble sculpture can be cleaned by an experienced operator in between one and three hours. A single pulse from the laser will clean a 25 mm (1 in) square area. This cleaning rate is comparable with the air abrasive pencil, when the few seconds interval needed for the laser operative to redirect the beam is taken into account. The advantage of the method is the absence of any mechanical contact with the surface of the sculpture.

Although this is an interesting and exciting development in the cleaning of fragile surfaces, and shows much promise, it is unlikely that laser cleaning will be of practical value outside the conservation studio for many years.

Removal of algal slimes, lichens, mosses

There are many circumstances in which lichen and some varieties of small plants may enhance the appearance of masonry without adverse effect. However in other circumstances sterilizing treatment is required for reasons of maintenance or appearance. Biological growths which should receive attention include unsightly algal slimes on vertical surfaces and especially on paving, and acid-secreting lichens which cause the deterioration of certain building materials, such as copper or lead sheet, or marble, limestone and glass.

An important point to remember when planning the consolidation and maintenance of many unroofed monuments, where the access to exposed wall heads is limited and expensive, is the function of lichens in nature as soil formers. Lichens, which are harmless in themselves, may assist the establishment of mosses, small plants and even trees. Complete cleaning of normally inaccessible areas during a consolidation programme is therefore of great importance. Due respect should be paid to the conservation of unusual or harmless flora where control and observation are possible.

Health and Safety regulations affecting biocides are becoming increasingly stringent, and obviously influence the use of some materials in some countries.

Treatment

In some situations, surface soiling by organic growth can be removed very simply by dry bristle or soft wire brushing, or by jetting with a high-pressure, low-volume water lance, provided that the substrate is sound enough to take this mechanical cleaning. However, rapid re-colonization is likely and some form of toxic wash will probably be needed.

A great variety of treatments which effect an initial kill is available. Unfortunately, some of the traditional treatments (for instance, the persistent use of calcium chloride or concentrated ammonia solutions) can build up residues of damaging soluble salts. Concentrated solutions of zinc or magnesium silico-

fluoride may produce hard surface skins on limestone, which are liable to spall off.

A long term inhibiting effect on biological growth on some walls may be obtained by the installation of narrow flashing strips of thin gauge copper. These strips are tucked into the length of horizontal joints in the masonry, approximately every metre. The effect of rain washing over the strips is to subject the face of the masonry to a mildly toxic wash. A certain amount of light green staining must be expected, which makes this system unsuitable for very light-coloured stones. In addition, it will not be effective where the detailing on the building tends to throw off the rain.

The best treatments currently available for controlling lichen are quaternary ammonium compounds ('quats'), used in conjunction with tin oxide (tri-*n*-butyl-tin oxide, TBTO). The following method is suitable for masonry covered with algae, lichen, mosses and small plants. It is designed to give the maximum inhibition against recolonizing growth. Simpler specifications may be limited to a single application of a quat.

1. Remove as much growth as possible in the form of plants and thick cushions of moss, using knife blades, spatulas and stiff bristle or non-ferrous soft wire brushes. If the surface below the growth is delicate, or liable to be marked or scoured in any way, this preparation must be limited to lifting off the moss only.
2. Prepare a solution of quat by adding water to the manufacturer's specification.
3. Fill a pneumatic garden-type sprayer two-thirds full with the diluted biocide. Adjust the nozzle to a coarse spray setting. There should be sufficient pressure at the wand nozzle after pumping the compressor to saturate the surface of the masonry causing excessive bounce back and drift of the spray.
4. Apply a flood coat. Start at the top of the vertical surface to be treated and move across horizontally and slowly, to allow approximately 100 mm (4 in) run down. The next horizontal pass should be made across the previous run down.
5. Leave the treated area for at least one week. Brush off as much dead growth as possible with bristle brushes, making sure that any adjacent gutters and hoppers are kept clear.
6. Prepare a solution of a proprietary quat, including TBTO. A typical concentrate is delivered in 1 litre containers and should be diluted with 19 parts of water by volume.
7. Fill a second pneumatic sprayer with the diluted biocide and apply as before.
8. Allow the surface to absorb and carry out a second application of diluted quat as a growth inhibitor.

Protection of other areas

Provided that the applications are made carefully, there should be little risk to grass or flowers below the area being treated. However, as there is always a risk of spillage, it is sensible to lay a plastic sheet over plants on the ground whilst working. It is preferable to use only mechanical cleaning in areas which are in close proximity to buildings, areas occupied by farm animals, or ponds containing fish and other aquatic wild life.

Coverage

Coverage will vary with site conditions. As an approximate guide, one litre of biocide treats $1.5\,m^2$ ($1.75\,yd^2$). There is some evidence that there will be a lessening of toxicity if the diluted biocide is stored for a long time. Only sufficient biocide for the day's work should therefore be prepared.

Failures with these treatments are not unknown, but, if the above procedures are followed, there should be no problems. In exceptionally dry periods it may be beneficial to revive dormant dry lichen, which tends to be water repellent, with light water spraying a day or two before applying the biocide. Applications of biocidal treatment should not be undertaken during wet weather, or when windy conditions lead to excessive drift of spray. It is important that products are applied in strict accordance with the manufacturer's recommendations, in order to ensure the safety and protection of the environment.

Removal of graffiti

The graffiti problem is not new, but since the availability of aerosol paint cans loaded with cellulose paint it has become an international nuisance of new proportions. Although most paints used for graffiti can usually be removed from the masonry surface it is very difficult to remove pigment which has been carried into the pores by a solvent. Sometimes the application of a solvent to remove the paint can drive the pigment more deeply into the stone, for example the application of cellulose thinners to freshly applied cellulose paint graffiti. Water-soluble paint strippers, 1:5 solutions of water and trisodium phosphate and pastes of sodium hydroxide in clay have all been used with varying degrees of success. The stripper must be left in contact with the paint for long enough to cause softening and to enable scraping and brushing to take place successfully. The application of a thick layer is essential, and a layer of thin plastic film may be necessary over the application. After the paint has been scraped off the surface must be washed thoroughly, preferably in warm water and liquid soap. Unfortunately, repeated attacks with paint and repeated removals build up an unsightly, patchy masonry surface which often results in despairing surrender to the apparently inevitable, either by inactivity or by overpainting.

Occasional graffiti attacks are not such a problem and may be dealt with as above (resorting to the caustic stripper only when all else fails), with the possible refinement of picking out some of the stubborn pigment with an air abrasive pistol or pencil and a fine abrasive such as aluminium oxide crystals. Sometimes, as after the graffiti attacks on the sarsen monoliths of Stonehenge, the ghosting left behind after cleaning may be further obscured by encouraging the development of lichen with organic washes of animal dung in water. The application of such material is not recommended on fragile or highly sensitive surfaces. The graffiti vandal is normally attracted to a sound surface rather than to a friable, decaying substrate. Thus lichen not only obscures the visual scars left after cleaning but tends to discourage further attacks.

Areas liable to repeated attacks have sometimes been treated with a barrier application to try to prevent the migration of paint into the surface pores of masonry and to facilitate removal. These applications attempt either to block the pores, or to cause temporary blocking by softening and swelling in the presence of moisture, or to line the pores with a water-repellent coating.

A recent project carried out for the Department of Ancient Monuments and Historic Buildings by the Colebrand Research Unit in the UK has shown that the pore lining technique is the most successful. In a series of tests simulating repeated graffiti attacks on surfaces of varying porosity and permeability, either a single-pack, moisture-cured polyurethane or a two-pack polyurethane-based material on a colour stable isocyanate prepolymer appeared to be the most promising. Cellulose paint was entirely removed by swabbing with MIBK. No retreatment with the barrier was found to be necessary after any of the paint stripping stages, unlike some currently available barrier treatments. In addition the treatment is colour stable and need not change the appearance of the substrate. It will inhibit the formation of organic growth and has good abrasion resistance during repeated cleaning. It allows simple and fast paint removal with non-caustic paint strippers and allow the passage of moisture vapour.

These barrier treatments must not be used on surfaces which are decaying or where there are major moisture movements. In such a situation it would be wiser to leave the surface alone. If intervention is essential it is best to use a deeply penetrating silane treatment which will serve to consolidate and give protection against paint attack.

Colourless water-repellent treatments

Recommendations to apply a colourless treatment after cleaning are often made by professional advisors and contractors. Such treatments are only rarely necessary. General assumptions about the permeability of masonry walls can lead to expensive and unnecessary treatments with water-repellent liquids. In some situations these treatments can actually increase the incidence of water penetration and, where there is a concentration of soluble salts, they may accelerate decay.

Colourless water repellents are intended to improve the resistance of masonry to rain penetration. Modern water repellents line the pores of the bricks, stones and mortar with water-repellent material, which inhibits capillary absorption. Treated surfaces will still absorb water during prolonged rainfall, but will allow the evaporation of trapped water because the treated zone remains permeable to water vapour.

BRS Digest 125[4] states that 'water-repellent liquids should be used with discrimination, having regard to the cause of dampness and the suitability of the surface for treatment.' The cause of dampness is often inaccurately diagnosed. If walls are unusually thin, or unusually permeable, water penetration through bricks and stones may take place, especially in conditions of extreme exposure. If penetration persists after all other sensible remedial work has been carried out, such as correct tamping and pointing of joints and cracks and repair of defective copings, gutters, downpipes and flashings, then there may well be a case for the use of water-repellent treatment. However, water repellents are not a substitute for other maintenance work and can, in some cases, increase the incidence of water penetration where there are cracks present. Experience has shown that there are relatively few situations where a water-repellent treatment alone has solved a major damp penetration problem. It should be noted, however, that trials carried out by the Building Research Establishment in the UK (BRE Report *Rain Penetration through Masonry Walls*, 1988) demonstrated that better resistance to water leakage through a masonry wall was obtained when water repellents were applied to pre-wetted surfaces. Pre-wetting appears to have satified the porosity of the masonry so that when the water-repellent solution was applied it was to treat interface cracks efficiently instead of being drawn into the surrounding porous materials.

The application of water repellents may exacerbate decay in some situations. This can happen as a result of the evaporating of water which contains salts in solution from behind the treated layer leaving salt crystals in the pores behind the treatment. Repeated crystallization cycles can then lead to disruption and spalling of the treated surface. In addition to this hazard, the thermal and moisture movements of the thin, treated surface layer may be sufficiently different from those of the underlying stone to generate shear stresses which eventually lead to failure. For these reasons, silicone or other water repellents must not be used as consolidants or preservatives. They must not be applied to surfaces which are friable or spalling as the result of salt crystallization damage.

Sometimes colourless water repellents are applied after cleaning masonry surfaces as dirt inhibitors. Such treatments are successful in this role for the duration of the surface repellency. However, this tends to deteriorate relatively quickly even though the repellence may persist in the surface pores of the treated layer. Retreatment is possible, but is rarely carried out in practice because of the expense of access to most building facades. Unfortunately, the deterioration of surface repellency is rarely uniform and a patchy appearance can result. Even the short-term benefits of water repellents as dirt inhibitors are therefore debatable and rarely justify the costs of materials and labour.

Although caution is advised in diagnosis of damp penetration and in the use of water repellents on decayed surfaces or as dirt inhibitors, there are many other situations where their use does no harm, but is simply an unnecessary expense. It can double the cost of a small cleaning contract. Therefore, any proposal for their use requires very careful consideration.

Examples of situations where silicone water repellents have proved their worth include masonry close to the sea where decay is taking place on the inside face of mullions, tracery or lintels, but the outside face is sound. Here, water repellents can usefully be applied to the sound external face only. On extremely exposed sites, where rain is driven through permeable stones and mortar, the use of water repellents may be justified. They have also been used successfully on brickwork where there is a history of staining from limestone dressings, since they encourage the calcium carbonate and sulphate to run off the surface rather than be deposited in the bricks.

BS 3826[5] (now being superseded by BS 6477[6]) sets out performance standards and offers user guidance. It is advisable to use materials which are manufactured to BS 3826, or which meet its performance requirements. Classes of silicone water-repellent appropriate for various substrates are:

Class A for use on sandstone, clay brick, terracotta, cement and cement-like stucco.

Class B for use on limestones, calcium silicate bricks, cast stone.

Class C for use on limestones and cast stone.

Other water repellents are based on stearates, to which the same general comments on use apply.

Protecting buildings from birds

Bird droppings are a major disfigurement on some buildings and the accumulations of ledges can lead to decay of the masonry surface. Excreta can also be a hazard on paving. A recently cleaned building in a zone frequented by starlings or pigeons may quickly become resoiled unless measures are taken to control the nuisance. The various methods of attempting to effect this control are listed below.

1. *Netting.* Synthetic mesh of unobtrusive colour can be stretched across potential roosting sites such as pediments, capitals and entablatures or even window openings. These nets must be knotted mesh and securely anchored at adequate intervals to stainless steel eyelets. Whilst not obtrusive at a distance extensive areas of netting do not enhance the appearance of a building. Properly installed it is a basic but effective system although probably a last resort from a visual standpoint.

2. *Gels.* Strips of gel can be extruded from a gun applicator along all ledges where birds may roost. On wide ledges a number of gel strips must be laid. The object is to provide an insecure footiing which discourages the birds from settling. Unfortunately, although this system has been widely used, it requires fairly frequent re-application; when the gel attracts dirt it becomes harder and less effective. The dried gel is difficult to remove and can itself become a major cleaning problem. The solvent leaches into stone causing dark, disfiguring stains. Even the non-staining gels which have been developed have the same limited life.

3. *Spikes.* Spikes are commonly in strip form in aluminium or stainless steel secured by stainless steel screws through lugs into the stone. They are difficult to use effectively and have been known to be used as permanent shuttering for nests! To be effective a ledge must be covered with enough rows of spiked metal to prevent the birds from settling. Less obvious are almost colourless cones of plastic which are fixed with a resin adhesive to ledges and even to sculpture. Because these are single spikes they are more versatile than the strips but a large quantity are still required to form a defence. Single spikes in the form of fine stainless steel rods are sometimes used as antennae around, for instance, figure sculpture in niches. These antennae are set into prepared drillings in the stone in an epoxy adhesive at approximately 45° to the face of the stone. As local defence these kind of spikes are effective and maintenance free.

4. *Low-voltage wires.* A small electric charge is run through wires stretched between insulators along ledges. Whilst working these systems are moderately successful but are liable to breakdown, even as a result of being covered, locally, with bird droppings. Maintenance can be frequent and costly.

5. The most effective of the anti-roost devices appears to be stretched and sprung stainless steel wire. Fine stainless steel wires are supplied to purpose-made lengths terminating with a tight coil at each end. The coil terminals are secured to stainless steel eyelets and maintain tension in the wire. Even when a number of wires are stretched in parallel formation along a wide ledge they are unobtrusive and relatively maintenance-free. Stainless steel antennae are also available (see the drawing on page 140).

Other types of intervention which do not rely on the modification of building detail include:

6. *Trapping.* A labour-intensive exercise involving basket traps and bait installed, normally, on flat roofs requires the trapped birds to be removed from the site at daily intervals. It provides only very local control and has attracted criticism from bird protection groups.

7. *Noise.* Intermittent loud reports from a tape recording can be transmitted over a speaker system to keep birds on the move and discourage roosting. This type of system is only really suitable in confined spaces such as grain stores.

8. *Shooting.* This is a local solution which is only applicable to remote sites and requires a resident custodian or official competent patrols. Shooting at buildings is to be discouraged!

9. *Predatory birds.* Pairs of kestrels or other birds of prey can be effective locally if they can be interested in taking up residence, but they will move on if the food source disappears. Some success has been reported on isolated sites with artificial birds mounted on flexible wands which cast a moving shadow on the ground.

10. More ambitious controls relate to attempts to feed pigeon populations with corn coated with sterility-inducing hormones. The chemosterilant Ornitrol (22,25 diazacholeatenol dihydrochloride) was found to be effective in inhibiting reproduction in pigeons for three months after treatment and remained up to 75% effective from four to six months after treatment. The major problem in the field is the nomadic habits of pigeon flocks.

No note on pigeon control would be complete without reference to a distinctly Italian solution, the *Piccioncelli con olive nere,* a dressed pigeon dish with veal stock, pepper, salt, white wine, brandy and olives!

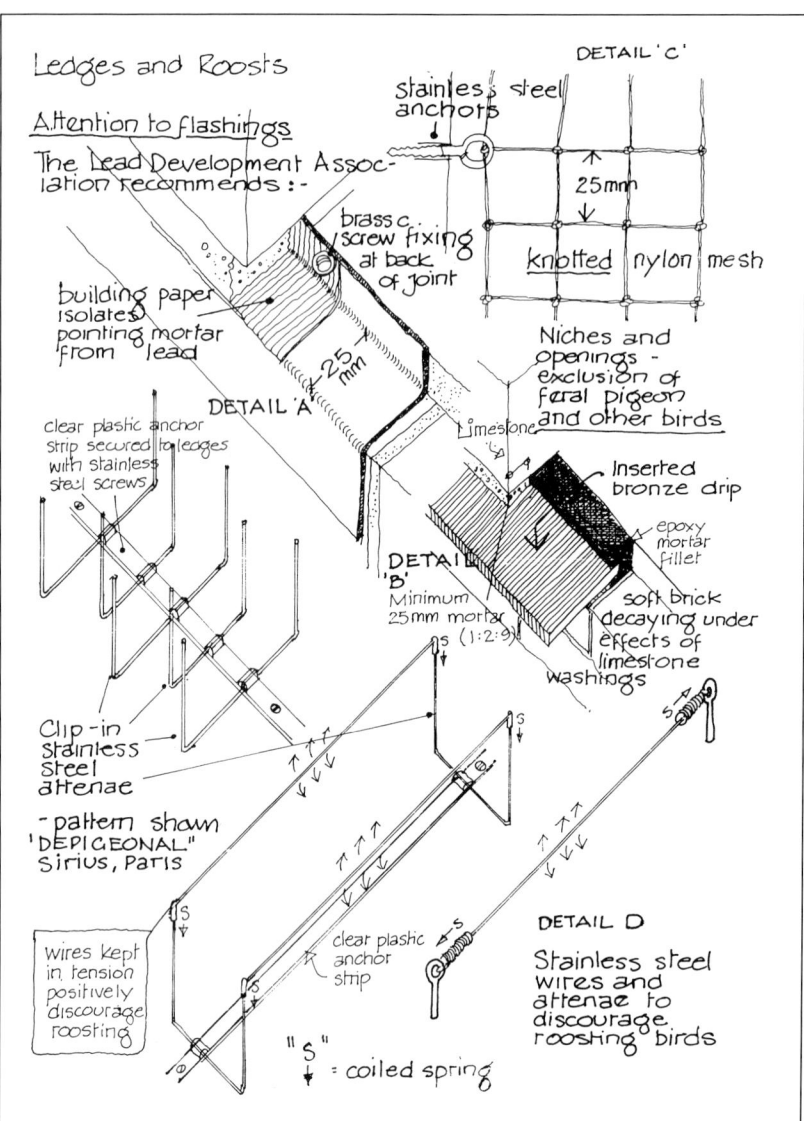

Ledges and Roosts

Attention to flashings

The Lead Development Association recommends :-

DETAIL 'C'

stainless steel anchors

25mm

knotted nylon mesh

brass c. screw fixing at back of joint

building paper isolates pointing mortar from lead

25 mm

DETAIL 'A'

Niches and openings - exclusion of feral pigeon and other birds

Limestone

clear plastic anchor strip secured to ledges with stainless steel screws

Inserted bronze drip

epoxy mortar fillet

DETAIL 'B'

soft brick decaying under effects of limestone washings

Minimum 25mm mortar s (1:2:9)

Clip-in stainless steel attenae

- pattern shown 'DEPIGEONAL' Sirius, Paris

clear plastic anchor strip

wires kept in tension positively discourage roosting

DETAIL D

Stainless steel wires and attenae to discourage roosting birds

"S" = coiled spring

Removal of soluble salts from masonry

The capillary movement of moisture through masonry is often associated with salt deposition, which tends to be mainly concentrated at or close to the wall surfaces. The disruptive forces associated with the crystallization of these salts cause decay, usually seen as pitting, powdering and flaking of the masonry. Drying out of the walls associated with a damp-proofing treatment or the elimination of a groundwater source may also lead to an increase in the amount of salt at or near the wall surfaces. Deterioration may increase rather than diminish unless measures are taken to reduce the salt content

of the masonry. Certain salts, particularly some chlorides, are hygroscopic and can take up moisture directly from the atmosphere. Dampness and deterioration may persist even after rising damp originating from the base of the wall has been stopped. In these circumstances the salts must be removed or at least substantially reduced from the masonry if deterioration is to be controlled.

Methods of removing salts

Two methods of removing some of the soluble salts from decaying masonry are the use of clay poultices and the use of a sand:lime sacrificial render. These systems have been used where the sources of soluble salts were rising damp, sea or estuarine sand in mortar, past flooding, storage of culinary salt, storage of gunpowder, storage of chemicals, human and animal urine, and caustic alkali cleaning and weed-killing treatments. The techniques are mainly suitable for large, plain areas of masonry or simple architectural detail. They should not be used (except in a limited way by trained conservators) on delicate, damaged surfaces of carving or sculptures, nor where the pre-wetting would create problems for plaster, painting or embedded wood or metal. Where poulticing or sacrificial rendering is considered to be appropriate it may need to be built into a long-term maintenance programme, perhaps every five or ten years, particularly if there is a persistent replenishment of soluble salts. In other situations, where the source of contamination has been removed, a single cycle of poultices may be sufficient to effect improvement.

Treatment of salt-contaminated masonry with a poultice

The form of deep washing of masonry which is usually described as desalination involves saturation and poulticing with an absorbent clay to try to reduce the level of potentially damaging soluble salts concentrated within the surface of decaying stone. To remove all soluble salts in a building is impossible, but a significant reduction in the outer 100 mm may have the effect of stabilizing a previously friable surface or may prepare the way for a consolidant whose curling process would be seriously inhibited by a high concentration of, say, sodium chloride. A further use of absorbent clay packs is as temporary plaster after the installation of a damp-proof course.

In principle the desalination technique is very simple. A wall is saturated for several days by spraying with mists of clean water, until wetting has occurred for the full, or a considerable, depth. During experimental work monitoring equipment is often set into the wall core. Plaster of Paris moisture gauges were used by the Building Research Establishment at the Salt Tower in the Tower of London in 1974.[7]

Fine sprays mounted on a boom delivering under 200 litres per hour are sufficient to feed six spray heads covering an area seven metres square. The setting up of the sprays should be designed to produce a consistent pattern of wetting. The wetting period is determined by construction of the wall and the porosity of the stone and mortar, but is likely to extend over three days and nights. Small areas may be persistently wetted from a back-pack sprayer, but this is labour intensive and tends to be less effective. In some situations it is sensible to carry out dry brushing before wetting. It is important to make sure

loose material is removed from the site. During the wetting process temporary gutters are required to collect the run-off from the wall surfaces and to conduct it to a gully or run-off point well away from the treatment wall base and any other walls. Heavy-gauge polythene sheet, PVC guttering, timber battens and a siphon tube may be all that is necessary to provide an effective water catchment and drainage system. Sheeting should also be used to minimize splashing.

When the wetting process is complete the absorbent clay or diatomaceous earth (usually attapulgite or sepiolite clays, 50 mesh) is added to enough clean water to make a soft, sticky paste. Water must not be added to the clay or a lumpy, unworkable mix will be formed. The clay poultice can be mixed by hand or with a small mechanical mixer, depending on the quantity required. When free of lumps the poultice is plastered onto the wet treatment wall in a single layer 20–25 mm (up to 1 in) thick using a plasterer's float or broad trowel. A 50 kg bag of clay will cover approximately three square metres. In its freshly mixed state the clay has very good adhesion and can be levelled reasonably accurately, even by a relatively inexperienced person. An important part of the technique is the ironing on to ensure good contact at all points. To help the clay keep its bond for as long as possible a light-gauge galvanized wire mesh can be pressed into it and tacked carefully into joints with galvanized staples. Any springiness in the mesh can be reduced by localized cutting with wire snips and pressing the cut ends into the clay. In some situations, especially where the wall surface is heavily contoured as in core-work, the overall adhesion of the clay will be assisted by cutting strips of open weave hessian soaked in a runny slurry of attapulgite clay and pressing these into the poultice. These strips, approximately 75 mm (3 in) wide, may be used alone or with wire. Wire is essential on a large area of flat surface where the weight of the clay tends to induce pulling away from the wall.

When the treatment wall is fully plastered it must be protected from direct sun or rain or, if internal, from any heat source which will produce rapid drying. Externally a ventilated space can most easily be set up with a tarpaulin or reinforced plastic sheet as a tent.

As the poultice dries out it draws salt laden water from the masonry. Water evaporating from the clay face leaves behind salt crystals which are usually seen in the form of efflorescences on the clay or wire. Drying conditions and the thickness of the wall dictate the contact time, which varies considerably from a few days to weeks. One month is not unusual for drying out, during which the clay lightens in colour, cracks, shrinks and detaches from the wall. At this stage the staples should be withdrawn with pliers, and the bulk of the clay may be rolled up on its wire reinforcement. The spent clay should be put at once into plastic sacks or otherwise removed safely from the site. Small amounts of clay still adhering should be brushed off the wall with a stiff bristle brush. These sweepings must also be removed from the site.

The cycle of wetting and poulticing may need to be repeated several times to reduce the salts to an acceptable level. Salt sampling and analysis may need to be carried out to determine the levels present. Clay poultice desalination is a lengthy process but it does not require a lot of supervision, expensive equipment or highly skilled personnel. It is best scheduled in with other works on or near the site.

Clay poultice desalination has mostly been used on stone walling. On brickwork or rubble, where there are plenty of keys for the poultice, special care needs to be taken when brushing down to remove all traces of dry clay from the joints. Any masonry which has been subjected to extended periods of salt crystallization may well require pointing at the completion of the desalination treatment.

Treatment with a sacrificial render

Where it is not possible to remove excessive amounts of salts with the poulticing technique, the application of a porous sacrificial render may provide a more practical method of overcoming the problem. A porous render is applied to the wall and evaporation of moisture from the wall results in soluble salts being transferred from the masonry to the render. The render will deteriorate with time and may require renewal, but the masonry will be protected against continued decay. A sacrificial render can be used either to reduce the salt content of a wall where rising damp treatment will also be carried out, or it can be used to protect a wall against salt attack where rising damp cannot be prevented.

The wall is first wetted and a render of one part slaked and screened lime putty to four parts fine sand is applied at least 12 mm ($\frac{1}{2}$ in) thick to both sides of the wall, (if possible) to a height 50 mm (2 in) above the salt crystallization/evaporation zone. The render should not be overworked with a trowel as optimum moisture evaporation and salt transfer will be obtained when the render has an open texture and a rough finish to increase the surface area. A practical and visually pleasing way of achieving this is to scrape the surface down after rendering with the fine-toothed edge of a hacksaw blade. This should be carried out after the surface has begun to stiffen.

As salts transfer to the render and crystallize there,

the render will begin to break down. Salt-contaminated render deposits at the base of a wall should be collected frequently. Where a contamination is severe, the application of only one render coat may be insufficient to reduce the salt context to a safe level and further treatment will be required. The remains of the first coat should be carefully removed, the wall re-wetted and the second coat applied.

Sacrificial sand:lime renders are a relatively slow method of masonry desalination. A period of several months may be required, depending on the level of salt and the amount of evaporation. Most success has been achieved on walls where rising damp was still present, before any damp proofing installation was carried out. The process is, however, inexpensive and easy to undertake. The method was developed in Australia where it has been used successfully on sandstone and brickwork.

Determining salt levels

If reasonable assessment is to be made of poulticing or sacrificial rendering, the level of salt within the masonry should be determined before, during and after a programme of work. Initially it may also be important to determine the types of salts and their hygroscopicity. The services of a laboratory will be required here. Samples should be taken at depths of 0–25 mm, 50–75 mm and 75–100 mm (0–1, 2–3 and 3–4 in), within the zone deterioration, which is usually about 900 mm (36 in) from ground level. After a clay poultice has been removed some drying and migration of salts will continue. Therefore the wall should be allowed to dry before further samples are taken for salt analysis.

References

1. Price, C.A., 'Industrial cooperation in the study of pollution effects', paper presented at the World Congress of the Heritage Trust in Toronto
2. Mansfield, T., 'Building cleaning and the stone cleaning industry', *Stone Industries*, April 1988
3. Lazzarini, L., Marchesini, L. and Asmus, J.E., 'Lasers for the cleaning of statuary: initial results and potentialities', *First International Symposium on the Deterioration of Building Stones*, La Rochelle, France, September 1972
4. BRS Digest 125, *Colourless treatments for masonry*, Building Research Station, January 1971
5. BS 3826, *Silicone-based water repellents for masonry*, British Standards Institution, 1969
6. BS 6477, *Water repellents for masonry surfaces*, British Standards Institution, 1984
7. Bowley, M.J., *Desalination of stone*, BRE Current Paper

Identifying soiling patterns

Figure 8.1 Soiling patterns indicate the nature of the stone. The limestone facade of St Margaret's, Westminster, in London exhibits clean parapets, cill and plinths. Wherever rain-washing is regular limestone is kept clean. Only the sheltered and semi-sheltered zones collect dirt

Figure 8.3 This limestone detail illustrates the two conditions very clearly. The rain-washed surfaces are roughened but sound and clean. The sheltered zones are crusted with dirt and the sulphate skin below is beginning to split, spall and blister. Maintenance washing could significantly overcome this problem in the sheltered zones

Figure 8.2 In some instances, as on the Old Palace retaining wall at Westminster, where there are repetitive elements, the light and dark contrasts have a strong architecture impact which is not always desirable. More importantly, the areas under soiling are the ones where acidic water sits in droplet form, reacting with the limestone to form a calcium sulphate skin

Figure 8.4 The soiling pattern in this illustration of a sandstone building in Leith (Scotland) is clearly different to that of Figure 8.1. In this case the most exposed features are the most heavily blackened

Figure 8.5 In contrast to Figure 8.2, repetitive elements on the sandstone of Lichfield Cathedral show reverse soiling. Cills, plinths and weatherings, the areas regularly washed by rain, are densely black, whilst the more sheltered zones remain clean

Figure 8.6 This detail illustrates the two conditions commonly to be found on external sandstone. Saturation zones, in this case the quoins of the buttress and the weatherings, are soiled in a way which clearly will not respond to water-washing. In these zones the dirt is bound to the surface with a siliceous matrix related to the etching of the stone by acidic rainfall. These are the same zones prone to suffer, through constant wetting and drying, from the decay phenomenon usually described as contour scaling. Failures of contour scaling related to pore blocking can be seen on the plinth weatherings. Although maintenance washing could not, by itself, avoid the development of contour scaling, there is some evidence that it could delay the problem if instituted from the early years of exposure and that it could, again if instituted early after exposure or mechanical or chemical cleaning, prevent the curious and unwelcome soiling patterns

Identifying soiling types

Soil types need to be properly identified and any associated deterioration accurately diagnosed before cleaning is advised. Figures 8.7 to 8.12 all involve soiled limestone, but each example requires a different treatment

Figure 8.7 Carbon deposits form the bulk of the soiling but conceal a calcium sulphate skin which is being disrupted along a 'tide-mark' under a cornice. The cornice and coping need to be pointed to prevent further water migration, and the salt activity zone washed and poulticed with attapulgite clay packs after the wall has been washed with nebulous water sprays assisted by bristle brushing. A refinement would fill the decayed area with a lime:stonedust:casein sacrificial layer

Figure 8.8 The soiling and associated decay in this illustration is primarily affecting the brickwork but is in part caused by the presence and detailing of the limestone flush bands. Calcium carbonate and sulphate deposition in the pores of the brickwork bring about disruption and flaking as salt crystallisation develops. The increased surface area of the decaying brick provides ample key for wind- and rain-borne dirt. It must be acknowledged that any realistic dry abrasive cleaning will further increase the surface losses and that any saturation technique will further distribute soluble salts and increase, initially, the incidence of efflorescence. Heavy encrustation may be lightly dressed off with sharp chisels and hand-held carborundum blocks. Potassium hydroxide in CMC (see Figure 8.10) packs achieves the bulk of cleaning followed by warm water washing using lances at less then 150 psi. Whilst still wet, the areas affected by efflorescence are poulticed with clean water and attapulgite clay to draw out mobilised salts. When dry, the clay is lifted and dry brushed off. Lead drips must be inserted in the bottom bed joint of all flush limestone dressings

Figure 8.9 The limestone detail in this illustration is almost totally obscured by plate lichen, to the extent that it had been mistaken for limewash. It is not always necessary to remove such growths, even if there is some light etching of the surface from secreted acid, but since at this stage there is no possibility of seeing the stone or its condition removal is advisable. The area of stone exposed by the removal of a small section of lichen shows a split calcium sulphate skin. If this is typical the lichen could play a role in exacerbating local decay. Small, round-edged plastic and wood scrapers will remove most of the lichen, supplemented with orange sticks, and bristle or nylon toothbrushes. Wet scrubbing should be avoided. A flood spray application of a quaternary ammonium biocide followed after twelve hours by bristle brushing will remove tenacious areas of growth. A further inhibiting flood coat, applied to dry stone, will inhibit further growth and may become a maintenance treatment

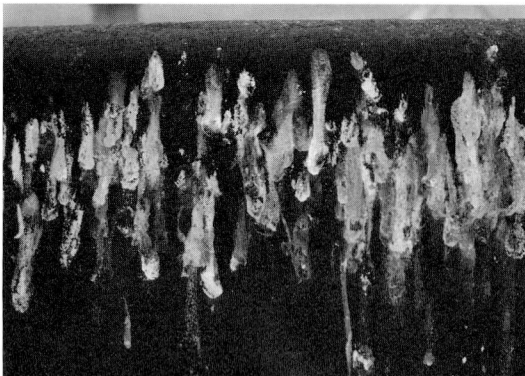

Figure 8.10 Dense, rather greasy soiling proved to be related to early linseed oil treatment (a ubiquitous water repellent/surface binder) which attracts particulate matter to it and inhibits natural rain-washing. Carbon deposits and especially soiling attributable to diesel emissions formed secondary deposits which were further soiled in some locations with bird excrement. Successful and safe removal of complex deposits of this kind inevitably involve more than one method. In this case a sequence of wood scrapers, non-ionic detergent and warm water used with bristle brushes was followed by potassium hydroxide in a carboxymethylcellulose pack and, finally, local areas of methylene dichloride poultice and efficient rinsing with clean water

Figure 8.11 The dark vertical staining is caused by rusting iron above the ashlar. Long-standing stains of this kind are not easily removed altogether but can usually be lightened satisfactorily by a poultice of clay (such as attapulgite or sepiolite) and sodium dithionite. The surface must be pre-wetted and several poultice applications may be needed before finally washing off. Of course, the source of staining should be treated to isolate it or removed before the cleaning process commences

Figure 8.12 The patchy appearance of this ashlar after washing was attributed to an earlier cleaning followed by the application of a silicone-based water repellent. The object of this application was apparently to encourage the wall to be self cleaning. Because the treatment had not been maintained and had begun to lose water-repellency unevenly, the new cleaning produced or enhanced a stain pattern. It is not wise to use water repellents for this purpose unless there is an assurance that regular retreatment (say 5–7 years) will take place

Feasibility studies for cleaning

Figure 8.13 For any but the most simple facade with an obvious soiling pattern some preliminary feasibility study including work on site as part of the diagnostic approach is highly desirable and may well be essential. Although valuable information may be gained by a cleaning demonstration such as the one shown in this illustration this must not be seen as a 'study' nor should any results obtained necessarily be regarded as typical. The clean area involves no real problems such as may be obtained at openings or in saturation zones

Figure 8.14 A carefully recorded feasibility clean of a piece of detail (top) which included oil, diesel soiling and paint and which showed (above) texture and mouldings unchanged in the process provided exactly the kind of information required for a detailed specification which required no speculation from contractors asked to submit competitive tenders

Figure 8.15 Feasibility studies should seek to anticipate all the problems which may be encountered during the main contract. These will include items on access, plant location and control of dust, water and noise. Left (above): shows window protection consisting of polyethylene sheets and heavy duty tape. Although cheap, during wet cleaning it may be confidently expected that this protection will peel off at frequent intervals risking water penetration and costly stoppages of the work. Left (below): shows alternative protection consisting of resin-bonded plywood templates set into tracery reveals in an improvised but effective gasket of pipe insulation. Although it was several times the cost of the sheet and tape, the study concluded that the template system was very much more effective and was likely to require no maintenance due to breakdown during the extent of the contract

Figure 8.16 The clean patches in this illustration are the result of trial cleaning with solvents and detergents in poultice media. Each patch has been placed on an area representative of the most difficult soiling problems and is referenced to a record sheet listing constituents, application method and conditions, contact periods and wash-off procedures. Results obtained in this manner are of real benefit in specifying and costing the work and reduce risks to the building

Washing

Figure 8.17 Removal of dirt from limestone by washing is traditional, often safe and often successful. Jets of water are played on the surface until the dirt is sufficiently softened to be removed by bristle or phosphor bronze wire brushes. Unfortunately, unless the building surface is very simple to clean, prolonged saturation can be involved in the process of removing substantial crusts of soil under projections or in detail, especially when the water jets are of the inefficient, large droplet type. The clean stone in the centre of the illustration responded to water spraying in five hours; the encrusted dirt in the detail required sixteen hours, during which time the building was subjected to considerable volumes of water

Figure 8.19 Unfortunately staining cannot be totally controlled by limiting the quantity of water, although this is a significant help. Staining shown in this illustration is random and was unpredictable, reflecting the surface condition and permeability of individual stones. Some staining, too, has already taken place during weathering. Light pre-wetting of the whole wall, to control absorbence, is advisable before concentrating water sprays on one horizontal lift. Much staining is encouraged by allowing soiled water to run down onto dry stones in the initial stages of cleaning

Figure 8.18 Other washing problems may be seen in the form of staining, especially of light coloured limestone and especially when the volume of water is left to do the work without any mechanical assistance in the form of brushing. Staining is usually the result of solubilised soiling being absorbed into some of the stones. As the wall dries out staining can become quite pronounced

Figure 8.20 Decayed stones, especially where small-scale detail is involved, are very vulnerable to washing with water sprays. Not only may water jets be responsible for mechanical damage, they will also mobilise soluble salts. Although the products of pollution, these salts may be performing a structural role in supporting critical flakes of weakened stone. On undercut, small-scale carving such as the example in the illustration, washing may actualy bring about the final destruction of some of the detail

Figure 8.22 Water lances operating at 20–25 psi with a small amount of fine abrasive are useful in cleaning simple ashlar. In this case the use of water is the vehicle for the abrasive, which distinguishes the technique totally from wet-grit blasting, where water serves only to contain dust generated by compressed air and abrasive

Figure 8.21 The ultimate mechanical damage to stone by water is brought about by the use of high pressure water lances. Water lances used much in excess of 500 psi clean mechanically by cutting the surface; if the stone is already weak, or is characterised by soft, sandy beds as the limestone in this illustration, wholesale destruction may be brought about

Figure 8.24 One of the most important washing developments of recent years has been the use of nebulous sprays. As the name implies, these nozzles are so designed to pass water through a fine brass gauze filter which atomises the water and delivers a wet mist through the nozzle. Nebulous water is easily caught by the wind and it is therefore necessary to place spray assemblies close to the wall surface and to screen the scaffold. There are many advantages to nebulous spraying. Dirt is softened progressively without cascades of water and the sprays can be mounted on straight booms, flexible bars or individual clusters just where they are most needed. A further refinement is to control the water by a pre-set timing device to deliver, for example, 8 seconds of water at 8 minute intervals. This 'intermittent' or 'pulse' washing is increasingly a feature of high quality washing

Figure 8.23 At the British Museum in London, the whole of the main facade of limestone was cleared using low pressure (20–25 psi) water as a carrier for abrasive. Because so little repair was required, the whole operation was carried out from a mobile hydraulic platform (Clearstone Ltd). In France, Thomann-Hanry use a similar access but enclose the cleaning platform on the end of the arm in a partial vacuum chamber, which 'sucks' itself to the surface of the facade. Within this chamber one or two operatives can work with low pressure dry abrasive guns to achieve safe dust-free cleaning with very low impact on the stone

Abrasive cleaning

Figure 8.25 The simplest mechanical cleaning involves abrading or scraping a surface by hand. Even with care this must be acknowledged as to some extent destructive of the original surface. The most severe treatment, that of spinning off the surface with power tools and abrasive discs, should never be described as cleaning but as re-dressing. Removal of an oil-stained surface by the use of mason's drags or small blocks of carborundum lubricated with water may be appropriate in skilled hands if the staining or soiling cannot be removed safely by poulticing

Figure 8.26 Few cleaning methods have caused more damage or evoked so much criticism as the mechanical system popularly known as 'sand-blasting'. This illustration (above) shows the characteristic conditions of commercial dry blasting. The cleaning operative wears a helmet with a visor which is fed by an air line to maintain positive air pressure. The hose delivers air from a compressor, at pressures typically between 40 and 80 psi, and an abrasive which might be sand or a non-siliceous type such as copper slag. The abrasive spread is too wide to be selective and the dust generated after the first two minutes largely eliminates visibility

Figure 8.27 Even when the dust is contained by a 'wet-head' system the most serious problems remain. In this illustration (left) a water line is brought up to the nozzle and feeds a perforated ring ('water-shroud') clipped over the nozzle. By this means visibility is much improved and there may be some slight cushioning effect from the water, but the system is still crude and, in terms of slurry generated, very messy

Figure 8.28 On any surface other than the simplest and most robust, standard commercial sand or grit-blasting on the scale shown in Figures 8.26 and 8.27 should not be employed. In this illustration a reasonable clean of ashlar, columns and flat fascia can be seen at the top of the picture; but the composite capital, the moulded architraves and, above all, the sculpture have been excessively torn and pitted. Cleaning such detail by such crude means is impossible, and should never be attempted

Chemical cleaning

Figure 8.29 The chemical cleaning of sandstone is usually carried out with proprietary products containing hydrofluoric acid, orthophosphoric acid and surfactants. In less sophisticated forms hydrofluoric acid has been used as a cleaning agent since World War I, so that it has almost become a traditional cleaning material. Because it is extremely hazardous, even in many proprietary forms, to personnel and to building materials such as glass and some metals there is a strict code of practice governing its use. This illustration (above) shows the valuable crown glass of Holyrood Palace in Edinburgh prepared for cleaning. The glass has two coats of peelable latex, a marine ply template and heavy duty polyethylene masking. Because even acid vapour can etch glass, scaffold tubes must be capped and washed off regularly during the cleaning

Figure 8.30 Holyrood Palace after cleaning and removal of temporary protection (left). The deep brown staining of some of the stones in the fluted pilasters has been enhanced by the action of the acid on the iron constituents of the stone. This effect may be caused by reaction with the acid, but it is more likely that it was already present to some degree and can often be detected on the soiled building by a darker soiling pattern

Figure 8.31 The dark coloured parapet on the Corn Exchange in Leith is typical of saturation zone staining. Water can migrate freely through free-standing features such as this, carrying soluble, staining material to the surface. Often this goes undetected until cleaning, when blame is unfairly placed on the contractor or the cleaning material

Figure 8.32 Other situations, where the cleaning material is clearly inappropriate, can be demonstrated by this illustration (above) of staining up to the party wall line on a sandstone terrace. In this case the colour of the entire unit within the facade has been changed from a cream colour to a rich orange-brown in the course of removing dirt with a proprietary hydrofluoric acid cleaner

Figure 8.33 Successful cleaning with hydrofluoric acid based cleaners or any other chemical depends on a proper diagnosis of the soil type, identification of the stone/s, detailed specification based on site and laboratory trials, competent, experienced operatives and adequate supervision. In this illustration (left) the operative is properly dressed in full protective clothing, including face and hands. The water lance, a flat 15° v-jet operating at 500 psi, is being used to remove a cleaning agent after a dwell time of five minutes. The same lance is used to pre-wet the wall before application of the cleaning agent to avoid the risk of dry stones or joints absorbing cleaning material

Figure 8.34 Failure to remove certain cleaning agents successfully can result in disfigurement or damage, or both. This illustration shows staining and efflorescence resulting from residues of sodium hydroxide left in limestone detail. Salt crystallisation damage is likely as wetting and drying cycles promote the distribution growth of sodium salts

Figure 8.35 Failure to remove hydrofluoric acid will result in the formation of colloidal silica bound to the surface of the stone. This illustration shows carefully applied hydrofluoric acid formulation permanently bound to sandstone after being left for over twelve hours instead of 5–15 minutes. This disfigurement could only be removed by spinning, blasting or otherwise redressing the masonry to remove the outer 2 mm

Figure 8.36 Successful cleaning with proprietary chemical products is quite feasible, but must be based on proper investigation and diagnosis of the cleaning problem, and not on a 'hit-or-miss' basis influenced by a particular range of products available. In general, more applications of material diluted down from the supplier's recommendations will achieve a better standard of cleaning. Very dilute hydrofluoric acid formulation was used to clean the flush banded brick and stone of St Pancras Station, London, with excellent results

154

Figure 8.37 Chemical cleaning agents are increasingly used in poultice form to effect safe, successful cleaning. This sequence shows a poultice cleaning of a limestone facade in Londonderry, Northern Ireland, using a formulation of the 'Mora' type, based on CDTA with sodium and ammonium bicarbonate in a carboxymethylcellulose (CMC) body. The heavily stained facade is wetted up, poulticed and covered in plastic film for periods which may range from seven to 24 hours. When the staining has been mobilised and has migrated into the poultice the material is removed with wooden scrapers into bins and any residue removed with low pressure water lances. The final illustration of the sequence shows a very successful level of clean with no staining and no harmful disfiguring by-products

9

Surface treatments

David Honeyborne, John Ashurst, Clifford Price and Keith Ross

Introduction

And as touching the stone of this cuntre, that shuld be for the jambes of your doores and windowes of your seid chapell, I dare not take upon me to sett no more therof upon your werkes, hit freteth and fareth so foule with himself, that, had I not ordained lynnessde oyle to bed hit with, hit wolde not have endured, ne plesed youre Highnesse. Wherefore I have purveyed xiij tons tight of Cane stone, for to spede youre werkes withall.

There is, of course, nothing new in the decay of building stones. The matter was as much of a concern to Roman builders as to Wren, and as much to us as to Henry V's Chief Mason writing his report on the building works at Calais in 1421, as recorded above. Writing in 1929, E.G. Warland gave the following summary on the subject of stone preservatives:

Preservatives may be grouped under three headings – oils, wax, or solutions giving rise to the formation of insoluble salts.

1. Boiled oil has been used extensively, but its use is accompanied by discolouration of the face of the stone.
2. Paraffin wax is an effective preservative, especially if driven into the stone by heat, but this presents a difficulty not easily overcome in practice.
3. Those preservatives which come under the remaining heading are solutions which are intended to act upon the carbonate of lime making insoluble compounds, such as silicate of soda and fluosilicic acid and its salts. These silicon derivatives certainly have some value if administered correctly and at the right time.

Little had changed in several centuries because oil was still the most commonly used 'preservative' and even now is used in some rare instances. As we now know, oil can be the most difficult material to remove from old stonework, has in some instances contributed to decay and has almost always been disfiguring in some way. However, it must be remembered that ancient coatings may have been applied as a ground for paint, which is usually the case where they are found on sculpture or architectural detail. These coatings may be lime alone, lime and cheese or lime and animal fat, or may be more sophisticated such as one of the 'secrets' of Timoteo Rossello, mixing colophony, honey, wax and mutton tallow.[2] Investigation of old surfaces must always take this possibility into account. Such coatings are normally distinguishable from later applications whose role was evidently to arrest decay.

The caution we have learnt from the lesson of applied 'preservatives' must be exercised in any other treatment we are considering; we must always think in terms of side-effects and long-term effects and, if possible, what we use as a treatment must be reversible. The dilemma for the conservator comes when the only hope for a stone 'patient' is a non-reversible treatment. In this situation the conservator must always take a second opinion, must be convinced that there are no possible alternatives, and must be prepared for criticism.

Our objective in applying surface treatments must be to 'enhance durability', but not in a speculative or experimental manner. 'Medicine' should be a last resort, when all other sensible remedial and protective work has been carried out and still a genuinely unacceptable rate of decay continues. This situation and condition is not always well defined and is usually the subject of some controversy; but if we look first to good housekeeping in the form of sensible and thoughtful maintenance and not too soon to advanced technology to get our stones out of trouble we shall not make many mistakes and will not be guilty of creating worse conditions and more serious maintenance problems than we found.

In the first part of this chapter David Honeyborne describes the ways in which stone surfaces are treated to try to extend their life. As an ever-increasing number of proprietary products and pseudo-scientific trade literature assails us it is increasingly important to have some basic understanding of decay mechanisms and treatments.

J.A.

Part 1 Surface treatments in general

David Honeyborne

When all decay-inducing defects in a stone building have been repaired and the best possible maintenance procedures are being regularly carried out deterioration of the stone and other exposed building materials will still inevitably occur. This is a consequence of nature's subservience to the Second Law of Thermodynamics. Fortunately the rate of deterioration is often imperceptible over the span of a human lifetime. Therefore human beings do not become so discouraged that they give up fighting the rearguard action that must be the task of every conservator.

Where the rate of deterioration is more apparent, those caring for a stone building or piece of sculpture often wish to apply some proprietary product to the surface of the stone in a desperate attempt to arrest or at least slow down the change. Such surface treatments have sometimes proved to be beneficial, but sometimes they are positively harmful to the stone and are often quite ineffective. This chapter reviews surface applications that can usefully be made to building and decorative stone in existing buildings.

While it is possible to formulate general rules that might reasonably be expected to remain valid for many years to come, guidance at a more detailed level might become outdated quite quickly as new products are developed. To overcome this problem the following important conservation organizations in Italy have agreed to collaborate in producing progress reports on the subject[1].

The National Research Council Centres for the Study of the Causes of Deterioration and of the Methods of Conservation of Works of Art (CNR Centro di Studio delle Cause de Deperimento e Metodi Conservazione delle Opere d'Arte) in Rome, Florence and Milan.

The Central Institute for Restoration (Istituto Centrale del Restauro) in Rome.

The International Centre for Conservation (ICCROM) in Rome.

Up-to-date information may be sought from ICCROM, 13 via di San Michele, 00153 Rome, Italy.

Water repellents

When masonry walls are unusually thin or unusually permeable, rainwater will sometimes penetrate the wall and cause staining of and/or damage by salt crystallization to interior surfaces. When the building is near the sea and sea-salt is carried to it by strong winds the damage can be particularly severe. If this kind of penetration occurs even after full attention has been paid to the maintenance of pointing, gutters, flashings and other details that are essential to ensure longevity for the building, there is a case for using some colourless water repellent treatment on those parts of the building where water is entering the structure. This can lead to a reduction in the rate of decay, if not a cure. It is essential that any such treatment should be applied with the aim of preventing water *from entering* the structure. There are many cases on record of the failure of attempts to prevent further damage from occurring by treating already decaying areas of stonework with some colourless water repellent. This approach often makes matters worse.

Several types of water repellent have been tried for preventing or reducing the entry of water into stonework. Most notable are waxes and silicones applied as solutions in an appropriate organic solvent. It is usually considered essential that the stonework should be dry at the time of application. In some ways waxes present more problems than silicones. It is often difficult to obtain adequate penetration if the wax solution is too concentrated. On the other hand the use of very dilute wax solutions can result in a failure to achieve adequate repellency. Moreover, even if adequate repellency is achieved, the wax-treated wall tends to become discoloured in course of time, either because the wax becomes yellow as it is chemically changed by the action of sunlight or because the waxy surface picks up more air-borne dirt than an untreated surface. These effects are usually avoided by the use of silicone solutions in organic solvents though even with this system erratic results can be obtained.

Silicone-based repellents seem to be more effective on sandstones and other siliceous stones than on limestones. However, unpublished work at the Building Research Establishment at Watford, England, indicates that the effectiveness of such treatments depends very much on the presence or absence of pore water lying several millimetres below the relatively dry surface. Treatment after a pre-wetting and partial drying is said to give good repellency even with limestone. The water resists an unduly deep penetration of the silicone solution. The water-repellent barrier is therefore deposited in a concentrated form in the outer layer of stone and in the masonry joints[2]. After drying, a second treatment without a water barrier is said to produce an enhanced effect. In the absence of an initial water barrier, the resulting water repellency is sometimes poorly developed or evanescent. The writer does not know of any confirmation of this effect in full-scale treatments. Naturally those applying water repellent treatments in attempts to prevent damaging water penetration are normally unwilling to leave a substantial area untreated to enable fair comparisons to be made.

Once water repellency has been established by a silicone treatment the treated areas tend to remain dry-looking for a long time and the darkening associated with wax-based treatments does not occur. However, it is important that treatments are applied to all stonework between natural projections in the building. Otherwise the demarcation line between treated and untreated areas may become apparent soon after treatment, and more apparent as time goes on because the two areas will differ for quite a long time in their tendencies to pick up dirt, even though the *surface* repellence tends to deteriorate relatively quickly with most formulations. Re-treatment is feasible.

A short discussion of silicone chemistry as applicable to stonework conservation is given later in this chapter. More details and many references have been given by Amoro and Fassina[3] and monographs on the subject have been written by Meals and Lewis[4] and by Freeman.[5]

A more recent approach to the problem of making sandstones water repellent involves the use of chemicals called perfluoro-polyethers. One of these materials, which has a molecular weight in the range 6000 to 7000 and is applied at a rate of $30\,g/m^2$ in the solvent trichloro-trifluoro-ethane, is reported[6] to be particularly effective and causes no discoloration of the substrate.

Water repellents as preservatives?

Because water plays an essential part in the main processes of stone decay, it is tempting to believe that the application of a water repellent treatment to a decaying stone face will arrest the degradation

processes. Unfortunately, the preliminary results often look very promising and this has led people to try this type of treatment on stonework of historical importance without waiting for the results of long-term trials on unimportant substrates. In fact, in the long term, wax-based treatments will give rise to often unacceptable discoloration, even in rural areas. Crystallizing salts will break through the treated surface or frost will cause a whole surface to break away. The final effects can be worse than those that would result from doing nothing. Schaffer[7] cites an example of stonework that was in a serious state of decay within a few months of being given a wax-based surface treatment. While silicone-based water repellents are unlikely to cause the same kind of discoloration when used in this way, the other consequences of their use are likely to be unsatisfactory. Clarke and Ashurst[6] reported the results of a comprehensive large-scale experiment which included 68 examples of the use of silicone-based water repellents on a large range of types of stone exposed under various conditions. Computations based on their report show that 92.6% of these treatments resulted in no change in or a worsening of the rate of decay; 75.4% resulted in no change in or a worsening of the appearance of the stonework and, of the cases that showed a reduction in the rate of decay, or an improvement in appearance, none showed a significant change. It thus appears that attempts to use colourless water repellents as stone preservatives are a waste of money. There is no reason to believe that the discovery of the value of perfluoro-polyethers as water repellents will lead to any modification of these conclusions.

Consolidants as preservatives?

It could reasonably be argued that since decay processes clearly weaken stonework, particularly near exposed surfaces, any kind of water-repellent treatment should be preceded by a treatment that would help to restore strength to the affected area and possibly give sound regions better strength to resist the weathering agencies. In fact, Clarke and Ashurst[6] included lime water and also silicon ester in their trials for this purpose. Lime water is a very dilute solution of calcium hydroxide which, on absorbing carbon dioxide gas from the atmosphere, is converted to calcium carbonate, the main component of limestone. The idea is that the calcium carbonate formed from the lime water will crystallize in critical positions in a limestone and strengthen it. Since calcium hydroxide has a low solubility, many coatings of lime water will always be necessary to achieve much in the way of strengthening, even if the crystals form at the most favourable positions in the stone. There is no value in applying lime water to a sandstone. Clarke and Ashurst reported[6] that 57% of the lime water treatments resulted in no change or in a worsening of the decay, and that all the treatments resulted in a worsening of the appearance of the stonework. In 43% of cases the treatment was successful in slowing decay, but none showed an improvement of any practical significance.

Silicon ester is a chemical product that is applied to stone in an alcoholic solution with the intention of hardening it. If some liquid water or water vapour is present, the silicon ester decomposes as the alcohol evaporates and a jelly-like material, silica gel, is developed which forms hard silica as it gradually loses water. Because silica is the main component of sandstones a treatment with silicon ester may seem more appropriately applied to sandstones than to limestones. However, Clarke and Ashurst's experiments[6] provide little evidence for this. Their results for silicon ester on all substrates show that 84.5% of all treatments resulted in no change or in a worsening in the rate of decay and 73.1% of the treatments resulted in no change or in a worsening of the appearance of the stonework. In trials involving only sandstone substrates 77.8% of treatments had no effect on the rate of decay and 100% had no effect on the appearance. The success in reducing the rate of decay was not of practical significance and in every case the effect on appearance was negative compared with the control panels.

A second reason sometimes put forward for the use of silicon ester on stonework is that, as a pretreatment, it will help a following silicone treatment to take better on limestone. Clarke and Ashurst's trials[6] were not intended to assess the efficacies of water-repellent treatments. However, of those treatments in their trials that involved the application of both silicon ester and a silicone to a limestone, 94.1% showed no improvement or possibly an acceleration in the rate of decay and 70.6% showed no change in or a worsening of appearance. Whether or not the silicon ester improves the effectiveness of the water-repellent treatment, it does not act as, or help the water repellent to act as, a preservative in these circumstances.

Is stone preservation by surface application impossible?

As long ago as 1932, Schaffer,[7] referring to failures of the stone 'preservatives' of that period, wrote:

The properties demanded of a perfect stone preservative are many and conflicting. For instance, a waterproofing agent is required to prevent penetration of moisture, but, at the same time, it should allow water which has gained access at some unprotected point to escape. A common cause of failure is that, even in porous materials, and under the most favourable conditions, the preservative penetrates only to a relatively small depth and a surface skin is formed which differs in physical properties from the underlying material; dangerous stresses are likely to be set up and ultimately the skin may flake off. The penetration of the preservative solution can only take place when the stone is dry ... and in cases where the deposition of solids depends on the evaporation of a solvent, the process of drying causes much of the dissolved substances to be drawn back to the surface. Another source of danger is that certain forms of treatment introduce soluble salts as by-products of the reactions involved; these salts may be extremely deleterious.

Forty years later Schaffer's second and third points (the importance of deep penetration and the need to ensure that a solvent carrying a preservative material did not withdraw the material while evaporating) were no doubt taken into account when Clarke and Ashurst[6] recommended in 1972 that 'a study of deep penetration of stonework with materials likely to avert or compensate for the harmful effects of time and the environment' should be carried out. This idea is now widely accepted. Thus Price[8], writing in 1975 about the failures encountered by Clarke and Ashurst, has said:

There are two main reasons for this. Firstly, water can invariably get behind the treated layer, either by passing through it in the vapour phase or by the absorption of rain or ground water at some unprotected point. This water evaporates from behind the water-repellent layer and any salts in the solution crystallize there. This can lead to spalling of the treated surface. Secondly, the thermal and moisture movements of the thin surface layer may be sufficiently different from those of the underlying stone to generate shear stresses that eventually cause failure. These effects would be reduced if the treated layer were sufficiently thick. The critical thickness is unknown but current research ... is aimed at impregnating stonework with a suitable material to a depth of at least 25 mm.

An impregnation treatment should serve both to consolidate friable stone and to prevent further deterioration caused by salt crystallization, either by making the salts inaccessible to water or by making the stone more resistant to crystallization damage. Increased resistance to crystallization damage could be achieved by an increase in the stone's tensile strength or by a modification of its pore structure. In order to achieve adequate penetration the treatment should have a high surface tension, a low contact angle and a very low viscosity at the time of application.

Schaffer's fourth point (that some treatments introduce soluble salts as by-products of the reactions involved) is certainly well recognized in authentic conservation work. Rossi-Doria, Tabasso, Torraca *et al.*[1] give a list of consolidants that they consider to be unsuitable for use on stonework, mainly because they give rise to soluble salts as by-products. This list and a list of materials they refer to as 'advisable consolidants' are presented in *Table 9.1*.

Is stone preservation by surface applications impossible? Probably not, if a suitable material can be found that will achieve adequately deep impregnation, will form a barrier against water movement but not against water vapour, and will not introduce soluble salts into the stonework either directly or as a reaction product. Available materials that are likely to meet these requirements are considered below.

Conservation of stonework by consolidants

The first four recommended groups of consolidants in *Table 9.1* are chemical products that are related to one another and to the 'silicon ester' used by Clarke and Ashurst[6] in their stone preservation experiments. All are compounds of silicon, carbon, hydrogen and oxygen, yet each plays a different role in attempts to preserve stone. It is virtually impossible to provide any satisfying explanation of their functions and potential without understanding a certain amount of structural organic chemistry. We will start with the group that is simplest in terms of molecular structure.

Ethyl silicates

There are many ethyl silicates, but the one that has been of importance in stone conservation is more strictly called tetra-ethoxysilane. Its molecular structure is shown in *Figure 9.1(a)*. In this figure the short straight lines are used to represent chemical bonds and the symbol 'R' is used to represent the group of atoms C_2H_5-, which is usually called the 'ethyl radical'. When this ethyl radical is combined with one oxygen atom to form C_2H_5O-, it is known as an ethoxy radical, hence the name tetra-*ethoxy*-silane. The simpler radical, CH_3-, is known as the methyl radical, and if the ethyl radicals in *Figure 9.1(a)* were replaced by methyl radicals as shown in *Figure 9.1(b)* the result would be known as tetra-*methoxy*-silane.

When tetra-ethoxy-silane has been used in stone conservation it has usually been fed to dry, or at least surface-dry, stone. If some water is present, either as a liquid or a vapour, the tetra-ethoxy-silane begins to decompose producing alcohol, C_2H_5OH (written as

Table 9.1 Consolidants for stone masonry

Recommended by Rossi-Doria et al.[a]	Not recommended by Rossi-Doria et al.[a]
Ethyl silicates	Sodium or potassium
Alkyl-trialkoxy-silanes	silicates[b]
Mixtures of the above	Sodium and potassium
Alkyl-aryl-polysiloxanes[d]	aluminates[b]
Acrylic resins	Zinc or magnesium
Barium hydrate (baryta)	fluorosilicates[c]
	Epoxy resins[e]

[a] Rossi-Doria, Tabasso, Torraca *et al.*[1]
[b] Because they give rise to soluble salts as by-products.
[c] Because they have poor penetration and give rise to soluble salts, mainly as a result of impurities.
[d] Either totally or partially polymerized.
[e] Because they penetrate poorly if they are not diluted with a solvent and block the surface pores. They also form shiny films which flake and turn yellow in time. Drawbacks substantially reduced if diluted with solvent, particularly with applications on very porous stone.

R−OH in *Figure 9.1(c)* since R− is C_2H_5- in that instance). The new product is called tetra-hydroxy-silane. This is unstable and each hydroxyl (−OH) radical will react if possible with an unchanged ethoxy radical or with another hydroxyl radical to form an −Si−O−Si− link and alcohol or water, respectively, as shown in *Figure 9.2(a)* or *(b)*. In either case the final solid product is silica, the crystals of which consist of a three-dimensional lattice of silicon and oxygen atoms in the ratio of 1 to 2. (Hence the common formula for silica is SiO_2.) This is the main constituent of sandstones. In the intermediate stages of these reactions, when the solid product is known as silica gel, a considerable number of water molecules are physically held in the silicon−oxygen lattice. The same solid product would have been obtained if the starting material had been tetra-methoxy-silane, but in this case the by-product would have been methyl alcohol rather than ethyl alcohol.

Amoroso and Pancella have shown that the compactness of the silica gel formed (and, by implication, the eventual binding power of the silica) is at its best if the reaction takes place very slowly as it would in dry stone in an atmosphere of low relative humidity. In practice, a very slow reaction might lead to an unacceptable loss of impregnating material by evaporation.

The product known as silicon ester differs from tetra-ethoxy-silane because some partial formation of a silica network has already been allowed to occur. The material is described as partially polymerized. It is fed to stonework in the form of a solution in alcohol, which must evaporate before hydrolysis and polymerization can take place.

H   represents a hydrogen atom
O   represents a oxygen atom
C   represents a carbon atom
Si represents a silicon atom
R   represents a group of atoms (a radical) as indicated in each case.

(a) Tetra-ethoxy-silane $R—O—\overset{\overset{R}{|}\overset{|}{O}}{\underset{\underset{R}{|}\underset{|}{O}}{Si}}—O—R$ where $R = H—\overset{\overset{H}{|}}{\underset{\underset{H}{|}}{C}}—\overset{\overset{H}{|}}{\underset{\underset{H}{|}}{C}}—$

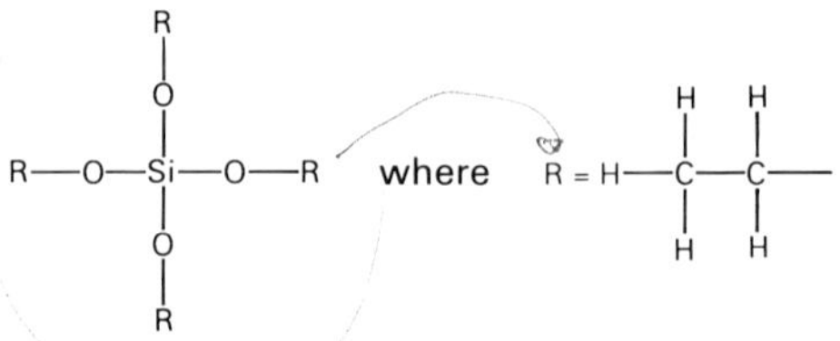

and is written as C_2H_5- for convenience. C_2H_5 – is called an ethyl radical.

(b) Tetra-methoxy-silane has the same structure except that $R = H—\overset{\overset{H}{|}}{\underset{\underset{H}{|}}{C}}—$

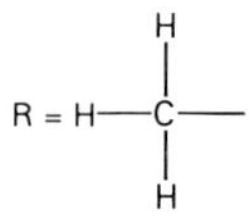

which is written CH_3 for convenience and is called a methyl radical.

(c) Hydrolysis of tetra-ethoxy-silane (dashed lines indicate where chemical bonds are broken).

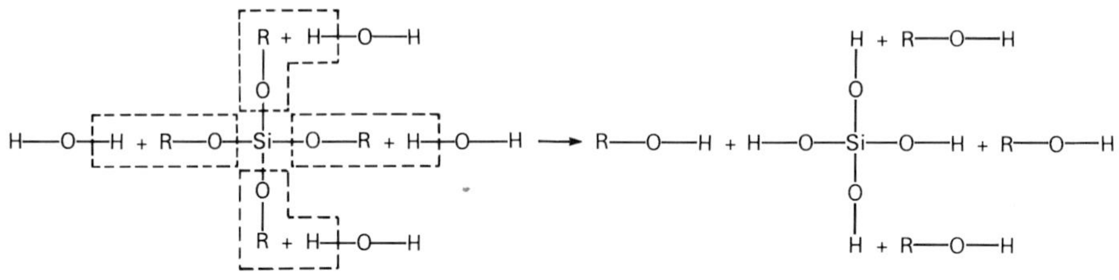

Tetra-ethoxy-silane + water → tetra-hydroxy-silane + alcohol. Since R is the ethyl radical in this case the alcohol is ethyl alcohol.

(d) Polymerization of tetra-hydroxy-silane.
The tetra-hydroxy-silane molecules will react *either* with other tetra-*hydroxy*-silane molecules (see *Figure 9.2(a)*) or with unchanged tetra-*ethoxy*-silane molecules as shown in *Figure 9.2(b)*. This process will continue until all the carbon present has been converted to alcohol. At that time the silicon and oxygen atoms in the ratio of 1:2 will have formed a complete network. This is silica, the essential material in sandstones. For this to happen the alcohol must be able to escape.

Figure 9.1 Structural chemistry of an ethyl silicate

Because of the considerable differences in the thermal expansion coefficients of silica (the main constituent of sandstones) and calcite (the main constituent of limestone) ethyl silicates seem far more likely to consolidate sandstones effectively than limestones. In fact, chemical manufacturers of products of this kind now normally claim that they act only as sandstone consolidators (see for example reference 9).

Alkyl-trialkoxy-silanes

The general structure of alkyl-trialkoxy-silanes is shown in *Figure 9.3(a)*, where R_1 and R_2 could independently be a methyl (CH_3-), an ethyl (C_2H_5-) or a propyl (C_3H_7-) radical, etc. The simplest member of this family would be methyl-trimethoxy-silane, the structure of which is shown in *Figure 9.3(b)*. Tetra-ethoxy-silane reacts with water

(a) By reaction between tetra-*hydroxy*-silane molecules. The dashed lines indicate where chemical bonds are broken.

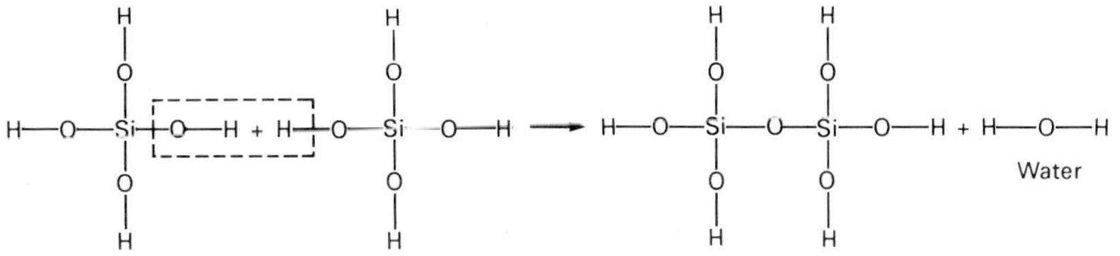

Each stage reduces the proportion of hydrogen and oxygen relative to silicon until no more hydrogen is left and the silicon:oxygen ratio is 1:2 in terms of atoms. When dry the final product is silica dioxide.

(b) By reaction between tetra-*hydroxy*-silane molecules and remaining molecules derived from tetra-ethoxy-silane (for example, dihydroxy-diethoxy-silane).

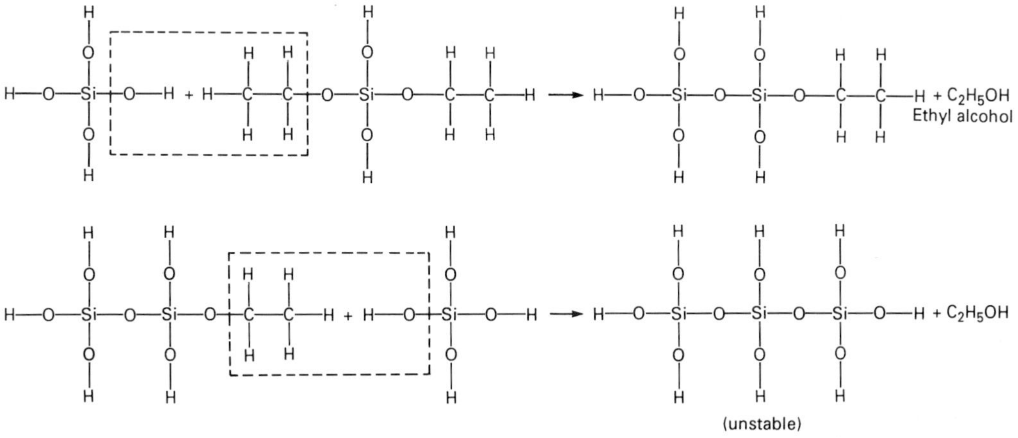

These and many other similar chemical reactions lead to reductions in the numbers of carbon, hydrogen and oxygen atoms present, relative to the number of silicon atoms, until nothing is left but silicon and oxygen atoms in the ratio of 1:2. This is silica.

Figure 9.2 Polymerization of tetra-hydroxy-silane

to form a network of silicon and oxygen atoms (silica). Methyl-triethoxy-silane or methyl-trimethoxy-silane also reacts with water to form a network of silicon and oxygen atoms. However, each silicon atom has one methyl radical attached to it and only three oxygen atoms. Because of the presence of the methyl radicals this material would have the property of water repellence at some sacrifice of consolidating power. An indication of the way the

hydrolysis and polymerization reactions proceed is given in *Figure 9.3(c)*.

A material with these characteristics has considerable potential for use as a conservation treatment for stonework if it can penetrate the stone sufficiently deeply and in a satisfactory concentration. Conservators have tried several techniques to achieve this. The application of a silane on its own to dry stonework can result in deep penetration but water

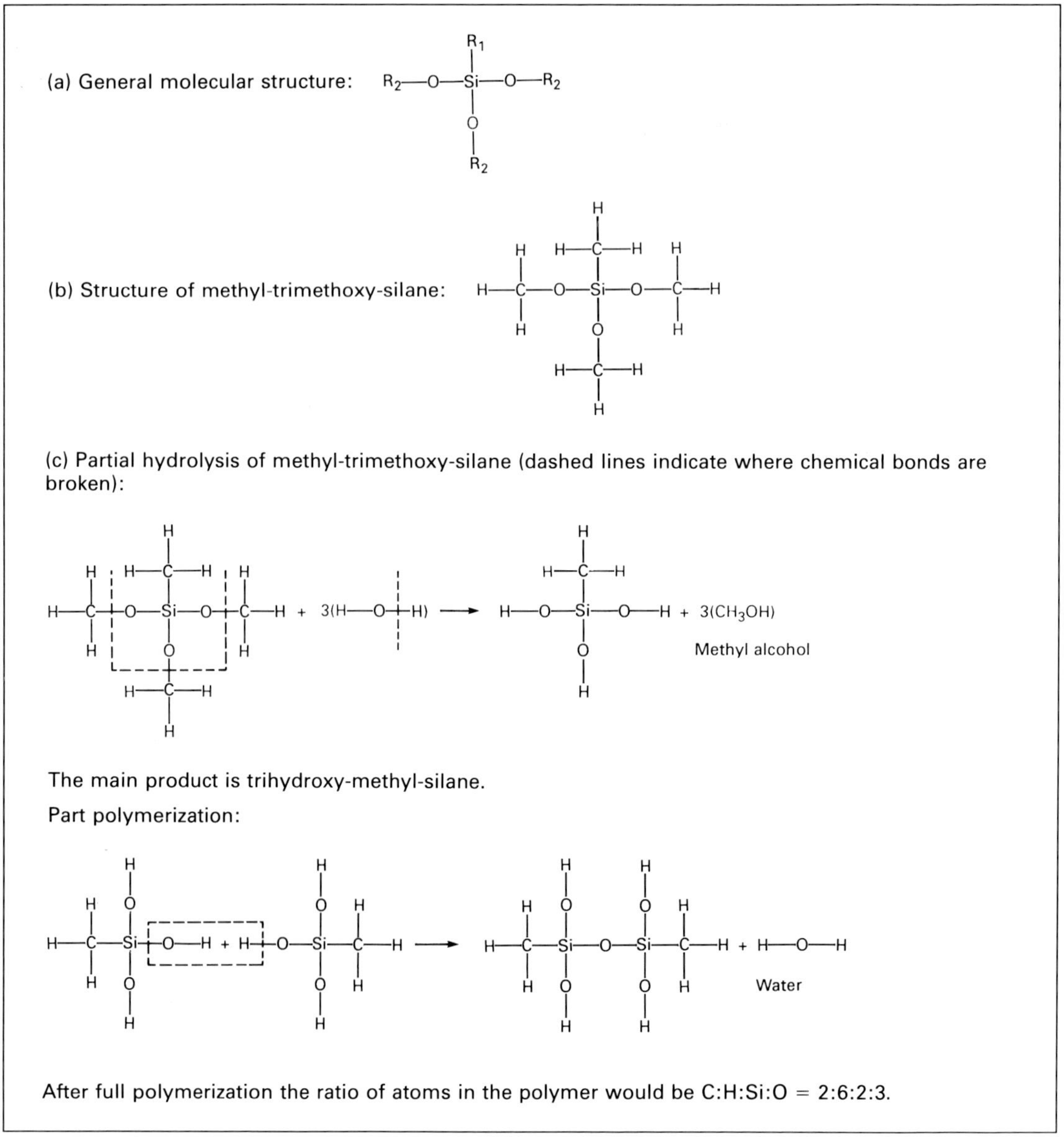

(a) General molecular structure: R₂—O—Si—O—R₂ (with R₁ above Si and R₂ below)

(b) Structure of methyl-trimethoxy-silane:

(c) Partial hydrolysis of methyl-trimethoxy-silane (dashed lines indicate where chemical bonds are broken):

$$H-C-O-Si-O-C-H + 3(H-O-H) \longrightarrow H-O-Si-O-H + 3(CH_3OH)$$

Methyl alcohol

The main product is trihydroxy-methyl-silane.

Part polymerization:

+ H—O—H

Water

After full polymerization the ratio of atoms in the polymer would be C:H:Si:O = 2:6:2:3.

Figure 9.3 Structural chemistry of alkyl-trialkoxy-silanes

is needed for the hydrolysis. To wait for moisture in the atmosphere to achieve hydrolysis would result in loss of most of the silane by evaporation. On the other hand, if the stonework is not dry, hydrolysis will take place but the resultant resin might not be deposited in an advantageous position. In the treatment of objects housed in museums or other buildings such as churches, it has been found to be useful to add acrylic resins to the uncatalysed silane.

The chemical significance of this is not entirely clear but it allows the conservator a long working time to deal with difficult jobs involving, for example, much surface readjustment of small pieces of stone that have become displaced by the decay process. It also allows for solvent cleaning of the surface. Solvent cleaning must be completed before the resin hardens, otherwise micro air-abrasive cleaning will be necessary.

Where consolidation is to be the last operation on stonework there is much to be said for using a *catalysed* silane system. In such systems water must be available from the start and additional substances must be added to make the silane and water miscible. Ethyl alcohol has been used for this purpose when caustic potash is used as a catalyst[10], and the rate of the reaction can be controlled by adjusting the amount of caustic potash used. This kind of system offers advantages for the treatment of external stonework, where conditions cannot be so well controlled as they can be in a museum laboratory or even in a church. However, one disadvantage is that the initial alcohol content can be as high as 38%. The alcohol takes no part in the reaction so it represents a severe dilution of the consolidant.

A later system which was developed at the Building Research Establishment and tried in Britain at a number of sites seemed to offer much greater advantages.[11] In this system, water sufficient for the hydrolysis is added to the alkyl-alkoxy-silane and the two liquids are rendered miscible by the addition of a very small quantity of acid. An organo-metallic catalyst is also added. The system is covered by a British Patent. The viscosity of the system remains low until a certain induction period has elapsed. After that it begins to rise rapidly as hydrolysis and polymerization take place quickly under the influence of the catalyst. This sequence reduces evaporation loss to a minimum and 'freezes' the advancing liquid so that it does not spread too far. The length of the induction period is controlled by selecting the appropriate initial composition. The system has been marketed under the trade name of Brethane since 1984. It is available only to licensed applicators who have successfully completed a two-day period of instruction.

Disadvantages of silane-based systems

The most important disadvantage of catalysed alkyl-alkoxy-silane systems is that once stonework has been treated and the silane has become hydrolysed and apparently polymerized there is a risk that any early retreatment with a fresh silane-based preservative will cause a previous immobile treatment to swell. This can be accompanied by such pressure that stone surfaces could suffer some disruption. For this reason conservators carrying out prolonged work on an object requiring more than one impregnation do not like to use silane systems. There is, however, reason to believe that polymerization continues for some time after the initial set of a catalysed silane system and it seems likely that a completely polymerized system would not swell in this way. Further investigation is needed.

In company with most other stone preservative systems, the residue left in the stonework after

Table 9.2 Theoretical maximum pore filling by some alkoxy-silanes

Preservative	Theoretical proportion retained (%)*
Methyl-triethoxy-silane	37.6
Ethyl-triethoxy-silane	42.2
Methyl-trimethoxy-silane	49.3
Ethyl-trimethoxy-silane	54.3
Phenyl-trimethoxy-silane	62.6

* These figures are only a guide because in calculating them it was assumed that the densities of the preservative and the polymerized product were equal.

hydrolysis and polymerization is just a fraction of the amount of polymer absorbed by the stonework. *Table 9.2* shows the fraction by weight for four relatively simple alkyl-alkoxy-silanes. The best retention is obtained with trimethoxy-silanes. Unfortunately these evolve methyl alcohol during the curing process and this is poisonous. Greater retention could be obtained by increasing the size of the alkyl radical but various difficulties then arise, either because the raw material is prohibitively expensive or the substituted radical confers less advantageous properties on the resulting preservative. For example, a phenyl (C_6H_5-) radical in an aryl-alkoxy-silane confers flexibility on a polymer rather than water repellence. In any event, the proportion of solid retained will be diminished by the extent to which any of the preservatives has been diluted with a solvent.

Because methyl alcohol is poisonous, all consolidation systems using an alkyl-methoxy-silane should be carried out under very well ventilated conditions.

Aryl-alkyl-polysiloxanes (partially or totally polymerized)

The fourth group of recommended consolidants listed in *Table 9.1* is the aryl-alkyl-polysiloxanes. The expression 'aryl' indicates the presence of a carbon ring radical such as phenyl, C_6H_5-. The phenyl radical confers flexibility on the product of polymerization of a silane. It also confers solubility on the polymer in organic solvents such as xylene or toluene. Therefore this type of silicone may be applied to stonework as a fairly concentrated solution. Nevertheless it is, in principle, less satisfactory than water-repellent/consolidation systems based on initially unpolymerized silanes to which no solvent has been added. Possibly Rossi-Doria *et al.*[1] recommend it because it has not been known to cause harm and because it was used with great success in stabilizing mural paintings on a gypsum ground at the Ghur Emir Mausoleum.[12] Poly-phenyl-methyl-siloxane was applied in solution in xylene to render

(a) For most purposes the starting point is an alkyl-methacrylate:

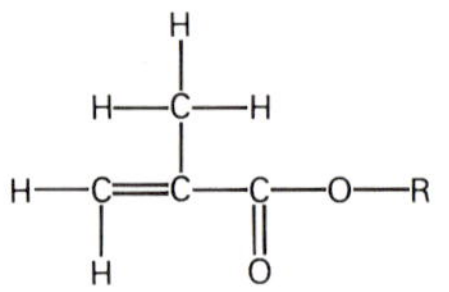

where R is an alkyl radical such as: methyl (CH_3-)
                                         ethyl (C_2H_5-)
                                         butyl (C_4H_9-)

This compound has a double chemical bond between two carbon atoms. This bond is easily broken and the material is very reactive. Under the influence of additives such as benzoyl peroxide and heat these double bonds will break and allow a large number of molecules to link up to form long chains. The result is a material that sets hard and is resistant to the weather when cold, but may be softened when heated again. Perspex is one example. The benzoyl peroxide is said to catalyse the reaction. It remains unchanged itself. Writing in a condensed form:

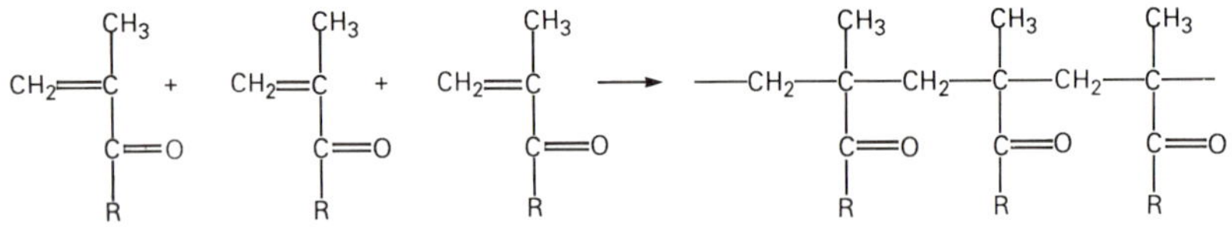

This is part of a chain molecule.

In consolidation work this thermoplastic material is usually introduced into the stone as a solution in a solvent such as tri-chlor-ethylene. The product is correctly referred to as poly-methyl-methacrylate or PMMA.

The solubility of PMMA is an advantage in consolidation work in some ways. An even more stable product can be formed by incorporating a cross-linking agent with the PMMA which will cause it to form a network of parallel chains.

Figure 9.4 Structural chemistry of acrylic consolidants

the gypsum ground-water repellent, and surface consolidation was then done by means of a suspension of 2-ethyl hexylacrylate in water. A solution of poly-phenyl-methyl siloxane was also recommended by Biscontin and Marchesini.[13] It was used to consolidate the terracotta facade of the Cathedral of S. Maria Assunta in Chivasso and for parts of the sandstone of the Re Enzo Palace in Bologna.

Acrylic systems

The essential structural chemistry of acrylic-based consolidating systems is given in *Figure 9.4*. A wide range of types are available, either directly or by blending. Methyl or ethyl methacrylates give rise to hard materials on polymerization; butyl methacrylate produces a softer polymer. The polymers formed are usually chain polymers, thermoplastic materials that

are fairly easily dissolved in some appropriate organic solvent such as trichlorethylene. However, cross-linked (thermoset) polymers can be produced by incorporating a catalyst such as benzoyl peroxide.

Probably the commonest attempts to use acrylics in conservation have involved the employment of polymerized materials in an organic solvent such as trichlorethylene. The solution must be fairly dilute or the viscosity will be too high to permit reasonable penetration. However, such systems suffer from a defect common in conservation work. The consolidant tends to be drawn back as the solvent evaporates and the polymer is concentrated in a thin layer near the surface. There are many records of partially or completely unsatisfactory results from conservation attempts of this kind (see, for example, references 14 and 15). However, Domaslowski and Lehman[16] claim that choice of an optimum combination of solvent and type of polymer, e.g. with a greater than 10% solution of polybutyl-methacrylate in white spirit, can achieve good results.

To overcome the difficulties arising with acrylic polymer *solutions*, many attempts have been made to consolidate stone using acrylic *monomers* and arranging for them to polymerize once they have penetrated the stone to an adequate depth. In the Soviet Union, for example, it is claimed that objects made of deteriorating wood or stone can be made more resistant to decay by impregnation with a solution containing nine parts of inhibitor-free methyl methacrylate monomer and one part of xylene to which has been added 20 g of benzoyl peroxide catalyst for each 983 ml of the solution. Decaying objects are then impregnated under vacuum, wrapped in polyethylene foil to prevent evaporation and heated to 120 °C (reference 17). Because of the need to evacuate and heat, this treatment can be applied only to objects of the kind normally kept in museums. Munnikendam has devised an easier experimental procedure by using technical quality methyl methacrylate monomer which sets in about one hour after the addition of 2% benzoyl peroxide and 0.6% dimethyl para-toluidine. The reaction takes place at room temperature. Spraying the treated object immediately with water thickened with starch or kaolin prevents loss of organic solvent or monomer. This coating can be removed with warm running water.[18] Under some conditions Munnikendam achieved 90% retention of polymer when impregnating a sandstone by this method. The use of gamma-radiation to polymerize the methacrylate is an interesting development.

This method seems very encouraging for museum conservation or the conservation of small externally exposed objects that may be removed from a building for treatment and then replaced. In general, however, acrylic materials do not yet offer the same hope as some silane-based systems do for the conservation of external stonework. Perhaps the most important use of acrylic materials for external conservation work at present is in the consolidation of loose flakes on carved stone. This is because acrylics weather well and have great transparency, and any excess can easily be removed from the treated surface by stroking it with solvent-saturated swabs. Nonformale[19] has developed a valuable restoration technique based on these properties.

Barium hydrate (baryta)

The barium hydrate shown in *Table 9.1* is more correctly called barium hydroxide or baryta. A solution of this material was proposed in the mid-nineteenth century by Church[20] as a preservative treatment for limestone or marble. Calcium sulphate, the sparingly soluble product of attack on limestone

or marble by sulphur-based acids in the polluted air of industrial countries, will react chemically with a solution of barium hydroxide to form the nearly insoluble barium sulphate. The chemical reaction is:

$$CaSO_4 + Ba(OH)_2 \rightarrow BaSO_4 + Ca(OH)_2$$

Calcium sulphate ⟶ Barium hydroxide ⟶ Barium sulphate (insoluble) ⟶ Calcium hydroxide

The theory is that not only is the calcium sulphate, which is the basis of sooty incrustations on lime-stone, thus removed, but the coating of nearly insoluble barium which takes its place forms some barrier to further attack on the limestone by the acidic sulphur-based gases. In practice the system proved to be a failure, probably because the barium sulphate formed a barrier of insufficient thickness.

Just over a century later this method of conservation was given a new lease of life by Lewin[21] who showed that a treatment *in depth* could be achieved by soaking the limestone in a solution that contained urea and glycerol as well as barium hydroxide. By this process the surface of the limestone itself is converted to barium carbonate and the underlying stone is said to consist of solid solutions of barium and calcium carbonates which gradually decrease in barium content until, at some considerable depth, pure limestone is reached again. The chemical reaction in this case is:

$$CaCO_3 + Ba(OH)_2 \rightarrow Ca(OH)_2 + BaCO_3$$

Attack by sulphur-based acids would be expected to be brought to a standstill by the insoluble layer of barium sulphate that would develop *in depth*. If the regions have compatible coefficients of thermal expansion and rather similar wetting and drying movements this treatment appears to be promising. However, little more seems to have been published about it in recent years.

Epoxy resins

As shown in *Table 9.1*, Rossi-Doria *et al.*[1] placed epoxy resins in the 'not recommended' category mainly because no reasonable depth of penetration could be achieved unless the resin was greatly diluted with some suitable solvent. In fact, diluted epoxy resins can also prove to be disastrous as stone preservatives because small perforations in the film of set resin can be sufficient to allow the passage of acidic sulphur-based gases.[22] Nevertheless two developments in this field deserve to be watched with interest. Domaslowsky[23] appears to have achieved success with limestones and sandstones by immersing them in a 10% epoxy resin solution in an alcohol–hydrocarbon mixture. However, the operation appears to be rather tedious and more suitable for museum specimens than externally exposed stonework. In the second development Munnikendam[24] achieved promising results using a resin based on a special low-viscosity epoxy resin (1,4 butanediol diglycidylether) and diluted with a silica-producing silane such as tetra-ethoxy-silane. Unfortunately this system went out of favour when some of the ingredients were found to be carcinogenic.

Treatments based on lime

There is much to be said for the view that the composition of a surface treatment should be close to that of the stone to be conserved. In practice, it is seldom possible to achieve this, but the use of lime water, and lime wash in the conservation of limestone seems, in principle, to be an ideal approach. This system has been used, apparently with most impressive success, in the conservation of the limestone figures on the West Front of Wells Cathedral, Somerset, England. See Part 2 of this chapter.

There appear to be three mechanisms involved, namely, consolidation of the limestone near the surface by lime water, fixing of loose particles of stone to the surface by lime mortar, and sacrificial protection of the limestone by lime wash.

Lime water is a solution of slaked-lime (calcium hydroxide, $Ca(OH)_2$) in water. A litre (0.22 gal.) of this solution contains about 1.7 g of solid. Carbon dioxide gas in the air will react with the calcium hydroxide to form calcium carbonate (limestone). The chemical change is represented by the equation:

$$Ca(OH)_2 + CO_2 \rightarrow CaCO_3 + H_2O$$

The 1.7 g of calcium hydroxide will become nearly 2.3 g of calcium carbonate.

The average piece of building limestone has a porosity of about 20%. That is, a bulk volume of five litres would contain one litre of interconnected air-space. Thus the volume of limestone required to absorb one litre of solution would be five litres and the volume of solid limestone would be four litres. At the normal solid density for building limestones of $2720 \, kg/m^3$ this would weigh 10.88 kg, i.e. 10 880 g. The 2.3 g of calcium carbonate deposited from the litre of solution on complete evaporation is thus little more than 0.02% of the weight of the dry stone. Clearly, an impracticable number of soakings and dryings would be necessary to have any appreciable effect on the strength of the stone, unless the calcium carbonate is deposited in exceptionally critical positions within the stone's pore structure. However, attempts to use lime water as a consolidant have failed. This suggests that even if conditions really exist that favour deposition of limestone in these critical positions, realization is difficult to achieve in practice.

Lime mortar is a thick paste of calcium hydroxide in water, with or without the addition of some inert sand as a filler. If the lime-mortar is to be used to fix back very small flakes on important carved stonework the sand will need to be very fine or omitted altogether. As the water evaporates from the mix the calcium hydroxide is converted by the carbon dioxide of the air to calcium carbonate (limestone), and this will join together all the limestone it is mutually in contact with (see equation above).

Unlike the deposits from lime-water, the position of the cementing deposit from lime-mortar is directly under the control of the conservator, who is responsible for the correct positioning of the flakes of stone in question.

Lime wash is a slurry of slaked lime, fine sand and stone dust in water to which casein has been added. It is applied to masonry that has otherwise been fully conserved. Its purpose is to fill small crevices and depressions caused by decay processes and then, by thinly coating the rest of the surface, to act as a barrier or sacrificial layer against future attack. Its use implies a rolling programme of conservation in which deteriorating sacrificial coats are renewed from time to time in the hope that this process will blunt the attack of aggressive gases and deposits and enable the precious masonry beneath to survive, or at worst decay more slowly. At Wells Cathedral, these are known as shelter coats. Coloured sands or stone dusts are included in the mix where this is necessary to moderate disturbing discrepancies between the colour of the shelter coat and that of the stone.

Lime mortar fillers and lime wash sacrificial coats appear to be useful conservation materials for use on limestones. They are not appropriate for use on sandstones because their conversion to calcium sulphate by sulphur-based acids in the air would soon enhance the rate of decay of all but the exceptionally weather-resistant sandstones.

Part 2 of this chapter describes the 'lime method' in detail.

Guidance through a maze

To those unfamiliar with chemistry and chemical terms, the range of chemical aids now available to those concerned with building conservation must often seem to be more confusing than helpful. *Table 9.3* is an attempt to clarify matters.

However, research aimed at the development of more effective aids is a more or less continuous process and better aids will no doubt appear as time goes on. The conservator will therefore be wise to keep in touch with international organizations such as ICCROM, as well as with national museums and building research organizations. However, it is the

Table 9.3 Consolidants in current use

1. *Acrylic monomers,* polymerized by (a) heat with a catalyst, (b) gamma radiation.

Acrylic polymers, e.g. acrylic polymer dissolved in silane.

2. *Alkyl-trialkoxy-silanes,* can be used (a) without catalyst, (b) with catalyst (e.g. potassium hydroxide and metal soaps).

3. *Aryl-akyl-poly-siloxanes,* e.g. phenyl-methyl-poly-siloxane as solution in xylene.

4. *Ethyl silicates and silicon ester*

5. *Epoxy resins,* e.g. Domaslowski's method[22] with alcohol-hydrocarbon solutions.

6. *Lime water,* described in Part 2 of this chapter.

Notes
1. Although they are primarily museum treatments, acrylic polymers are used increasingly externally for securing flakes of limestone or marble.
 (a) Without a catalyst, requires handling by an experienced conservator.
 (b) Has behaved excellently with patented catalyst in trials on external limestones and sandstones and achieves good penetration. It was not commercially available until 1984. If an alkyl-trimethoxy-silane is used there must be good ventilation during treatment because poisonous methyl alcohol is released.
2. Success has been reported on terracotta and sandstone.
3. These are sandstone consolidators and are generally not very effective on limestones.
4. Successes have been reported but the method seems more suitable for museum work than external application
5. Successes have been claimed on limestones. Not suitable for sandstones.

unenviable lot of the conservator to be the one to decide whether to act now with any particular problem or wait for the better treatment to become available.

Philosophy of conservation by surface application

Ideally, any surface treatment applied to stonework of artistic or historical merit should be reversible. No present treatments are perfect and, judging by the past, better ones will be devised in the future. It is almost inevitable that the more effective and more long-lasting a treatment is in resisting the forces tending to destroy stone, the less likely it will be that the treatment can be removed without damage to or serious discoloration of the stone. Acrylic resins might seem to approach the ideal because they are normally removable by organic solvents, but at present they have not been proved to be as good at deep consolidation as treatments based on silane monomers. No safe methods have yet been devised

to remove silane treatments once they have polymerized. Ideally, no conservator should make an irreversible mistake with any treatment, but unfortunately mistakes do occur.

Fears that the irreversibility of silane-based treatments and mistakes by conservators using them might cause irreparable damage to ancient stonework has led a number of people to ask if some conservators are not pressing ahead too rapidly. Indeed, the Society for the Protection of Ancient Buildings (SPAB) has gone so far as to call for a moratorium on the use of silane-based treatments on ancient stonework until sufficient experience of their use on unimportant stonework can give assurance that present fears are unfounded[25]. The Society has advocated, and is ready to initiate, a *Register of Treated Stonework.* This would list all buildings or objects on which silane treatments have been used, together with all relevant information on date and type of treatment, method, etc. This might seem to be overcautious. However, the SPAB 'recognizes that those responsible for the care of stonework of historical importance are sometimes faced with the certain loss of stone substance if nothing is done. In such circumstances a choice has to be made between the short-term risk of possible loss of irreplaceable carving and the long-term risk' that irreparable damage will be caused. The Society goes on to recommend that the following procedure be adhered to in these exceptional circumstances.

1. Make sure that the deterioration causing concern is not caused or aggravated by faulty rainwater channels, decayed pointing or other defects that are causing the stonework to be wetter than necessary.
2. If the above does not apply there are two alternatives:
 a. Consider whether it would be feasible to remove the affected stonework to museum conditions and replace it with a cast copy to preserve the architectural concept. An alternative might be to provide temporary shelter for the historic stonework in its original position.
 b. Consider the use of a stone preservative system but only under the conditions outlined above.
 No system should be considered unless:
 i. It has support from at least one non-commercial body that does work in the field of conservation;
 ii. An example can be inspected of its use on exposed stone that is of the same kind or very similar to the stone in question;
 iii. The person who would apply the preservative can show an example of his or her work on similar stone. [The writer would add: 'carried out under at least as hostile ambient conditions'.]

The SPAB document continues: 'In these special circumstances silane-based preservatives would merit consideration together with other preservative systems. *It is essential* that all details are recorded of the use of any preservative system that is adopted.'

Although these conditions may always be met before any irreversible impregnation of historically important stonework is carried out, it is valuable to express this formally. It could well be argued that the Register should be kept internationally as well as nationally. Perhaps the International Centre for Conservation in Rome would be the best body to hold the International Register.

Silicone terminology

Since 1907, when Kipping made the first recorded synthesis of silicon–carbon compounds in which chains of carbon atoms occur, the terminology has evolved in several directions and some terms have changed their original meanings. Even those well acquainted with other fields of chemistry might become confused. The following is a brief description of what appears to be present usage.

Silane. The basic material in this branch of chemistry is silicon tetrahydride, commonly called silane. A molecule of silane is represented by:

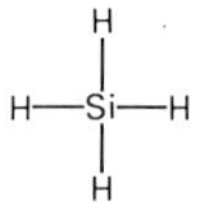

When any or all the hydrogen atoms in silane are replaced by some other atom or by a group of atoms including carbon the term silane is still retained in the name of the new material. Thus if one of the hydrogen atoms is replaced by a methyl radical, that is, a carbon atom with three hydrogen atoms attached to it, the new material is called methyl silane and the reaction could be represented by

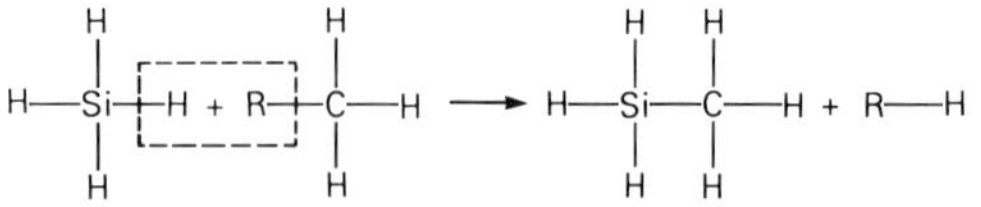

Silane   Methyl   Methyl
                radical   silane

R could represent the chlorine atom, for example. The dashed lines indicate where chemical bonds are broken.

If another of the hydrogen atoms attached to the silicon atom is replaced by a methyl radical dimethyl silane is formed, thus:

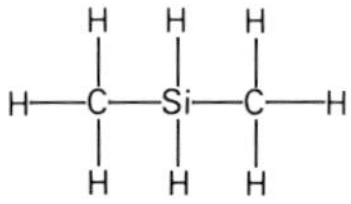

Other silanes include tetramethoxy-silane and methyl-trimethoxy-silane.

Siloxanes. All materials with molecules containing the –Si–O–Si– group of atoms are known as siloxanes, except pure silica, the basic ingredient of sandstones, which contains nothing but silicon–oxygen links. An example is tetra-siloxane, which would have the following molecular structure:

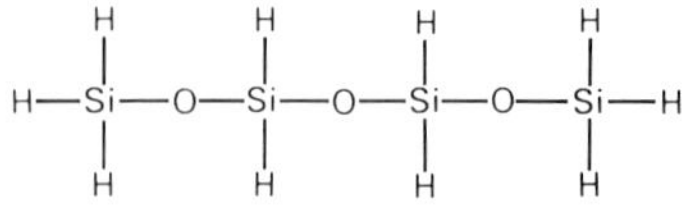

Organo-siloxanes. When some of the hydrogen atoms in a siloxane are substituted by radicals containing carbon atoms, e.g. methyl radicals or methoxy radicals, the material is known as an organo-siloxane.

Polyorgano-siloxanes. When some of the radicals containing carbon atoms in a siloxane are radicals such as methoxy (CH_3O^-) which allows cross-linking of organo-siloxane chains the result of such cross-linking is known as a poly-organo-siloxane. An example is:

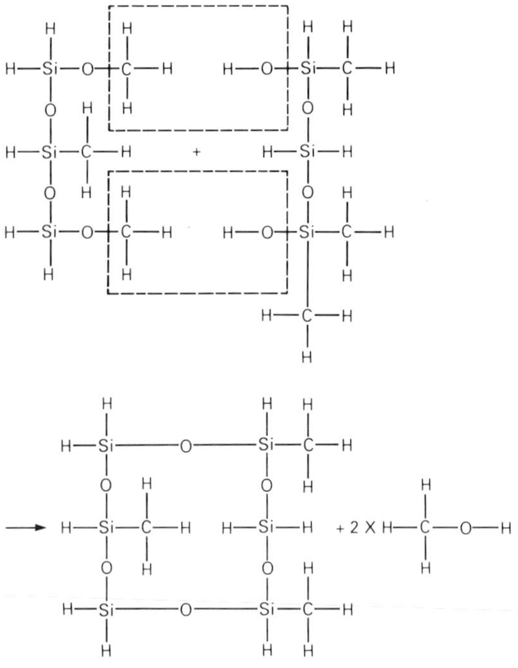

The last term would normally be written 2 CH_3OH (methyl alcohol). The main product would be known as a *silicone*. Unfortunately the term silicone is also sometimes used to denote materials that

consist of organo-siloxane chains *before* cross-linking. Most useful polyorgano-siloxanes have much longer chains than the example shown.

Alkyl. The term alkyl implies the presence of a radical containing straight chains of carbon atoms with hydrogen, e.g. methyl (CH_3^-) or ethyl ($C_2H_5^-$).

Alkoxy. The term alkoxy implies an alkyl chain plus an oxygen atom, e.g. ethoxy ($C_2H_5O^-$)

Aryl. The term aryl implies the presence of a radical in which carbon chains form an aromatic ring structure, e.g. phenyl ($C_6H_5^-$). This is represented formally as

$$
\begin{array}{c}
\text{CH} = \text{CH} \\
\diagup \qquad \diagdown \\
\text{CH} \qquad\qquad \text{C} - \\
\diagdown\diagdown \qquad \diagup\diagup \\
\text{CH} - \text{CH}
\end{array}
$$

Part 2 The cleaning and treatment of limestone by the lime method

John Ashurst

The West Fronts of Wells and Exeter Cathedrals and the ruined West Front of the Abbey of Crowland have undergone interesting transformations over the past few years. Heavily soiled, badly repaired limestone sculptures, which are fragile and have spalling sulphate skins, have been pulled back in some cases from the apparent brink of destruction. The dirt and all the wreckage of iron, copper and cement associated with past remedial work has gone. Some observers see a new warmth, clarity and stability in these façades; others see an unnatural uniformity, a blurring of detail and an uncertain future. These façades and others have been cleaned, repaired and consolidated using techniques generally known as the lime method.

In 1904, Lethaby examined the sculptures on the West Front of Wells Cathedral and commented: 'Sooner or later the question of preserving the statues from surface decay must be considered. It would, I believe, be desirable to cover them by degrees with distemper.' However, Lethaby did not have his way. The suggestion was rejected by the Dean and Chapter on the advice of their architect, Edmund Buckle, who foresaw a danger of blocking the pores of the stone if the surface was painted. The distemper suggested by Lethaby was probably a mixture of whiting (crushed chalk) and water, bound with a size made from parchment clippings and coloured with burnt umber or yellow ochre. However, in the absence of a precise specification for the distemper, it is difficult to estimate how much harm the execution of Lethaby's suggestion would have caused.

Lethaby's idea has some aspects in common with the lime method, especially the idea of replacing the protection once afforded by the gesso and polychrome with a substitute medium. Although distemper has been removed successfully from medieval polychromed sculpture elsewhere, for example from the figures of the Virgin and Gabriel flanking the Annunciation Door of Westminster Abbey Chapter House when it was cleaned in 1983, it is likely that damage would have been caused during the application of the distemper. Some of the effects of pore blocking would have exacerbated the decay of the sculptures, especially in sheltered areas.

Some critics of the recent work at Wells Cathedral have expressed similar doubts about the application techniques used and the possibility of pore clogging during the course of the recent restoration. Some do not find the finished work visually pleasing.

The lime method, which is also known as the Baker or Wells method, was developed on a few important sites over the past two decades. However, there is still much misunderstanding about what it really entails and what it sets out to achieve. Opinions which may have been formed about the lime method seven or eight years ago should be reviewed in the light of the evolution of the technique due to its increasing use and the accumulation of experience and discussion. Credit for this development must go to the originator of the complete lime method, Professor Robert Baker, to the architects, Alban and Martin Caroe, who were responsible for the West Front at Wells Cathedral, to members of the West Front Committee, and especially to the growing team of conservators who have shared their experiences and made their findings available.

What does the lime method involve? There is nothing new in the use of lime mortars for 'plastic repair' or in the use of lime washes for external weather protection. Although all these processes relate to the lime method, they do not actually describe it. The method is based on good common sense and traditional materials, but requires skill and experience to apply it successfully. Its lack of sophistication has led to great interest among conservators. However, all techniques, even those based on traditional materials, must stand close scrutiny and come under review from time to time. Success with one project should not stimulate unqualified commitment to the lime method as a solution to all stone problems, or even all limestone problems.

The lime method consists of several operations which are described below.

Preliminary survey

Any activity should be preceded by a careful survey of the general and detailed environmental influences and the condition of the subject. The survey should cover the following:

- *The environment:* the effects of the prevailing wind, exposure to direct sunlight, exposure to rain, water run and drip effects, humidity patterns, local pollution levels, proximity to heating outlets and nuisance from roosting birds.
- *The structural condition:* the presence of soft beds or open vents, failures due to edge or face bedding, damage from impact, diagnosis of other crack patterns, identification of position and type of fixings, especially ferrous fixings, type of any corset, existing stiffening or strengthening.
- *The surface condition:* the type of stones and description of any original covering, such as gesso and polychrome; pattern of decay and soiling; identification of existing repairs and fillings, especially those associated with decay; identification of later treatments, such as wax or limewash; description and analysis of any visible efflorescences; description of organic growth in the form of algae or algal slimes; identification of any areas too weak or too vulnerable to be cleaned by poulticing.

If the subject is very important and the conditions complex, the conservator may call in the services of other specialists. For instance, it may be advisable for an art-historian to make an assessment of a sculpture before it is touched, or a consultant to look at the conservation of fragmentary polychrome. What is vital for the conservator is thorough familiarity with the subject before work commences; for this reason, the survey should always be part of the conservation exercise and not carried out by someone other than the conservator.

The completed survey must include adequate photographs and drawings to record and explain all the information listed above, in addition to notes and appropriate measurements.

Structural repair

Although structural repairs are sometimes the first operation, most do not take place until the cleaning has been completed. They are not described here in detail, as they do not relate specifically to the lime method, but they commonly include the removal of at least one large iron dowel (in the case of figure sculpture) and other iron pins, copper straps, bars and nails. Where pinning and support is needed, it can be provided with threaded stainless steel dowels or non-ferrous pins, made of phosphor bronze, delta metal or fibreglass, set in a grout of synthetic or lime mortar. All dowel and pin heads should be set well below the surface of the stone and the outer part of the drilling filled with repair mortar. Removal of old fixings is normally carried out by careful drilling. Temporary support is provided as required. Staining from copper and iron is removed as much as possible during the cleaning operation.

Cleaning

Large areas of limestone, including ashlar and architectural moulding, are cleaned by traditional washing. Large amounts of water are very undesirable in situations where there is polychromed sculpture and many natural traps which will hold water. Various ways to protect vulnerable areas and figure sculpture have been devised, including polythene sheeting and rigid catchments, temporary gutters and downpipes. Experiments with controlled washing were commissioned by Alban and Martin Caroe at Wells Cathedral in about 1980 and some pioneering work was carried out by R.H. Bennett with sensor-controlled and clock-controlled washing.

Clock-controlled systems were subsequently developed by the Wells Cathedral conservators under the direction of Professor Baker and Mr Peter Cooley. They are still in use, on a four-second wetting time with dry intervals of four to five minutes. It is not sensible to specify the wetting-interval time too precisely, as it can only be determined on site by trial. The object is to achieve a progressive softening of the dirt deposits to enable them to be removed by brushing. Experience has shown that this does not require constant sheets and cascades of water running over the face of the building, with all the attendant risks of staining, loss of friable or fragile material and other problems associated with salt migration and water penetration.

Some areas of detail will require more positive protection from water than sheets or catchments. Obvious areas of polychrome, for instance, or areas likely to have surviving colour under dirt layers, should be covered with tissue pads under a thin plastic film, which is taped or tied in position. Delicate areas such as fleurons may now be cleaned with dry air abrasive and protected from subsequent washing. Once the washing of masonry has been completed, cleaning of the sculpture can begin.

The traditional method of cleaning associated with the lime method is by hot lime poultice. Quicklime should be used for the poultice. It should be broken into small pieces to pass a 12 mm (0.5 in) sieve and bound against the stonework with either sheet or strip sacking. This should be taped down so that no lime escapes at the bottom. The thickness of the lime should be 12–25 mm (0.5–1 in). The sacking should be covered with medium-heavy polythene, taped at the bottom and sides, but with a hole left in the top. Water should be poured slowly through the hole to allow the lime to slake. When the lime softens to the consistency of putty, sufficient water has been used. The hole should be covered and the poultice left for a week to ten days. The poultice may then be removed. It will be shaped like a mould of the object and will be stained by the bituminous material that covered the stone. The object should then be lightly sprayed for a few hours to remove any remaining deposits.

In the early days of the restoration of Wells Cathedral the lime was slaked against the surface of the stone. It is not surprising that Mr W.A. Wheeler, the Clerk of Works at the time, reported dramatic happenings during the slaking process when the string binding burst under the expansion of the lime and the hessian began to burn!

Hot lime is still in use, but it is now applied by gloved hand and trowel. The putty is pressed well into the surface of the pre-wetted stone. When a thick plaster is applied it is bound with scrim and wet sacking or underfelt which is secured with string. Finally, a heavy-duty polythene sheet is tied loosely in position. From time to time, over a period of two to three weeks, the polythene is lifted and the sacking surface is sprayed with water to ensure that the poultice remains damp and soft. If the poultice dried out it would render the lime useless, or bind it to the surface of the stone.

When the packaging is finally removed, the lime is carefully lifted off over small areas at a time with spatulas or small trowels, taking with it some of the dirt from the contact surface. Water sprays are used to assist in the removal of the lime and to further soften the dirt. In common with most other poultices, not very much dirt actually detaches with the poultice material. The softened deposit must be worked at with hand sprays, dental picks and small toothbrushes or stencil brushes to achieve a relatively clean surface. In the past, some areas were scraped down, but this practice no longer continues. The scrubbing stage is long and laborious. Added to perhaps three weeks of poulticing, the cleaning of a life-size figure may well take a month or six weeks before any repair work is undertaken. In 1965–66, Mr Wheeler was experimenting with alternatives to hot lime after the unsuccessful and literal baptism of fire, a line of enquiry which has still to be pursued.

A report by one of the Wells conservators draws attention to the fact that the air abrasive unit preserved more of the polychromy than a lime poultice would have done, particularly in view of the risks involved with removal of the water during removal of the poultice. With hindsight, it is a pity that the early use of small air abrasive tools at Wells Cathedral attracted so little interest and that superficial assumptions about the technique ruled it out on the grounds that 'sand-blasting' would be too destructive. (Statue 117 was cleaned by R.H. Bennett under the direction of the Directorate of Ancient Monuments and Historic Buildings with wet attapulgite clay packs, an air abrasive pencil and aluminium oxide abrasive in 1977.)

Wet poulticing combined with careful mechanical cleaning using dental tools and brushes or air abrasive seems to be the best option for both economy and the safety of the surfaces and operatives. Whether or not the poultice should be lime, hot or cold, or attapulgite clay, or some other medium is still open to debate. Any wet pack which can remain in intimate contact with the stone without drying out or adhering to the surface will have a softening effect on dirt and make it more responsive to gentle washing and brushing.

Does the lime poultice, which is initially hot, have any other beneficial effect during its two or three week contact period with the stone? It has been claimed that it increases the permeability of a sulphated layer and makes the surface more receptive to the lime water applications that follow. It is also claimed that initial strengthening of friable areas is noticeable after the poulticing and as the stone dries out. This phenomenon is related to the strengthening claimed to be achieved after multiple applications of lime water.

Removal of old fillings

The cleaning processes will reveal the full extent of the damage due to weathering and decay and the amount of filling of spalls and cracks which has been carried out in the past. Almost invariably these fillings, including some crude remodelling, were carried out in Roman Cement, a strong, brown coloured hydraulic cement much favoured in the nineteenth century for restoration repairs. More recently, equally strong Portland cement-based mortar has been used. These fillings are completely unsuitable as a visual match for the stone; but, more seriously, their dense, impervious nature encourages moisture and salt concentrations around them, thus extending the area of decay still further.

Removal of old fillings is essential, but it is slow and careful work. The old fillings must be drilled out, with only the minimum use of impact tools such as sharp masonry chisels and fluted plugging chisels on large areas. Small chisels and air abrasive tools should be used to assist cutting and to enlarge the cavities slightly by undercutting to improve the keying effect. The maximum amount of surviving surface should always be retained. Only where the original surface is already lost should any further dressing-off take place, to avoid the retention of water traps.

Once all old fillings have been removed, their cavities recut and new cavities formed where newer spalls and splits had developed, all loose dust and debris must be removed by flushing with clean water. If algae are present a few drops of formalin may be added to the water. This will provide a sound, clean and sterile area in which the new mortar can be placed. Flushing out is most conveniently carried out with trigger-operated hand sprays which have a simple adjustable nozzle to vary the jet from a fine pencil to a coarse spray pattern as required.

At this stage much of the sculpture looks very leprous, but all deleterious material which can be removed has been scrupulously excised. Once the cleaning has been completed any structural repairs can be carried out.

Consolidation by lime water

The cleaned surfaces with open cavities are next treated with lime water to attempt to consolidate the more friable areas. Lime water contains small quantities of calcium hydroxide (0.14 g in 100 ml of water at 15 °C.) Traditionally lime water is siphoned from the slaking tank after the lime has been slaked in an excess of water and after all slaking has ceased and the water is clear. Now the lime putty is usually stirred into a container of water and left to stand until the water is clear.

It is important to protect the lime water from the air, otherwise it will carbonate and become ineffective. A number of different methods have been used to achieve this. The most recent development is the covering of the surface of the lime water with a float of polystyrene sheet, pierced only by a siphon tube fitted with a filter. The lime water is drawn off when required by a hand pump into spray bottles or directly to a lance with a control valve and adjustable nozzle. It is necessary to check from time to time that the water has not accidentally become clouded through disturbance of the lime in the bottom of the bin. Any cloudy water should be rejected and the water allowed to stand until it is clear again.

Approximately forty applications of lime water must be flooded onto the surface of the limestone over a period of several days. Application can continue as long as the surface will absorb, but excess lime water should not be allowed to lie on the surface of the stone. It should be removed by sponges which are then squeezed out in clean water.

Over many years consolidation effects have been reported as a result of multiple applications of lime water to lime plaster, Doulting, Bath, Clunch, Barnack, Beer, Salcombe and Chilmark limestones. However, attempts to record or quantify the phenomenon have met with a disappointing lack of success. For example, in Wells Cathedral trial treatments with lime water (27 applications over a six-day period) were carried out by Mr W.A. Wheeler in 1967 on the south side of the south doorway and by the author and Mr Brian Clarke of the Building Research Station with Mr Wheeler on the blind arcading of the central tower in 1970. Neither of these produced any evidence that lime water had any strengthening effect on the stone.[6] The central tower experiment compared forty applications of lime water with forty application of distilled and of tap water.

Surface repair

The consolidation treatment is followed by the placing of mortar repairs. This is the stage in the lime method where perhaps the greatest skill and the most experience are needed. The mortar repair is the core of the method and, when well executed, is the work which evokes the greatest admiration.

All mortar repairs are based on lime; no Portland cement of any kind is used. If a weak hydraulic mortar is needed, then a small addition of high temperature insulation (HTI) powder, a pale coloured ceramic powder, is used as a pozzolana. At Crowland Abbey, Professor Baker used finely crushed Cambridge White brick dust as his pozzolanic additive in order to match the Barnack limestone of the building.

All limes should be of a high calcium, non-hydraulic type. Lime should be brought to the site after burning and be slaked as soon as possible in a suitable tank by adding it to water, raking and hoeing it through until all visible reaction has ceased. An excess of water should be used, so that the soft mass of lime putty formed during slaking is kept well covered. Experienced lime practitioners express preferences for different limes according to the kind of work and the type of stone they are working with. However, this should be an indication of very considerable practical experience and not an affectation! The lime putty must be left in its tank under water for as long as possible. It should be left for at least one week to ensure that all slaking is finished, but any days, weeks, months or even years that can be added to this period can be looked on as a bonus, especially if the lime putty can be mixed and stored in wet, air-tight conditions with the aggregates. The lime putty will never 'set' or harden too much if it is kept from the air, and even if it has stiffened it can easily be softened again when needed without the addition of water; with sufficient working it will soon become a soft gelatinous mass again. Pozzolanic additives must only be added just before use, and then mixed in very thoroughly.

Aggregates should be selected and graded for colour and function. Often considerable time must be spent in their selection and many sands and crushed stones will be tried in the process of finding the right combination. Stone pieces can be crushed by hammer or roller on a concrete slab, or even in a corn grinder, and then carefully sieved and graded for storing in a 'bank'.

The mortars have a number of different functions to fulfil. They are all likely to be a combination of lime and the same aggregates, but the lime:aggregate proportions may vary and so will the size of aggregate. A pozzolanic additive is required only for some functions. The basic proportions are summarized below:

	Lime	*Aggregate*
Repair mortar	1	2
Adhesive mortar (for fixing spalls)	1	1
Grouting mortar (for crack filling)	1	1.5
Shelter coating	1	3

A ten per cent pozzolanic additive (HTI powder) should be included in the basic aggregate proportion and in the adhesive and grouting mortar. A lower percentage is required in the repair and shelter coat

mortars. Finer aggregates are used for adhesive and grouting mortars. The finest are used for shelter coating. Some examples of aggregate sizes related to mortar function are given in *Table 9.4.*

The lime putty should always be screened through a 1.18 mm mesh after slaking. Further screening takes place according to the function of the mortar.

The final colour of the repair depends on the selection and blending of the aggregates and the proportion of lime used, the method of placing the repair and the rate of drying out. Minor variations in colour continue to take place indefinitely just as the colour of a stone surface will continue to respond to variations in humidity. Successful 'instant effects' are not necessarily the most satisfactory after a period of weathering. Only with considerable experience can this be anticipated and the mortar constituents selected accordingly. At Wells Cathedral experience has been primarily concentrated on matching Doulting and Dundry stones.

Dundry and Doulting limestones weather in subtly distinct ways and are always distinguishable in colour. The workers at Wells Cathedral have developed a palette of mortars which can be used as repair mixes or as shelter coats and which make use of the same aggregates in varying proportions.

Dundry stone varies from a light cream to dark brown and light grey. Doulting varies from a pale buff to different and often darker browns and greys. The aggregates used to match these colours are not obtained by crushing stones of the same kind but rather, richer coloured stones with good staining properties. In particular, use is made of Hornton, a ferruginous limestone with a distinctive blue grey and golden brown colour from Edgehill in Oxfordshire, and of Guiting, especially the dark buff-orange Guiting from Gloucestershire.

Table 9.5 shows how typical colours are made up.

Before the conservator goes onto the scaffold to place the repair mortar a number of pre-mixed mortars, sometimes as many as thirty for two stone types, will have been prepared in separate plastic tubs and covered with a piece of wet cloth. The tools

Table 9.4 Mortar composition

Mortar function	*Lime*	*Aggregates*				*Pozzolanic additive*	
		BS sieve sizes					
		1.18 mm	600 μm	400 μm	300 μm	600 μm	300 μm
Mortar repair	3	1½	1½	¾	¾	½	—
	3	3	2	1	—	½	—
Adhesive mortar	6	—	—	—	6	1½	—
	6	—	1	1	4	½	1
Grouting mortar	3¼	3	—	1	1	½	—
	2	—	½	1¼	—	—	¾
Shelter coat	3	—	—	—	8	—	—
	3	—	—	2½	4½	—	—

Table 9.5 The composition of coloured mortars

Aggregates	*Dundry stone*		*Doulting stone*	
	Repair mix	*Shelter coat*	*Repair mix*	*Shelter coat*
Guiting	3	2½	2	2
Blue Hornton	¾	½	2¼	3
Brown Hornton	1½	1¼	2	1½
Gold sand	1	¼	1	1
Red sand	—	⅛	—	½
Lime	4	1	3¼	3
Pozzolanic additive	½	—	—	—

and materials necessary for the operation should be conveniently laid out on a board ready for use. These include hand-spray bottles full of water, cotton wool packs, a small trowel, dental picks and plugging tools, spatulas, two or three small bristle brushes and rubber gloves. The following sequence of working is typical.

1. Cavities and cracks are flushed out again with water from the hand sprays to avoid an otherwise dry stone surface de-watering the repair as it is pressed into position. The surface should be damp without water actually shining on the surface.
2. Deep cavities are treated at the back with a slurry of repair mortar followed by a filling into which small pieces of Bath or Doulting stone are inserted to reduce the thickness which needs to be built up in fine repair mortar.
3. A thin slurry of repair mortar containing HTI powder is brushed into the cavity or fracture to provide an additional key for the repair.
4. After one or two hours, when the slurry has dried, the cavity is wetted up again and the first repair mortar is kneaded and pushed into place with the fingers, exerting as much pressure as possible. With few exceptions, not more than 5–6 mm should be pressed in at one time. Dental plugging tools and spatulas are used to assist in the filling. Throughout the entire sequence compaction of the amalgam by pressure is absolutely essential to achieve good adhesion and minimum shrinkage.
5. As each filling is completed, precautions must be taken to avoid rapid drying out by protecting the area from direct sunlight or strong draughts. When dry, the cavity must again be wetted and step 4 repeated until the cavity has been filled completely. Overfilling is a useful aid to compaction and surplus mortar can be trimmed off with a spatula to the desired profile on completion. A texture matching the stone can be achieved with a dry sponge, hessian pads, stencil brushes and purpose-made plastic scrapers. It is important not to press hard and absorb moisture from the repair.

As a general rule no modelling is carried out using repair mortar. Its role is to fill cavities and cracks and to provide a weak, porous capping to vulnerable, friable areas. It is designed to draw moisture, and therefore soluble salts, to itself and finally to fail before any further stone is lost. Ideally it will then be replaced. To ensure slow drying, wet cotton wool packs are laid over the finished repair and left in position for as long as is thought necessary.

Shelter coating

The final stage of the work is to apply a thin surface coating to all the cleaned and repaired stone. This is intended to slow down the effects of weathering on the surviving surfaces by providing a sacrificial layer which may be removed by direct rainfall or disrupted by salt crystallization associated with wetting and drying cycles. In the case of stones which were once covered with gesso and coloured with tempera, the shelter coat may be seen as a substitute protection. It has been suggested that the shelter coat may also provide a warmer surface than the untreated stone and that this may inhibit the formation of condensation. Whilst this might conceivably be the case with a thick lime wash, it is difficult to believe that a fine shelter coat could have such an effect. One of the most obvious and striking developments of the technique is the increasing fineness and subtlety of the shelter coat. One observer, only slightly misquoting Hans Christian Andersen's story *The Emperor's New Clothes*, insisted that the stones 'had nothing on at all'! Thicker coats are still applied to ashlar and simple architectural mouldings, as they have been at Wells since 1980. Shelter coats have been applied to figure sculpture as a general policy since 1977, and were pioneered by Professor Baker twenty years before then.

Practitioners insist that a shelter coat is not a paint, largely because of the method of application. It is, however, a coloured surface treatment which requires periodic maintenance. The shelter coat is of similar or the same composition as the repair mortars, but the aggregate to lime proportion is slightly higher and sand and stone dust are crushed more finely (see *Tables 9.4* and *9.5*). Water is added to the fine lime and aggregate mix until a consistency of thin cream is reached. Thorough mixing continues for 20 to 30 minutes. At Wells Cathedral Mr Martin Caroe has introduced the use of a heavy-duty food mixer to carry out this part of the operation. At the end of the mixing period casein and formalin may be added.

More work needs to be carried out to establish the roles played by casein and by formalin in the shelter coat. Casein paints have been used since antiquity. Lime and casein form calcium caseinate, a useful binder for whiting and pigment. A readily available source of casein is milk, but there is some confusion on how best to obtain casein from milk on site.

Milk is the primary food for all young mammals. It is a mixture consisting of butter fats (3.8%), lactose (sugar, 4.7%), minerals (0.8%), water (87.4%) and solids (3.3%) which contain the protein casein. To ease digestion the milk is coagulated in the stomach by the enzyme rennin, which is secreted by the stomach wall. A similar process is used in the production of curds and whey. The addition of rennet (impure rennin) to milk will cause it to coagulate, forming curds (a calcium casein compound) which separate from the whey (a clear sugary solution with no casein present). Another method is simply to allow the milk to stale. In this situation coagulation is brought about by the action of bacteria digesting the protein, which leaves a clear liquid containing no casein.

Shelter coats gauged with whey have been used extensively at Wells Cathedral and elsewhere and have produced very satisfactory results. This suggests that perhaps casein has no role to play. Some lime method practitioners do not use any milk at all and include finely ground ceramic powder with the lime. However, lime casein mixtures continue to be of interest and skimmed milk or skimmed milk powder are still being used.

Skimmed milk is simply milk from which the cream has been removed. A typical composition for powder provided by the Milk Marketing Board contains lactose (52%), protein (mostly casein) (36%), ash (0.8%), moisture (3.2%) and fats (0.8%). Skimmed milk powder may be reckoned, therefore, to contain about one-third part of casein. Other experiments have used colostrum, the milk produced by cows for the first forty-eight hours after a calf is born, which contains more protein (casein) and less sugar and fats than ordinary milk.[26]

Lime casein paints use a proportion of about one part casein to ten parts lime. A paint with excellent binding properties was mixed at Old Gorhambury in 1979 for protecting weak badly decayed limestone based on three parts skimmed milk powder to ten parts lime putty. However, such applications are intended to lay on a relatively thick coat. Formalin is included in these paints and in shelter coats.

Formalin is a saturated solution of the gas formaldehyde in water. Casein plastics are produced by immersing casein in a solution of formaldehyde. A gelling effect occurs if formalin is added quickly to a solution of casein and lime. However, the minute proportions of formalin traditionally used in shelter coats are unlikely to have any effect other than a transitory sterilization of the milk and lime mixture. This is probably a useful property and 5 ml of formalin in one litre of lime and skimmed milk shelter coat seems to have an inhibiting effect on the development of mould spots.

Careful colour matching of cleaned, weathered stone should precede the full application of a shelter coat. This matching can be carried out on a separate piece of the same stone in similar condition, but it is better to lay the samples on the stone itself or on, for instance, an adjacent moulding. Considerable skill is required in colour matching, as it is in matching repair mortars. All trial colours must be completely dry before a decision can be made about its accuracy. Sometimes a hot air-blower may be used to hasten the drying of the trial colours.

The surface is prepared for application by careful but thorough spraying with water. Spraying is carried out with hand bottles until water begins to sit on the surface and is no longer absorbed into the stone. At this stage, as soon as the water has ceased to glisten on the surface, the shelter coat can be laid on with a soft bristle brush. A second, short haired or worn bristle brush is used to work the shelter coat into the texture of the stone. Traditionally, pads of hessian sacking were used for rubbing in to achieve the maximum compaction possible. The hessian must have been washed to remove the starch and any impurities. Compaction by rubbing is a very important part of the process and serves to fill the minute hollows of textured stone whilst wiping off all but a smear from the high spots. The treatment is always applied to complete stones, and sometimes, as in the case of sculpture, is carried across joints as well.

Drying out must be as carefully controlled as the drying out of mortar repairs. Polythene shrouds are often used, and intermittent mist spraying by hand during the first few hours avoids any risk of rapid drying which can result in a powdery and useless shelter coat and undesirable modifications in colour. During the first stages of drying out, small additions of colour in the form of finely ground stone dust or even powdered charcoal may be dusted on to achieve minor, subtle variations in the final appearance.

Shelter coating is the most visually striking part of the lime method but should never be too obvious. Inexpert handling can result in a bland, woolly appearance, which on the scale of the West Front of a cathedral would be an aesthetic disaster. However, properly carried out, with sufficient sensitivity to the colour and tonal variations of the worn stones, it can greatly enhance their appearance.

As with any other technique the principle of shelter coating can be misunderstood or misused. There is, in the stone cleaning trade, an expression used to describe covering up dirt, old paint and poor repairs with a lime and stonedust or coloured cement slurry. This technique, known as 'toshing' in England, is disliked by reputable cleaning contractors. However, in one recent case the covering up of the heavily soiled underside of a cornice, which should have been cleaned, with a thick cement slurry, was described defensively as 'shelter coating'!

The lime method is here to stay. Its continued use and the scientific scrutiny which is now being applied to it ensure that it will develop and will be refined. The following questions still have to be answered.

1. *Cleaning.* Should clay of the attapulgite type be used instead of lime and could the poultice contact period be much reduced? Would another poultice be more appropriate to delicate surfaces? Should more of the cleaning be carried out with air abrasive pencils?

2. *Consolidation.* How much consolidation is achieved by multiple lime water applications? Does a lime poultice have any consolidating effect? Could lime water be applied through long fibre tissue facings, enabling wet flakes to be gently pushed back onto the surface to achieve better consolidation?

The second question was taken up by Dr Clifford Price and Mr Keith Ross (both, at the time, of the Building Research Establishment). Which parts of the treatment had caused the changes observed, and how had they worked? How long would the apparent benefits last? An investigation was undertaken to provide a technical rationale for the treatment and to compare the performance of the lime poultice with air-abrasive and washing techniques.

Technical appraisal of stone conservation techniques at Wells Cathedral
Clifford Price and Keith Ross

Ideally, the entire investigation should have been based on a single piece of stone, in order to eliminate variations in properties from one piece of stone to another. In practice, however, it was not possible to find a single piece of stone that was uniformly weathered and large enough to permit the necessary sampling. The investigation was therefore carried out on three pieces of stone cut from three mullions of the unglazed west cloister walk of the cathedral. They were each in Doulting limestone, the stone from which the majority of West Front figures are carved. The mullions were believed to have been installed around 1470, and were equally dirty and decayed. The pieces cut out for experiment were 900 mm (36 in) long, with a cross-sectional area of about 180 cm² (28 in²).

The first stage of the experiment was to clean the mullions, using a lime poultice, air abrasion or water washing. The design of the experiment, shown in *Figure 9.5*, permitted direct comparison of any two techniques on a single piece of stone. A central portion, approximately 20 mm (0.8 in) thickness, was cut out using a dry saw and served as a control. The remaining six pieces were then cleaned by the conservation team; two pieces were cleaned using each technique. Every effort was made to ensure that the cleaning was carried out in a realistic manner. The lime poultice cleaning and the air abrasive cleaning were carried out on the scaffold alongside a figure that was being cleaned by the same technique. The water washing, normally used for the architectural stonework but not for the figure sculpture, continued until the stone was clean and lasted around two days.

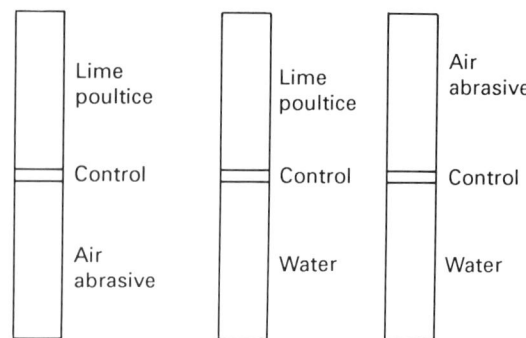

Figure 9.5 The design of the experiment permitted direct comparison between any two cleaning techniques on a single mullion

When cleaning was completed and the stone had dried a 20 mm (0.8 in) slice was cut with a dry saw from the centre of each of the six pieces. This slice was set aside for laboratory examination. Of the two pieces that remained from each of the original six pieces, one piece was treated with around forty applications of lime water whilst the other was left untreated *Figure 9.6*. The lime watering was carried out by the conservation team in exactly the same way as the lime watering of the figure sculpture.

When the lime watering was completed, a 20 mm (0.8 in) slice was cut from the centre of each of the lime-watered pieces and set aside for laboratory investigation. One of the two remaining pieces was covered with a shelter coat. The blocks that had not been lime watered were simply cut in half and one half was covered with a shelter coat. A sample for

Figure 9.6 Quarter-length mullions after treatment with lime water

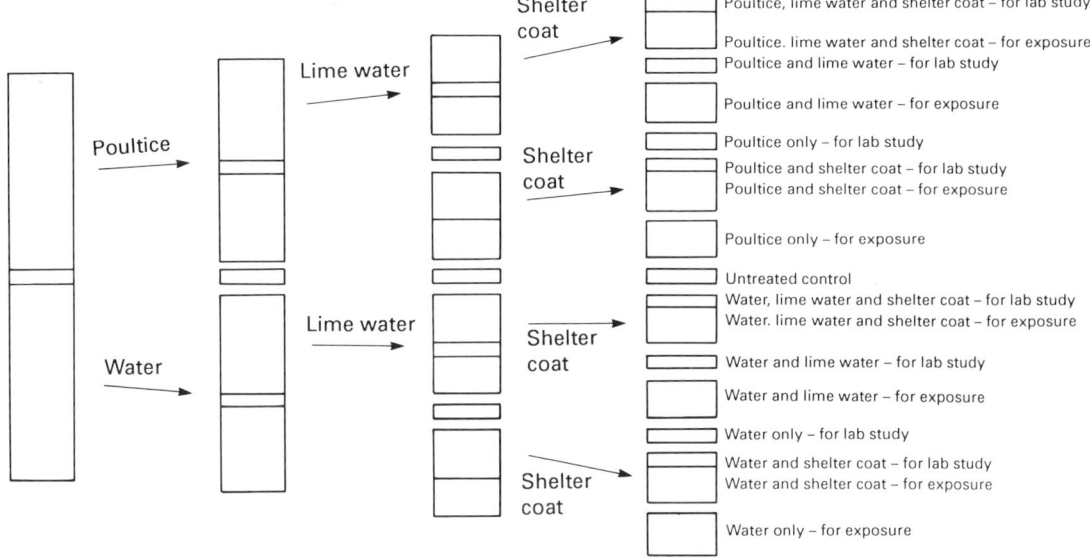

Figure 9.7 Stages in the treatment of one mullion

laboratory study was then cut from each of the shelter-coated pieces, and all the remaining pieces were exposed to the weather. Their condition will be monitored over the next few years. This seemingly complicated procedure, illustrated for a single mullion in *Figure 9.7*, enabled each part of the conservation treatment to be studied, either in isolation or in conjunction with other parts. End effects were eliminated in the cleaning and lime watering stages by cutting the specimens for laboratory study from the centre of each treated piece. This precaution was not necessary in the shelter coat stage.

Laboratory investigation of specimens

Each 20 mm (0.8 in) slice of mullion was sampled as shown in *Figure 9.8*. All cutting was done dry, to prevent any redistribution of calcium sulphate or calcium hydroxide.

Distribution of calcium sulphate

The majority of investigators agree that calcium sulphate plays a major role in the decay of limestones, the calcium sulphate being formed by reaction of the limestone with sulphur oxides in the air. There is remarkably little understanding, however, of the precise mechanisms by which the calcium sulphate causes decay, and little can yet be added to Schaffer's summary of 1932.[7]

On first sight, it would appear to be beneficial to the stone if all the calcium sulphate could be removed from it. However, this is not necessarily so. When stone is in a very advanced stage of decay, the calcium sulphate may actually be serving to bind the stone together. If the calcium sulphate were to be removed, the stone would disintegrate altogether (see *Figure 9.9* and *9.10*). This phenomenon was in

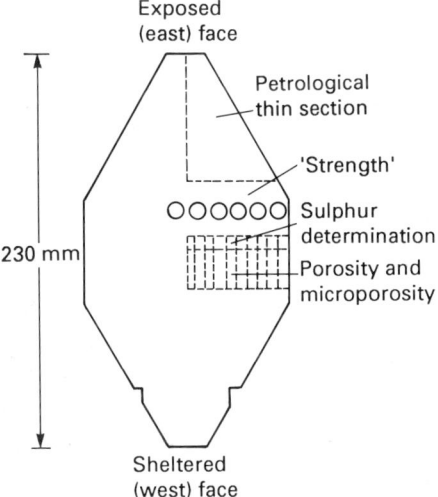

Figure 9.8 Sampling of mullion sections

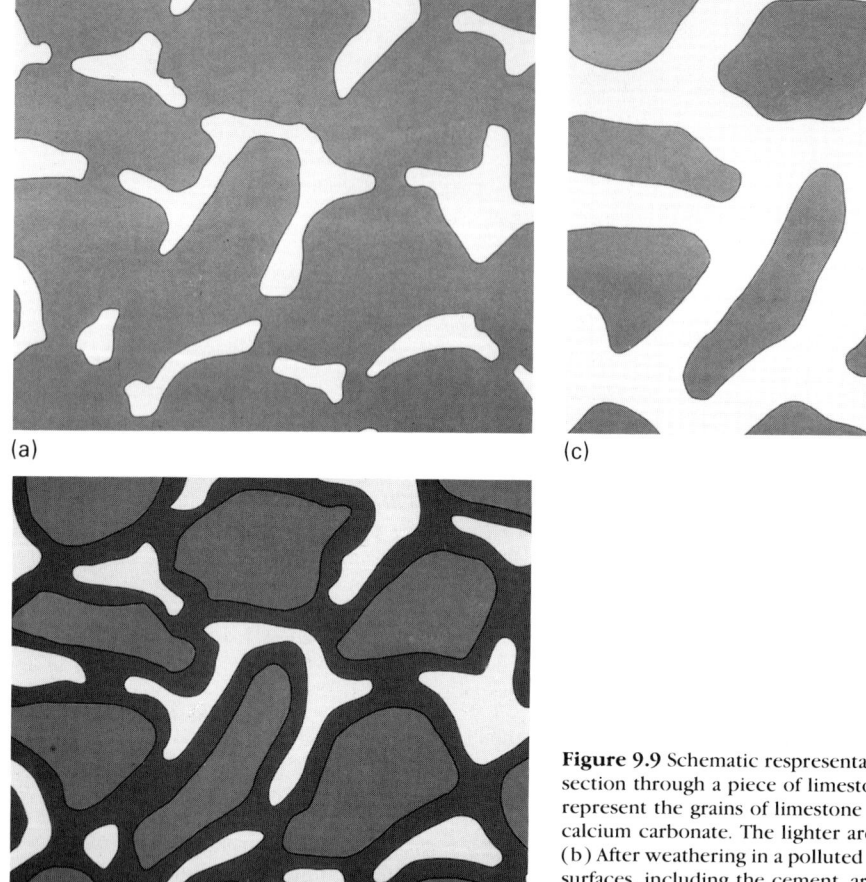

(a)

(c)

(b)

Figure 9.9 Schematic respresentation of a magnified cross-section through a piece of limestone. (a) The darker areas represent the grains of limestone cemented together by calcium carbonate. The lighter areas represent the pores. (b) After weathering in a polluted atmosphere, the exposed surfaces, including the cement, are converted to calcium sulphate. (c) After prolonged washing, the calcium sulphate dissolves and the stone disintegrates.

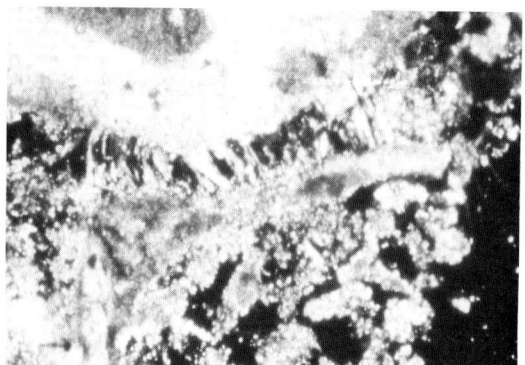

Figure 9.10 Petrological thin section: calcium sulphate crystals form a line of bridges between two grains of stone (× 130)

fact observed at Wells, when conventional water mist sprays were used to clean highly undercut architectural detail. The prolonged washing leached the calcium sulphate from the stone, which was reduced to a soft mass. (This experience led to a refinement of the technique for washing architectural stonework, in which water was sprayed onto the stone for only a few seconds at a time, with intervals of several minutes in between. The spray was controlled either by a time switch or by electronic sensors placed on the stone. This refinement enabled the stone to be kept wet, thus softening dirt, without the calcium sulphate being leached out.) One must conclude that removal of the sulphate is not necessarily beneficial, despite the fact that one would prefer the calcium sulphate not to be there in the first place.

The effects of the three cleaning techniques on sulphate distribution are shown in *Figure 9.11*, which gives the results for two of the mullions. The results show beyond doubt that none of the cleaning techniques has any influence on the quantities of sulphate contained *within* the stone. It should be remembered, however, that these results relate to specimens which are typically 7 mm (0.3 in) thick; they thus represent the average sulphate content within a 7 mm specimen. If there were to be any redistribution of the sulphate within such a specimen, it would not be discernible from these results. Nevertheless, the results clearly refute any claim that the lime poultice serves to draw calcium sulphate out of the depth of the stone.

The situation is different when the amount of sulphate on the *surface* of the stone is examined. *Table 9.6* contains the results of sulphate analyses on

Table 9.6 Sulphate content of surface scrapings, following the initial cleaning stage

	Cleaning technique	*Sulphate content* (% SO_3)
Mullion 1	Lime poultice	26.5
	No treatment (control)	28.0
	Air abrasive	22.1
Mullion 2	Lime poultice	4.4
	No treatment (control)	26.0
	Water	4.8
Mullion 3	Air abrasive	12.8
	No treatment (control)	26.3
	Water	3.8

scrapings from the surface of the various samples. In both cases of water washing, the washing removes more than 80% of the sulphate skin. The effects of the air abrasive and the lime poultice, on the other hand, are more variable. In one case, the air abrasive reduced the sulphate content by 21%, in the other case by 51%. The lime poultice reduced it by 5% in one case and by 83% in the other, an even greater reduction than that caused by water washing. The variability of the results is not surprising, for some areas of stone will come clean more readily than others. In the case of the lime poultice, in particular, water is used to assist cleaning after removal of the poultice, so areas that had required a good deal of washing would be expected to give results similar to those for water washing alone.

The results of *Table 9.6* are borne out by examination of petrological thin sections. The sulphate skin is largely absent from samples that have been water washed, whereas it is present in variable amounts in those that have been cleaned by air abrasive or lime poultice.

These data confirm that water washing is potentially harmful to the stone, because it can remove the sulphate that binds surface grains together. The air abrasive and the lime poultice, on the other hand, permit a reduction in the sulphate skin without disrupting the stone below. This will facilitate the subsequent absorption of lime water but will also make the stone more vulnerable to further attack by acid rain water unless the protective shelter coat is applied. One advantage of the air abrasive over the lime poultice is that the air abrasive is more selective. It is possible to clean around traces of pigment, for example, without affecting the pigment itself.

Deposition of calcium hydroxide

This part of the investigation was aimed at detecting any calcium hydroxide or calcium carbonate that had been deposited in the stone. The lime poultice

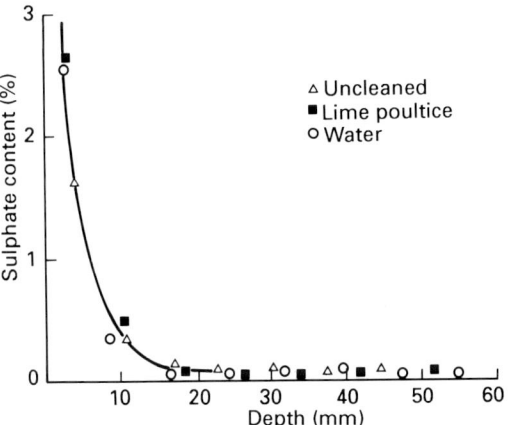

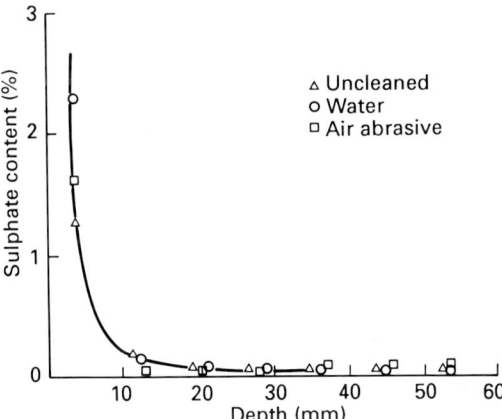

Figure 9.11 Variation of sulphate content with depth; analysis was by carbon/sulphate combustion, all sulphur being taken as sulphate

consists of calcium hydroxide, and the lime water is a solution of calcium hydroxide. Either the poultice or the lime water could thus lead to the deposition of calcium hydroxide, which would subsequently react with carbon dioxide in the air to form calcium carbonate. Ultimately, the calcium carbonate would react with sulphur dioxide in the air to form calcium sulphate.

The search for calcium carbonate/hydroxide was based mainly on examination of petrological thin sections, in the expectation that this would reveal the precise points at which deposition had occurred and would also give some indication of whether the deposition had occurred largely at the surface or in depth. In the event, the search was disappointing. In the majority of specimens, no deposits could be seen in the treated specimens (after either poulticing or lime watering) that could not also be seen in the controls. *Figure 9.12* shows one of the few specimens in which deposition was possibly evident. This particular specimen had been lime watered after cleaning by air abrasion. Nevertheless, it was disappointing and puzzling that convincing evidence of deposition could not be seen in each of the specimens.

The failure to detect calcium hydroxide/carbonate does not necessarily mean that no carbonate or hydroxide has been deposited or that the lime treatment is worthless. It is possible that very small quantities of carbonate/hydroxide could have a marked effect on the strength of the stone if deposited in just the right places. The petrological examination may not have been sensitive enough to detect such deposits. Alternatively, it is possible that the calcium carbonate/hydroxide has already been converted to calcium sulphate, which is indistinguishable from pre-existing calcium sulphate.

Porosity and microporosity

The porosity of a stone is defined as the volume of the pores that it contains, expressed as a percentage of the bulk volume of the stone. The 'microporosity' gives a broad indication of whether the pores are mainly coarse or fine. Microporosity is defined as the volume of water retained (expressed as a percentage of the available pore space) when a suction equivalent to a 6.4 m head of water is applied to the specimen. The concept is discussed in reference 27; the detailed test procedure is given in reference 28. A high microporosity indicates a high proportion of fine pores and is normally associated with low durability; conversely, a low microporosity indicates a high proportion of coarse pores and is normally associated with high durability. In the present

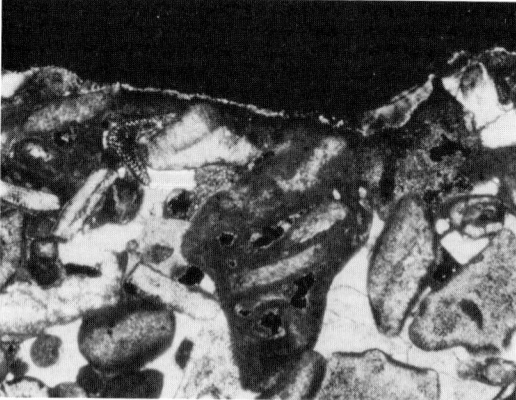

Figure 9.12 Petrological thin section of specimen after air abrasive cleaning and treatment with lime water. The calcium sulphate skin has been stained red, using Alizarin Red S in hot alkaline soloution. Magnification × 20; viewed under crossed polars. The white crust visible on the outer surface, and to some extent on the sides of the pores, may be a deposit of calcium hydroxide

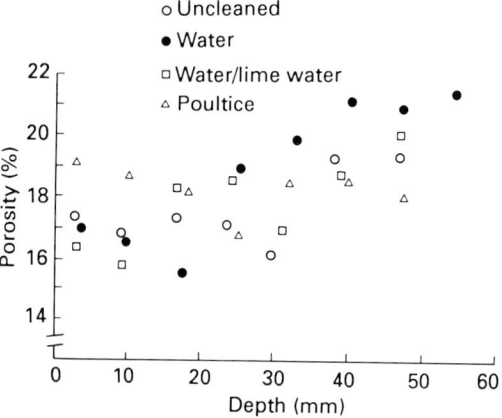

Figure 9.13 Variation of porosity with depth

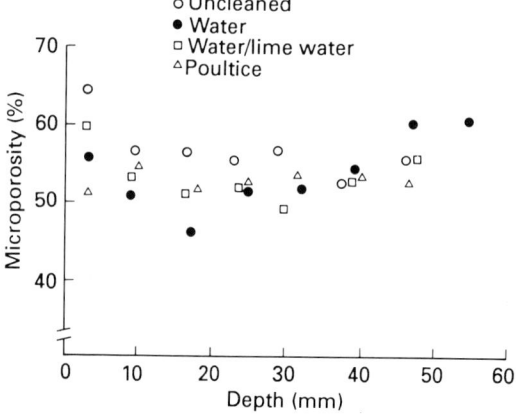

Figure 9.14 Variation of microporosity with depth

investigation, it is not so much the absolute values of microporosity that are of interest as the relative values, before and after treatment. Any marked change in the microporosity would indicate a significant change in the pore structure of the stone, with a consequent change in durability.

A representative selection of the results is depicted in *Figures 9.13 and 9.14*. As one would expect, particularly in the absence of major deposits in the petrological thin sections, neither the poultice nor the lime water has any discernible effect on the overall porosity of the stone. (Bear in mind, when examining the data, that the stone itself is not uniform and that fluctuations will inevitably occur from one part of the stone to another.) The microporosity data, likewise, show no effects attributable to the lime treatments.

Strength

One of the main benefits claimed for the lime treatment is the increase in strength that it brings about. Strength measurements, before and after treatment, are therefore essential to any assessment of the treatment. However, strength measurements are normally carried out on large cubes of stone, e.g. 80 mm (3.1 in) side, and many measurements must be made in order to eliminate statistical fluctuations. To avoid this a technique attributed to Butterbaugh[29] was tried instead. This entailed placing the stone in the jet of an air abrasive gun and measuring the size of the hole that was made in a given time.

The abrasive used was a silica sand of 100 FG mesh. The gun had a 5 mm (0.2 in) nozzle and was operated at 40 psi. It was held in a clamp 100 mm (4 in) away from the surface of the stone. A thin sheet of metal, with a 7 mm (0.3 in) diameter hole drilled in it, was placed on the surface of the stone. The gun was operated for two minutes, and the metal sheet was then moved on to another position. In this way, it was possible to make a line of holes, at approximately 10 mm centres, from the outer edge of each mullion slice to the centre. The size of each hole was measured by filling it level with 120 mesh carborundum grit, weighing the grit and converting to volume.

Examination of all the mullion slices by this technique is not yet completed, but the results for one of the mullions are shown in *Figure 9.15*. Disappointingly, the results are inconclusive. There appears to be a lot of scatter, which is not surprising in view of the inhomogeneity of the stone. Many more results would be required in order to confirm the statistical validity of any apparent trend. Even in the 'best' instance, the size of the outermost holes after lime watering is not very much lower than those of the control.

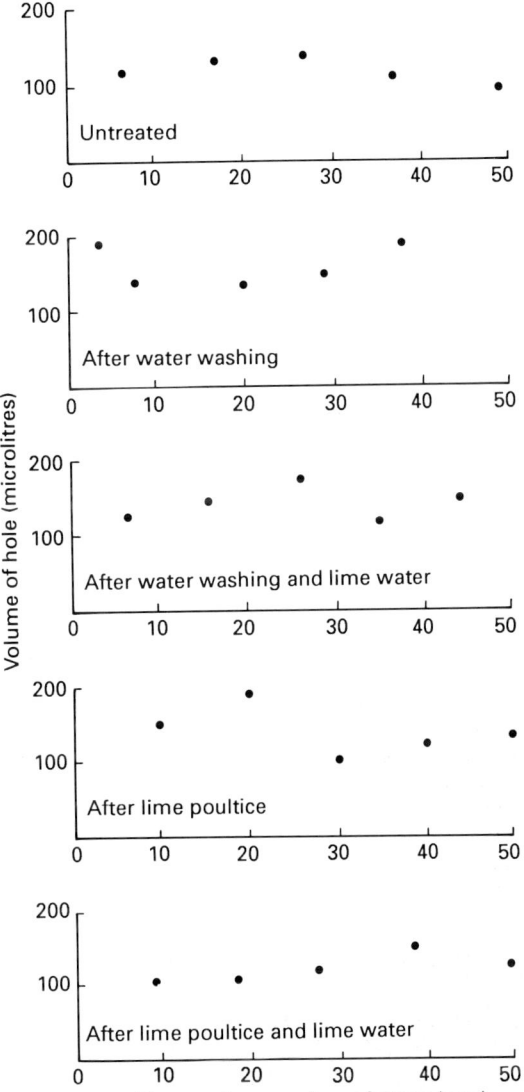

Figure 9.15 Estimation of strength by abrasion resistance

Consolidation of crushed stone

In the absence of conclusive data on strength, an attempt was made to consolidate crushed stone with lime water. Clearly, any consolidation so achieved would represent an increase in strength, since the initial strength was zero. Two types of stone were used, Doulting limestone and Monks Park limestone, which is an oolitic limestone mined near Bath. A silica sand (Ham River sandstone) was also tried. In each case, a carefully graded mix was prepared, in accordance with British Standard BS 1200. The proportions retained by standard meshes were as follows: 2.36 mm, 10%; 1.18 mm, 20%; 600 μm, 20%; 300 μm, 20%; 150 μm, 15%; 10% passed a 150 μm sieve. The moist mixture was placed into the filter funnel shown in *Figure 9.16*. It was next dried and weighed. The tip of the filter paper was then dipped into lime water until the crushed stone was all visibly wet. This took five to ten minutes. This procedure was adopted in order to avoid the fine particles in the mixture from being washed to the bottom, as would have happened if the lime water had been poured in from the top. The stone was then allowed to dry at room temperature. The drying period was never less than 24 hours and was usually several days. The cycle of wetting and drying was repeated thirty times over a period of six months. On each occasion, a control specimen was treated with distilled water.

At the end of the experiment, the Doulting and Monks Park specimens had increased in weight by 0.38 and 0.40% respectively. The sand had increased in weight by 0.22%. The control specimens had not changed weight significantly.

Despite the increase in weight, none of the lime-watered specimens showed any significant consolidation. All of them crumbled at the slightest pressure from a spatula. The Doulting specimen was perhaps marginally stronger than its control, but the Monks Park specimen was, if anything, even more friable than its control. Certainly none of the specimens showed the slightest degree of useful consolidation.

It is generally assumed that any consolidation would be achieved by carbonation of the calcium hydroxide, in a manner analogous to the hardening of lime mortars. Lime mortars harden when carbonation yields an interlocking mass of calcite crystals which binds the aggregate particles together.[30] By comparison with a lime-watered sample of stone, however, the amount of calcium hydroxide available for carbonation in a lime mortar is enormous. The reason for the failure of the lime water to achieve consolidation in this experiment may simply be that insufficient calcium hydroxide is deposited in the stone.

An alternative suggestion was contained in a Building Research Station Digest published in 1959 which reported that appreciable strengthening effects were obtained on friable stone by repeated applications of clear lime water. Repeated applications of lime water in the laboratory had no measurable effect on the strength of friable marble but it was suggested that any consolidation that might be achieved *in situ* might be due as much to the solution and redeposition of calcium sulphate already present in the stone as to the lime introduced into it. This tallies with the later observation that distilled water could sometimes achieve as much consolidation as lime water.[6]

It is clear that the mechanism by which lime water can consolidate porous building materials is not yet understood. There are certainly instances where useful consolidation has been achieved, especially with lime plasters, but equally there are some instances where there has been no apparent effect.[6] It is hoped that the present study will stimulate other workers to a further investigation of the general problem.

Conclusions

1. A lime poultice, and associated washing, does not serve to extract calcium sulphate from the depth of the stone.
2. A lime poultice, and associated washing, can reduce or remove the calcium sulphate skin on the surface of the stone. This may assist the subsequent absorption of lime water, but it also makes the stone more vulnerable to attack by acidic rainwater unless a protective shelter coat is applied.
3. There is no evidence that a lime poultice serves to consolidate friable stone.
4. A lime poultice should be regarded as one of a range of possible cleaning techniques (e.g. clay poultice, air abrasive), each of which has its own strengths and weaknesses. It should not be regarded as a technique of unique stature.
5. On the basis of the laboratory experiments described, there is no conclusive evidence that multiple applications of lime water serve to consolidate friable limestone.

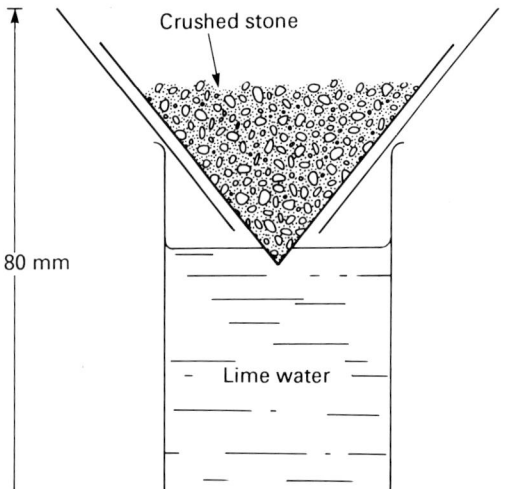

Figure 9.16 Attempted consolidation of crushed stone

6. Despite these rather negative findings, the lime technique can undoubtedly produce a dramatic change in the condition of decayed limestone. It is possible that part of this change, at least, is attributable simply to the meticulous care and attention which the stone receives, principally the painstaking preparation of the stone and the placing of carefully designed mortars. In view of the evident benefits of the technique its continued use at Wells Cathedral is recommended, but it is clear that further investigation into the technique is required.

Acknowledgements

The work described has been carried out as part of the research programme of the Building Research Establishment of the Department of the Environment, and this section is published by permission of the Director.

The work would not have been possible without the collaboration of the conservation team and the masons at Wells Cathedral. In particular, gratitude is due to Mr Peter Cooley, Superintendent of Works, who supervised the work carried out at Wells, and to Mr Martin Caroe, architect for the West Front, who commissioned the investigation. The Dean and Chapter of Wells kindly gave their consent to the work. The use of grit-blasting for estimating strength was developed in collaboration with Mr Bob Bennett of Bennett Masonry Cleaning.

Further appraisal of the lime method
John Ashurst

A further appraisal of the lime method was made by Clifford Price, now head of the Ancient Monuments Laboratory of English Heritage, Keith Ross, still of the Building Research Establishment, and Graham White, lecturer in biochemistry at University College, Cardiff (Wales, UK).

They carried out an experiment on a limestone mullion removed from the cloister of Wells Cathedral (Doulting limestone) which had a typically decayed and friable surface. Cleaning and consolidation was carried out under the direction of Richard Marsh, then manager of the Wells Conservation Centre, to ensure that the techniques were correctly applied. After a light cleaning with an Airbrasive tool, the mullion was cut into five 100 mm lengths and treated with lime poultice (14-day contact) and forty applications of lime water (over 44 days). To enable the deposition of calcium hydroxide to be detected, a radioactive tracer, ^{45}Ca, was added to the lime. The experiment has been recorded in detail in *Studies in Conservation*.[32]

The conclusions of the experiment, and the experiment itself, are of interest. Important points were that some lime could be traced in every case to a depth of at least 26 mm and that at least half of the deposited lime was found in the outer 2 mm. The poultice deposited some lime, but four to five times more was deposited during the lime watering. How useful is this deposition in terms of consolidation? Based on the experiment and on observations of weight gains in limestone powder consolidated with lime water, the authors concluded that only the outer 1–2 mm can have experienced any appreciable consolidation attributable to lime. Further into the stone the amounts deposited are so small that no consolidating effect can reasonably be expected.

Overall, the results seemed to confirm observations and speculations made in previous years. The lime water application, by virtue of lime deposited, or soluble salt mobilisation and crystallisation, or a combination of both, created a surface firm enough to receive a shelter coat of lime, casein and stone dust. In all cases the vital element for success was the skill, patience and experience of the conservator.

References

1. Rossi-Doria, P., Tabasso, M., Torraca, G. *et al.*, Note on conservation treatment of stone objects, *UNESCO-RILEM Colloquium*, Paris, 1978.
2. Sharp, R.W., private communication, 1981.
3. Amoro, G.G. and Fassina, V., 'Stone decay and conservation', *Material, Science Monograph II*, Elsevier, Amsterdam, 1983
4. Meals, R.N. and Lewis, F.M., *Silicones*, Reinhold, New York, 1958
5. Freeman, G.G., *Silicones*, Iliffe, London, 1962
6. Clarke, B.L. and Ashurst, J., *Stone Preservation Experiment*, Building Research Establishment, Watford, WD2 7JR. England, 1972
7. Schaffer, R.J., *The Weathering of Natural Building Stones*, Department of Scientific and Industrial Research Special Report 18, HMSO London, 1932 (available from Building Research Establishment, Watford WD2 7JR, England)
8. Price, C.A., *Chemistry in Britain*, **11**(10), 350–353, 1975.
9. Herwig Fritsch, *The Preservation of Sandstone*, Central Research and Development Department, Thomas Goldschmidt AG, Essen, Germany
10. Stambolov, T. and de Boer, J.R.v.A., 'The Deterioration and Conservation of Porous Building Materials in Monuments', ICCROM, Rome, 1976
11. Price, C.A., *Brethane Stone Preservative*, Current Paper 1/81, Building Research Establishment, Watford WD2 7JR, England, 1981
12. Ivanova, A.V., Lelekova, O.V. and Filatov, V.V., 'Choosing materials for and developing methods of stabilisation of Mural Painting in Mausoleum Ghur-Emir',

Communication No. 21, United Central Laboratory for Research on Conservation and Restoration of Museum Valuables, Moscow, 1968, 42–54

13. Biscontin, G. and Marchesini, L., 'Techniques d'intervention pour la protection des oeuvres d'art en pierre: resultats obtenus', *Lithoclastia*, Special issue, 51–56, Sept. 29–Oct 30, 1975

14. Rossi-Manaresi, R., 'Causes of decay and conservation treatments of the tuff of Castel dell'Ovo in Naples', in Boloyannis, N. (ed.), *Proc. 2nd Int. Symp. on Deterioration of Building Stones*, Sept 27 to Oct 1, 1976, pp 233–248, NTU, Athens

15. Alessandrini, G., Giambelli, G. and Peruzzi, R., 'Prove sull'efficacia di un trattamento conservativo effetuato sul Duomo di Milano', RP 76/6/31, Politecnico, Milan, 1976

16. Domaslowski, W. and Lehman, J., 'Recherehes sur l'affermissement structural des pierres au moyen de solution de résines thermoplastiques', in Rossi-Manaresi, R. and Torraca, G. (eds) *Proc. Meeting of the Joint Committee for the Conservation of Stone*, Bologna, Oct 1–3, 1971, Centro C. Gnudi per la Conservazione delle Sculture all'Aperto, Bologna, 1972

17. Fedorovich, E.F., Khusnitdinkhodzhaev, Kh. and Ruzybaev, D., 'A new method for consolidation of archaeological objects of unbaked clay and other porous materials' *United Central Laboratory for Research and Conservation of Museum Valuables, Communication No. 17-18*, 113–116, Moscow, 1966

18. Munnikendam, R.A., 'Preliminary notes on the consolidation of porous building materials by impregnation with monomers', *Studies in Conservation*, **12**, 158–162, 1967; also Munnikendam, R.A. and Wolscgrijn, Th. J., 'Further remarks on the impregnation of porous materials with monomers', *Studies in Conservation*, **14**, 133–135, 1969

19. Nonformale, O., 'A method of consolidation and restoration for decayed sandstone', in Rossi-Manaresi, R. (ed.) *Proc. Int. Symp. the Conservation of Stone I*, Bologna, June 19–21 1975, Centro C. Gnudi per la Conservazione delle Sculture all'Aperto, Bologna, 1976

20. Church, A.H., 'Improvements in the means of preserving stone, brick, slate, wood, cement, stucco, plaster, whitewash and colour wash from the injurious action of atmospheric and other influences', British Patent 220, 28 January 1862

21. Lewin, S.Z., 'Preservation of limestone structures', United States Patent 3577244, 4 May 1971; also Lewin, S.Z., 'Rationale of the barium hydroxide–urea treatment of decayed stone', *Studies in Conservation*, **19**, 24–35, 1974

22. Gauri, K.L., 'Efficiency of epoxy resins as stone preservatives', *Studies in Conservation*, **19**, 100–101, 1974

23. Domaslowsky, W., 'Investigation on the consolidation of stones with solutions of epoxy resins', *Biblioteka Muzealnictwa i Ochrony Zabytkow*, Seria B, **15**, Warszawa, 1966

24. Munnikendam, R.A., *Studies in Conservation*, **18**, 95, 1973

25. Anon., *The Development of Silane-Based Preservatives—their Use and Abuse*, Society for the Protection of Ancient Buildings, (now at) 34 Spital Square, London E1 6DY, 1980

26. Henson, D., 'Experiments with milk and lime on limestone surfaces', 1983

27. Anon., 'The selection of natural building stone', *British Research Establishment Digest 269*, 1983

28. *Proc. Int. Symp. on the Deterioration and Protection of Stone Monuments*, Volume 5, Test I.4, UNESCO/RILEM, Paris, 1978

29. Phillips, M.W., 'Acrylic precipitation consolidants', *IIC Congress on Science and Technology in the Service of Conservation*, Washington DC, 1982

30. Lea, F.M., *The chemistry of cement and concrete*, 3rd edn, 252, Edward Arnold, London, 1970

31. Anon. 'Stone preservatives', *Building Research Station Digest 128* (First series), 1959

32. Price, C., Ross, K. and White, G., 'A further appraisal of the "Lime technique" for limestone consolidation, using a radioactive tracer', *Studies in Conservation*, **33**, 178–186, 1988

10

The conservation of stone monuments in churches

John Larson

Introduction

The term monument can cover a very wide range of carved memorials that can be as simple as an unadorned inscription tablet, or as complex as some of the great eighteenth century tombs that possess the scale of miniature buildings. However complex or simple the monument may be, all monuments share one basic feature: they are inevitably wedded to the fabric of the building that they inhabit and, of necessity, must suffer the same changes in fortune. Those architects and conservators who have to deal with decaying monuments and buildings must, if they are to succeed in preserving them, attempt to understand the complex interactions that take place, often over a period of centuries, between a monument and its environment.

It is fundamental to any sensible programme of monument conservation that hopes to achieve any enduring results to possess a knowledge of the basic forms of monument construction.

Monument construction

Tomb building in England, combining both sculptured and architectural detail, really began in the thirteenth century and carried through on an ever-increasing scale until the early years of the twentieth century. Throughout this time the basic pattern of construction remained similar. There is a supporting core surrounded by facings of carved stone, usually fixed to the core by cramps or, in a few cases, simply adhered with lime mortar. This basic simplicity of construction, however, has, over many centuries, been elaborated upon by architects and sculptors to the point where certain monuments attempt to achieve forms of construction that would be more

suitable in wood than stone. Even in the most elaborate monuments, the same basic elements of construction recur and these can be categorized as follows.

The free-standing box tomb

The free-standing box tomb was very popular throughout the medieval period until well into the seventeenth century. The basic elements of this type of construction can be seen in *Figure 10.1*. A core of brick, stone blocks or rubble was constructed, to form a solid platform around which the monument was built. The core was usually built onto the floor of the church, and therefore may well stand on a bed of cut stone. In many cases, however, the core simply stands on earth, particularly if there is a vault below. With time this obviously creates problems of movement in the core and also allows the penetration of moisture and soluble salts.

Although the cores are usually hollow and make efficient use of mass to strength ratio, particularly clumsy constructions, where the core is a solid conglomerate of rubble, earth and mortar, are often found. It is obvious that there is little chance of either introducing air circulation or eliminating damp in such a structure.

Once the foundations, if they exist, and the core were constructed, the carved facing slabs of the monument were attached to the core. A wide variety of carving stones used for such monuments are found, ranging from Purbeck 'Marble' and alabaster, to limestones, sandstone and marbles. In general, the thickness of these facing slabs does not vary greatly. On average, they are 50 mm (2 in) to 75 mm (3 in) deep. Where the workmanship is poor, or the monument is very large, the stone may be 150 mm (6 in) to 300 mm (12 in) deep. The whole strength of this pattern of tomb lies in its core. The visible

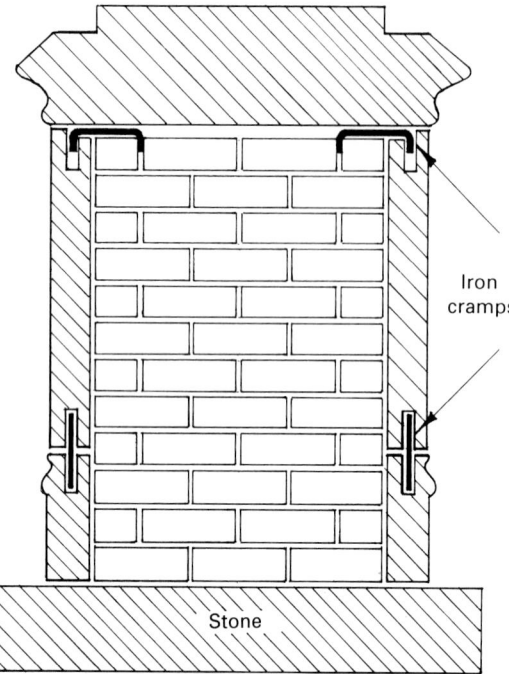

Iron
cramps

Stone

Figure 10.1 Traditional construction of box tomb.
Although some medieval tombs have a brick core (as shown
here) many are supported by a crude rubble, mortar and
earth infill

elements of the monument rarely have a structural
role; they are simply cladding.

The carved elements of the tomb are attached to
the core by means of cramps and dowels. These are
nearly always made of ferrous metal and little
evidence is found to suggest that any other metal,
such as copper, brass or bronze, was ever used on a
regular basis. The cramps and dowels that are found
in small medieval tombs vary little in character from
those that are found in the enormous constructions
of the eighteenth century. The cramps, whether
retaining or supporting, fit into slots cut into the
edges of the facing panel and are bedded into a
suitable adhesive.

Insufficient research has been carried out to
determine the difference in type between medieval
and later adhesives, but it would be unwise to
assume that the only adhesive available to masons of
that period was lime mortar. In tombs of all periods,
shellac and wax-resin mixtures are found being used
as adhesives, but the constant moving and rebuilding
of tombs that has occurred in so many churches over
the years makes such evidence unreliable.

The box tomb acts as a support for a large slab on
which there is often an embedded brass or, most
commonly, a recumbent effigy or pair of effigies. The
true box tomb is often further embellished above the
level of the effigy with decorated finials, coats of
arms, or other heraldic devices. However, when the
construction goes beyond this, the structure really
comes into the category of the canopy tomb.

The box tomb basically relies on the strength of
its own construction and is therefore most often a
free-standing monument. Tombs of similar construction are often built against walls in churches, but
they are rarely fixed to the wall by cramps or other
constructional devices. They simply lean against the
wall and are fixed by mortar joints. In this case, there
is no back panel to the tomb and the core is in direct
contact with the wall of the building. In certain cases,
notably St George's, Colegate, Norwich, where a
tomb has been moved from a free-standing site, there
is a carved panel facing into the wall, which would
originally have been visible.

The wall tomb

This category of monument can be broken down into
two types; the full wall tomb and the cantilevered
wall monument. The full wall tomb, which has at its
base the solid foundation of the box tomb, becomes
a partially cantilevered construction as it ascends the
wall, and derives its support from the wall behind
(*Figure 10.2*). This type of construction can be found
throughout the medieval period and is echoed in
many Easter sepulchres and sedilias. It reaches its
greatest technical extravagence in the vast tombs of
the eighteenth century, constructed by such sculptors as Rysbrack and Roubiliac. The cantilevered wall
monument (*Figure 10.3*) owes its origins to the
sculpture of the Italian Renaissance, but is only fully
exploited in baroque England.

The difference in construction between these two
tomb types is very basic. The first relies on the firm
foundation of the box tomb with its core to provide
a platform for the elements of the superstructure,
which are then tied back to the wall with cramps.
The second has no support other than the cramps
which secure it to the wall. In the seventeenth
century, the cantilevered wall tomb tended to be
very solidly constructed and relied heavily on large
corbels (often penetrating 300 mm (12 in) deep into
the wall) at the base of the monument to support the
upper elements. Such a construction becomes very
much a part of the wall into which it is constructed
and often cannot be dismantled without considerable reconstruction of the wall behind. In the
eighteenth century, when marble became the
fashionable material for monuments, as opposed to
limestone and alabaster, its inherent strength and
expense led sculptors such as Francis Bird (*Figure
10.4*) to undertake daring experiments, whereby a
monument was merely hung on the surface of the

Figure 10.2 Eighteenth century wall tomb by Roubiliac: Warkton Church

Figure 10.3 Example of eighteenth century cantilevered wall tomb

wall with cramps and was not corbelled back into the stone behind.

The canopy tomb

This type of monument employs the basic forms of construction found in the box tomb and the wall tomb. It was used throughout the medieval period, and is shown at its most elaborate in the Percy tomb, but reached its greatest constructional daring in the seventeenth century in tombs such as the St John monument at Lydiard Tregoze.

The free-standing canopy tomb usually has as its basis a box tomb construction and may have a reclining or kneeling effigy on top. Above this, the construction may rise to form an arched or domed canopy, although in many cases the termination is a stone tester supported on vertical columns. In this form, a pyramidal or rectangular format is essential to achieve stability in the tomb. However, when the tomb is adjacent to a supporting wall, the canopy may be cantilevered from the wall and may derive little support from the box tomb below. In such cases there is often a very complex arrangement of ironwork embedded into the canopy, in an attempt to replace the strength that would normally be derived from supporting columns. The ironwork in these tombs is not always original. Very often it is the work of the nineteenth century architect or engineer, who has tried to preserve the rash constructions of the seventeenth century.

Causes of decay in monuments

Structural problems

The very fact that monuments are of composite construction, containing a variety of materials of different thicknesses and weights bonded together by iron, is enough to ensure that they will, at some time, suffer some form of movement or collapse. Moisture in all its forms is the main agent of decay in all stonework. In monuments, moisture causes

Figure 10.4 Monument to Orlando Gee by F. Bird: Isleworth Church. This monument has a completely flat back and is only supported by irons in the walls. The corbel brackets at the base of the monument are not inset into the wall

disruption of the ironwork by the process of rusting and expansion. The expanding cramps and dowels exert an enormous pressure when they are trapped in stone; several tonnes of marble can be lifted by the expansion of a few iron cramps within a monument. This expansion causes such pressure that the brittle stone cracks and becomes structurally unsound. Movement in one part of a monument will also affect other parts of the structure and gradually create tension throughout the monument.

Structural pressures can also be exerted on a monument from outside. If the monument has inadequate foundations, or is built above a slowly collapsing vault, the shift beneath the monument will result in opening of the joints and the collapse of the core. If the monument is fixed by cramps to the wall, as well as to the ground, any movement will cause tremendous tensions that can result in the total collapse of the monument. The monument conservator may be the first to discover some serious

weakness in the structure. Such weaknesses, even if only suspected, should be made known to the client immediately.

Pressures on the monument can also come from the wall into which it is fixed. Many churches have undergone structural alterations over the years and it is not uncommon for a door or window to have been blocked in to provide wall space for a monument. The filling of such an aperture is often of the roughest kind and sometimes consists of rubble bonded with mud and plaster. Monuments bedded into such structures, or sited above them, usually develop structural problems at a later date when the wall begins to sag under the weight of the monument.

One major factor in structural decay can often be blamed on the monument's designer. It is particularly apparent in some tombs of the seventeenth century, when alabaster was often the chosen medium, that the artist attempted to stretch the material beyond the limit of its tensile strength. In some cases this has resulted in partial collapse of the monument. In others alabaster has cracked or simply warped (*Figure 10.5*).

Figure 10.5 Alabaster monument: Bletsoe. One can see clearly that the support provided for the continuous alabaster architrave (1.5 m) has been inadequate and the stone has gradually warped

Decay from soluble salts

Perhaps the most insidious and least understood form of decay in stone monuments is that caused by the migration and crystallization of soluble salts. All old churches that do not have damp proof courses are contaminated by salts of one form or another. The most common types are sulphates and nitrates. Chlorides are less common and are most often found in maritime areas.

Salts in a monument tend to come from the ground on which they are built, although they can be introduced into a monument by the use of contaminated mortars. The classic pattern of salt contamination can, however, be broken down into several simple stages (*Figure 10.6*). If the source of moisture derived from rising damp caused by flooding, changes in the water table, blocked drains or, more commonly, from raising the ground level outside the church above that of the inside, then the salts will rise from the ground and be drawn into the walls of the church. If the cause is falling damp, e.g. broken gutters, decayed mouldings, or a damaged roof, then the rise of the salts will follow the moisture up the wet walls, but, because the monument may also be saturated with water from above, the breakdown will usually be even more rapid than that caused by rising damp.

The progress of salt migration depends on cycles of wetting and drying to provide the migratory impetus. The walls of a church act as a wick. They are basically a column of stone standing on wet earth, and above ground level they act as a membrane between the outer and inner environments. As part of the outer environment, they are exposed to all the dramatic changes of weather, temperature and humidity. The inner environment changes less rapidly and may remain wet and cold, even when the outside environment is warm and dry. Generally the wall will be drier than the earth on which it stands. Therefore moisture will naturally tend to rise up into the dry stone above, carrying with it the salts in solution. While the salts remain in solution, they will cause little harm. However, when they crystallize near the surface as a subflorescence, or on the surface as an efflorescence (due to changes in temperature, or humidity, or wall thickness), damage will occur.

One thing that is certain about the presence of salts in a structure is that they will not simply disappear. Monuments do not mysteriously get better. It is possible to reduce salt activity in a wall by careful drainage of the ground, but as long as the salts remain they will always pose a threat. Once salts are in stone, the changes in relative humidity and temperature in the atmosphere around the stone will be sufficient to continue the growth of salts. Recent work in Switzerland[1] has shown not only that salts continue to migrate as long as moisture is present, but that the salts themselves will change the chemical balance of the stone they inhabit, attracting moisture to it. In some cases this will actively change the temperature within the stone.

Although salts display slightly different patterns of behaviour in different stones, their effect on a monument is equally destructive whether it be made of marble, alabaster, limestone or sandstone.

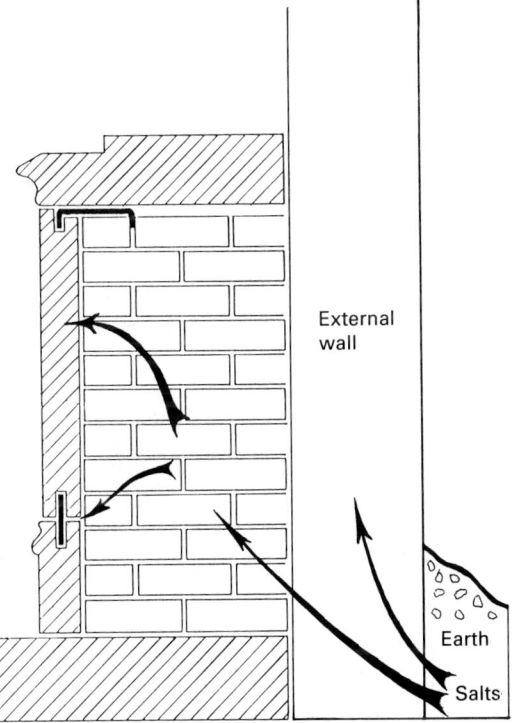

Figure 10.6 Progress of salt contamination. The most common source of salts is in the ground around or underneath the church. Where earth has been allowed to build up against an outside wall, the salts seep into the wall, gradually migrate into the core of the monument and then attack the mortar joints and fabric of the monuments. The mortar joints in both core and monument act as an absorbent pathway along which the salts can easily move

Condensation and heating

Unfortunately, the climate within most churches is not controlled in any way. Very few churches possess adequate ventilation and many of them are overheated for very limited periods of time. As a result, much of the damage that occurs to monuments is due to condensation and surface moisture. One of the stones most readily affected by condensation is Purbeck 'marble'. Because the stone presents a cold, polished surface, moisture condenses readily on it and, lying on the surface, slowly seeps into tiny fissures which are often found in this shelly limestone. The moisture is absorbed slowly into the surface, combining with salts from within the stone. Over a period of time the polish will disappear and the Purbeck 'marble' will become rough and take on a grey appearance, superficially similar to cement.

Black limestone and slate (usually used for inscriptions) will also be attacked by condensation; this often shows as dribbles etched into the surface where the moisture has formed persistently. Carrara marble and alabaster are also attacked by condensation, because they are both relatively impervious. However, most limestones, which are porous, will accept the moisture vapour into their pore structure without visible damage. The recurring movement of water droplets over a polished surface causes an erosion similar to that of a river in a valley, although a chemical reaction between water and stone is also involved.

Heating the interior of a church for a short period draws moisture through the walls and aggravates the condensation problem. Gas heaters are perhaps one of the worst forms of heating, as they give off many litres of water into the atmosphere in a few hours.

The greatest disasters occur when radiators or hot water pipes are placed near monuments. The heat will draw salts and moisture into and, eventually, through the monument. This creates an exaggerated rate of salt crystallization and an accelerating rate of stone decay.

Damage from restoration

A great part of the damage to monuments is man-made and not the result of natural causes. Whether a restoration is good or bad, whether from the aesthetic or technical viewpoint, is always debatable. However, on the technical side, there is positive evidence that certain treatments lead to decay.

Cleaning

Alabaster (calcium sulphate) is water soluble and therefore should never be cleaned with soap and water, which will slowly erode the surface. As alabaster is also very soft it should not be cleaned with abrasives, such as commercial abrasives containing pumice and bleach. Acid and caustic solutions should also be avoided because they will erode the surface and create, or exacerbate, staining.

Marble (calcium carbonate) is not readily soluble in water, and therefore the majority of cleaning treatments are based on water and liquid chemical treatments. It is unsafe, however, to use large quantities of water on marble for extended periods of time, because this can create iron-staining and will eventually cause loss of detail in fine carving. Acid and caustic solutions will both erode and discolour

statuary marble. Abrasives such as pumice, or wet and dry paper, will remove any traces of original polish or fine detail.

Limestones and sandstones are used in a wide variety of types for monument construction. They differ from alabaster or marble in that some are porous. It is very noticeable in churches that it is the highly polished marble and alabaster monuments that suffer from surface erosion caused by condensation. The more porous limestones and sandstones absorb atmospheric moisture quite readily, and will also absorb any water from a cleaning treatment. Liberal washing can, for this reason, encourage salt crystal growths and staining from salts and iron. Similarly, the use of bleach, acids and powdered detergents can create problems in the surface pores of the stone which may not become apparent until several years later.

Generally, in the cleaning of all carved or decorative stone in churches, it is best to use a very controlled approach. Cleaning should proceed in small, manageable sections, using the minimum quantity of cleaning agent, so that there is never any danger of the treatment damaging a large part of the monument. Where a monument is still in contact with the fabric of the church during cleaning and has not been dismantled, great care should be taken not to saturate it with water, because this will create problems with salts that may eventually cause structural damage.

Pigmentation

One of the misunderstood areas of monument conservation, simply because it arouses strong aesthetic prejudices, is that which centres around the treatment of polychromy on monuments. If a monument is painted or gilded, it cannot be cleaned as though it were made of plain stone. It is surprising, however, how often this does occur and much of the understanding of the history of sculpture in this country has been blurred by such inept treatment. Water washing of painted stonework is a certain way of losing pigment, either from direct action of the water or from later salt growths. The cleaning of painted monuments is a specialized task and requires the expertise of a skilled conservator.

Although the current opinion is that monuments should not be repainted to simulate original colour schemes, a considerable amount of repainting does still occur. This is usually aesthetically disastrous because no one can hope to recreate the original painted scheme on top of decayed stonework. From the conservation point of view, it can also damage the monument. In some cases, oil paints and enamel paints have been used on monuments. These not only stain the stone, they also encapsulate the stone in an impervious film. Salts can build up under this film to cause irreparable damage. The application of new paint over original paint also creates problems and may result in the loss of the original paint fragments.

Cements

Portland cements should never be allowed to come into contact with old stone. So much damage has been caused to monuments by rebuilding with cement that it is surprising to find that this practice still occurs in churches. Long observation has proved that cements create or aggravate salt activity in old stone and will eventually lead to its destruction. Wherever cement or concrete has to be used near a monument, the monument should always be isolated from it by a suitable membrane.

Consolidation treatments and damp-proof courses

There have been many attempts over the past hundred years to consolidate crumbling monuments *in situ*. Materials such as wax, lime water, shellac, oil, epoxy resins and silicones have all been used for this purpose. In one way or another, they have all largely proved ineffective. The main reason is that deep-seated disruption, which is usually caused by soluble salts, cannot be treated by forming a casing of hardened stone on the surface. In fact, all research has shown that such impervious barriers accelerate decay. Even lime water, which remains permeable, can activate rather than neutralize salt activity. The injection of a liquid damp-proof course or the partial fitting of a solid one, will hasten decay, because salt is trapped and causes local tensions within the stone.

The treatment of monuments

The monument and the environment

When formulating a programme of conservation for a monument in a church, the problems that exist within its environment must be considered first. Faults in the building, such as bad drainage, broken gutters, decayed pointing, leaking roofs, condensation and structural movement, should all be dealt with before the monument is treated. The commonest failing is the gradual rise of the outside ground level above that of the floor in the church. This inevitably leads to problems with rising damp and salts. When all these problems have been dealt with, the treatment of the monument can begin.

The crucial question is really whether or not to dismantle. In most cases where a monument shows serious signs of breakdown, due to the presence of iron cramps or salts, there is very little choice but to dismantle. There are cases where local consolidation,

removal of visible cramps, or partial dismantling, may solve or at least arrest the decay. However, it generally makes better long-term economic sense to carry out a full treatment, involving full dismantling, rather than to patch a monument and then undertake the full treatment at a later date. There are many examples where expensive surface treatments on salt contaminated monuments have not proved effective. As a result, the monuments have had to be dismantled and properly treated later. This makes monument conservation unnecessarily expensive and subjects the monument to further years of decay.

In cases of salt contamination (*Figure 10.7*), the monument can only be effectively de-salinated if it is fully dismantled and each individual block of stone is treated by poulticing. If the basic structure of a tomb is affected by expanding ferrous cramps (*Figure 10.8*), partial dismantling, or repointing of joints, would be ineffective.

To dismantle a large, finely carved monument by a sculptor such as Rysbrack or Roubiliac may be considered by some people to be vandalism.

Figure 10.7 Marble monument: Kirkleatham.
Crystallization of salts has caused expansion in the core. Because the marble facings are cramped to the core, they have gradually cracked under the pressure.

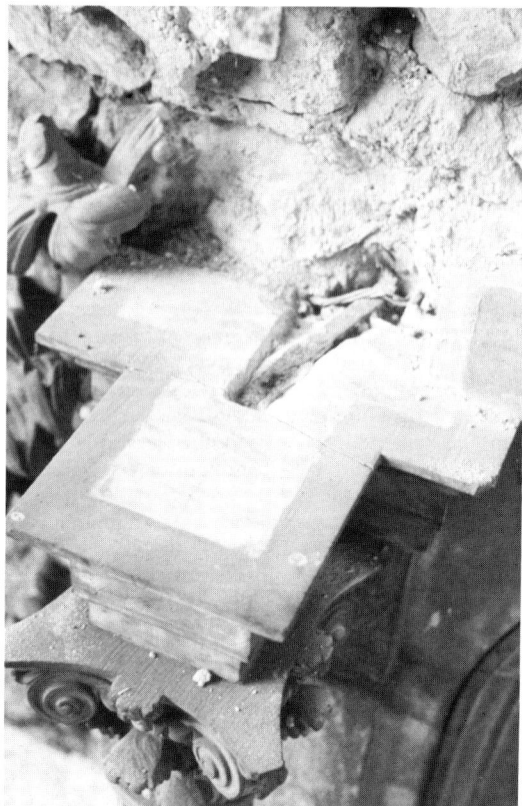

Figure 10.8 Expanding iron cramp causing splitting in marble 12 cm thick

Figure 10.9 Seventeenth century painted stone monument: Colyton. The monument was originally painted and then repainted in the nineteenth century. All mortar joints had also been covered with paint.

However, with modern conservation techniques, it is possible to dismantle, conserve and re-erect such monuments without damage. Even large polychrome monuments with pigment actually covering the mortar joints, such as the monument at Colyton (*Figure 10.9*), can be dismantled without pigment loss. By 'facing up' friable stone (*Figure 10.10*) with a reinforced tissue before dismantling, the retention of all fragments of paint and stone can be ensured. This type of treatment allows the monument to be either partially or wholly transported off-site, if necessary, in order to be more fully treated in the safety of the conservation studio.

In any programme of monument conservation, record keeping is of the utmost importance. When a monument is to be dismantled, a complete record of the operation is vital. At the very least, good black and white photographs should be taken before, during and after the operation. These should be related to a measured drawing of the monument before conservation and to a written record of the condition before treatment. There should be a full record of treatment listing all the products involved,

however basic. In some cases, photogrammetric surveys and corrected photography will be useful. Whenever polychromy exists, colour photography is essential.

Very few monuments contain buried remains. However, in some cases, bones or evidence of earlier remains do turn up during dismantling. Therefore it is wise to inform the local archaeologist when work of this nature is to be undertaken.

Membranes

Once a monument has been dismantled, the site that it occupies in the church should be treated so that damp or structural movement will not affect it again. The wall behind the monument should be repointed and any structural faults corrected. The floor beneath the monument may be perfectly sound, but the monument may be standing on little more than a bed of earth and rubble. In some cases, it may be supported only by the roof of a collapsing vault. In

Figure 10.10 Detail of Colyton monument, showing tissue 'facing-up'. By covering the painted surfaces with tissue and size (polyvinyl alcohol) the joints could be revealed by making incisions through the tissue and paint layers. When the paint had been peeled back on either side of the joint, the joints could be cut with a chisel. During rebuilding, the paint could be laid down and ironed with a heated spatula over the new joints

the majority of such situations it will be necessary to provide a new base for the monument. This usually consists of a concrete raft about 150 mm (6 in) deep. In some cases, slabs of stone are used for the base.

Whatever the condition of the wall or floor, all monuments must be isolated from them by a substantial waterproof membrane after refurbishment. There are many forms of membrane available today, ranging from thick polythene, epoxy resin and glass-fibre mat, to metal foils and bitumen laminates and even some polyester foams. Many of these membranes are suitable for small-scale domestic work or buildings where a life-span of thirty years is envisaged. However, when conserving church monuments, a life of a hundred years should be expected. Therefore, proven materials are needed that will ensure long-term service.

Lead has many advantages. A Code 4 to Code 6 lead sheet has sufficient thickness to keep out moisture and salts. It also has considerable flexibility, so that it will withstand compression without tearing. In one example, a two-hundred-year-old lead membrane which had been situated beneath a 15 m (45 ft) high medieval market cross was removed without any sign of damage. When coated with bitumen on both sides to protect it from alkali attack from mortar, a lead membrane will provide long-term protection for any monument and will isolate it from a potentially hostile environment.

Although lead can tear from its fixings when hung on a wall, this can be minimized if the lead is given adequate support, and is wedged and screwed into mortar joints. If this is done when it is pinned behind a monument, experience has shown that the movement is negligible.

Where a monument has to be cramped to a wall and the membrane has therefore to be pierced, the area around the point of pentration can be sealed with a suitable waterproof mastic such as Akemi, or 'General' resin mixed with sand.

Cores

The core is a basic structural feature of nearly all types of monument. When rebuilding a monument, the main concern is to produce a core that will not be a reservoir of moisture in the very heart of the monument. A dry system that does not use aqueous mortars has been evolved using Celcon blocks bonded with a sand and polyester mortar (*Figure 10.11*). In certain cases, where damp is not a great problem, a polyvinyl acetate emulsion (such as Unibond) and sand mix can be used. Apart from the obvious advantage of this system in excluding water, it also allows the core to be built up rapidly and does not require a long period for drying and settlement.

The core should be built slightly smaller than the internal dimensions of the monument, so that an air gap of 25–50 mm (1–2 in) can be allowed between the core and the monument. Where horizontal members have to bear directly onto the core, they should be isolated from the core by a lead and bitumen membrane (*Figure 10.12*).

Dowels, cramps and mortars

As there is a basic logic in the dismantling of a monument, in that it should be dismantled from the top down, so there is a logical pattern to reconstruction. Once the core has been constructed, building up is from the base mouldings. The individual elements should be cramped back to the core, making certain that the dimensions of the monument coincide with the original scheme.

Figure 10.11 Detail of monument at Lingfield during rebuilding. Here one can see the new core on its lead damp-proof course and the bottom stages of the monument during rebuilding. The monument is also on a damp-proof course and there is an air gap between it and the core of about 40–50 mm (1½–2 in)

Figure 10.12 Detail showing lead damp-proof course

When reconstructing a monument, the architect and conservator are faced with certain basic problems, arising from the use of both synthetic and traditional materials. The difficulty is in producing a balance between rigid and flexible materials, movement and stability. For instance, in traditional monument construction, the following pattern would be typical:

1. Core (brick and rubble and lime mortar), which is flexible
2. Monument (stone facings and lime mortar), which is rigid and flexible
3. Cramps (usually ferrous) which are rigid and brittle
4. Adhesives (shellac or wax/resin) which are initially soft, but become brittle

These materials, which are allied to the possible movement between the monument and supporting building fabric, are significant factors in the deterioration of monuments. When reconstructing a monument, all these factors must be taken into account and appropriate materials chosen.

None of the materials used in reconstruction must be affected by damp. Therefore, for cramps and dowels, the most satisfactory material is stainless steel. Non-aqueous, or at least water-repellent, mortars should be used for bedding the components of the monument. These are best made from mixtures of polyester, acrylic or PVA, mixed with silica sands.

Of course, stainless steel is highly inflexible. Some degree of movement around a cramp or dowel can be designed for, by sleeving in a thick polythene or nylon tube. Where necessary, the flexibility of the adhesive can be increased by using an acrylic or PVA resin instead of an epoxy or polyester resin. All of these changes will allow some small movement in the monument, but they will not weaken the retaining power of the cramps.

Whenever possible, the conservator should reuse the slots for cramps made by the original mason. Only where recent breaks have occurred will new

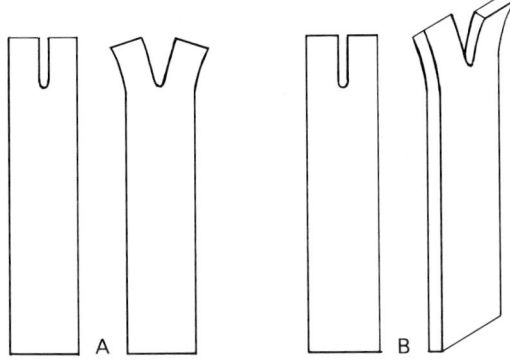

Figure 10.13 Two basic forms of cramp. Both cramps are made from flat stainless steel bar. A saw cut (about 15 mm long) is made at one end. In 'A' a chisel is inserted in the saw cut and tapped until a V-shaped is formed. In 'B' the two prongs are tapped away from each other with a hammer

holes be necessary. There are two basic shapes for cramps, which have not changed since medieval times (*Figure 10.13*). These can easily be cut on site in a vice and can be bent cold.

Fillings, repairs and retouching

There are widely differing views on the extent to which a monument should be restored. Some feel that it should look as new, while others feel that a strictly archaeological approach should be taken and no cosmetic work is necessary beyond essential structural repairs. The grant-awarding body of the Church of England, The Council for the Care of Churches, has a positive, though slightly flexible, view. In effect, it feels that the harmony of the monument should be retained, but no unnecessary cosmetic work should be undertaken, particularly if it is likely to blur the original intention of the artist. Thus recutting large areas of a monument, putting back garlands, hands, feet, armorials, or large areas of moulding, would be regarded as unethical. Generally, areas of moulding can be filled with a suitable filler when a disturbing break occurs in a line of moulding. Recutting a whole line of moulding and disposing of the original would not be sanctioned.

Over the years, considerable progress has been made in producing fillings that look very like marble, alabaster or limestone and will survive in a church environment for many years without deterioration. The advantage of a plastic repair, rather than splicing in new stone, is obvious. Plastic fillers can be modelled *in situ* and have a minimal effect on the original stone, whereas to piece in a new block of stone would require the loss of a certain amount of

original material. The plastic filler has the added advantage that, from the ethical viewpoint, it will always be recognizable as a synthetic addition. A stone indent may look like an original repair, and possibly lead to historical confusion.

The most suitable fillings are based on mixtures of synthetic resins (polyesters and acrylics), mixed with ground stone dust, silica sands and alabaster powder. They can be mixed to a thixotropic putty and worked in place with a spatula. If carefully matched to the colour of the original, there should be no need to paint over the filling to blend it with the original. This is always an advantage for future maintenance, because it allows washing with water or some weak cleaning solutions at a future date.

In the past, plaster fillings could not visually match the marble or alabaster on which they were used. Their porosity also meant they were a breeding ground for salts and they tended to soften and crumble when attacked by rising damp.

Where re-touching is necessary, usually to preserve heraldic colour, or to tone down unsightly patches, the best medium is an acrylic. Acrylics produce a paint that will form a skin on the surface of the stone and will dry rapidly. These paints also have the advantage that they do not stain the stone and can easily be removed at a later date, should taste or practical necessity require it.

Consolidants and surface finishes

Stone consolidation is a subject which arouses a great deal of passion. There are many myths surrounding the treatment of decaying stone and the subject must be looked at logically if a sensible approach to the problem is to be formulated.

The basic factors that need to be borne in mind when looking at a crumbling stone monument include:

1. The major cause of all stone decay in churches is damp, either rising or falling.
2. Migrating soluble salts are the agency through which damp creates the greatest damage.
3. If stone is to 'breathe', it will go on absorbing moisture, salts and atmospheric pollutants.
4. It is dangerous to stop stone from 'breathing', when it is part of a major structure such as a church, if it does not have a damp proof course.
5. It is likely that, if a deteriorating monument is consolidated *in situ*, the damage caused by salt migration will be accelerated.

Once these factors have been assessed, a decision can be made on the desirability of full or partial consolidation. It is only possible to treat a monument successfully when full dismantling has been undertaken and the source of damp removed.

The consolidant must completely isolate each block against the further penetration of moisture, and the depth of penetration must be sufficient to ensure that the protection is not merely on the surface of the stone. Partial consolidation is only permissible where the element treated can be fully isolated from the rest of the monument, as in the case of an isolated figure.

The most widely used consolidants for marble, limestone and sandstone monuments are the silanes. These are deep-penetrating consolidants which give, on average, 3.5 cm (1.4 in) penetration. Silanes deposit silica in the stone and impart a high degree of water repellency. They can be applied by brushing, spraying, pipette and drip feed, but it must be stressed that they should *only* be applied by a skilled conservator who understands the full implications of this radical treatment.

There are two basic silane systems in use in the UK at the moment. One is a catalysed silane, which gels within a few hours and has a short working time. It is therefore mainly suitable for the treatment of large, plain surfaces. The second system is a mixture of acrylic and silane. This method allows the conservator a long working period and is suitable where more intricate work is involved, such as sculpture or ornament. It also allows a much wider range of cleaning treatments to be used, which is

essential in cases where stonework has to be consolidated before it can be cleaned. The catalysed silanes, once cured, will only respond to air-abrasive cleaning: the acrylic-silane system allows the use of solvents and other more controllable treatments.

In cases where consolidation is not required, but where it would be advantageous to apply a protective coating to the stone after conservation, a varnish of cosmolloid wax, ketone 'N' resin and white spirit can be applied. This should only be used on the more impervious stones, such as marble, alabaster or compact limestone. It should never be applied to the more permeable limestones and sandstones. There is also a range of acrylics available, which can be mixed with wax or sometimes with silicones. These have proved very durable, even when subjected to external weathering tests. They have the added advantage that they can easily be removed with white spirit or acetone.

References

1. Arnold, A., 'Rising damp and saline minerals', paper presented at 4th International Congress on the deterioration and preservation of stone objects, 7–9 July 1982, University of Louisville, Kentucky
2. Larson, J., 'Conservation of alabaster monuments in churches', *The Conservator*, **3**, 28–33, 1979

11

The conservation of stone sculpture in museums

John Larson

Stone in the museum environment

There are many misconceptions regarding the role of the museum-based conservator. The greatest of these is that the sculpture in his care must be in good condition and will require little attention apart from cleaning. Nothing could be further from the truth. The origins of museum collections are threefold:

1. Objects from churches, castles or temples
2. Objects from tombs or archaeological sites
3. Objects from private houses and collections

In the first case, the objects will have been subject to many of the aggressive conditions mentioned in the preceding chapter. In the second, they will have been subject to burial and may be in an advanced state of decay when acquired by the museum. In the third, they will have been treated according to the whim of the owner and may well have been cleaned by unskilled staff over many years, usually with abrasives, bleaches and strong caustic solutions.

Therefore much of the stone sculpture in national museums is in a state of decay, and although much of it is housed in reasonably stable conditions it continues to decay.

The enemies of stone in museums are much the same as those in churches, namely moisture and salts. In the museum environment, however, these cycles of decay become extended and often produce less dramatic results. Even in very controlled conditions, only small changes in relative humidity and temperature are required to continue the cycle of salt growth. Even strict environmental control is unable to stabilize this condition. Therefore the stone conservator is required to take positive action to treat a great many of the stones in his care.

It is ironic that one of the main reasons why so much stonework in museums is deteriorating is not from neglect, but from too much attention. A stone that has been in a museum collection for a hundred years or more may well have been treated more than once during that time. In the past, waxes, baryta water, shellac, soluble nylon and all manner of synthetic resins were used to consolidate stone, often without any real understanding of the nature of stone decay. Large-scale installations, using cement for the fixing of large stones (*Figure 11.1*), were also responsible for the decay of many important objects.

The museum approach

One great advantage that the museum conservator has over the conservator working on his own in a church is that of continuity of practice and availability of records of treatment. The museum conservator can constantly reassess his treatments by comparing them with past treatments. He is also surrounded daily by his successes and failures. Such a concentration of experience, coupled with the demands of an active curatorial staff, allowed the museum conservator to develop techniques of examination and treatment that, until recently, were unknown in the world of the church conservator.

The use of the binocular microscope for the regular examination of sculpture surfaces (*Figure 11.2*) has heightened the conservator's awareness of the wealth of historical and artistic detail that cannot be seen by the naked eye. To preserve such detail, a more refined approach to stone cleaning and preservation has been evolved in museums. Many of the cleaning techniques listed below have been in use in museums for over twenty years. During that time, the results of their use have been monitored, so that some assessment can be made as to their long-term effect.

Figure 11.1 Detail of carved plinth, showing spalling caused by the migration of soluble salts in cement

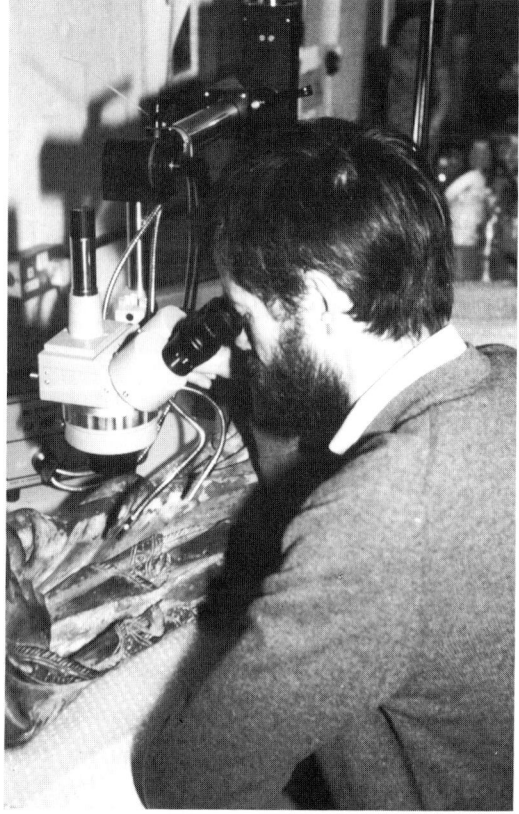

Figure 11.2 Sculpture being examined under binocular microscope: (magnification range ×10 to ×40)

Cleaning techniques

See pages 202–207 for case histories.

Poulticing

The idea of using a poultice to draw out dirt from stone evolved from a technique described by Plenderleith[1] for drawing salts out of stone with poultices of paper pulp. The advantage of using a poultice, rather than soaking, for cleaning is considerable. Cleaning a stone by soaking is not only dangerous, it is also unnecessary. Soaking may disrupt salt and minerals deep within the stone, thereby setting up salt movement, or iron-staining. It is also wasteful. In cleaning, only the stone surface need be wetted. Deep cleaning is rarely necessary. By using a poultice of deionized water and sepiolite (magnesium silicate), a layer of water can be suspended over the surface of the stone and kept there while it dissolves the dirt layer. As the poultice dries (*Figure 11.3*) the water evaporates and pulls the dirt back into the poultice. After about twelve

hours, the mud begins to fall away. At this stage, the rest of the poultice can be removed and the stone cleaned with swabs and deionized water. This treatment may need to be repeated on badly blackened stone (*Figures 11.4, 11.5*), but careful use of this treatment is sufficiently gentle to allow even areas of painted stone to be cleaned without loss. The same sculpture immersed in a bath of water for several weeks, following the traditional treatment, would have lost much surface detail and a great deal of paint before it could be declared clean.

Water poultices are mainly used for cleaning marble, limestone and some sandstones. Alabaster can be cleaned with poultices composed of clay and white spirit.

Air-brasive

This machine (*Figure 11.6*) provides a dry abrasive cleaning, which is very useful in cases where water could be disruptive. However, the machine has severe limitations. It is essentially a micro-

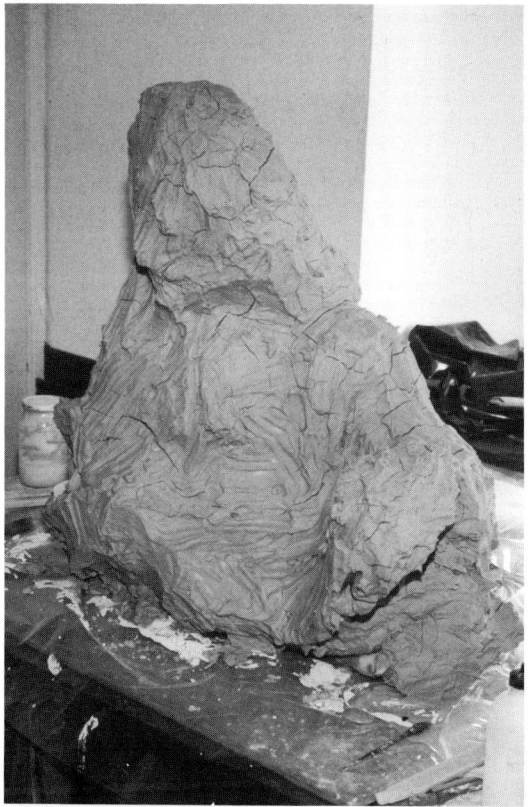

Figure 11.3 Bust of Orlando Gee covered with clay poultice. One can see cracks in the clay as it begins to dry out

Figure 11.4 Sutton Valence reredos: before cleaning

sandblaster. Microscopic beads of aggregate (glass beads, or aluminium oxide are the most commonly used) are fired by compressed air from a tiny nozzle at the tip of a small, pen-like gun. Although in skilled hands this machine can be carefully controlled, it undoubtedly has a deleterious effect on the stone surface by weakening and causing surface abrasions. In many cases where thick sulphation layers cover the surface of a sculpture, it is the only tool available to conservators which will remove the encrustation without wetting the surface.

Cavitron

This machine (*Figure 11.7*) is an ultrasonic, dental de-scaling tool. It is a wet process and it functions by producing a delicate, ultrasonic vibration in the working tip, over which a jet of water is played. As the water runs under the tip it forms a gentle bubbling action, and when the tip is placed just above the surface of the stone, the machine will rapidly disperse the dirt. This machine is ideal when used in conjunction with poulticing techniques (*Figure 11.8*) and is very good for removing particles of dirt trapped in undercuts and crevices (*Figure 11.9*). It can be dangerous when carelessly used. If the vibrating point is pressed against a stone, then a small pit will result. This can be avoided if the point is kept moving over the surface.

Chemical treatments

Conservation of paintings is the conservation discipline with the longest history. Sculpture conservation has borrowed many of its techniques and materials from this discipline. The types of solvents and reagents used for removing dirt and varnishes on paintings have proved useful on sculpture. Also, the practice of cleaning only small patches at a time, using small cotton wool swabs, has proved effective in introducing a degree of care and delicacy into the treatment of stone surfaces.

Chemicals such as white spirit, liniment of soap and ammonia wax paste are very useful for cleaning

Figure 11.5 Sutton Valence reredos: poultice partly removed showing cleaned areas

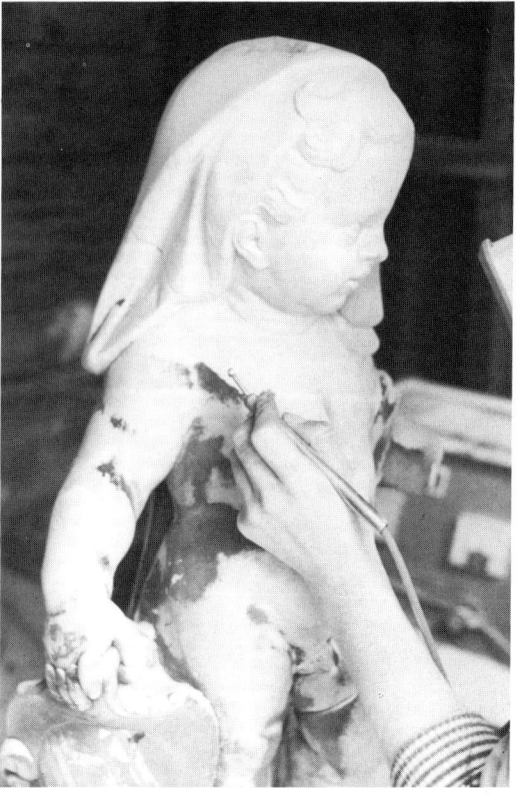

Figure 11.6 Detail of an eighteenth century marble putto, showing sulphation removal with air-brasive

alabaster because the surface is relatively impervious. On limestone, mixtures of acetone or white spirit with water are more effective. On marble, methylene chloride, solvol autosol, white spirit and acetone are all effective. Used in a disciplined manner, all these chemicals can be used safely, but brushed on carelessly and not properly neutralized, they can be very harmful.

Steam cleaning

Although steam cleaning has been an accepted method for the external cleaning of buildings, it is only recently that small-scale steam machines have become available for the cleaning of sculpture. Steam is an ideal cleaning treatment because it is controllable, causes minimal wetting and the pressure of the jet forces dirt out of undercutting and details that would otherwise be laborious to clean.

In England, the steam cleaner used most widely is a Derotor GV. This instrument is actually manufactured for use by dentists for degreasing and steriliz-

ing their instruments. The steam pressure can be raised or lowered by the use of a regulating valve. When full steam pressure is reached the machine at first produces some excess water. This should be drained off before use. To clean effectively, the nozzle should be held near the surface of the stone so that dirt can be blown off. Although the steam pressure is not as great as on many large industrial models, it is dangerous to use the steam cleaner on powdering or friable surfaces. Where surfaces are damaged or fragments of paint remain, it is possible to lay Eltoline tissue on the suface and then pass the jet of steam over it. In this way the surface will be protected and the dampened paper will absorb the dirt.

The advantage of steam is that the surface dries rapidly after cleaning and therefore does not delay other processes such as consolidation or bonding. However, some water will be produced on the surface of the object, and this should be swabbed off with cotton wool or tissue to avoid pooling and possible staining.

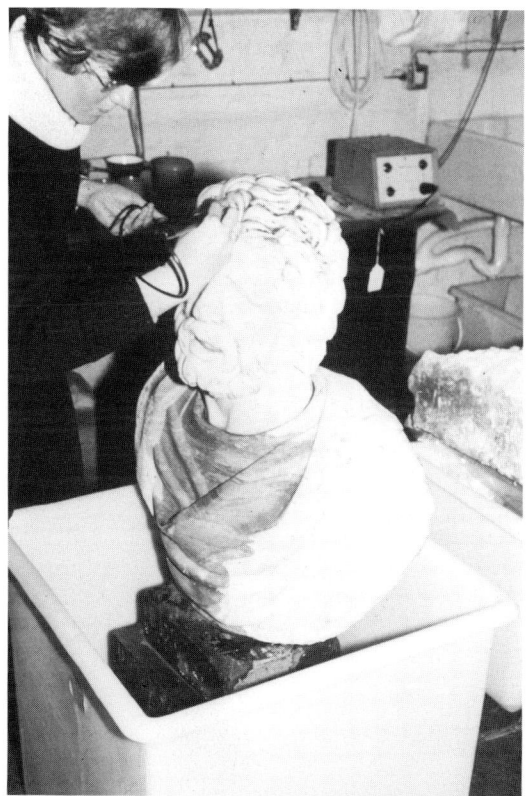

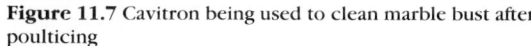

Figure 11.7 Cavitron being used to clean marble bust after poulticing

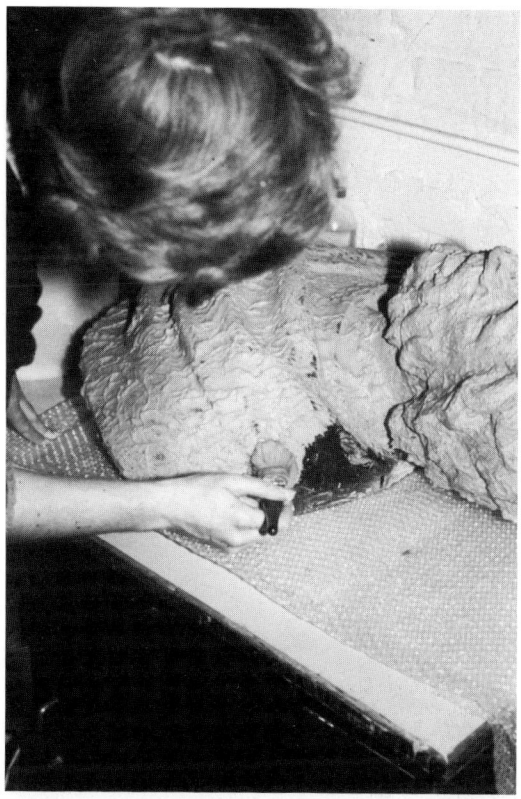

Figure 11.8 Clay poultice carefully applied to marble bust

Laser cleaning

Although this is not a widely available cleaning technique and may never become commercially viable, it can be used in the museum environment. The advantage of using a beam of laser light in contrast to an air-brasive or steam lies in the minimal contact of the beam with the stone surface. Most cleaning techniques leave dust or moisture on the surface, tending to obscure the conservator's view. The laser beam does not leave any deposit on the surface and simply removes the area of dirt at which it is aimed.

The use of laser energy for cleaning sulphated surfaces on decayed stone is not a new idea. Kenneth Hempel and John Asmus carried out experiments on blackened stone in Venice in 1970 and again at the Victoria and Albert Museum a year later. At that time Asmus was using a large, expensive and slow Ruby laser; although it produced impressive results it did not seem practical for museum use.

Over the years, as laser technology has advanced, more adaptable and cheaper lasers have been produced. The most suitable would appear to be a neodymium laser, and it is this type which is now the focus for cleaning research. The laser beam cleans by vaporizing the organic deposits contained in the black crust that forms on polluted stone. The beam will continue to burn away the black crusts until it meets the lighter stone surface beneath. When it does, the beam is reflected back and the laser automatically cuts out. It is this mechanism which makes the laser a very safe tool for cleaning. The laser beam can be focused down to very small sizes. In experimental work the beam size has been as small as 0.5 mm. However, the usual operating size is 4–10 mm.

It is possible, with care, to pass a laser beam over the most friable of surfaces, whereas an air-brasive or steam cleaner would damage the weakened surface. This is an advantage in that it does not constrain the conservator to use pre-consolidation, which is often necessary with other techniques and can inhibit the use of other consolidation treatments.

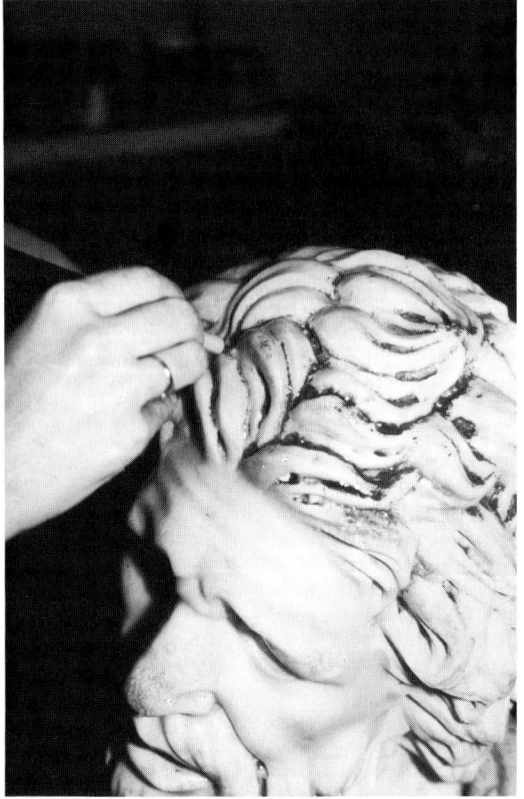

Figure 11.9 The cavitron is ideal for removing small areas of sulphation caught in undercuts

Figure 11.10 Sculpture of Virgin and Child from Minster-in-Sheppey (twelfth century, English)

Case history A

A twelfth century figure of the Virgin and Child. English. Limestone (Caen stone). Dimensions: height 85.5 cm (33.7 in); width 19.5 cm (7.7 in).

This sculpture *Figure 11.10* was acquired by the Victoria and Albert Museum in 1973, from the church of St Mary and St Sexburgha, Minster-in-Sheppey, England. It was placed on display in the museum galleries without receiving any conservation treatment, as it was considered to be in a stable condition. The sculpture was re-examined in January 1979, because some concern had been expressed regarding the powdery nature of the surface.

Although originally described as a white sandstone, on re-examination with a magnifying glass (×8) it was clear that the stone was, in fact, a cream coloured limestone, covered by a dense layer of sparkling white crystals. The sculpture was then removed to the Conservation Department for further examination and treatment.

Examination

When examined under a binocular microscope, the crystals on the surface of the sculpture could be clearly identified as salt crystals (*Figure 11.11*). Samples of the crystals were tested in the laboratory and were found to contain sodium, potassium, calcium, sulphates, nitrates and some carbonates. The high concentration of nitrates was extremely worrying, as these are particularly damaging to stone. It was therefore obvious that the sculpture would have to be de-salinated.

Cleaning

Before any other treatment could take place, a careful surface cleaning of the sculpture was undertaken under a binocular microscope (×10–×40). The purpose was to remove the surface salts and to reveal any fragments of pigmentation that might remain on the surface. The cleaning was carried out by rolling small cotton-wool swabs, dampened with

Figure 11.11 Salts on surface of sculpture, seen at ×10 magnification

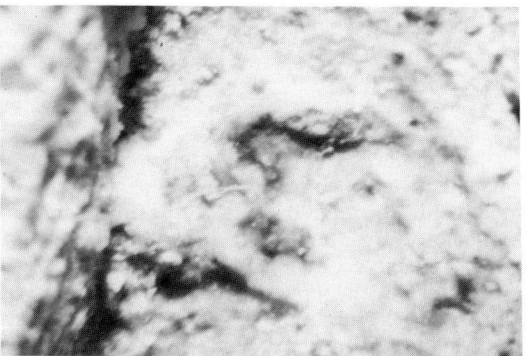

Figure 11.12 Pigment emerging from beneath salts during initial cleaning and examination

The real difficulty with using some silanes is that they will not allow any further treatment once the resin has cured. Experience with catalysed silanes in the past has revealed that attempts at re-treatment can be problematical. For a stone that has been previously consolidated with silane, the introduction of fresh resin can cause swelling in the gel that has already been formed by the cured resin. In some cases, this has caused noticeable disruption of the consolidated stone and produced cracks and surface flaking.

In an attempt to overcome this problem, tests were carried out with a silane (Dow Corning T 40149) to which a catalyst had not been added. By using silane in this way, it was found that it could be applied to decayed stone over a period of months without any signs of swelling or disruption. The only disadvantage was that the consolidation was not as effective as that obtained by using a catalysed resin. However, by leaving some T 40149 in a beaker, so that the solvent could evaporate, a more viscous solution was obtained. It was found that if the stone was first treated with the normal T 40149 and then with the more viscous T 40149 a more satisfactory consolidation resulted. Generally it was found best to apply the partially evaporated silane (reduced to half of its original volume) once the stone had begun to show signs of saturation, because it acts as a sealing coat, holding the volatile silane deep in the stone.

On the basis of these tests, it was decided to treat the sculpture in the same way, beginning with the larger figurative section.

Consolidation of the figurative section

Before consolidation began, a beaker containing 300 ml of silane was left in a fume chamber to partially evaporate. Unthickened silane was then carefully applied to the surface, using brushes and pipettes. The resin was measured out in 100 ml batches, and at the end of four hours 700 ml had been applied. The sculpture was then tightly wrapped in polythene and left overnight. This process, known as 'gassing', meant that the stone was completely enveloped in silane fumes for at least twelve hours. Over a period of years, it had been observed that this preliminary treatment greatly increased the capacity of the stone to absorb resin, presumably by ventilating the pores within the stone.

On the second day, a further 500 ml of silane was applied to the sculpture, including 100 ml of partially evaporated silane. Although at the beginning of the treatment the stone had quickly reverted to a dry appearance, now it was beginning to stay wet for much longer periods.

During the two following days, further batches of silane totalling 465 ml were applied. Of these, 165 ml was partially evaporated silane. As the absorption of

de-ionized water, over the surface of the sculpture. During cleaning, several traces of paint were discovered (*Figure 11.12*). These consisted of traces of vermilion and a dark iron oxide, less than 1 mm in width. The pigment was secured during cleaning by feeding an acrylic resin (Racanello E0057) under the flakes with a small pipette.

Cleaning revealed the true surface appearance of the stone and subsequent examination by the Geological Museum revealed that the stone was Caen stone.

Consolidation
The arguments for and against de-salination have already been discussed. In this case the surface of the sculpture was too fragile, and the fragments of pigmentation too precious, to attempt any form of de-salination. It was therefore considered that the least dangerous course of action was to attempt the encapsulation of the salts in the stone by introducing a deeply penetrating silane.

resin was now extremely slow, it was decided to stop the treatment. The total quantity of silane absorbed was 1665 ml.

The sculpture was then left in the storeroom so that the resin could cure over the normal six weeks period. The sculpture was examined after four weeks, when it was, surprisingly, found to be covered by a film of tiny water droplets resembling dew (*Figure 11.13*). The relative humidity (RH) and the temperature in the room were noted as being 63% and 14°C (57°F) respectively.

The surface of the sculpture was carefully dabbed with dry cotton-wool swabs and all visible traces of moisture removed. The stone was left in the same room for a further week and, when inspected, was again covered with beads of moisture. The RH was then 45%, but the temperature remained at 14°C (57°F).

Samples of the water droplets were removed from the surface and tested for salt content. They contained nitrates, sulphates and chlorides. The tests produced very positive reactions, suggesting a fairly high level of concentration. Given such levels of contamination, it was considered dangerous to allow the formation of more droplets on the surface, as this would inevitably create disruption of the stone.

The formation of this surface moisture was at first puzzling. It was assumed that it was merely condensation. However, when the sculpture was removed to a much warmer and drier environment, the moisture still formed on the stone. The fact that this water contained large quantities of salts suggested that the silane had not completely encapsulated the salts in the stone and that moisture, or at least moisture vapour, could still enter the pores in the stone. The droplets resulted from the partial water-proofing of the stone by the silane. The normal transpiration of moisture, attracted by the salts, through the stone no longer occurred and the water was therefore settling on the surface in the form of

Figure 11.13 Moisture droplets on the surface of the sculpture

droplets. At this time, the canopy section, which had not been treated, was showing no signs of similar disruption, even though it was exposed to the same humidity and temperature.

It seemed that the technique of salt encapsulation was, in this case, a failure. Although the silane had hardened the stone, it was obvious that the sculpture would never be stable without some form of de-salination.

De-salination

As the surface was now reasonably sound, poultices of de-ionized water and sepiolite (magnesium silicate) were applied to the sculpture, to draw out the salts. The poultices completely covered the sculpture to a uniform thickness of about 1 cm (0.4 in). They were allowed to dry to a craquelure over a period of about 48 hours. During this time, white salt crystals formed on the peaks of the clay poultice. When these salts were removed and tested, they matched those that had been found in the water droplets.

The poultice treatment was repeated ten times and, although some minute grains of stone were undoubtedly lost from the surface, the tiny fragments of pigment were still completely intact. Throughout the treatment, each poultice was tested for salt content and, by the tenth application, no evidence of salts could be found. At this point, it was assumed that a stable situation had been reached.

Re-consolidation

Once the sculpture had been allowed to dry, it was re-consolidated with an acrylic-silane resin, to give it greater strength and to seal it against moisture.

The decision to use an acrylic-silane mixture was based on the results of experimental work conducted at the museum during the previous year. This had shown that limestone consolidated by this method could be considerably strengthened without any noticeable colour change, or without the disruption that could occur when catalysed silanes are used for retreatment. Other advantages of this system were that it reduced the evaporation of the silane and that it allowed the use of other acrylic resins for the consolidation of paint, or large flakes of stone. It was also possible to use solvents, such as acetone, for cleaning, even after consolidation. With catalysed silane, cleaning is only possible with an air-brasive once the resin has cured.

For this consolidation, a combination of Racanello E 0057 (acrylic silane) and Dow Corning T 40149 (silane) was used. The materials were simply mixed together in the proportion of 5% E 0057 to 95% T 40149.

The consolidant was generally applied with a white bristle lacquer brush. In very fragile areas it was dripped from a pipette. During the first two days,

1270 ml of the 5% mixture was absorbed. Over the next two days, the rate of absorption declined and the 5% mixture was changed to one which contained 10% of the E 0057. The reason for this change was to reduce the evaporation of the silane and to ensure that the maximum consolidation was achieved at the surface. In all, 965 ml of the 10% solution was absorbed. The total quantity of acrylic silane used was 2.235 litres. This, added to the previous silane consolidation, meant that the sculpture had accepted 3.9 litres of consolidant.

Poulticing of the canopy section

At this stage, the canopy section had received no treatment other than local consolidation of one area of pigment and light cleaning with a swab and deionized water. No pre-consolidation of the sculpture was required, as the surface was very sound and it was thought that poulticing would not cause any damage. The same procedure for poulticing was adopted as had been used on the figure section. Ten poultices were applied until a neutral state was achieved.

Consolidation of the canopy section

As this part of the sculpture was in better condition than the rest, it was thought unnecessary to attempt complete penetration of the stone. A mixture of 10% E 0057 to 90% T 40149 was therefore used throughout the consolidation of this section. It was again applied by brush and, in total, 500 ml of resin was absorbed by the stone.

Humidity tests

Although no evidence of further salt movement could be seen during the curing period of six weeks, tests were carried out to establish the stability of the sculpture in the face of wide fluctuations of temperature and humidity. During the month of March, the sculpture was left in an unheated room and was subjected to humidity ranges of 40–70% and temperature changes between 8°C and 19°C (46–66°F). At no time during this period did any moisture appear on the surface of the stone, nor was there any sign of surface disruption.

Final cleaning

The sculpture was once again examined under a binocular microscope and any traces of sepiolite left on the surface were removed with a dry stencil brush and dental tools.

Case history B

Neptune and Triton. Bernini (1622). Carrara marble. Lifesize.

This important carving (*Figure 11.14*) was once the centrepiece of an elaborate water garden. It had

Figure 11.14 Seventeenth-century Italian marble group: Neptune and Triton by G.L. Bernini

functioned as a fountain and therefore, from its earliest days, had suffered from a certain degree of surface erosion. In the eighteenth century the sculpture was brought to England by Joshua Reynolds. It was displayed in various gardens during the next two hundred years and finally arrived in the collection at the Victoria and Albert Museum in 1950. Some cleaning and some minor repair work was carried out at that time, but the sculpture was never fully conserved.

In 1979 the sculpture had to be moved due to redecoration of the Costume Court. As the condition of the sculpture was unknown, it was decided to examine the piece before removal. Once the sculpture had been scaffolded, the true condition of the marble became apparent (*Figure 11.15.*) The surface showed all the symptoms of Carrara marble that has long been exposed to weathering and pollution. The surface was very granular ('sugary') to the touch. The

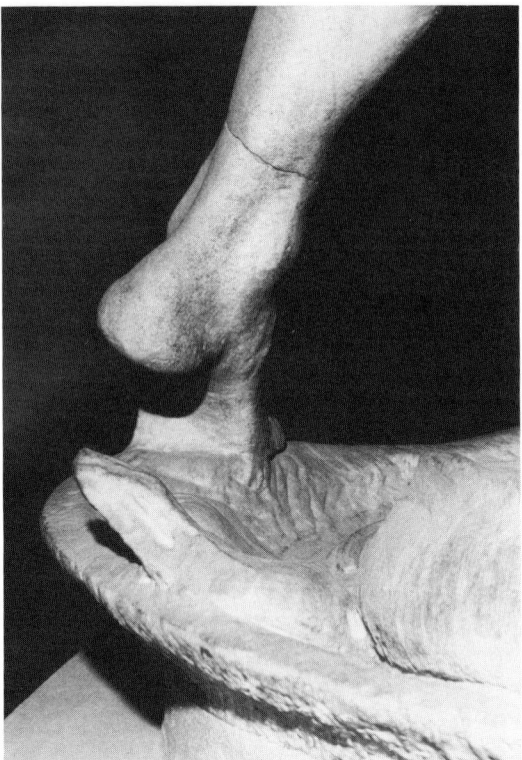

Figure 11.15 Neptune and triton: note the weathered condition of the surface

company so that they could make preparatory tests for material density and exposure time for the film. When they came to film the Bernini, the technicians were surprised to find that, on average, they only required about half the exposure time to penetrate the decayed Carrara that they needed to penetrate the sound samples.

Several important points could be deduced from the radiographs:

1. The raised arm had been dowelled on with a metal cramp, the end of which showed on the radiograph (*Figure 11.16*).
2. The cracks in Neptune's ankle did not penetrate right through the marble.
3. It had been known that the sculpture had functioned as a fountain and the radiograph showed the pipes clearly, still inside the body of Triton (*Figure 11.17*).
4. The ease with which gamma rays penetrated the marble gave some indication of its porosity and its very weak state.

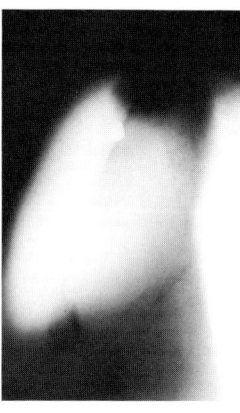

Figure 11.16 Radiograph of left shoulder: the outline of the bent cramp; the white blob is the end of the cramp where it is embedded in mastic

detail of the carving was blurred and a great many of the fine edges were completely blunted. Dirt had penetrated deeply into the very open structure of the marble and a thick brown film, resulting from pollution, covered the entire surface. There were cracks in the ankle of Neptune and it was obvious that the raised arm had been repaired at some time and had been incorrectly realigned with the shoulder.

Gamma radiography survey

Due to the lack of conservation documentation, it was decided to examine the sculpture as thoroughly as possible to try to uncover information regarding its past history. X-radiography is usually helpful when trying to reconstruct changes that might have taken place in the structure of an object. In this case, with 500 mm (22 in) of marble to penetrate, X-rays were insufficient. It was therefore decided to carry out a survey using the more powerful gamma radiography.

The work was carried out by a commercial company. They used a partial system in which the radiation source was an Iridium pill, which gives off a power of about 600 kV. Samples of sound marble with embedded iron dowels were given to the

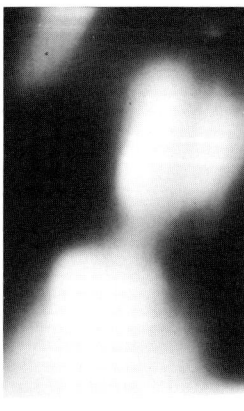

Figure 11.17 Radiograph of Triton's torso. The lead pipe still runs through the figure and can be faintly seen as two parallel lines running vertically through the centre of the body

Cleaning tests

A range of chemicals was tried on various areas of the sculpture. These were applied on cotton-wool swabs and included:

1. Acetone: little effect; some removal of surface dirt.
2. Acetone and water: slightly more effect; the brown staining remained unaffected.
3. White spirit/Lissapol/water solution: a noticeable cleaning effect, but the pollution staining remained unaffected.
4. Water soluble Nitromors: some cleaning effect, but really little more than the white spirit solution.
5. Sepiolite and deionized water: little or no effect.
6. Cellosolve (2-ethoxy-ethanol): used on swabs, this had the most promising cleaning effect. When left on wads of cotton-wool for one minute and then rinsed off with Cellosolve, it was even more effective.

On the basis of these tests, it was decided to use Cellosolve mixed with sepiolite and to poultice the sculpture in areas roughly 600 mm × 300 mm (2 × 1 ft) at a time. The poultice was left on the sculpture for an average of 12 hours before removal. The results were quite startling. Although the ingrained dirt could not be drawn out, the uniform brown layer on the surface was completely removed.

The final cleaning was completed by using an air-brasive with an aluminium oxide aggregate. This removed some traces of black sulphation that still remained on the sculpture from its external exposure. It also helped to pull the surface together, giving the sculpture a much greater sense of unity.

Consolidation

Before any cleaning had taken place, some minor areas of the sculpture, which were very weak, were treated locally with Racenello E 0057. This allowed cleaning to take place without hindrance and did not affect the final full consolidation.

For the complete deep consolidation of the sculpture, a mixture of 90% Dow Corning silane T 40149 and 10% Racenello E 0057 was used. The consolidant was applied with a brush and a total quantity of 8 litres was applied over a period of two days.

After a week, the sculpture was found to be firm to the touch, although the colour was still a little dark. After a period of a month, the sculpture was very hard, with no sign at all of powdering, and had returned to its natural colour.

Reference

1. Plenderleith, H.J. and Werner, A.E.A., *The Conservation of Antiquities and Works of Art: treatment, repair and restoration*, 2nd edn, pp. 304–305, Oxford, 1971

12

The museum display of architectural features

Deborah Carthy

Introduction

The removal of architectural detail from a building of historic importance fortunately is no longer common practice. Sometimes, however, such details are all that remain of buildings which have been demolished, having survived because of the interest and intervention of a collector, or because they have been removed through a less creditable acquisitiveness. Alternatively, an historic building may be so badly neglected that it cannot be saved. A detail such as a fireplace, a door case, a window or a balustrade may be all that can be preserved. Architectural details need to be re-used, or displayed, according to their importance and taking account of their original setting. If no record survives, informed speculation about the relationship of the architectural element to the building of which it was part may be all that is possible. If, however, a detail is to be salvaged from a derelict building, there are procedures to be followed if valuable information about the architectural context and history is not to be lost. Without this information, the rescued piece can become meaningless, or lose much of its architectural and structural significance.

Planning

Many factors may influence the decision on the best procedure to be followed. These may be structural, contractural, or simply physical, if the labour or equipment available for the project is limited. Since planned conservation work of this type has not taken place to any great extent, little has been written on the subject. The following procedures, therefore, have been based on experience gained in recent projects. A well-planned programme needs to be

formulated at the start, in order to avoid much later investigation and researching of information.

The importance of recording and handing on information must be emphasized, particularly when the object to be conserved may pass through a number of hands before being reinstated in a new site. Even when the processes of taking down, storage and re-erection are in direct sequence, a project may take several years. Therefore detailed records should be kept throughout.

Survey

Ideally, a project begins with the architectural element concerned still in its original context. An architect, a conservator and a stone mason should be involved, because each has knowledge of the relevant conservation techniques. They should work closely together from the start. If further specialists are required for some aspects of the work, they should be consulted at the earliest possible stage. If the element to be conserved is free-standing, only the problems immediately relating to the element need be considered. If the element is an integral part of an already unstable structure, however, the situation is more complex.

A detailed survey of the element to be removed is of the utmost importance. This survey should include some, or all, of the following: a measured drawing showing all dimensions, including joint thicknesses and with all the stones numbered; photographs taken before and during taking down; a photogrammetric or corrected photography survey; use of a metal detector to indicate the positions of any iron fixings; the use of gamma radiography (X-ray) to indicate voids and all non-ferrous fixings, such as slate or timber dowels; consideration of

Figure 12.1 Back view of late 12th century English limestone doorway, dry built. In the Burrell Collection, Glasgow

relevant building techniques; and research into any historic accounts of the construction.

Before the scaffolding is erected, it is very important that all who are to be involved are properly briefed on site. Any particular requirements, such as areas to be kept free of scaffolding, whether or not the scaffold is to be tied to the structure surrounding the element to be conserved and any limitations on loading, should be discussed and understood. This is particularly important when stones are to be removed and lowered to the ground.

Some immediate stabilization of the surface of the stone may be needed in order to minimize the risk of damage during taking down. Most stabilization treatments require the stone to be as dry as possible and this must be allowed for in the programme. Further treatment may need to be carried out in a more suitable environment before the element is rebuilt.

At this point, the conservator should be able to make a realistic assessment of the visible problems and of the overall treatment likely to be needed, although the full extent of problems within the structure may not be revealed until the taking down is in progress. Surface problems are most likely to be those caused by weathering, atmospheric pollution, salt migration, iron stains from cramps or dowels within the structure, or cracking of the stone caused by movement or the expansion of concealed iron dowels and cramps. Any structural problems must be assessed as far as possible before taking down is started, in the interests of safety. Any temporary supports required should be put in position as soon as possible, and certainly before taking down is started.

Taking down

When an arch is to be dismantled, centering which is capable of taking the weight of the stone without deforming should be provided. It should be constructed just below the daylight size of the arch (the width of the opening at the springing line by the height from the springing line to the head), from the ground, or from a level surface below the arch. Final adjustments can be made with wedges at the springing line, to ensure that the stonework is fully supported; the wedges should be pushed in to make the adjustment but not forced in. Centering is not needed for a tympanum arch, unless the tympanum has been damaged in such a way that it has become structurally unsound. In principle, the same method of support applies to a split-lintel, but the supporting timber should be shaped to the profile of the lintel. In all cases, the stone must be protected from direct contact with the timber by a padding of polystyrene, or other non-slip, water-resistant material.

The original construction of the element to be conserved must be considered before taking it down. For example, when dismantling an arch, the keystone should be removed first and control then kept of the order in which the stones on either side are taken down. In some split-lintels, these stones act as a counter balance and this should be remembered when removing them. Equilibrium should be maintained and as little strain as possible put on the structure below.

The importance of marking stones as they are taken down cannot be emphasized too strongly. The method of numbering and marking should be recorded on the measured drawings and reference to compass points may be necessary when dealing with a free-standing structure. All identification marks should be made on the back, or the bedding, face of the stones; never, under any circumstances, on an exposed face. Marks need not be removable, but they must be readily distinguishable from any place or mason's marks already on the stones. The recording of any place or mason's marks will also help to identify the stones. This is important, since these marks may not be visible once the structure is rebuilt.

Transportation

When an architectural element has been dismantled and numbered, and is awaiting transportation, the stones should be stacked neatly off the ground on pallets and covered with black polythene, or tarpaulin, with air spaces in between. In wet conditions this will reduce condensation, help drying out and lessen the risk of algal growth on the stones. For transport, the stones should be packed in a non-staining material, such as polystyrene. Straw or wood shavings should not be used because these are likely to stain the stone if moisture is present. This staining can take place in a matter of days and, although superficial, is disfiguring.

An approximate estimate of the weight of the dismantled structure may be made at this stage for the purpose of designing foundations or calculating the loading on a new floor to carry the structure. This estimate can be obtained quite simply by driving first the unladen and then the laden transport onto a weighbridge.

Reassembly

If the architectural element has been dismantled already and detailed records of its original form are not available, the approach to reassumbly must be quite different and can be extremely time consuming. If the element has been numbered from the base upwards, it is likely to have been numbered on the ground and not in the sequence in which it was taken down. If the element has a complex structure, the dismantled stones may well be upside down or misleadingly positioned. All such possibilities must be anticipated and checked, either by laying out the stones in a sand box, or by erecting them without mortar in a 'dry-build'.

A sand box is a strong timber construction of sufficient superficial area and depth to contain the re-assembled stonework. The stones are laid out in the box on a bed of well-washed, dry, sharp sand. Iron or salts present in unwashed, damp sand can easily stain the stone, or even transfer soluble salts into dry stones. If, for any reason, it is impracticable to dry the sand, then a tough, easily flexible plastic film should be laid over the sand to avoid these risks. In some cases, additional support is provided in the sand box in the form of bricks, blocks, or timber framing. During laying-out, clues to the original bedding of the stones and their relationship to each other may be provided by the tooling pattern or building marks, all of which should be carefully recorded. Overall dimensions of the complete element can be taken once the stones have been set out, but allowances must be made for the width of bedding, vertical and radial joints.

If a 'dry-build' approach is made, rather than setting out in a sand-box, enough information must be available beforehand to determine the sizes of the supports and centering which will be required. Consideration must also be given to the ability of the stones to withstand the process. A dry-build with weak, fragile material would be most unwise. Dry-building is usually preceded by laying the stones out on a floor, to enable dimensions between jambs and the sizes of centering required to be established. At this stage, any missing stones can be sized and worked. These will be necessary for reasons of

Figure 12.2 Sixteenth-century sandstone arch from Hornby Castle, Yorkshire; new stones are Cat Castle sandstone. In the Burrell Collection, Glasgow

structural integrity or for completeness of a design element. They should be of a new or second-hand stone which will match the original, weathered material as closely as possible in colour and texture. The ideal replacement stone should not be obvious on casual inspection, but should be easily identifiable on closer examination. During the dry-build, non-staining wood slips or wedges can be used to cushion the stones and to take up the joint widths which will later be occupied by mortar. In some situations, new elements will have to be introduced to substitute for the function of masonry masses in the original structure. Stainless steel threaded tension bars, for instance, may be needed to take the place of masonry abutments opposing the thrust of an arch. Bars of this type are anchored to plates at springing level on, or near, the extrados of the arch and are tensioned *in situ.*

When setting out has been satisfactorily concluded either in the sand-box or as a dry-build, and all missing and new elements have been identified and supplied, erection, or erection and building-in to the new environment, can proceed. Because new masonry construction takes a long time to dry out completely and because there is likely to be differential settlement between, for instance, new brickwork and antique masonry (if only because of the difference in number of joints), it is essential that an isolating membrane and an air space are provided. If the architectural element is built in to a new wall, the foundation of the wall will need to be modified to take the increased size and loading. It may also be necessary to incorporate a new lintel or a brick relieving arch over the element, to ensure that loads from the new construction are not transferred to the museum piece. A 25 mm (1 in) air space is normally provided between new and old construction. The isolating membrane is usually of Code 4 lead, or of heavy-duty polythene. It must contain the historic element completely. When the element is free-

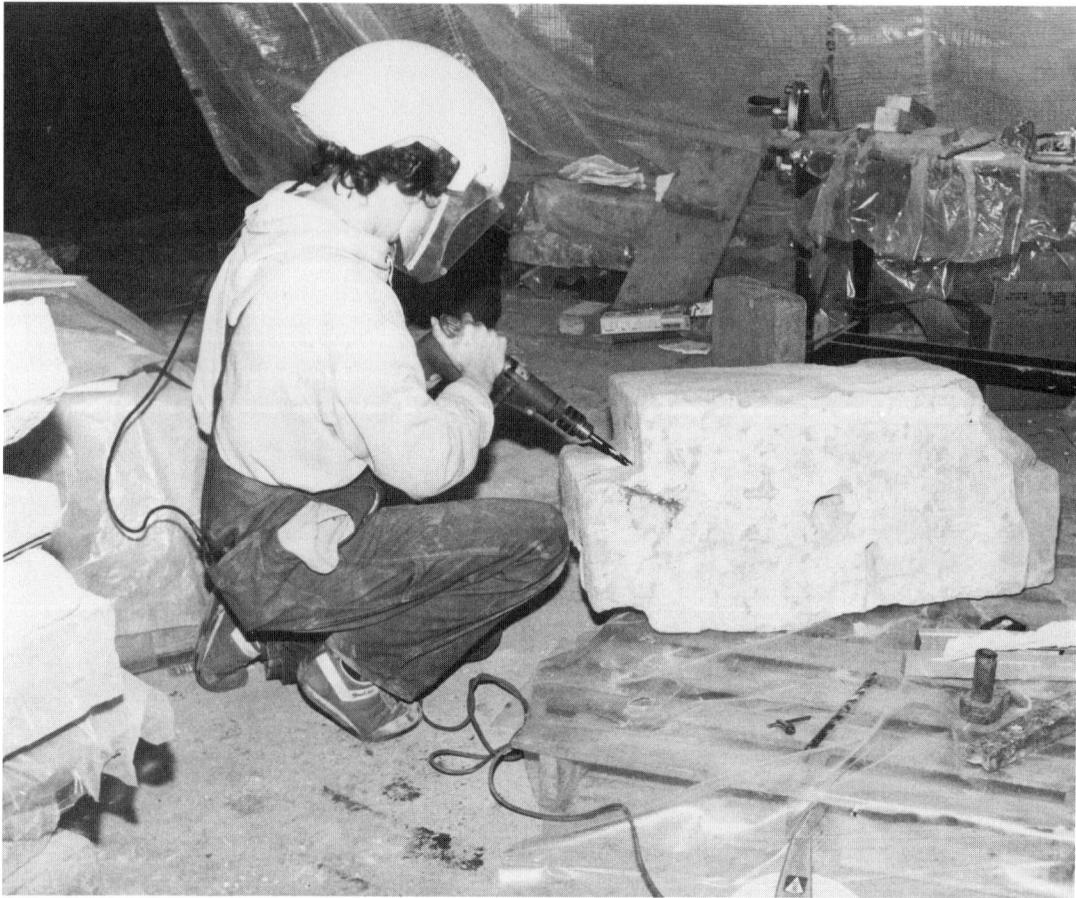

Figure 12.3 Lead being extracted from hole for hinge bracket (bracket visible at lower right). In the Burrell Collection, Glasgow

standing its base should be isolated from the ground surface with lead pads. All lead should be coated with bitumen where it will be in contact with fresh mortar and carefully lapped at least 50 mm (2 in). Where a membrane is pierced by ties or other fixings, a potential bridge for moisture and salt migration is established. This must be closed off. Polyesters, bitumen-coated polythenes and some of the silicone-based sealers have been used successfully for this purpose. When the element has an irregular surface, polythene is usually the most practical form of membrane since it can be easily cut and trimmed and the overlapped sheets heat-sealed or joined with a sealant. Where the surrounding walls are to be plastered, the membrane must be brought to the face of the plaster to avoid moisture bridging at the surface.

Any ties or dowels used should be austenitic stainless steel, or delta bronze. When stonework needs to be drilled through the beds, the mortices

formed should be oversized to allow the dowels to fit loosely. The dowels should be no more than 70 mm (2.75 in) in length and should be dropped into the mortices dry, without mortar or mastic. This will provide a movement tolerance and will avoid any risk of localized stress.

The mortar used should be compatible with the stone; that is to say, it should not be too strong. A mortar such as one part of white lime, mixed with three parts of well-graded sand, to which a small proportion of white cement or pozzolanic powder has been added, will be quite adequate. If the architectural element concerned is to be completely protected from the weather, as in most museum environments, the cement or pozzolana is hardly necessary, but a weak hydraulic set may be necessary in order to take the loading imposed by heavy masonry units.

The planning stage of a museum project will have considered fire regulations and discussed the layout proposed with the regional authorities. If an historic element, such as an arch, is to be incorporated into a wall, fire doors may have to be inserted in the opening. If this is so, the doors must be designed to hang on an independent frame or pivots and be free of the historic element.

Free-standing structures

When the historic structure to be conserved is to be free-standing, different problems must be resolved. Some structures, such as arches, can stand quite satisfactorily on their own in many circumstances. Other elements, such as traceried windows, are difficult to display in isolation, without the physical and visual support of embracing walls. The physical support can be provided by a frame around all or part of the free-standing element, by floor to ceiling stanchions on either side, or by plating the back and top of the element. Physical and visual support together can best be provided by panels of stonework. Any metal used should be stainless steel or delta bronze. The method of support must, of course, be adequate for the size and weight of the element, and the design of the supports will need to be considered in relation to the relevant fire and building regulations. It should be remembered that regulations which may be waived in the context of an existing historic building may not necessarily be waived in relation to historic elements re-sited in a new building.

Conclusions

The conservation and display of historic details in a new environment is often a complex and always a challenging undertaking. It is essential for an experienced team and appropriate specialists to be consulted from the start of a project. Fortunately such an approach is increasingly adopted now. This follows significant developments in research on materials which are suitable for this type of work, and a greater general appreciation of the importance of conservation techniques.

13

The cleaning of painted stone

Clare Finn

Introduction

The purpose of this chapter is not to describe the treatment of polychromed sculpture, but to outline some of the problems and techniques which may be encountered in the cleaning and repainting of painted architectural detail and wall surfaces. In essence, the investigation of painted layers, their consolidation, cleaning and treatment, is the same whether the substrate is stone, plaster, or even wood. The process is often complex but for the sake of completeness this chapter will attempt to provide some information for those who find their masonry problems involve paint as part of a decorative scheme. This is particularly relevant to the large public buildings of the nineteenth century, such as town halls, museums and hotels.

Once it has been determined to clean, repair or refurbish a building which included painted stone, a careful survey and analysis of the painted areas should be put in hand as soon as possible. Without such a survey, much information about colours and techniques relating to different periods in the building's history may be lost. In addition, damage to the existing paint may be caused through ignorance about its type and the nature of discoloration and soiling.

Whilst there is little justification in most cases for carrying out extensive sampling as an academic exercise, by sensible and selective sampling it should be possible to establish, to some extent, the techniques and paints used to produce a specific finish at any given point in the history of the building. Additional examination of the stratification of the paint layers may be informative when structural alterations have taken place. Mistakes in re-colouring, based on assumptions made on the existing appearance, can be avoided by careful examination. The value and the extent of sampling carried out will vary with different situations and will need to be related to the information available on the history of the building and its decoration. Building records and other technical literature contemporary with the construction will often provide, in advance, a good idea of what the survey is likely to uncover. Sometimes a specification may survive from the period of building, but it should not be assumed without checking that the work carried out necessarily conforms with the printed intention!

Where samples are to be taken from should depend on:

1. The architectural detail
2. The known possibility of decorative paint
3. The amount of known alteration which has taken place

The sampling should be carried out only after available building records, or other literature contemporary with the building, have been searched. The more samples that can be examined, the more complete and accurate will be the picture obtained.

The survey should provide the following information:

1. An identification of the paint materials and the substrate
2. A description of the original colour schemes
3. A description of the paint stratification and characteristics of the surface finish
4. A description of the condition of the paint and substrate. Attention should be drawn to causes of deterioration and damage, alterations and additions

This information should be systematically recorded because it is the basis on which the restoration, or reconstruction, recommendations will be made. If a building has been altered it may be desirable to restore it to the historic finish dating from a particular alteration, and not back to the 'original' scheme.

Under item 4 above, the survey report must make clear which improvements are essential and which are desirable, before money is spent on painted surfaces. This may mean drawing attention to open joints, leaking gutters, soil levels and humidity problems. It may also mean advising that extra time must be allowed for drying out after remedial work before work on the painted surfaces can commence. 'Restored' paint can never hope to overcome basic environmental problems.

Temporary protection

In addition, measures such as improving ventilation and reducing humidity levels, and some 'first aid' protection of painted surfaces, may be necessary while other work is in progress.

Where the paint is more fragile, it will be necessary to secure it by a facing. This technique consists of brushing a suitable consolidant (see Annex) onto the wall through Japanese mulberry tissue, calendered eltaline tissue, or other suitable soft tissue. The paper remains in place, securing the paint, until work on the surface can be commenced. The paper can be removed by the appropriate solvent for the consolidant. However, there are some consolidants which cannot be removed, such as a catalysed silane system, and there are some solvents which would also remove the paint.

During major building works, it is expedient to cover the painted surfaces with thin sheets of hardboard, held in place with battens. Protective work of this kind needs close supervision to ensure that no avoidable abrasion or impact takes place and that no fixings are inadvertently made to the painted wall.

Paint types

Stone may be covered with thin gesso and painted, or prepared in some other way, or painted direct. Frequently, stone is part of a complex wall surface, and the colour scheme extends across stone and plaster.

Early production of building paint was largely in the hands of master painters, whose apprentices were taught to prepare colours for the craftsman's use. A prestigious market, however, often generated more organized production, as in the case of Richard de Welton of York, who was in business as a colour maker in 1591.

During the eighteenth century, paint production became more organized and centralized. Factories were established for the production of pigments, such as white and red lead, Prussian blue, vermilion and verdigris, in addition to various varnishes.

The nineteenth century saw the introduction of a wide range of pigments. Zinc oxide, lithopone, chrome yellows and Brunswick green appeared. Extenders, such as china clay and barium white, were added to reduce the yellowing tendency of pigments, by lowering their oil absorbency. Extenders increased and improved the durability of paints. However, sometimes they were added in such quantity that they became adulterants which significantly lowered tinting strengths. The range of binders based on modified drying oils alone, or combined with various resins, similarly increased.

Before 1930 there were two basic categories of building paint available: oil-based and aqueous. Oil paints, or oil/varnish paints, purchased in paste form for dilution on site, were mixed to the painter's own specification for the job in hand, although pre-mixed paint had been available from the eighteenth century. A wide range of materials were available, formulated from drying oils or modified drying oils, e.g. stand or blown oil, or combinations of drying oils with natural or fossil resins, such as rosin or Congo copal. All these were used for decorative purposes.

Thin oil mastic is another protective and decorative finish which was applied to stone externally from the last quarter of the eighteenth century. Although these mastics were most commonly used in the same way as stucco, lined out in imitation of masonry and painted with various stone colours, they were sometimes applied directly to stone after saturation priming with linseed oil, as a protective rather than a decorative finish. All were based on litharge (lead monoxide) and linseed oil, with fillers such as ground brick, porcelain clay, sand and glass.

Aqueous paint includes limewash and cement paints, lime-casein paints, and distempers and whitewashes based on whiting and glue size. Distempers and whitewashes were internal finishes. They had poor durability, but they were sometimes used externally and frequently renewed. This kind of repeated maintenance anticipated the kind of sacrificial coat now used to slow the effects of weathering on newly cleaned stone. Distemper was sometimes recommended as a preservative measure on external masonry which was decaying, although limewash, with or without tallow, was the more common treatment.

Generally speaking, the pigments found in building paints are cheap to produce. More costly pigments are sometimes included in interior schemes, such as the vermilion identified in the Morris Green Room at the Victoria and Albert Museum.

After the 1920s the development of the petrochemical industry brought about great changes with the introduction of vinyl, acrylic, alkyd and other synthetic resin-based paints.

Methods of application

Oil paint was usually applied to previously unpainted stone highly diluted with oil. When applied to previously painted stone, it was highly diluted with turpentine. The paint layer, as a rule of thumb, was built up in four to five layers. The first layer was the most dilute and subsequent layers increased in concentration as the stone became saturated. The first layer was the priming coat, followed by two or three undercoats and a finishing coat.

Over the base, a variety of decorative techniques might be applied including:

1. Striation with heavy brush marks
2. Hand rubbing to simulate enamel
3. Marbling to imitate marble (or porphyry or granite)
4. Graining to imitate wood (more common on plaster)
5. Stencilling with decorative motifs
6. Hand-painted elements
7. Gilding (generally oil mordant gilding or japan gilding)

The identification of these finishing techniques is as important as the identification of the colour scheme.

Sampling techniques

The simplest technique is to scrape 'windows' through the paint layers with a sharp scalpel, with the aid of suitable solvents if necessary. These 'windows' will expose the finishes *in situ*. Considerable care and experience are necessary to obtain the required information in this way. In addition to the visual information gained from the 'windows', analysis of samples removed from each layer may provide valuable supplementary data on the colour and material.

A study of the substrate layering, carried out by making cross sections, will provide a knowledge of the accumulated build-up of paint in different areas.

Ideally, these techniques should be used together. To use one method alone, especially the 'window' method, may lead to misinterpretation. The intensity of colour can be distorted, optically, by considering only a small sample area.

Cleaning and restoration

There may well be a considerable gap in time between the initial survey of a painted interior and the implementation of any remedial work, while proposals are considered, grants applied for, money raised and general building work put in hand. This time may well be useful, but it may also represent increasing danger to a threatened interior. The importance of the survey in drawing attention to causes of deterioration can be readily appreciated. Whilst it should not be the responsibility of the painting conservator to point out that a roof needs repairing, or that penetrating damp is the main problem, it should never be taken for granted that these items are all in hand.

Methods and dangers of cleaning

Cleaning should only begin when the maximum amount of information has been gained on the surfaces to be cleaned, and after careful visual examination and testing under good lighting conditions. Experience is crucial to the recognition of technique, aging effects, surface deposits and degree of attachment, and to the determination of what the original appearance and final aspect were and should be. There are specific practical limitations to cleaning. These are imposed by the sensitivity of the original surface (which may yield to cleaning more readily than the discoloration) or, for example, by the tenacity of a layer of oil paint laid over an aqueous distemper.

A basic decision must be made at the start on which layers are to be removed and which are to remain. Any necessary consolidation should be completed before cleaning commences, bearing in mind the problems of binding dirt layers to the substrate, on the one hand, and the risks of removing the consolidated layer during cleaning, on the other.

Loosely adherent dust should be removed first, by cleaning with a soft brush.

Greasy deposits, such as surface dirt associated with smoke from chimneys, lamps, candles, cigars and tobacco pipes, can usually be removed by swabbing gently with a mild alkali solution, such as ammonia water: 5% ammonia water (35% NH_3) in water. Suitable swabs for cleaning include sponges, soft paper tissue pads, or cotton wool. An alternative to ammonia water is a saturated solution of bicarbonate of soda, but ammonia is to be preferred. If the paint is sensitive to water, white spirit may be used.

Ingrained surface dirt can usually be broken down with a potassium oleate soap (Vulpex) in a solution of water, white spirit, or 1,1,1-trichloroethane. The solution may be applied, left for a short interval (determined by observation) and then removed with ammonia water. Both Vulpex and ammonia water solutions can be varied in concentration, as can the contact time. The cleaning action can be arrested with white spirit. Of course, extreme care must be taken to ensure that not more than is intended is being removed!

Wax can generally be removed with an aromatic solvent, such as xylene or toluene. If the wax has been applied recently, a less toxic petroleum distillate may be used. Unfortunately, if the wax was applied to a rather porous surface, it may not be possible to remove it all.

Resins, and oil-resin varnishes

Resins may be removed with a suitable organic solvent (see Annex for list of solvents in general use). Oil-resin varnishes may sometimes be swollen with solvents, in which case their removal must be carried out by careful scraping. The use of gelators may be helpful in holding a solvent in contact with a vertical or overhead surface. Methyl cellulose and laponite, which form a gel in water, are useful in this context. Sometimes, proprietary brands of paint strippers may be used successfully, but the constituents must always be known and great caution applied. An exact knowledge of what is supposed to be below the surface is absolutely vital, because too many layers can all too quickly be removed. It is essential to have adequate ventilation and to wear a filter mask, including eye protection, when working with solvents and toxic chemicals. Smoking is prohibited in such a work area.

Proteins, such as animal glue, milk, casein, or egg, may remain soluble in warm water. If they prove resistant, however, as may be the case with casein or egg white, small quantities of a dilute organic acid, such as formic or acetic acid, may be used.

Gum arabic is removable with warm water, if it has not been mixed with something such as egg or oil. If this is the case, then acid and alkali solutions, as described above, should be used alternately.

Organic deposits, such as bird and bat excreta or mould growth, may usually be removed by an alkali solution such as a weak ammonia solution.

Efflorescent salts should be removed, as far as possible, by gentle brushing, followed by washing in water or solvent, according to the sensitivity of the paint. If the paint is very fragile and friable, a poultice of soft paper tissue may be more appropriate. The reason for the efflorescence must be established at the time of the survey and a salt analysis carried out, if necessary. Remedial building work and humidity control may be required. Non-soluble efflorescences may sometimes be removed mechanically (see Chapter 8) bearing in mind the fragility of the paint layer.

Lime wash can be one of the most difficult surface coatings to remove, especially when sulphated. Gentle mechanical flaking is often the only answer.

Consolidation

In addition to consolidating areas of flaking and powdering paint before cleaning, it may be desirable to apply a weak fixative to the entire painted surface, once all dirt and unwanted deposits are removed, such as a weak solution of Paraloid B-72 (2% or 3% Paraloid in an aromatic solvent such as toluene). This not only improves the adherence of the paint to the surface, but will remove the white cloudy bloom, which may remain in patches after cleaning.

The choice of a suitable fixative should be governed by its surface gloss, flexibility, permeability to moisture, liability to discoloration, reversibility, and compatibility with the surface to be treated. Cost and availability will also influence the selection. In the past, beeswax or limewater were the usual consolidants and limewater is still used. However, beeswax is impermeable to moisture and should not be applied to a porous substrate. More commonly today the following materials are used as fixatives:

1. Acrylic resin, methacrylate in solution, e.g. Paraloid B-72 in xylene or toluene, or Bedacryl in xylene or toluene.
2. Polyvinyl acetate emulsion in water with a surfactant or in solution in alcohol or acetone, e.g. Vinamul, Mowilith, Gelva.
3. Soluble nylon in methanol, e.g. Calaton.
4. Polyvinyl alcohol in water.
5. Acrylic silane mixtures, e.g. Dow Corning, Racanelio.

Not all these consolidants meet the criteria listed above. For instance, both soluble nylon and polyvinyl alcohol cross-link and discolour. Both the methacrylates and polyvinyl acetate may darken the appearance of the surface in which they are applied. The consolidants may be brushed, sprayed or injected, depending on the detachment problem. The application of localized heat, using a heated spatula, aids reattachment.

Filling of losses

After consolidation, losses should be filled ready for reintegration with a material compatible with the original surface. Lime putty and sand should be used in lime plaster, or lime putty, sand, stonedust and ceramic powder in masonry. Such repairs must be built up in thin layers of 5 mm at a time and pressed well home. Smaller losses in stone may be better filled with synthetic filler (e.g. marble dust in a synthetic resin binder) which does not require water in the mixing process, nor pre-wetting of the repair area.

Reintegration

Reintegration should be carried out in paints compatible with the existing surface. Water colours or acrylic paints are the usual choice, although oil paint, from which the excess oil has been bled, is still used. Factors governing the choice are similar to those described for selecting consolidants. The reintegration of a decorative technique must be carried out by a suitably skilled technician, under the general guidance of a fully trained, competent conservator.

Very few buildings of importance have retained original colours and are rarely seen as they were intended. Regular maintenance, perhaps preceded by rubbing down or caustic washing, may have obscured or destroyed all evidence of original paintwork. New colours may also have been applied as determined by changing fashions. Soiling patterns may suggest a completely misleading range of colour and tone. Paint, such as distemper, may have disappeared altogether, except, for instance, under the protection of an oil-stencilled motif. Many repaintings fill the texture of the stone surface and affect the amount of reflected light. In all these situations, recorded descriptions or illustrations of the original interior may be the only guide as to how to proceed with a reconstruction. In many cases, interiors can only be restored by reconstruction because of the way in which they have been subjected to changing use. In these situations, the skill of the conservator is paramount in importance.

When trying to determine the colours to be used for a reconstruction, the metameric qualities of colour should be borne in mind. This should also be a major influence in designing the lighting system of an historic interior.

The artistic traits of all the parts of an interior should be matched with one another to the fullest extent possible, so that the complete effect, a single artistic unit, is achieved. Where some elements are to be conserved and others reconstructed, the approach to the reintegration exercise may be determined by the most seriously deteriorated areas.

Factors such as the intended use of the building, the new environment conditions and, in some cases, availability of the types required will also affect the choice of paints. Modern emulsion paint is wipe-proof, distemper is not. Pure mineral silicate paints have a better durability record than lime paints. These advantageous properties must, however, be weighed against the visual differences which will be involved. The sheen of a modern synthetic paint will look quite out of place in some historic settings.

Conclusion

The complexity, condition and importance of the painted surfaces will determine the appropriate approach to the cleaning, repair and consolidation of painted stone interiors. The cost of correct and careful cleaning, restoration or reconstruction may well be prohibitive, and a more economic option may have to be adopted. If this is the case, then priorities related to the survival of threatened areas must be established and original surfaces must not be jeopardized by the application of unsuitable, 'temporary' redecoration layers.

In some cases, where a full conservation scheme has to be postponed, displays of the sampling 'windows' can be made and left. Such displays may be seen in the cast court at the Victoria and Albert Museum in London. Alternatively, or in addition, economically produced reconstructions showing the original scheme, as at the Roman Painted House at Dover, England, may be commissioned. Both are ways of making use of necessary preliminary exercises to inform and create interest in the project.

Most important of all, short cuts imposed by the need to economize must not be allowed to destroy any historic material or potential source of information. Financial situations may improve, but surfaces damaged or destroyed by inexpert or unsuitable cleaning and painting cannot be recovered.

Annex

Some solvents in common use for the removal of resins and oil resin varnishes are listed below.

Aliphatic hydrocarbons
Petroleum distillates, e.g. white spirit, V M and P naphtha

Aromatic hydrocarbons
Xylene
Toluene

Alcohols
Methanol (methyl alcohol)
Ethanol (ethyl alcohol)
Industrial methylated spirit
Propan-2-01 (isopropyl alcohol, or isopropanol)
4-hydroxy-4-methylpentan-2-one (diacetone alcohol)

Ketones
Propan-2-one (acetone)

Ethers
2-ethoxyethanol (Cellosolve)

Chlorinated hydrocarbons
Dichloromethane (methylene chloride)

Amides
Dimethylformamide

Alkalis
Ammonia solution

14

The cleaning and consolidation of the stonework to the Annunciation Door, Chapter House, Westminster Abbey

Keith Taylor, Christopher Gradwell and Teresa McGrath

Introduction

The Chapter House of Westminster Abbey, which has been used as the meeting place of the English parliament and as a library since its original function became obsolete, was completed some time during the first half of the thirteenth century. It is approached from the cloister through an outer and inner vestibule. At the top of a flight of steps the Annunciation Door forms the entrance into the Chapter House itself. The entrance wall is largely filled by the doorway and is a mixture of thirteenth-century work and nineteenth-century restoration by Scott. Pevsner[1] has this to say about Scott's work: '... a last word ... on Scott and his much attacked restorations. There is one thing at least that ought to be remembered. He found the Chapter House full of bookcases, staircases, galleries. If we have an idea today of its noble original beauty, Scott has given it to us'.

The Annunciation Doorway was cleaned and consolidated most recently during the period February to May 1983, by Ian Clayton Ltd.

The Annunciation doorway

The Gothic arched entrance to the Chapter House from the vestibule is made up of a double doorway divided by a central Purbeck 'marble' pillar, with a circular feature in the centre of the arch above. The jambs to the arch contain four large Purbeck 'marble' shafts on their outer side. On either side of the arch, facing the Chapter House, are sculptures of Gabriel on the left and the Virgin on the right. In the spandrels are two trefoils, each containing two angels: one large censing angel and one small angel. The orders on both sides of the arch are an extremely intricate design of openwork foliage containing small figures. The design continues in the jambs between the Purbeck 'marble' columns. In the central quatrefoil a Victorian addition, showing Christ in Majesty with angels, has blocked what was thought to be open tracery. This would have lit the stairs and given a view through to the Chapter House from the vestibule.

The entire Reigate Stone surface of the doorway, excluding the two large figures, was covered in a heavy limewash, which was later found to be a gesso mix applied in the 1950s. It was very dirty and dusty. After careful brushing of the surface with soft bristle brushes to remove dust, cleaning tests, using an S.S. White air abrasive machine at about 50 psi, with 50 µm aluminium oxide powder, were carried out on the right-hand trefoil, the upper arch order and the diaper flowers.

Fortunately, the tests showed that the gesso was soft and reasonably easy to remove at moderate air pressure and powder flow. The surface of the stone underneath the gesso was very friable with a great deal of flaking. However, with careful use of the air abrasive, the gesso could be removed gradually without disturbing the friable stone. Particularly friable areas were consolidated immediately, using Raccanello Acrylic Silane 55050. Pre-consolidation (applying the consolidant through the gesso and trying to clean back to the stone) was not successful because it hardened the coating too much and made it difficult to remove.

Tests also revealed that the stone was covered with a linseed-type oil, which presumably had been applied during the Victorian restoration, in an attempt to blend in the additions with the original work. Although this coating was lightened by air abrasion, the oil had penetrated the stone and was impossible to remove mechanically. Also, the need for immediate consolidation meant that the oil could not be removed by solvents, without disturbing the consolidant and the friable stone. Some tests were carried out with solvents such as white spirit, acetone and ethoxyethanol, but the results were not successful enough to risk damaging the unsound stone.

The method of work that evolved from these tests was to remove all limewash carefully and to consolidate where necessary, using Raccanello 55050. The possibility of re-limewashing certain areas after consolidation was discussed, because of the uneven appearance of the stone. However, as work progressed and the original detailing was revealed, it seemed inappropriate to obscure such fine detail as those on the front left-hand order by recoating. There was also some doubt about the compatibility of the consolidant and the limewash.

The working programme was planned by dividing the doorway into areas of differing conditions and for ease of working. These basic areas were:

The decorative arch orders and adjacent moulding and the four decorative jambs
The two trefoils with censing angels
The diaper flowers
The two large sculptures of Gabriel and Mary
The Victorian Christ in Majesty and surrounding moulding
The ashlar and niches
The Purbeck 'marble' columns

These basic areas are illustrated in *Figures 14.1* and *14.2*.

The arch orders and jambs

There are three intricately carved arches of moulding on the Chapter House side and two on the vestibule side. The dominant order of the arch on both sides of the doorway contains small figures surrounded by a continuous tendril of deep-cut foliage. Each order starts from a half figure on the Purbeck 'marble' capital and consists of 26 full figures (13 on each side), 270 mm (10.5 in) high. The order is 240 mm (9.5 in) wide.

Chapter House side

Arch orders
The arch orders figures were numbered from left to right as follows:

1–8. Original figures, with Victorian moulding on 2 and 7.
9. Head and shoulders are Victorian, as is adjacent moulding. The torso is original.
10. The figure is original with Victorian moulding.
11. Victorian figure.

12. Original figure, with some Victorian piecing in the moulding.
13. Victorian head.
14. Victorian figure, with some original moulding.
15. Original moulding and torso, Victorian head.
16–26. Mostly Victorian figures.

Figures in jambs
Left-hand jamb. The eleven figures, which were numbered 1 to 11 from top to bottom, are all original, with a great deal of surviving detail. By comparison, the original figures of the dominant order of the arch are in a much worse condition. They have none of the surviving crisp detail that can be seen on the figures in the jamb. There has been some flaking on the jamb figures, mainly on the fine detail such as the folds of garments and faces, and there is physical damage, with heads missing from figures 6, 7, 8, 9 and 11. Although the damage probably occurred before the Victorian restoration (as there is linseed oil and limewash covering the breaks), no attempt has been made to replace missing sections, leaving the whole jamb as original stonework.
Right-hand jamb. This jamb consists of deeply undercut foliage motifs, all apparently original, with a small architectural niche and a bird at the top. The detail is fairly good overall but there are some missing parts and some spalling.

Vestibule side

Arch orders
The vestibule side has a similar dominant order to the Chapter House side, with an outer order of foliage motifs. The left side of the foliage order is apparently mostly original and is in much the same condition as the original figures on the arch order on the Chapter House side. There are three badly damaged and missing motifs in the lower half. From the apex to the right the order is largely Victorian, but small sections of original work survive, for example a 15 cm (6 in) strip between the third and fourth motif from the apex. The inner order of figures is again made up of original pieces with Victorian additions, but on this side of the doorway most of the figures have been restored. The main part of the original work remaining seems to be on the right hand side of the arch. There is a section of foliage missing between the original figure 20 and figure 21.

Figures in jambs
The figures are similar to those on the Chapter House side. There are eleven small figures on the right-hand side and foliage motifs on the left. The condition of the carving is also similar to the Chapter House side. A great deal of untouched original detail survives,

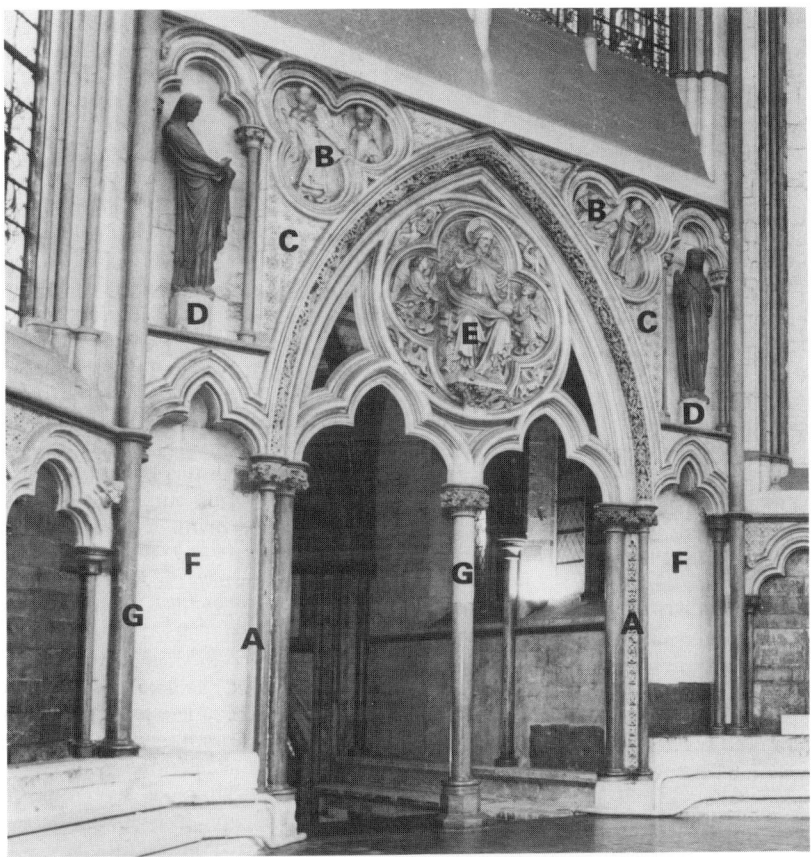

A Decorative arch orders and adjacent moulding, and four decorative jambs
B Two trefoils with censing angels
C Diaper flowers
D Large sculptures of Gabriel and Mary
E The Victorian Christ in Majesty and surrounding moulding
F Ashlar and niches
G Purbeck 'marble' columns

Figure 14.1 The Annunciation Doorway, Chapter House side

Figure 14.2 The Annunciation Doorway, vestibule side

especially on the figures, which are not so damaged as on the Chapter House side.

The work carried out on these areas consisted of removing all limewash with air abrasive and then consolidating with Acrylic Silane where necessary (see *Table 14.1*). Fillings on larger fractures in the stone were made up of acrylic silane and dry Portland stone dust with pigment to match, and were mainly applied to the left-hand of the Chapter House side.

The two trefoils with censing angels

Each trefoil contains two angels; the larger angel (1090 mm (43 in) high) holds a censor towards the two life-size figures in the niches. To the inside of these are the smaller angels (560 mm (22 in) high).

Both panels have flaked badly, especially the left-hand side, which has lost most of its detail. The right-hand panel, despite a great deal of flaking, has quite a lot of detail remaining; the face of the large angel and the censor are still recognizable. The small angel has lost its head, but has a lot of detail remaining. The Victorian restoration is confined to the moulding of the trefoil.

The work carried out on the panels consisted of removing limewash with air abrasive and consolidating the surface with acrylic silane where necessary.

The diaper flowers

The diaper patterns which make up the background of the spandrel around the trefoils are original and, although badly flaked, have a reasonable amount of detail left, especially in the lower parts. The work carried out was similar to that on the trefoils.

The figures of Gabriel and the Virgin Mary

The two large figures, described as 'unique in importance and preservation among the whole body of Gothic sculpture in England' and 'perhaps the most significant surviving single works of English medieval sculpture,' stand on pedestals in niches and are fixed to the ashlar near the shoulders by overlapping wedged bars. Both figures are heavily waxed, and this has badly discoloured with age and surface dirt.

The figure of Gabriel is in almost perfect condition, with only one or two very small flakes on the drapery folds. The flakes reveal a chalk-like substance, probably gesso. This may have led to the belief that the figure was made from Chalk.

The figure of the Virgin is in a much greater state of decay. There are large areas of flaking on the face and hands and on many of the edges of the drapery. However, the flakes are not recent, as they are all obscured by the beeswax.

The finer surface detail on both figures was covered by the layer of beeswax. Therefore, test areas on both were initially carried out by fine air abrasion. These tests on the folds, the unfinished back and the scroll of Gabriel and the drapery areas of the Virgin did not reveal any pigment, but did reveal the possibility of a gesso covering.

The surface of the wax was cleaned, and was actually removed only in small areas. On Gabriel, the overall cleaning showed on inspection with a magnifying light a change of surface levels (especially on the face). This indicated the presence of some sort of covering on the stone below the wax. Inspection of the Virgin had similar results. After further wax was removed from the face of the Virgin, definite pigment layers were revealed. Several layers, with a flesh tone on top, are obvious on the forehead, as is an eyebrow in black. There are also details on the eye itself, to the left of a large flake. There is also a brown and black colouring on the hair, with a bright pink (probably undercoating) in two small areas. Tests, carried out by removing the wax slowly with a solvent as above, revealed a white layer, possibly gesso or pigment. On close inspection, two smooth 'high spots' are evident about knee level on the drapery, indicating further pigment layers.

The discovery of pigment on the figures was important, particularly when considering the significance of the sculpture, and it was essential that the pigment should be preserved. It was necessary to examine the surface of the figures carefully in order to determine the exact nature of the surface coverings and, from that information, to determine how to clean back safely to the original pigment layer. Discussions were held with John Larson, of the Victoria and Albert Museum Conservation Department, who indicated that an adequate examination could only be made by using microscopic techniques and by thorough testing in studio conditions. This would involve removal of the figures from the niches and their transportation to a suitable environment. This would be a complex undertaking, requiring careful supervision. Until this examination could be arranged, no cleaning work on the sculpture could be attempted because this could make future work difficult at best and, at worst, endanger the remaining pigment. If the figures were to remain in the niches for the time being, the test areas could be touched in so as not to detract from the overall appearance by sealing the surface with acrylic and then colouring with pigment. A photographic record of the test areas was made. Subsequently the sculptures were cleaned and conserved as described below.

Table 14.1 Acrylic silane record

Date	Quantity applied	Area applied
		Chapter House side
24/2/83	100 ml	Right-hand trefoil and sculpture: small angel. Mainly on right-hand wing and right arm and edges of folds around waist. Small spalls on left-hand wing and neck.
24/2/83	100 ml	Right-hand trefoil. Moulding of left lobe of trefoil in stone adjoining main arch.
25/2/83	50 ml	Left-hand trefoil. Small angel. Mainly wings, head and upper torso.
25/2/83	50 ml	Right-hand trefoil. Large angel. Mainly right arm and drapery fold edges.
25/2/83	50 ml	Right-hand trefoil. Larger angel. Head, left hand and right thigh.
26/2/83		Small figures in the dominant arch order of the Chapter House side, numbered from the left up over the apex and down the other side.
	20 ml	Figure 8: mainly upper half.
	35 ml	Figure 9: mainly lower torso.
	35 ml	Figure 10: foliage on right-hand side.
	150 ml	Figure 12: overall and foliage.
	25 ml	Figure 17: small exfoliations overall.
	25 ml	Figure 18: small exfoliations overall.
	20 ml	Figure 19: small exfoliations.
	35 ml	Figure 15: overall.
28/2/83	200 ml	Left-hand trefoil. Lower and right-hand moulding.
1/3/83	50 ml	Figures 21–26 on small sculpture.
	+50 ml	Dominant orders overall, small exfoliations.
	100 ml	Figure 8.
		Vestibule side
1/3/83	300 ml	Figures 1–4 of the dominant order.
	100 ml	Lower orders figures 1–3.
	50 ml	Figure 4 on lower order.
8/3/83	100 ml	Upper order rosettes.
9/3/83	350 ml	Lower left-hand rosette order. Small exfoliations.
9/3/83	300 ml	Upper rosettes and figures 8–13.
10/3/83		
(a.m.)	100 ml	Dominant order figures 13–18.
(p.m.)	150 ml	Dominant order figures 18–26. Small spalling.
11/3/83	150 ml	Reapplication dominant order figures 13–26.
15/3/83		
(a.m.)	100 ml	Right-hand lower dominant figures 5–8.
(p.m.)	100 ml	Lower dominant order figures 8–11.
(p.m.)	100 ml	Foliage order left-hand side.
16/3/83		
(a.m.)	100 ml	Foliage order left-hand side.
17/3/83		*Chapter House side*
(a.m.)	100 ml	Dominant order right-hand side figures 1–3.
	100 ml	As above, figures 4–7.
	100 ml	As above, 7–11.
(p.m.)	100 ml	Reapplication figures 1–11.
	100 ml	As above figures 1–11.
18/3/83	100 ml	Dominant order. Reapplication overall figures 1–26 where necessary.
20/4/83	100 ml	Dominant order. Reapplication to figures 10 and 12.
21/4/83		
(a.m.)	150 ml	Inner moulding above capital on left-hand side.
(p.m.)	100 ml	As above.
22/4/83	200 ml	Outer moulding overall and reapplication.

The Victorian Christ in Majesty

The space above the subarches has been blocked in by two large back-to-back seated figures of Christ, one facing the vestibule and the other facing into the Chapter House. On the Chapter House side Christ is flanked by two censing angels, on a similar scale to the large angels in the trefoils. The cusps of the circle contain the symbols of the Apostles. On the vestibule side the design is simpler, with four angels in the cusps.

The figures were covered in limewash. When this was removed in tests with air abrasive, there was also a layer of beeswax, similar to the wax on the Annunciation figures, underneath the limewash. The air abrasive removed the wax to a certain extent. However, the wax had obviously penetrated the stone, so a solvent cleaning method was thought to be more appropriate. The stone itself, on the whole, was in good condition with some flaking on the outer, presumably original, moulding. A dichloromethane type of paint stripper was found to remove the wax. This was swabbed off with white spirit. On flaking areas of moulding, it was considered safer to use the air abrasive pencil because the paint stripper had to be worked into the wax with stiff bristle brushes. No consolidation of any of the Victorian carving was needed.

The ashlar in the niches

The ashlar on the Chapter House side was brushed down with stiff bristle brushes to remove any old, flaking limewash. It was then recoated with lime–casein paint (see Appendix 1) using Mars Yellow and black artists' dry ground pigment to give a satisfactory colour. Care was taken not to interfere with the remains of wall paintings in the right-hand niche. Two stone columns on the vestibule side were also recoated with lime–casein paint.

The Purbeck 'marble' columns

These were treated with Renaissance wax after washing with Vulpex soap and rinsing with water.

Conservation work to the Annunciation Figures

Keith Taylor and Graciela Ainsworth

Following the conservation of the doorway, it was decided in 1988 that, because of the importance of the discovery and rarity of the polychromy on the sculpture the figures should not be worked on until they could be removed from their niches and be examined in a studio environment, where full and detailed analysis could be carried out under magnification. Only then could a specification for conservation be decided. The stone of the Virgin was very friable, with small areas of spalling stone evident particularly on the edges of folds in the drapery. Because of this, the more friable areas were treated in situ with acrylic consolidants as a holding operation until the detailed work could begin.

The difficult task of removing the sculptures without damage was achieved by sliding the statues on to the bases of travelling cases on the scaffolding. The figures were then braced into position with padded timber supports and the sides of the cases were constructed around them. In this way they could be lowered to the ground and safely transported in their frames without the need to touch the surface of the sculptures. They were transported to the studio for initial inspection. This inspection permitted the backs of the figures to be examined and photographed for the first time.[2] Both figures are flat and unfinished at the back. The figure of Gabriel has a large diagonal channel cut into the back behind the left shoulder and a slot with a dowel fixing hole in the right shoulder. Further fixing slots occur on the left arm, suggesting that originally the figure had wings (probably wooden) and possibly a scroll. The figure of the Virgin has a section of stone let into the top of the head above the hair line. This piecing-in does not appear to be a restoration and is probably an original addition to give the necessary height to the block of stone for the design.

The statues were carefully lowered into a horizontal position for the conservation work. The major part of the work was to remove the thick layer of beeswax covering the sculpture without disturbing the polychromy underneath and to consolidate this polychromy as it was exposed, as well as consolidating the extremely friable and spalling stonework of the Virgin. Cleaning tests were carried out to determine suitable solvents which would be required to remove the wax from a variety of conditions (e.g. friable stone, paint etc.) without disturbing any layers beneath the wax. Several solvents from white spirit, toluene and ethanol to dichloromethane were used overall to slowly remove the thick layer of wax until the stone and paint layers were clearly visible. Careful recording on a grid system with photography logged each minute trace of paint so that the remaining wax could be safely and thoroughly removed. It was found that although the surface of the figure of the Virgin was in a much more advanced state of decay, there were extensive areas of original polychromy. Gabriel, structurally, was in near perfect condition, with original tool markings still visible over the surface, but with only traces of polychromy in areas like the recesses of the nose and mouth.

The dissimilarity in the amount of surviving polychromy could be a result of the differing histories of the sculpture. The figure of Gabriel was taken down and placed in the vestibule, presumably after the Chapter House was turned into a Public Records Office in 1540, following the dissolution of the abbey. The Virgin, however, remained hidden behind a press until the Victorian restoration of the building by Sir Gilbert Scott between 1866 and 1872. It may be that Gabriel was cleaned before being put on display in the vestibule, resulting in the loss of the orginal polychromy in all but the deeper recesses.

The dissimilarity in the condition of the stone can be attributed to their differing origins. Core samples were taken from the bases of the statues and analysis (see below) has shown that the Virgin is carved from Reigate stone, a pale coloured calcareous sandstone from the Upper Greensand. Gabriel, however, is carved from Caen stone, a fine-grained French limestone widely used in England at the time. The reasons for the sculpture using different stones can only be guessed, but the size of blocks needed for the statues would have been difficult to obtain in Reigate (this might also explain why the top of the Virgin's head is pieced in) and as the figures were intended to be completely painted the choice of stone, as far as its appearance was concerned, would have been immaterial.

Six paint samples were taken from differing areas of the figures and polished cross sections were prepared and examined at × 175 by Jo Darrah of the Victoria and Albert Museum. The sections from both figures have been confirmed as simple, finely applied and consistent with a medieval date.

The very friable surface of the Virgin was locally consolidated as the wax was removed using an acrylic consolidant (Raccanello 55050). The Caen stone of Gabriel was sound over the whole surface and did not require any consolidation. The paint layers were also consolidated using the acrylic consolidant.

When all the wax had been removed from the Virgin and the stone was sound, the hollow edges of the spalled areas were carefully filled with finely sieved stone dust in acrylic binder to give maximum protection to the surface. The completed figures are now reinstated in the Chapter House at Westminster Abbey.

Determination of samples from the Annuciation sculptures

Francis G. Dimes

As received the specimens comprised two small cylinders of stone (identified as RTAS/88/1/S The Virgin and RTAS/88/8/2/S Gabriel) each about 14 mm

in diameter and each with an axial hole about 7 mm in diameter, not symmetrically drilled along the axis of the cylinder. That of RTAS/88/2/S Gabriel did not penetrate the length of the cylinder.

The specimens were first inspected 'by eye' and with the aid of a ×10 lens and a stereoscopic microscope. Simple non-destructive physical and chemical tests were carried out. In veiew of the statements made that the determination of the stone was of archaeological and artistic importance, permission was sought, and received, to have thin-sections cut for microscopic examination to support and confirm the determinations made by eye. The thin-sections were prepared by GAPS of Putney, London. The petrographical descriptions are given below. The pieces of stone removed from the cylinders (to prepare the thin-sections) were impregnated in blue-dyed epoxy resin. The thin-sections were then made. They were stained with Alizarin Red S and potassium ferricyanide in order to differentiate between carbonate phases present. The photomicrographs were shot in plane polarized light.

The Virgin Mary (Figure 14.3)

Fine- and even-grained, highly calcareous, mostly of fine grains of quartz. Abundant grains of dark-green colour determined to be the mineral glauconite. Scattered planar flakes of the white mica muscovite may be seen. From its general appearance and mineral content, and from direct visual comparison with material from known provenance and geological horizon, the specimen is determined as being a piece of 'Reigate Stone', from the Upper Greensand, Cretaceous in age. Around Reigate, Gatton, Godstone and Merstham, Surrey, the Upper Greensand occurs as a pale-coloured calcareous sandstone. In this area it was commonly referred to as Malmstone or Firestone and it was extensively used for major building works during the Middle Ages in and around London. The stone taken from the Upper Greensand of the Reigate area is recorded under a number of names such as Reigate, Gatton, Merstham and Godstone stone, which ostensibly indicates its source area. However, these names probably are sheer guesswork. The rock is lithologically similar along considerable distances of its outcrop and no absolute technique is currently available to distinguish stone from one quarry from that of another in this area.

The petrographic description given below supports the determination of the specimen as 'Reigate Stone'.

Archangel Gabriel (Figure 14.4)

Fine-grained, highly calcareous evenly-granular, homogeneous, yellow-white coloured, with areas of crystalline calcite commonly in optical continuity.

Figure 14.3 Sculpture of the Virgin Mary (Courtesy John Larson)

Figure 14.4 Sculpture of Gabriel (Courtesy John Larson)

The specimen was compared with material from known geological horizons and provenances and for overall appearance and mineral content matches specimens of 'Caen Stone'.

Caen Stone is the name given to stone extracted from beds of middle Jurassic, Lower Bathonian age found in the Caen plain, Calvados, Normandy, France. There were three main areas working in Caen and the adjoining communes:

La Maladrerie – Bretteville/Odon – Corpiquet belt
Fleury/Orne or Allemagne – Grâce de Dieu belt
Rue Basse – rue de Calix – eastern Caen Hérouville belt

Caen Stone has been used since Gallo-Roman times, with large-scale exploitation developing in the 11th century boosted by the conquest of England by William, which opened up a huge new export market. Trade with England continued into the nineteenth century with production effectively ceasing in 1914, although there is some record of extraction up to 1930, up to 1952 and up to 1966 at various quarries.

Petrographic descriptions

Archangel Gabriel. Fine grained well sorted biopelsparite (Folk) or grainstone (Dunham) containing many small micritic peloids (?fecal pellets), typically 100 μm across, and brachiopod valves and spines. These lie in a medium to coarsely crystalline sparry calcite mosaic zoned to ferroan calcite in places. The brachiopod fragments show internal structures characteristic of spiriferoids or pentameroids, and punctate forms are also observed. Other skeletal grains identified include echinoderms (echinoid spines and plates), foraminifera and rare bryozoa and ostracods. The foraminifera comprise trocospiral, planispiral and biserial as well as undiagnostic types. A minor micritic matrix is stained with carbonaceous impurities. Minor quantities of phosphate are also observed. The sparry calcite is probably a cement; some, at least, occurs as epitaxial outgrowths from echinoid fragments.

Virgin Mary. A sandy biomicrite (Folk) or wackestone (Dunham) containing, in approximate order of abundance, very fine quartz sand and silt grains, siliceous spicules, glauconite pellets, planktonic foraminifera, calcispheres, muscovite and biotite flakes, bioclast moulds, phosphatic clasts and ?bivalve fragments in a calcareous matrix consisting of ?microspar crystallites, typically 15 μm across. The spicules are mainly monaxon, but also include diaxon and triaxon forms and may show ribbing. The foraminifera include *Heterohelix*, *Hedbergella* and *Praeglobotruncana*. Carbonaceous materials occur locally dispersed within the matrix.

References

1. Pevsner, N., *The Buildings of England: London*, Volume 1, 3rd edn, Penguin, London, 1973
2. Williamson, P., 'The Westminster Abbey Chapter House Annunciation group', *Burlington Magazine*, **CXXX**, February 1988

Appendix 1

Limewashing

John Ashurst

The practice of limewashing is very ancient. Limewash is one of the simplest, but also one of the most effective external 'paint' treatments which can be applied to historic masonry, rendering or plaster. Frequently it is the only treatment which should be applied. Limewash cannot be matched in appearance, except in the most superficial way, by any paint system, whatever claims may be made to the contrary. First-time limewashing should not be carried out on sandstone, even though there are good historical precedents for this. Limewash should also not be used as a preservative treatment on sandstone, as recommended in the earlier part of this century, unless regular maintenance can be guaranteed. Flaking limewash on decaying sandstone will only exacerbate the situation, because water washing off the lime is carried into the sandstone. This encourages the stone to behave as a calcareous sandstone, with less resistance to a polluted atmosphere.

The milky suspension of hydrated lime in solution with water is mildly antiseptic. It was used extensively in the past for this reason, as well as for decorative reasons and its light-reflecting properties.

Limewashes

Slaked lime mixed with water will rub off rather easily, so some additional ingredients are usually needed. Whiting (crushed chalk) and lime were traditionally mixed with glue, or size water, to bind them and to improve adhesion. Sometimes common salt, or crude commercial calcium chloride, would be added to tallow washes to assist the emulsification of the tallow. Because salt is hygroscopic, it can also assist the carbonation of the lime on exposure. A common proportion was 7 kg (15 lb) of common salt to 27 kg (50 lb) of hydrated lime. These salt mixes are not recommended for historic fabric; apart from the risk of introducing an unwelcome soluble salt crystallization cycling, such mixes are not strongly adherent. Mixes which include tallow are not recommended for interior situations, where they may inhibit the drying out of a damp plastered wall. Walls liable to development of mould growth should be treated with a quaternary ammonium fungicide, such as Murosol 20, rather than by the traditional inclusion of carbolic acid.

Lime–glue formulations are another traditional wash which should be discarded, even when improved with the addition of alum (for better working properties) and formaldehyde (for resistance to rubbing), because they require frequent maintenance.

Recommended washes are of three types:

1. Lime–tallow
2. Lime–casein
3. Lime–cenosphere (PFA)

Lime–tallow limewash

Ingredients
High calcium lime, in the form of lump lime: 5.0 kg
Tallow: 0.38 kg
Pigment (if required): as much as necessary to produce the intended colour.

Quantities given here and below are those recommended in references 1 and 2.

Procedure. Break the fresh quicklime into small lumps and shred the tallow. Fill a galvanized tank with about five litres of hot water, to a depth of about 300 mm and add the quicklime slowly, taking all necessary protective precautions. While stirring the

229

boiling liquid, add the shredded tallow and pigment. Keep stirring until all activity has ceased. Screen the limewash through muslin. A consistency of thick cream is required to start with. Subsequent thinning with water may take place.

Lime–casein limewash

Ingredients
High calcium lime, in the form of lump lime as above, or soak 12.5 kg hydrated lime in 14 litres of water.

Casein:	0.9 kg
Trisodium phosphate:	0.57 kg
Formaldehyde:	0.5 litre
Pigment as required	

Procedure. Soak the casein in hot water for two hours. Ordinary commercial quality casein, prepared from separated milk, is adequate. Dissolve the trisodium phosphate in two litres of water. Add the pigment to the lime, stirring vigorously. When the solutions are quite cool, add the trisodium phosphate solution to the casein solution and then, as slowly as possible, mix in the lime solution. The formaldehyde should be dissolved in seven litres of water and added just before use, stirring constantly. Rapid addition of the formalin will result in a gelling of the whole mixture. Thin with water as required. This mix should be used at once and not stored for more than one day. A simpler lime–casein limewash can be produced by substituting skimmed milk for the commercial quality casein and trisodium phosphate. Both lime–casein washes have excellent rub resistance.

Lime–cenosphere (PFA) limewash

A form of ready-mixed limewash, which has shown itself to be useful over the past six years, is composed of hydrated lime with 10% of pozzolanic PFA added (cenospheres). Powdered pigment may also be added to the mix. A 'polyox' thickening agent is also incorporated. This mixture is bagged and delivered by Pozament Cement Limited. It only requires the addition of cold water. This limewash is quite resistant to rubbing and to normal external exposure. Adhesion is markedly better on porous surfaces, such as old lime plaster or brickwork, than on fresh gypsum plaster. Because of the variations which occur in fly ashes, fine, light-coloured ash should be specified.

Pigments

Lime-fast pigments, complying with BS 1014, should be used. Trial samples are always advisable. Traditional colours for limewash may be prepared with the following mixes:

Cream:	1.8–2.7 kg (4–6 lb) of ochre to 36.3 litres (8 gal) of lime putty.
Fawn:	2.7–3.6 kg (6–8 lb) of umber, 0.9 kg (2 lb) indian red and 0.9 kg (2 lb) lamp black to 36.5 litres (8 gal) of lime putty.
Buff:	2.7–3.6 kg (6–8 lb) raw umber and 1.35–1.8 kg (3–4 lb) lamp black to 36.5 litres (8 gal) of lime putty.

Hydraulic limes

Hydraulic limes should not generally be used for limewashing. They tend to flake on drying out, and have poor resistance to rubbing.

Application of limewash

Brush down the surface to be limewashed with a stiff bristle brush to remove dust, old scaling limewash and loosely adhering particles of stone. Treat with a quaternary ammonium fungicide if there is any evidence of organic growth. The surface should be damp on application, and direct heat on a warm day should be avoided. The limewash should be applied when cool, in thin applications, with a large 100 mm brush (grass brush). Four and a half litres (1 gal) should cover approximately 18 square metres (200–300 square feet). An application rate of 17 to 32 square metres per hour, with the above size brush, is average. The limewash should be worked well into the surface and allowed to dry. A second and third application may then be made in the same way.

References

1. Building Research Establishment, *Lime and Lime Mortars*, DSIR Special Report No. 9 (Cowper), HMSO, London, 1927
2. Anon., *Lime in Building*, British Quarrying and Slag Federation Ltd, Croydon, 1968

Appendix 2

Effects of large numbers of visitors on historic buildings

David Honeyborne

People can inadvertently harm buildings in the following ways:

- By direct contact (feet, hands, clothing)
- By polluting the air inside the building with tobacco smoke
- By increasing the relative humidity of the air inside the building to an extent that causes some kind of condensation of moisture on the fabric

Minor effects

Minor risks arise from vibration, if many people step in unison, or from an increase in the concentration of carbon dioxide in the air inside the building. Vibration risks can normally be eliminated, however. Also the risk from an increase in the carbon dioxide content of the air is unlikely to be serious; this is partly because people become noticeably physiologically affected if the carbon dioxide content of the air rises very much, and partly because the only significant effect on the building of a higher concentration of carbon dioxide in the air would be an increase in the rate of dissolution of very wet limestone surfaces. Limestone inside a building normally has a nearly dry surface unless severe rain penetration or rising damp is occurring or the wall is subject to condensation of moisture. Even then, the rate of dissolution caused by the acid-forming sulphur oxides in polluted air and its natural carbon dioxide content will far outweigh any effects caused by the carbon dioxide exhaled by people.

Effects of direct contact

The wearing away of paving and flooring materials by the passage of many feet is a well-recognized hazard. In general, the damage is done mainly by hard particles embedded in the soles or heels of shoes or boots. Damage will tend to be greatest where people turn sharply. In some circumstances the damage can be minimized by arranging for people to have to take smooth curves rather than sharp turns. In others, it may be possible to lead the visitors along routes paved with hard-wearing contemporary materials of no historical value. Eventually it might be necessary to require visitors to replace their outdoor footwear with slippers before entering some historic buildings. This will pose many problems and probably necessitate the introduction or the raising of entry charges. In churches, where right to free entry is more than just a custom, the problems of policy will be particularly difficult to solve, but they concern matters of policy rather than technology and will not be further discussed here.

The rubbing of clothes against the fabric of a building can produce a polishing and staining of the fabric. This is often particularly noticeable in spiral stairways. Even granite can be affected in this way, but limestones and lime- and gypsum-based plasters are more quickly polished. Sandstones are relatively immune. Lighter coloured materials naturally show staining more readily than darker ones. Staining in these circumstances is generally attributed to oil from woollen clothing. However, some of the staining may well be due to a polishing in of dirt particles already on the surface.

Oil naturally present in the skin has a similar effect to oil from clothing. This may often be seen on stone hand-rails and on carved features that people tend to finger out of curiosity. Some of the stains to be seen on marble, particularly on white statuary marble, no doubt originate in this way. There is no reason to believe that oil stains of this kind will lead to any deterioration of the building material. Indeed, there is some evidence that the oil has a tendency to preserve the material. However, such stains are usually considered to be unsightly and there are sometimes calls for their removal.

The relatively cheap methods available for cleaning the masonry of ordinary buildings are seldom appropriate for cleaning the general masonry, much less the carved work in historic buildings. The special methods required instead, for example micro-scale grit blasting or poulticing with special solvents, are slow and need very skilled people to operate them. Hence removal of stains caused by visitors can involve considerable expense and may absorb money that is needed for other conservation activities.

Effects of tobacco smoke

The staining that may be caused on marble counter and table tops by cigarettes that are left smouldering in contact with them is well known. It is not so generally realized that a more wide-spread staining may occur as a result of large numbers of people smoking inside buildings. This has been established as being the most likely cause of otherwise unexplained staining of marble in at least one large building in London. There is no reason why tobacco smoke should not cause similar stains on porous stone or brick surfaces, though stains are likely to be noticeable only on a light-coloured limestone or marble. The removal of such stains from a porous limestone building would present grave difficulties. If an area of polished marble of no great historic value is involved, the best method of removing the stains is by repolishing the surface. Where, for historical or other reasons, this method is not appropriate, poulticing methods must be used. These will involve the use of organic solvents which may well present a health hazard if inhaled.

The removal of stains may absorb money needed for other purposes.

Effects of increasing relative humidity

Air is able to absorb a certain amount of water vapour and hold it invisibly, but its capacity is limited. When air contains the maximum quantity of water vapour it is capable of holding, it is said to be saturated. The amount of water that a given volume of air can hold varies with the temperature of the air, rising as the temperature rises and falling as it falls. In air that is not saturated, the amount of water present is usually expressed as a percentage fraction of the amount that would be present if the air were saturated at that temperature. This is the *relative humidity* of the air.

When unsaturated air is cooled, its relative humidity rises. When the relative humidity reaches 100%, the air will be saturated and further cooling will cause a separation of moisture. This takes the visible form of mist if the air is being cooled by radiation of heat to a cold region (such as a clear night sky), but if the air is being cooled by an impervious surface, moisture will appear on that surface in the form of water droplets. This process is called condensation and the cold body is called a condenser. Window glass is the commonest condenser in buildings with single glazing. The temperature at which condensation first appears is known as the dew point of that body of air. If the air is initially nearly saturated with water the dew point will be high. That is to say, the dew point will be near the air temperature and little cooling will be needed to produce condensation. If the air is initially rather dry its dew point will be far below the air temperature. If the dew point is below the freezing point of water, any condensation will appear as frost.

With every breathing cycle people exhale air that contains more moisture than the air they inhale. They also pass some moisture into the air in the form of perspiration. Hence, if people enter a building in sufficient numbers they will cause the relative humidity of the air to rise significantly, particularly if the ventilation rate of the building is relatively low. In consequence, the dew point will also rise and so will the probability that condensation will occur on the coldest parts of the building. The greater the number of people involved, the greater the risk.

In his analysis of the moisture balance in King's College Chapel, Cambridge, Lacy[1] assumed that, on average, a person walking around an historic building produces 50 g of moisture per hour. A large building of internal air capacity of 50 000 m^3 (rather larger than King's College Chapel) with air at 15 °C and relative humidity 65% will contain 8.26 g of water per cubic metre of air. The dew point will be about 8.1 °C. If, over a period of three hours, 1000 people move quietly round the building they will contribute 3 g of moisture to each cubic metre of air. Assuming negligible loss by ventilation, the total moisture content will become 11.26 g per cubic metre of air, the relative humidity will become 88.6% and the dew point 13 °C. Thus, before the visitors came in, a window would have needed to be at least 6.9 °C below the air temperature to cause condensation. At the end of the three hours in question, condensation would form on the window if it were just over 2 °C below air temperature. The basis of this calculation is given in *Table A2.1* to illustrate how to carry out analogous calculations with data appropriate to other buildings. What happens to the additional moisture introduced by visitors will depend not only on the temperatures of the solid surfaces within the building but also on the nature of those surfaces.

Table A2.1 Calculation of effect of a heavy influx of visitors on the moisture conditions in a large building with a negligible ventilation rate

In this example the building has an air capacity of 50 000 m³ and the relative humidity of the air is 65% before the entry of the visitors. The temperature of the air is assumed (rather unrealistically) to remain at 15°C throughout the period under examination.

From tables of physical constants (e.g. Kaye and Laby), saturated air at 15°C contains 12.71 grams of water per m³. Thus, at 65% RH the air must contain 0.65 × 12.71 = 8.26 grams of water per m³. The dew point is then found by inspecting the table below to find the temperature at which 8.26 grams of water per m³ will saturate the air. This is found to be 8.1°C.

For three hours after opening, there are an average of 1000 quietly moving people in it. If each visitor contributes moisture at the rate of 50 g/h the total moisture added to the air in the building by the end of the three hour period will be 50 × 1000 × 3 = 15 000 g. The contribution per cubic metre of air will then be 150 000/50 000 = 3 g so the moisture content of each m³ of air goes up to 3 + 8.26 = 11.26 g. The air at 15°C will still require 12.71 g for saturation, so the new relative humidity will be 11.26/12.71 × 100 = 88.6%.

From the table below, 11.26 g of water will saturate one m³ of air at 13°C, which is the new dew point.

Temperature (°C)	Water (g)
5	6.76
6	7.22
7	7.70
8	8.21
9	8.76
10	9.33
11	9.93
12	10.57
13	11.25
14	11.96
15	12.71
16	13.50
17	14.34
18	15.22
19	16.14
20	17.12
21	18.14
22	19.22
23	20.35
24	21.54
25	22.80

Effects on impervious surfaces

Moisture condensing on an impervious surface will normally be very pure and initially very reactive chemically. Some attack on window glass may take place. If this is repeated often it will cause deterioration of some medieval window glass, particularly glass with a high content of potash. Modern glass is unlikely to be affected significantly.

Condensation running down window panes can also cause damage to putty and to timber framing in the long run. If condensation runs over gypsum-based plaster it can cause softening or the appearance of blisters. If it runs into brickwork it can often transfer soluble salts from the brickwork to other building materials which may be damaged if the salts crystallize on subsequent evaporation of the water. Staining of the surface from which the evaporation occurs may also take place.

Effects on porous surfaces

It may be shown by thermodynamical reasoning (see for example Croney *et al.*[2]) that water held in the pores of a porous material has a lower vapour pressure than water at the same temperature lying on a plane impervious material. It follows that moisture from humid air will condense in the porous material at relative humidity below 100% and at temperatures above the dew point. Condensation will occur first in the finest pores. The relative humidity at which water will begin to condense in a pore of given diameter may be calculated if the angle of contact of the water surface with the solid surface of the pore is known (see *Table A2.2*).

Unfortunately the angle of contact when water is advancing in a pore is not precisely known for any porous masonry. In consequence, only a crude estimate of the relative humidity at which moisture will condense in a pore of any given size can be made. However, it is possible to calculate the relative humidity below which water will *not* condense in pores of a given diameter. This is the relative humidity at which water will just begin to leave the pore. This calculation is possible because, under drying conditions, the angle of contact becomes so near zero that its cosine is 1 for all practical purposes. The relative humidity required to cause condensation in this pore will theoretically always be equal to or greater than that calculated in this way.

To obtain a picture of what will happen in a real porous material, as opposed to a single pore, under given conditions of relative humidity it is necessary to know the pore size distribution. The equations in *Table A2.2* were used by Croney *et al.*[3] to obtain estimates of pore size distributions in soils. Honeyborne and Harris[4] obtained estimates of pore size distributions by carrying out similar analyses on some British building stones. However, too few were examined to allow conclusions to be drawn from their results. The only other workers in Europe known to have employed this technique are in Portugal (see, for example, de Castro[5]); their work naturally concerned Portuguese stone. Owing to the lack of sufficient experimental data it would be better to obtain data about British stones by direct

Table A2.2 The relationship between the maximum diameter of the pores that would be filled with water when the material is in equilibrium with air of a given relative humidity

Croney et al.[3] state that:

$$h = -\frac{R\,t}{M\,g}\log_e\frac{H}{100} \tag{A2.1}$$

where h is the height (cm) of the column of water that the pore will just support by capillarity
H is the relative humidity (%)
R is the universal gas constant (8.315 J/mol K)
M is the molecular weight of water (18.0 g/mol)
t is the absolute temperature (K)
g is the gravitational acceleration (cm/s^2)

From Laplace's equation:

$$h\rho g = \frac{4\sigma\cos\theta}{d} \tag{A2.2}$$

where σ is the surface tension of water (dyn/cm)
d is the pore diameter (cm)
θ is the angle of contact between water and solid
ρ is the density of water (g/cm^3)

Rearranging this equation:

$$d = \frac{4\sigma\cos\theta}{h\rho g} \tag{A2.3}$$

Combining Equations A2.1 and A2.2:

$$d = \frac{4\sigma\cos\theta M}{\rho t R\log_e(100/H)} = \frac{4\sigma\cos\theta M}{\rho t R 2.303(2 - \log_{10} H)} \tag{A2.4}$$

At a temperature of 20°C $t = 293$; $\rho = 0.9982$; $\sigma = 72.8$. Hence:

$$d = \frac{0.00000009359\cos\theta}{2 - \log_{10} H}$$

If the diameter is expressed in micrometres we have

$$d = \frac{0.0009359\cos\theta}{2 - \log_{10} H} \tag{A2.5}$$

The amount of residual water in the pores is often plotted against a factor designated as pF. This is the common logarithm of the value of h in cm. Thus:

$$d = \frac{4\sigma\cos\theta}{\rho g\ \text{antilog}(pF)}$$

Table A2.3 Relationship between relative humidity and density of sulphuric acid solution in a closed vessel

Relative humidity (%)	Density of acid at 20°C (kg/m^3)	Suction (pF) $\log_{10}$ (cm)
20	1475	6.34
30	1416	6.22
40	1377	6.10
50	1336	5.98
60	1293	5.85
70	1245	5.69
80	1194	5.49
90	1130	5.16
93	1103	5.00
98	1030	4.45

Source: references 3 and 6.

A limited amount of useful information can be drawn from published results. Because de Castro[6] gives simple water absorption properties of the stones tested as well as their cumulative pore size distributions (CPSD) it is possible to judge if any of them are sufficiently like any British stone for useful comparisons to be drawn. The limestone from Anca is sufficiently like Monks Park limestone from Wiltshire to justify examination of the results obtained when de Castro tested it. *Figure A2.1* shows CPSD graphs for Monks Park stone and Anca stone. The Portuguese results have been recalculated to fit the unit system usually employed in this field of work in Britain. The graphs have a similar shape, but the Portuguese stone has a finer pore structure (Monks Park stone has the finest pore structure of any British limestone so far studied). De Castro's moisture take-up measurements for Anca stone at a range of relative humidities have also been recalculated to fit the unit system usually employed in Britain. They are shown in *Table A2.4* together with an estimate of the diameters of the pores involved. Column 4 is the most informative.

Over the range of relative humidities from 50% to 70% the pick-up is relatively small. Even at 90% relative humidity the volume of water taken up would occupy only 0.35% of the bulk volume of the stone. Since British stones generally have coarser pores, their moisture pick-up at these relative humidities will probably be distinctly lower.

In his examination of moisture conditions at King's College Chapel, Lacy[1] deduced that about 15 tons (15 240 kg) of water exhaled by visitors passed into the walls of the building during the summer and about 5 tons (5080 kg) of this passed back into the building during the winter when the heating was on. It seems most likely that the water was held in the pores of the masonry. It might also be of interest to note that at equilibrium with an atmosphere of 90%

measurement of the amount of water taken up by initially dry test pieces when exposed to controlled atmospheres covering a range of relative humidities. The simple desiccator/sulphuric acid system used by Croney et al.[3] and by Honeyborne and Harris[4] for studying the drying cycle can be used just as easily to study the wetting cycle, as shown by de Castro[6]. There seems to be scope for even small conservation laboratories to carry out useful work along these lines. *Table A2.3* gives the densities of the sulphuric acid solutions that may be used to give a range of useful relative humidities.

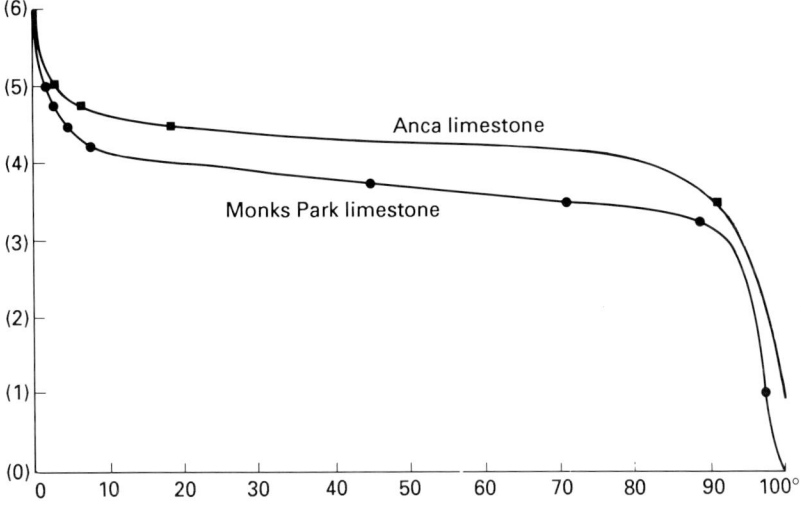

Figure A2.1 Suction-based cumulative pore size distribution (based on reference 4, Figure 8, and reference 6, Figure 3)

Table A2.4 Hygroscopic properties of limestone from Anca, Portugal

Relative humidity (%)	Moisture absorbed			Max. pore diameter affected (nm)
	g water per 100 g stone	% saturation	% volume of stone	
20	0.013	0.09	0.025	1.3
30	0.022	0.15	0.043	1.8
40	0.031	0.22	0.061	2.4
50	0.038	0.27	0.074	3.1
60	0.048	0.34	0.094	4.2
70	0.063	0.44	0.12	6.2
80	0.102	0.71	0.20	9.7
90	0.18	1.2	0.35	20
95	0.56	3.9*	1.1*	42

Data taken from ref. 6, figure 19
*Value less certain

relative humidity each cubic metre of Anca stone would hold 3.5 kg (3.5 litre) of water and in an atmosphere of 50% relative humidity it would hold 0.74 kg.

It is debatable whether water held in this way causes harm to the stone, even if it is a limestone and the ambient air is polluted with oxides of sulphur. De Castro[6] assumes that there must be a connection between the amount of hygroscopic moisture, as she calls it, and the rate of attack by aggressive agents in the air. However, there does not appear to be evidence to support this view. Intra-porous condensation must occur in the stonework of many older churches, yet damage to interior stone can seldom be found away from areas suffering from rising damp, rain penetration, massive dew-point condensation, or

the action of some of the more aggressive soluble salts. Any liquid held in very fine pores (see *Table A2.4*, column 5) will be subjected to intense molecular forces. Crystallization of any salts present will be highly suppressed and the normal chemical behaviour will be much modified, so abnormally passive behaviour is possible.

Effects on walls when hygroscopic salts are present

The situation is entirely different when hygroscopic (i.e. moisture-attracting) salts are present on the surfaces or in the larger pores of the stonework. Such salts will induce condensation of moisture from the air at relative humidities well below 100% and at temperatures well above the dew point. In this respect they resemble the fine pores. However, instead of being held harmlessly, the water so condensed will dissolve part or all of the salts involved. Damage to the fabric will almost certainly occur on subsequent drying out, if the accompanying crystallization takes place within the coarser pores. Such damage can occur with nearly all kinds of porous building materials.

Unfortunately there is no available theory that can quantify hygroscopic condensation. Each salt or mixture of salts is characterized by an equilibrium relative humidity (ERH) above which hygroscopic condensation will occur. The ERH is affected by temperature as well as by the kinds of salts involved. *Table A2.5* lists the ERH for a few simple salts at room temperatures. However, mixtures of salts

Table A2.5 Equilibrium relative humidity (ERH) of a number of simple common salts

Salt	Chemical formula	EQRH (%)
Calcium chloride hydrate	$CaCl_2 \cdot 6H_2O$	31
Magnesium chloride hydrate	$MgCl_2 \cdot 6H_2O$	33
Potassium carbonate hydrate	$K_2CO_3 \cdot 2H_2O$	44
Potassium chloride	KCl	85
Potassium nitrate	KNO_3	93
Potassium sulphate	K_2SO_4	98
Sodium carbonate hydrate	$Na_2CO_3 \cdot 10H_2O$	90
Sodium chloride	NaCl	76
Sodium nitrate	$NaNO_3$	75
Sodium sulphate hydrate	$Na_2SO_4 \cdot 10H_2O$	93

The ERH of a salt tends to rise with a fall in temperature. The effect is more striking with some salts than others. The EQRH may sometimes reach a maximum at some mid-range temperature. The values given have been rounded off and apply approximately within the temperature range 20–25°C.

behave in anomalous ways and it is not possible to deduce the ERH of a mixture from the known properties of its constituents. When a mixture of salts is present in a building material and changes of relative humidity are believed to be causing damage, the best way to investigate is to measure the ERH of the mixture experimentally. This can be done using a small sample and the same kind of controlled-humidity vessels as are used for measuring the hygroscopicity of materials. The initially dried and weighed test sample is placed in the driest atmosphere first and, after an appropriate time, is removed, weighed and placed in the vessel with the next higher relative humidity, and so on. A plot of gain in weight against RH will soon reveal the ERH of the material. (This measurement can be done more precisely with an absorption balance, if one is available.) If the ERH found is within the RH range normally found in the building, crystallization damage is likely to occur.

Different salts have different degrees of aggressiveness when crystallizing. For example, sodium sulphate tends to be more damaging than sodium chloride, which tends to be more damaging than calcium sulphate. However, mixtures of salts have an aggressiveness that appears to be unrelated to the aggressiveness of the constituents. These properties are not yet understood.

Changes in relative humidity that lead to the solution and recrystallization of salts and mixtures of salts are likely to be as damaging to the internal fabric of a building as rain penetration or rising damp.

References

1. Report of special investigation No. 2143 on atmospheric humidities in King's College Chapel, Cambridge, Building Research Station (Department of Scientific and Industrial Research), 1963 [No author of this report is named but it is well known that the principal investigator was R E Lacy.]
2. Croney, D. and Coleman, J.D., Soil thermodynamics applied to the movement of moisture in road foundations, *Proc. 7th International Congress for Applied Mechanics*, **3**, 163–177, 1948
3. Croney, D., Coleman, J.D. and Bridge, P.M., 'The suction of moisture held in soil and other porous materials', *DSIR Road Research Technical Note No. 24*, HMSO, London, 1952
4. Honeyborne, D.B. and Harris, P.B., 'The structure of porous building stone and its relation to weathering behaviour', *Proc. 10th Symposium of Colston Research Society*, pp. 343–365, Butterworths, London, 1958
5. de Castro, E., 'Determination of pore size distribution in stones by means of moisture suction', *Memoria No. 441*, Laboratoria Nacional de Engenharia Civil, Lisbon, 1974
6. de Castro, E., 'Evaluation de l'hydroscopicité des pierres', *Memoria No. 526*, Laboratoria Nacional de Engenharia Civil, Lisbon, 1979

Appendix 3

The use of air-abrasive cleaning techniques for stone building surfaces

Peter Moss

Air-abrasive or 'blast' cleaning is not an appropriate technique for all stone building surfaces, and there is no doubt that bad experiences associated with poor specification and inept operatives have, on many occasions, led to prejudice against the system. Successful cleaning with compressed air and abrasive, with or without water, depends on a correct and detailed specification, properly trained operatives and well maintained equipment. A full understanding of the principles of the 'blast' methods, by both specifier and operative, will ensure that they are used only in the correct way on appropriate surfaces, in a safe and cost-effective manner.

'Blast' cleaning methods include (in descending impact effect):

1. Wheel type (electric). Metallic grit or shot abrasive. Suitable only for removing surfaces, descaling and cleaning of some pavings.
2. Air pressure blast (portable). Various abrasives. Typical pressures at the nozzle range from 20 to 100 psi. When air-abrasive cleaning is used, most building surfaces are cleaned by this method.
3. Air suction blast (lightweight portable). Fine abrasives only. Typical pressures at the nozzle range from 20 to 100 psi, but the design type has the effect of reducing impact to about half that of the air pressure blast at the same air pressures. Architectural detail, especially if small-scale or multi-faceted, is frequently cleaned by this method.

All air blast cleaning equipment should be fitted with a pressure regulator, complete with a (working) gauge. High pressure water may also be used with suction-feed abrasive, but is generally only suitable for lightly soiled, flat surfaces.

Applications and use

The pressure machines can be fitted with water injection or water shroud type fittings. The 'Klean-blast' water injection unit need only inject one litre per minute, which is ideal for damping down dust, without the use of running water, on the surfaces or base of a building. Generally, the work rate is equal to that of dry blasting.

The wet blast head (water shroud) uses substantial amounts of water, because it has six or eight jets of water around the nozzle. The centre area is dry, but the water volume washes the surface. The work rate is slower and general visibility less than with the water injection unit. The water injection unit is preferred by most contractors.

The advent and availability of water injection units such as the KB80 means that there should be no reason for a dust nuisance to be experienced on any site cleaned by this system, even when the scaffolding is unsheeted. Suction blast guns, such as the SG300, can only be fitted with the shroud type water attachment.

For safety reasons, all blast cleaning machines should be fitted with remote control. Building cleaning requires a system capable of enabling the operator to shut the abrasive flow off and on as required, in order to avoid the risk of damage to the surface. Electric or electronic remote controls are available, and they give instant response even on the longest of high-blast hoses. These controls are not affected by liquids and always fail-safe. A common malpractice is to check the flow of abrasive by folding the blast hose. This is extremely dangerous and should be absolutely prohibited. Remote control grit valves are also available, which enable operators to blow or wash down the surface intermittently during the cleaning process.

Abrasives and nozzles

Abrasives, nozzle types and sizes and air pressures must be selected and specified for particular applications. In general, round abrasives, such as shot, beads and some types of sand, hammer the surface. These are ideal where the soiling is hard and brittle on a fairly hard substrate, for example a sulphated film on granite. Angular abrasives, such as blasting grits, quartz sand or flint grit, have a cutting effect. These are suitable where a soft or resilient soiling covers the substrate.

Blast cleaning uses kinetic energy ($1/2$ mass $\times$ velocity^2). The size or the specific gravity of an abrasive and its impact velocity will determine the cleaning work rate. In building cleaning, the emphasis should be not on the fastest, but on the most effective work rate. Therefore, a trial area should be specified and the contractor should always start with the lowest pressure and the smaller, lighter abrasives. These factors can then be modified to determine the optimum work rate, abrasive type and size and pressure.

The 'Health and safety and the blasting of castings' Act and others forbid the use of abrasives containing 'free silica' (sands and flint grit). Even the use of water does not prevent dust risks. There is some evidence from the USA that wetted sand is absorbed more easily into the lungs than dry dust. The ready availability of building cleaning grits, such as Stone-grit, in many different sizes, now means that there is little need to use banned grits.

Nozzles must be chosen carefully. Long venturi nozzles are more efficient and give an even particle spread over a greater impact area (at a constant distance from the surface) at any pressure. They are ideal for flat areas, or consistent soiling conditions. Long and short straight nozzles, whilst less efficient, provide a more pencil-shaped blast, which is ideal for window seals, channels and taking out poor pointing. Angled nozzles are also available.

An important aspect of nozzle choice, for consistency of application and economic reasons, is the selection of nozzles which will stay the same shape throughout the job. The design life of some nozzles is only 20–25 hours. With a constant air-feed pressure, the abrasive will cut differently between the start and the finish of a 25 hour job. If the air supply is constant, the pressure will be reduced. This will gradually reduce the impact on the surface. If, as is more common, air is available to maintain pressure, then the impact area will be reduced and more energy will be expanded within this reduced area. This means there will be a greater chance of

substrate damage. These nozzles are generally of the cast alloy or ceramic type.

A comparison of work carried out with venturi nozzles of different orifice sizes shows:

If $1/4$ in $= 100\%$ area:
    $5/16$ in $= 157\%$ more area than $1/4$ in nozzle
    $3/8$ in $= 220\%$ more area than $1/4$ in nozzle
    $7/16$ in $= 320\%$ more area than $1/4$ in nozzle
    $1/2$ in $= 400\%$ more area than $1/4$ in nozzle

This relates to any specific nozzle pressure. A comparison of air requirements, nozzle size and pressure for pressure machines is given in Table A3.1.

Suction gun jets require approximately 28% more air, but are only available in $1/16$ inch to $1/4$ inch sizes. Suction gun nozzles should be at least twice the diameter of the jet size.

The air/grit mix at any pressure should be as lean as possible, but should give an even, constant flow of abrasive to the work. All blast cleaning machines used for building cleaning should be fitted with a flat 'sand' valve, not a 'steel' grit valve.

Table A3.1

Nozzle diameter (in)	Nozzle pressure (p.s.i.)						Compressor size (cubic ft/min)
	50	60	70	80	90	100	
$1/8$	11	13	15	17	18	20	25
$3/16$	26	30	33	38	41	45	60
$1/4$	47	54	61	68	74	81	100
$5/16$	77	89	101	113	126	137	160
$3/8$	108	126	143	161	173	196	250
$7/16$	147	170	194	217	240	254	325
$1/2$	195	224	252	280	309	338	450

Summary

Both clients and specifiers must insist that work is carried out at specific and appropriate pressures, and site supervision should ensure that these are adhered to. 'Blast' cleaning can be considered as an even area cleaning method, which is fast and suitable for much building cleaning. It is not a spot cleaning method. The characteristics of soiling on buildings are infinitely variable, particularly the tenacity of adhesion to the substrate. Although 'blast' cleaning systems are very flexible, they cannot be expected to provide a total cleaning of all areas. Other techniques and methods may be used in conjunction with 'blast' cleaning. This includes the use of fine water sprays as a preliminary treatment, where the soiling has been absorbed and the substrate is not at risk from water damage. If the substrate is weak and friable, with a hard dirt crust on the surface, a chemical cleaning agent may be appropriate as a preparation for careful air abrasive treatment. In this case pre-wetting is essential and some washing on completion will also be necessary. Flame cleaning should precede the use of air abrasive where hard paint films or resilient bitumen paints have to be removed from weak substrates.

Note Peter Moss is a member of Hodge Clemco Limited of Sheffield, England, a company which supplies the stone cleaning industry with most of its blast cleaning equipment and materials. The equipment and abrasives mentioned are trade names of Hodge Clemco Limited. The company provides a free advisory service to customers and specifiers on application and techniques, and has a training school for operatives and supervisors.

Appendix 4

The analytical approach to stone, its cleaning, repair and treatment

Nicola Ashurst and John Kelly

The belief that the identification of a stone as, for instance, 'sandstone' is sufficient basis for an understanding of the processes of alteration or decay is an erroneous one. It is equally inadequate in the formulation of a program of remedial work. The term 'sandstone' is a generalized term for those rocks representative of a section of the arenaceous rocks— that is, those detrital, quartz-rich sediments with a grain size of 2.00–0.0625 mm. This does not reflect the wide variation of chemical, mineralogical and physical characteristics found within the generalization. A failure, or inability, to recognize this variation prior to cleaning or other remedial treatments can often lead to damage in the form of discoloration or accelerated decay rates.

An analytical approach, involving a geologist and a competent architect experienced in stone weathering deterioration and repair, can avoid many of the problems which have become all too familiar. Their correct interpretation of on-site factors and laboratory analysis, and the meaningful and accurate synthesis of the data obtained, may be translated into appropriate recommendations for remedial work.

On-site investigation/analysis

On-site investigation of stonework should be directed towards obtaining visual identification of the apparent stone types present. This will, of necessity, be based on colour and such characteristics as may be observed with the naked eye or hand lens—for example, grain size or other large textural features such as banding or lamination. The occurrence of any alteration of the stone surfaces due to the action of algae, lichen, pollutants or efflorescence, together with granulation, scaling or exfoliating elements, should also be noted.

Above all, no local consideration of a particular problem should exclude an assessment of the condition of the whole facade. Decay and staining frequently relate to poor building maintenance and remedial work to joints, flashings, copings and rainwater disposal goods. The effect of these as well as the design of the facade should always be taken into account.

Sampling

On the completion of preliminary assessment of stone types present and the range or nature of their alteration, samples should be taken which reflect these variations and will be useful in the proposed program of analysis. With due consideration for the aesthetic integrity of the masonry, it is usual that the larger the number of samples available the more the results of analysis will be representative of the materials present. However, even relatively small, carefully selected samples, with proper preparation and analytical techniques, can provide an adequate data base.

The location of samples on the structure and their relationship to any failures of structure or detailing should be noted. A description of the sample methods should accompany each sample. Also, each sample should be packed separately and be clearly labelled with all relevant information.

It is preferable that the sampling is carried out by personnel from the analysing facility who can be expected to be responsible for correct sampling. This should, of course, always follow discussion with the owner or the owner's delegated agent.

Laboratory analysis

While some simplified analysis may be carried out on-site as an aid to sampling procedures, meaningful results can only be obtained by proper laboratory-based work to fully elucidate the physical and chemical characteristics of the stones.

Petrological analysis[1]

This basically entails the systematic examination of stone sample, both in thin section and hand specimen. The purpose is to identify or classify the stone type under consideration. Even where the stone type is identified in historical records such an investigation is recommended for the purpose of confirmation or to note any variation from an expected norm.

The work is generally carried out using a stereoscopic and petrological microscope with plane-polarized light. Due to the limits of magnification and resolution inherent in light microscopy, the analysis may need to be supported, where appropriate, by other methods. Those most commonly employed are X-ray diffraction (XRD) and the scanning electron microscope (SEM). From the application of these techniques the mineralogy of the individual elements and their textural relationships can be determined.

The identification and quantification of the mineralogy allows the determination of the gross chemistry of the stone; it also clearly indicates the direction of further analysis and the choices available for the future remedial work. At this stage of analysis the fundamental classification of the sandstone is established.

Physical analysis

While the differences apparent in the various sandstone types will be determined from petrological analysis, it is the physical characteristics which will largely control the ingress and movement of water. The majority of processes which are detrimental to stonework require the presence of water for their operation, and it is the physical characteristics of porosity and capillarity which determine the rate and amount of water uptake.

Capillarity determination

The capillary characteristics are generally calculated from the uptake of deionized or distilled water into a stone sample by surface contact with a wetted, absorbent pad. The amount of water taken up is calculated against the dry weight of sample and recorded against time. From these measurements a capillary curve may be plotted. When such measurements are carried out under similar conditions, a graphic illustration of the capillarity of a sample may be compared to other stone types or to modified samples of same stone. Furthermore, from these results the capillary coefficient of the stone type may

be determined. The observations may, of course, be applied to the determination of a drying curve.

Porosity determination

The uptake of water into a stone will be determined largely by its capillary system. However, the effect of the water within the stone, either alone or together with contained contaminates, will depend on the extent and nature of the pore system.

Two methods may be used to determine the porosity:

1. Water uptake at atmospheric temperature and pressure (APT) and under vacuum. Unlike capillary testing, these tests are carried out by controlled immersion and saturation of the sample.
2. Mercury porosimetry. Using this method mercury is forced into a small sample. The amount of mercury intruded and the force required are indicative of the volume of pores penetrated and their diameter.

Both these methods have positive and negative aspects, which must be correctly interpreted.

With the water method the pores are either filled completely or not. From the amount of water taken up under both ATP and vacuum, effective and total porosity may be determined together with water absorption coefficient, saturation coefficient and density. This information is useful in several ways, particularly for assessing the susceptibility of the stone to frost damage. The use of mercury porosimetry allows the determination of both the total porosity and the relative amounts of pores of known diameter. This allows a calculation of the relative amounts of macro-pores to micro-pores. The division between these is an arbitrary one based on earlier petrological work. The present division at 5 mm diameter is under review. Again, this data is significant as an indicator of the ability of the stone to withstand internal pressure originating from either freezing water or salt hydration. The shortcomings of the mercury porosity method are that certain assumptions must be made concerning the pore geometry of the stone, and that the size of the mercury molecule limits measurements to pores of 32 Ångstroms (3.2 nm) diameter or greater.

However, both methods have their application in determining the characteristics of the stone and with careful interpretation can provide a valuable insight into the material and its alteration.

Chemical analysis

This involves determination of the water-soluble, acid-soluble and solvent-soluble contents of the stone.

Chemical analysis can be developed to a considerable extent by interpretation of the results of petrological analysis. Unfortunately, contaminants, whether derived from alteration of the original chemistry of the stone or by ingress of extraneous matter, are often extremely fine-grained. They may be dispersed through an area relatively large in relation to their amount. In addition, the amount of contaminants present may be small relative to the damage caused by their presence. These factors tend to make their identification by direct observation time-consuming and problematical.

With few exceptions the stones utilized for building and monumental work do not contain appreciable amounts of water-soluble material, and therefore where such material is present it may be regarded as a contaminant. Similarly, by the use of other solvents the chemistry relevant to decay processes may be more closely defined.

Water-soluble content

Using deionized water, soluble materials may be extracted for analysis. Total analysis may be carried out, but it is considered sufficient to determine the cations and anions which constitute the main classes of soluble salts known to occur within inorganic building materials. It is essential, however, that such analysis be quantitative with regard to the total water-soluble contaminants and to their relative amounts. The techniques most readily available for this determination are atomic absorption and inductively coupled plasma spectroscopy and ion chromatography.

Acid-soluble content

The acid-soluble content is relevant where the stone type under analysis has been previously noted as having a calcareous content. The determination of the total calcareous content is needed in order to assess the response of the stone to a polluted environment. The loss of a calcareous mineralogy will have a direct effect on the stone, owing to loss of its cementing mineralogy or its conversion to a different mineralogy. In the latter respect the dissolution of the stone in acidic water may also have a detrimental effect on adjacent non-calcareous stonework, similar to that observed at times between limestones and sandstones. Futhermore, sandstones with a clay content may have a greater susceptibility to acidic waters.

Sovent-soluble content

The solvent-soluble content aspects of the chemical analysis is mainly directed to the nature of soiling of pollutants other than those mentioned above. While the presence of unburnt fossil fuels and their residues is thought of largely in terms of surface disfigurement, they can contain materials which catalyse or assist other decay mechanisms. As their presence as the dark components of soiling crusts is often the reason for the intiation of an intervention program, determination of their nature is an important preliminary to the selection of appropriate cleaning methods.

Conclusions and the approach to cleaning

With the completion of a sequence of analysis as outlined above, an understanding of the nature of the stone substrate and its alteration will be available, upon which a programme of intervention may be reasonably based. This will allow a choice of methods and materials applicable to the problems of the stonework as determined rather than as perceived. It will also preclude the use of inappropriate stone for replacement or indenting repairs based on a superficial assessment of colour alone.

From the examination of correctly selected thin sections and from the use of chemical profiling it will be apparent that soiling or alteration are not confined to the surface of the stonework. Furthermore, cleaning as the removal of damaging as well as disfiguring contaminants may have to be carried out on delicate or weakened stonework. The damage caused by the widespread and seemingly indiscriminate use of abrasive or harsh chemicals has led to radical reassessment of cleaning methods.

There are no universal sandstone cleaners, just as there are no universal limestone or granite cleaners. Note must be taken of the nature and the specific condition of the stone substrate so that the cleaning approach can be tailored to suit.

In the light of this it may be seen that building cleaning should, ideally, be an extension of museum cleaning methods based on extremely weak solutions of the appropriate chemicals. Serious consideration should also be given to the use of chemicals together with absorbent packs to form gels and poultices, as these allow a much greater control of the chemical action.

Poultice cleaning

The principles of a poultice are that it not only acts as a vehicle for the chemical but also functions as a capillary system exterior to the stonework but intimately associated with it. This means that, once the soiling is dissolved, it is absorbed by the poultice and drawn away from the stone rather than moving into the body of the stone, Using the poultice approach, combinations of chemical solvents can be brought into contact with the soiling; these combinations will relate to the nature of the substrate and the nature of the soiling. The intimate contact of the cleaning materials means that smaller quantities of chemicals have to be used, and these may be of much lower concentration. Typically, concentrations of less than 0.5% hydrofluoric acid in poultice form have been effectively used on sandstone against levels of 5% to 10% hydrofluoric acid used in many other available systems. In addition, the use of poultice techiques greatly reduces the amount of water required.

To conclude, it is very important that the testing of any proposed cleaning materials is viewed as an integral part of the programme of analysis and assessment. In addition, a post-cleaning analysis of all affected stonework is another essential element in the analytical approach to sensitive and proper stone cleaning.

It must be reiterated that the success of the process described relies heavily on the quality of the professional interpretation given to the many factors.

Reference

1. Kelly, J., 'The petrographic microscope as an aid to stone conservation', *Microscopy and Analysis*, June 1989

Index

Page numbers in *italics* refer to illustrations or tables. Some textual matter may also occur.